Microsoft Dynamics CRM 2011 Cookbook

Includes over 75 incredible recipes for deploying, configuring, and customizing your CRM application

Dipankar Bhattacharya

[PACKT] PUBLISHING enterprise
professional expertise distilled

BIRMINGHAM - MUMBAI

Microsoft Dynamics CRM 2011 Cookbook

First published: May 2013

Production Reference: 1170513

Published by Packt Publishing Ltd.
Livery Place
35 Livery Street
Birmingham B3 2PB, UK.

ISBN 978-1-84968-452-1

www.packtpub.com

Cover Image by Vivek Sinha (vivek.ratan.sinha@gmail.com)

Credits

Author
Dipankar Bhattacharya

Reviewers
Ian Grieve
James Wood

Acquisition Editor
Rukhsana Khambatta

Lead Technical Editors
Rukmini Iyer
Ankita Shashi
Sharvari Tawde

Technical Editors
Jalasha D'costa
Saumya Kunder
Varun Pius Rodrigues

Copy Editors
Brandt D'Mello
Insiya Morbiwala
Aditya Nair
Laxmi Subramanian

Project Coordinator
Anurag Banerjee

Proofreader
Ting Baker

Indexer
Tejal Soni

Graphics
Ronak Dhruv

Production Coordinator
Shantanu Zagade

Cover Work
Shantanu Zagade

About the Author

Dipankar Bhattacharya is a Dynamics CRM consultant and Microsoft technology evangelist. He is a Certified Professional in Microsoft Dynamics CRM, the Microsoft Dynamics Sure Step methodology, and core .NET technologies, such as .NET 3.5, ADO.NET, WPF, and WCF. He has been working with Microsoft technologies for around nine years and his primary focus has been solution architecture, system integration, computer telephony integration, and data migration. Currently, he is associated with Microsoft Services Global Delivery as a Business Solution Consultant and he is working with various enterprise customers, assisting them with architecting a solution till its deployment. He has been architecting, developing, and deploying business solutions across the globe using Dynamics CRM, xRM and Customer Care Accelerator for Dynamics CRM, and so on.

> **Disclaimer**
>
> The opinions expressed in this book are solely my personal understandings and do not represent the thoughts, intentions, plans, or strategies of my employers.

Acknowledgments

Writing this book has been quite a journey, and during the evolution of this book, I have accumulated many debts, only a few of which I have space to acknowledge here.

I would like to offer a big thanks to Packt Publishing for publishing this book. Special thanks to the Project Coordinator, Anurag Banerjee, for his continuous support since the very beginning. I must thank Sharvari Tawde and Rukhsana Khambatta who helped me with proofreading and styling, and offered valuable comments to make this book better. Thanks to the entire team of Packt Publishing for their help and dedication.

I wanted to offer my sincere thanks to Ian Grieve and James Wood for their insightful feedback and excellent technical review. They have helped me fill the gaps and improve the overall quality of the book.

I have been fortunate enough to work amid a very passionate set of people; they have all helped me enrich my knowledge base. I want to offer thanks to them for their help with writing this book.

I have spent most of my time writing when my little daughter, Dishita, expected me to spend time with her. Finally she will have her papa back with her. Dishita, you surely deserve packets of chocolates. My wife, Sangeeta, has been a consistent support, and without her help and encouragement, this book would not have become a reality. I want to thank my family immensely for their best wishes, which have always provided me strength and encouragement.

Last but not least, I beg forgiveness of all those who have been with me through the course of writing this book and whose names I have failed to mention.

I hope readers will have at least half as much fun reading this book as I've had writing it. Readers can reach me at `b.dipankar@outlook.com`.

About the Reviewers

Ian Grieve is a Microsoft Dynamics GP and CRM certified consultant specializing in the delivery of Microsoft Dynamics GP and CRM projects. He is a senior consultant at Perfect Image Ltd, a Microsoft Partner and VAR in the North East of England.

Ian has worked with Microsoft Dynamics GP since 2003, and over the past nine years since then, has dealt with all aspects of the product life cycle, right from presales, to implementation, to technical and functional training, to post go-live support, and subsequent upgrades and process reviews. Alongside his work with Microsoft Dynamics GP, he has fulfilled a similar role dealing with Microsoft Dynamics CRM, with especial emphasis on project delivery and training of end users in the management of sales, marketing, and service.

In his spare time, Ian runs the *azurecurve | Ramblings of a Dynamics GP Consultant* blog dedicated to Microsoft Dynamics GP and related products, and tries, often unsuccessfully, to squeeze in extra time for the blog related to Dynamics CRM, called *coralcurve | A Consultant's Dabblings In Dynamics CRM*.

James Wood is a consultant at Gap Consulting with skills in the end-to-end implementation of enterprise-level Microsoft Dynamics CRM solutions. He graduated from the University of Huddersfield with a first in Computer Games Programming before making the switch to business applications.

He has worked with Microsoft Dynamics CRM for three years and is an able developer of bespoke applications. He has worked on a number of small to large implementations in sectors including local and regional government, education, defense, banking, manufacturing, and welfare.

He has also worked as a technical reviewer for *Microsoft Dynamics CRM 2011 Application Design* and on an upcoming book on Microsoft Dynamics CRM 5.0 Reporting by *Packt Publishing*.

You can read his blog at `www.woodsworkblog.wordpress.com`.

I would like to thank my family and friends, especially Georgia, for everything.

Table of Contents

Preface 1

Chapter 1: Installing Dynamics CRM 2011 7

Introduction 8
Installing Dynamics CRM Server 10
Installing Microsoft Dynamics CRM Reporting Extensions 24
Installing Dynamics CRM for Outlook 28
Installing a Dynamics CRM language pack 35
Installing Microsoft Dynamics CRM E-mail Router 40
Configuring Microsoft Dynamics E-mail Router 44
Installing Microsoft Dynamics CRM E-mail Router on multiple computers 52
Deploying Microsoft Dynamics CRM on multiple servers 54
Creating a new organization 60
Editing the organization's details 62

Chapter 2: Maintaining and Optimizing Microsoft Dynamics CRM 2011 Server 65

Introduction 66
Backing up Dynamics CRM 2011 Database Server 67
Backing up Dynamics CRM 2011 Server 74
Recovering from a Dynamics CRM 2011 Database Server failure 75
Recovering from a Dynamics CRM 2011 Server failure 78
Enabling server-level tracing 79
Enabling deployment-level tracing 82
Enabling tracing on the Microsoft Dynamics CRM 2011 E-mail Router machine 84
Monitoring Dynamics CRM 2011 Server performance 85
Optimizing Dynamics CRM 2011 Database Server performance 87
Optimizing Dynamics CRM 2011 Server performance 98

Chapter 3: Administering Microsoft Dynamics CRM 2011 107
Securing Dynamics CRM 2011 deployment with SSL/HTTPS 108
Configuring Claims-based authentication (AD FS) for Microsoft Dynamics CRM 2011 111
Configuring Internet-facing Deployment (IFD) 122
Creating a new deployment administrator 127
Creating a new system administrator 131
Creating a new business unit 132
Configuring a security role 134
Creating a custom administrator security role 139
Creating a field-level security profile 141
Adding a new user account in the Dynamics CRM 2011 system 142
Adding multiple users in the Dynamics CRM 2011 system 146
Creating a new team in the Dynamics CRM 2011 system 148
Configuring autonumbering formats 150
Configuring system-wide settings 152
Configuring fiscal-year settings 156
Configuring error-notification preferences 157

Chapter 4: Data Management 159
Introduction to data import 159
Importing data into Dynamics CRM 2011 with Import Data Wizard 160
Exporting Dynamics CRM 2011 data to Microsoft Excel 170
Cleaning data using Bulk Deletion Wizard 172
Creating duplicate detection rules 175
Scheduling duplicate detection jobs 180
Enabling auditing in the Dynamics CRM 2011 system 183
Viewing and cleaning audit records 187

Chapter 5: Solution Management 191
Introduction to solution management 192
Creating a solution publisher 193
Creating a new unmanaged solution 194
Adding an item in the unmanaged solution 196
Removing/deleting an item from the unmanaged solution 198
Exporting a solution 200
Importing a solution 203
Updating a managed solution 206
Deleting components from a managed solution 208

Uninstalling or deleting a solution 209
Exporting translations from an unmanaged solution 210
Importing translations to an unmanaged solution 212

Chapter 6: Entity Customizations 215
Introduction to entities 215
Creating a custom entity 218
Updating the icon of an entity 226
Creating a custom field for an entity 229
Creating a global option set 234
Creating a new one-to-many (1:N) or many-to-one (N:1) relationship 237
Creating a new many-to-many (N:N) relationship 242
Creating a relationship field mapping 247

Chapter 7: Form and View Customizations 251
Introduction 252
Creating and customizing an entity main form 254
Controlling form behavior using JScript 269
Customizing the process-driven form (Dynamics CRM 2011 Online only) 272
Creating and customizing the mobile form 280
Configuring a form to be role-based 282
Creating and customizing a public view 284
Customizing search criteria for the Quick Find view 290
Creating a user's personal view 292
Deactivating or deleting a user's personal view 295

Chapter 8: Site Map and Ribbon Customizations 297
Introduction to Site Map and Ribbon 297
Editing the Site Map 299
Preparing for editing the ribbon 307
Adding a new button to an existing ribbon group for all entities 310
Adding a new button to an existing ribbon group of a specific entity 316
Hiding a ribbon button 327
Importing the modified ribbon definition 330

Chapter 9: Office and SharePoint Integration 333
Introduction 333
Creating Mail Merge templates using Microsoft Word 334
Integrating Microsoft SharePoint Server (2010/2013) with Dynamics CRM 2011 342

Chapter 10: Processes 351
Introduction to processes 351
Creating a workflow using the Dynamics CRM 2011 web interface 352
Creating a dialog using the Dynamics CRM 2011 web interface 361
Querying Dynamics CRM data in a dialog 371
Monitoring the workflow execution status 376
Index 381

Preface

Microsoft Dynamics CRM 2011 Cookbook is a hands-on guide with clear, step-by-step instructions to deploy, maintain, optimize, and administer the Dynamics CRM 2011 system along with advanced configuration and customization processes.

This book introduces Dynamics CRM 2011 by describing the important aspects of the system. It will take you through a number of clear and practical recipes, right from successful deployment, hassle-free maintenance, and effective administration to advanced level configuration and customization techniques.

This book details the various customization techniques; for example, solution management, data management, entity-form-view-relationship customization, Site Map and ribbon customization, integration with Microsoft Outlook and SharePoint, workflow and dialog configuration.

This book also discusses the technical details around every recipe, which will provide the reader with a deeper understanding of how the recipe actually works.

What this book covers

Chapter 1, Installing Dynamics CRM 2011, is a step-by-step guide to installing Microsoft Dynamics CRM 2011 server components. This chapter covers the installation of Dynamics CRM in both single server mode and multiserver mode. Additionally, it also covers the installation of Reporting Extensions, Outlook extension, Language Pack, and E-mail Router. Finally, the creation of Dynamics CRM Organization is also discussed.

Chapter 2, Maintaining and Optimizing Microsoft Dynamics CRM 2011 Server, provides step-by-step guidance for backing up the Dynamics CRM database and application server. This chapter also describes how to recover from a failure of the Dynamics CRM database and application server. Additionally, it covers server-level tracing, deployment-level tracing, monitoring, and optimizing Dynamics CRM 2011 database and application server performance.

Chapter 3, Administering Microsoft Dynamics CRM 2011, explains how to securely deploy Internet-facing Dynamics CRM 2011 using AD FS. This chapter explains how to create a new deployment administrator, system administrator, business units, security roles, and field-level security profiles. The steps to create a custom administrator security role are also discussed here. Additionally, this chapter explains how to add users to the system, how to create and manage teams, and how to configure system-level settings, fiscal settings, autonumbering formats, and error notification settings.

Chapter 4, Data Management, covers data import techniques using Import Data wizard and data maps and data export techniques using Microsoft Office Excel. Additionally, it also covers bulk data deletion, duplicate detection, and the auditing feature in the Dynamics CRM 2011 system.

Chapter 5, Solution Management, describes the Dynamics CRM 2011 solution framework using recipes for creating a solution publisher and unmanaged solution. This chapter also covers the configuration and customization of the unmanaged solution, the export and import of solution files, solution uninstallation, and deletion techniques. Additionally, it describes the export and import technique of translations using an unmanaged solution.

Chapter 6, Entity Customizations, shows how to create custom entities and custom fields inside the Dynamics CRM 2011 system. Additionally, it also shows how to create and configure new relationships between entities in the Dynamics CRM 2011 system.

Chapter 7, Form and View Customizations, discusses how to create and/or customize the main form of an entity, the new process-driven forms of Dynamics CRM Online, and controlling the behavior of a form using JScript. This chapter also discusses how to configure forms to be security role based, and how to create and/or configure various system views and personal views in the Dynamics CRM 2011 system.

Chapter 8, Site Map and Ribbon Customizations, covers the recipes for editing Site Map and ribbon components of the Dynamics CRM 2011 system.

Chapter 9, Office and SharePoint Integration, explains how to configure Dynamics CRM 2011 to be integrated with Microsoft Office and Microsoft SharePoint Server.

Chapter 10, Processes, describes how to configure a business logic step by step, using workflows and dialogs in the Dynamics CRM 2011 system.

What you need for this book

You will need the following software to install Dynamics CRM 2011 on-premises, and the same deployment can further be used for the remaining recipes in this book. The required software is:

- Microsoft Windows Server 2012 or 2008 (x64 architecture) running Active Directory and Internet Information Services (IIS) 7.0 or higher

- Microsoft SQL Server 2012 or 2008 (x64 architecture)
- Microsoft Office 2003 or higher
- Microsoft Exchange Server 2010 or later
- Microsoft SharePoint Server 2010 or later

You can also use a 30-day trial version of Microsoft Dynamics CRM 2011 Online to carry out most of the system administration and customization recipes that are common in the Online and On-premises versions. To create a Dynamics CRM 2011 Online trial version, please visit `http://crm.dynamics.com`.

Who this book is for

This book is great for Microsoft Dynamics CRM 2011 professionals who have a beginner-level understanding of the system and who are looking to get a good grounding in how to deploy, maintain, configure, and customize a Dynamics CRM 2011 application efficiently.

It's assumed that the reader has a basic understanding of IT infrastructure topologies along with a functional knowledge of Dynamics CRM 2011 Sales, Marketing, and Services modules.

Conventions

In this book, you will find a number of styles of text that distinguish between different kinds of information. Here are some examples of these styles, and an explanation of their meaning.

Code words in text are shown as follows: "The form layout definition is actually stored as an XML file called `Form Xml` in the `SystemForm` entity"

A block of code is set as follows:

```
</Descriptions>
<Group Description="string"
        DescriptionResourceId="string"
        Icon="string"
        Id="string"
        IsProfile="" ["0" | "1" | "true" | "false"]
        License="string="
        ResourceId="string="
                Url="string=">
    <Titles />
    <Descriptions />
```

Any command-line input or output is written as follows:

```
AllowHtcExtn.ps1 http://<server_name>:<port_number>
```

New terms and **important words** are shown in bold. Words that you see on the screen, in menus or dialog boxes for example, appear in the text like this: "Select the **Start Auditing** checkbox to enable auditing at the system level."

> Warnings or important notes appear in a box like this.

> Tips and tricks appear like this.

Reader feedback

Feedback from our readers is always welcome. Let us know what you think about this book—what you liked or may have disliked. Reader feedback is important for us to develop titles that you really get the most out of.

To send us general feedback, simply send an e-mail to `feedback@packtpub.com`, and mention the book title via the subject of your message.

If there is a topic that you have expertise in and you are interested in either writing or contributing to a book, see our author guide on `www.packtpub.com/authors`.

Customer support

Now that you are the proud owner of a Packt book, we have a number of things to help you to get the most from your purchase.

Downloading the example code

You can download the example code files for all Packt books you have purchased from your account at `http://www.packtpub.com`. If you purchased this book elsewhere, you can visit `http://www.packtpub.com/support` and register to have the files e-mailed directly to you.

Errata

Although we have taken every care to ensure the accuracy of our content, mistakes do happen. If you find a mistake in one of our books—maybe a mistake in the text or the code—we would be grateful if you would report this to us. By doing so, you can save other readers from frustration and help us improve subsequent versions of this book. If you find any errata, please report them by visiting `http://www.packtpub.com/submit-errata`, selecting your book, clicking on the **errata submission form** link, and entering the details of your errata. Once your errata are verified, your submission will be accepted and the errata will be uploaded on our website, or added to any list of existing errata, under the Errata section of that title. Any existing errata can be viewed by selecting your title from `http://www.packtpub.com/support`.

Piracy

Piracy of copyright material on the Internet is an ongoing problem across all media. At Packt, we take the protection of our copyright and licenses very seriously. If you come across any illegal copies of our works, in any form, on the Internet, please provide us with the location address or website name immediately so that we can pursue a remedy.

Please contact us at `copyright@packtpub.com` with a link to the suspected pirated material.

We appreciate your help in protecting our authors, and our ability to bring you valuable content.

Questions

You can contact us at `questions@packtpub.com` if you are having a problem with any aspect of the book, and we will do our best to address it.

1

Installing Dynamics CRM 2011

Dynamics CRM 2011 is a piece of **customer relationship management** (**CRM**) software by Microsoft. It provides a powerful business application platform for marketing, sales, and services modules. The Microsoft Dynamics CRM 2011 software solution works as a web client, while it can also be embedded within an Outlook client.

This chapter will explore recipes for installing the various components of Microsoft Dynamics CRM 2011. With the installation of Dynamics CRM, the process of exploring the world of Dynamics CRM 2011 will begin.

In this chapter, we will learn how to install various components of Microsoft Dynamics CRM 2011 step by step.

The chapter includes the following recipes:

- Installing Dynamics CRM Server
- Installing Microsoft Dynamics CRM Reporting Extensions
- Installing Dynamics CRM for Outlook
- Installing a Dynamics CRM language pack
- Installing Microsoft Dynamics CRM E-mail Router
- Configuring Microsoft Dynamics CRM E-mail Router
- Installing Microsoft Dynamics CRM E-mail Router on multiple computers
- Deploying Microsoft Dynamics CRM on multiple servers
- Creating a new organization
- Editing organization details

Introduction

Microsoft Dynamics CRM 2011 Server is a .NET-based web application that works exclusively with Microsoft SQL Server databases. It uses **Windows Communication Foundation** (**WCF**) as the communication protocol. Microsoft Dynamics CRM 2011 supports three types of deployment, namely, **on-premises deployment**, **Internet-facing Deployment** (**IFD**), and **CRM Online**. Each deployment supports a choice of client applications, which are as follows:

- Microsoft Dynamics CRM 2011 Web Client
- Microsoft Dynamics CRM for Microsoft Office Outlook
- Microsoft Dynamics CRM for Microsoft Office Outlook with Offline Access
- Mobile Express for Microsoft Dynamics CRM

The on-premises and IFD deployment types are deployed using the data center or hardware capabilities of the customer or a hosting partner. On the other hand, Microsoft Dynamics CRM Online is a powerful solution that provides customers with the benefits of Dynamics CRM in a Microsoft-hosted environment.

In this chapter, we will dive deep into the recipes for on-premises deployment of Microsoft Dynamics CRM 2011, and in *Chapter 3, Administering Microsoft Dynamics CRM 2011*, we will discuss how to configure a CRM deployment for IFD.

Single server versus multiserver

Microsoft Dynamics CRM 2011 can be installed on a single server as well as on multiple servers. While a single-server deployment is mainly recommended for development purposes or small-user-based production deployments, a multiserver deployment is more suitable for most production environments because multiserver environments provide a better balancing of processing load across several servers. Load-balanced multiserver deployment can increase the performance, availability, scalability, and throughput of the system. In addition, it also can increase the resilience of the system to server failures.

To begin with, we shall start with a recipe on the installation of Microsoft Dynamics CRM 2011 on a single-server box with all its required components. Upon successful installation on a single box, we will find the recipe on the installation of a multiserver machine more useful.

One limitation of single-server deployments is that the server machine on which Dynamics CRM 2011 is installed cannot function as an Active Directory directory service domain controller unless the operating system of the server is **Windows Small Business Server**.

Hardware and software specifications for Microsoft Dynamics CRM 2011 Server

Like any other software, Microsoft Dynamics CRM 2011 also comes with minimum recommended hardware and software specifications. Based on the Microsoft guidelines, the recommended hardware specifications for a Full Server deployment is as follows:

- Quad-core x64 architecture
- 2 GHz CPU or higher, such as Intel Xeon or AMD Opteron systems
- 8 GB of RAM or more
- 40 GB or more of hard disk space

Hardware sizing greatly depends on nonfunctional requirements such as total user base, maximum number of concurrent users, required page load time, initial data volume, data growth, and data archival policy. Microsoft Dynamics Lab has released **Performance Toolkit** for Dynamics CRM 2011, which can be used to collect performance-related data that then can be used for sizing the related decisions in on-premises deployment. Performance Toolkit can be downloaded at `http://pinpoint.microsoft.com/en-gb/applications/performance-toolkit-for-microsoft-dynamics-crm-2011-12884915630`.

The Microsoft-recommended hardware specifications for the SQL Server-based Dynamics CRM database are as follows:

- Quad-core x64 architecture
- 2 GHz CPU or higher, such as AMD Opteron or Intel Xeon systems
- 16 GB of RAM or more
- SAS RAID 5 or RAID 10 hard disk array

> This specification is based on an estimated top load of up to 320 users on the system. Computers with more than 16 GB of memory will require more disk space for paging, hibernation, and dump files.

Microsoft-defined hardware requirements for Dynamics CRM Server 2011 can be found at:

`http://technet.microsoft.com/en-us/library/hh699840.aspx`

The recommended operating systems for Dynamics CRM 2011 Server are Windows Server 2008 (Standard/Enterprise/Datacenter editions), Windows Server 2008 R2, Windows Small Business Server (Premium/Standard), and Windows Small Business Server (Standard/Essential Update Rollup 13 of Dynamics CRM 2013 also supports Windows Server 2012.).

Internet Information Services (**IIS**) 7.0 or 7.5, along with Indexing Service, IIS Admin service, and **World Wide Web Publishing Service** (**W3SVC**), need to be installed and running. **Windows Data Access Components** (**Windows DAC**) 6.0, and **Microsoft ASP.NET 4** are also required for the installation of Microsoft Dynamics CRM 2011 Server.

The Microsoft Dynamics CRM 2011 Server machine must be a domain member of a domain that is running in one of these Active Directory directory service domain modes: Windows 2000 (Mixed/Native), Windows Server 2003 (Interim/Native), and Windows Server 2008 (Interim/Native).

Microsoft Dynamics CRM 2011 only supports the x64 version of Microsoft SQL Server 2008 with SP1 (Standard/Enterprise/Datacenter editions) / Microsoft SQL Server 2008 R2 (x64 version). Update Rollup 6 (and higher) also supports SQL Server 2012 (Enterprise/Business Intelligence/Standard versions).

> Active/Active SQL Server clustering is supported in Dynamics CRM Server 2011 from Update Rollup 1 onwards but not as a load-balancing configuration.
>
> Other than that, 32-bit versions of SQL Server and **SQL Server Reporting Services** (**SSRS**) are not supported.

Microsoft defined hardware requirements for SQL Server for Dynamics CRM Server 2011 can be found at:

`http://technet.microsoft.com/en-us/library/hh699808.aspx`

Installing Dynamics CRM Server

The installation of the on-premises version of Microsoft Dynamics CRM 2011 involves a little more than the standard Microsoft wizard process. Here we will discuss how to install the on-premises version on a single-server machine.

Getting ready

Microsoft Dynamics CRM is designed so that its components (**Application Service**, **Deployment Service**, **Sandbox Processing Service**, and **Asynchronous Processing Service**) can run under separate identities. It is recommended that you use separate Active Directory accounts for running these components and **SQL Server Reporting Services**. Additionally, these accounts should be set up as **service accounts** in Active Directory and should only be granted the permissions necessary to enable a particular component to function. By this, we can help secure the system and reduce the likelihood of exploitation.

[**Managed service accounts**, introduced in Windows Server 2008 R2, are not supported for running Microsoft Dynamics CRM services.]

We will now take a look into these identity accounts and the privileges to be granted to them for proper functioning. It is very important to set up these accounts before starting the installation of Dynamics CRM 2011. After the installation of Dynamics CRM, these accounts *should not be added* to Dynamics CRM as users. This might create authentication issues and unexpected behavior in the application. These service accounts should be granted the following permissions:

- Application service account:
    - Should be a member of the Active Directory Domain Users group and the local machine's Performance Log Users group
    - Should have administrative access on the computers that are running Microsoft Dynamics CRM website and SQL Server
    - The service account may need a **service principal number** (**SPN**) for the URL used to access the website that is associated with it

[By default, websites using IIS7.0 or later versions are configured to use kernel-mode authentication. When a Microsoft Dynamics CRM website is run using the Kernel-Mode authentication, SPNs for the Microsoft Dynamics CRM Application Pool identities are not required.]

- Deployment Web service account:
    - Should be a member of the Active Directory Domain Users group
    - Must be granted the **Logon as service** permission in Local Security Policy
    - Should have administrative access on the computers where Dynamics CRM 2011 Deployment Web Service and SQL Server are running
    - Should have **sysadmin** permission on the instance of SQL Server to be used for the configuration and organization databases
    - The service account may need an SPN for the URL used to access the website associated with it

- Microsoft Dynamics CRM Asynchronous Processing service account:
    - Should be a member of the Active Directory Domain Users group
    - Should be a member of the Performance Log Users group
    - Must be granted the **Logon as service** permission in Local Security Policy
    - The service account may need an SPN for the URL used to access the website associated with it
- Microsoft Dynamics CRM Sandbox Processing service account:
    - Should be a member of the Active Directory Domain Users group.
    - Must be granted the **Logon as service** permission in the Local Security Policy.
    - The service account may need an SPN for the URL used to access the website associated with it. To set the SPN for the Sandbox Processing service account, run the following command at the command prompt on the computer where the service is running:

      ```
      SETSPN -a MSCRMSandboxService/<ComputerName> <service account>
      ```

      Replace `<ComputerName>` with the name of the computer running this service and `<serviceaccount>` with the name of the service account.
- Dynamics CRM 2011 Installation User account:
    - Should be a member of the Active Directory Domain User group.
    - Should have administrative access on the computer where the Dynamics CRM 2011 setup will be run.
    - Should have read and write permissions to the local `Program Files` folder.
    - Should have administrative access on the computer where the instance of SQL Server that will be used to store the Microsoft Dynamics CRM databases is located.
    - Should have **sysadmin** membership on the instance of SQL Server that will be used to store the Microsoft Dynamics CRM databases.
    - Should have organization and security group creation permission in the Active Directory directory service.

- If Microsoft SQL Server Reporting Services is installed on a different server, the **Content Manager** role must be added at the root level for installing the user account. We must also add the **System Administrator** role at the site-wide level for the installation of the user account. Also make sure that port 80 (the default port on which Reporting Services is installed) accepts connections.

How to do it...

In the previous sections we have discussed the minimum recommended software and hardware specifications and service account requirements. Now we will discuss how to install Dynamics CRM Server components on a single-server machine.

During the installation, if a machine restart is requested by the setup, it is recommended that one selects the **Restart** option before proceeding with the installation.

It is usually recommended that one creates separate **organization units** (**OUs**) for each CRM deployment, especially for production or production-like deployment environments. Dynamics CRM 2011 Server installer creates security groups within the specified OU, and hence, it is advisable to create separate OUs for deployment isolation purposes.

Follow these steps to install Dynamics CRM 2011 Server in a single-server machine:

1. Log in to the machine using the installation user account setup using the recommended privileges.
2. Run the Dynamics CRM 2011 setup.

   Alternatively, navigate to the installation directory for Dynamics CRM 2011 Server and run the Dynamics CRM 2011 setup file at `\Server\amd64\SetupServer.exe`.
3. It is recommended that you run the setup using the **Run as Administrator** option by right-clicking on the `.exe` file.
4. On the **Welcome to Microsoft Dynamics CRM Setup** page, select **Get updates for Microsoft Dynamics CRM (recommended)** in the latest update rollups that have to be applied during the installation; otherwise, select **Do not get updates**. Press **Next** to continue.

   It is recommended that you assess the impact of the update rollups before applying them because they can break any existing code or the rollup itself can have defects.
5. On the **Product Key Information** page, enter the product key.
6. On the **Accept License** page, accept the license agreement.

7. If the setup detects that a few of the required components are missing, the **Install Required Components** page will appear. The missing required components can be installed by clicking on **Install**. When the components are installed, the status column will change from **Not Installed** to **Installed** and we can click on **Next** to continue as shown in the following screenshot:

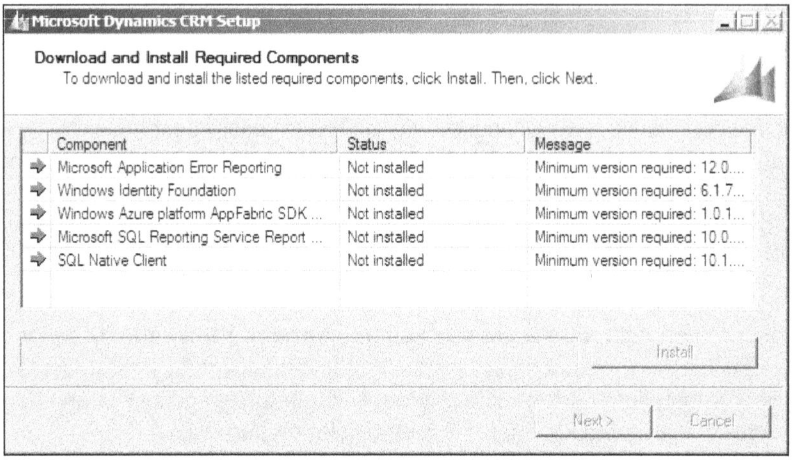

8. The **Select Installation Location** page provides us with the option of choosing the installation directory. Accept the default location or enter a different file installation location, and then click on **Next**.

9. The **Specify Server Roles** page appears. By default, **Full Server** is selected. For a single-server deployment, we will go with the **Full Server** option.

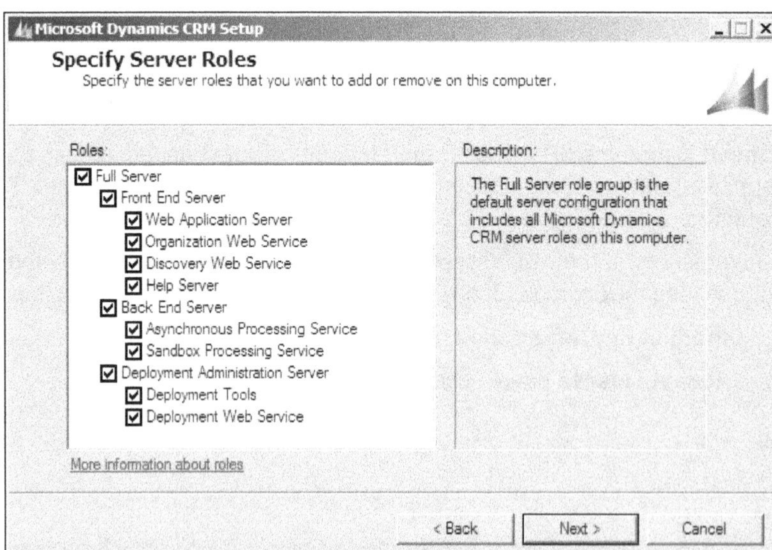

10. On the **Specify Deployment Options** page, select the **Create a new deployment** option. In the **Enter or select the name of the computer that is running SQL Server to use with the deployment** box, type or select the instance of SQL Server that will be used to store Dynamics CRM 2011 databases.

    In case there already exists an `MSCRM_CONFIG` database from a previous CRM deployment that is intended to be used here, select the **Connect to, and if necessary, upgrade an existing deployment** option. But, if an `MSCRM_CONFIG` database does not exist in the SQL Server instance, an error will occur.

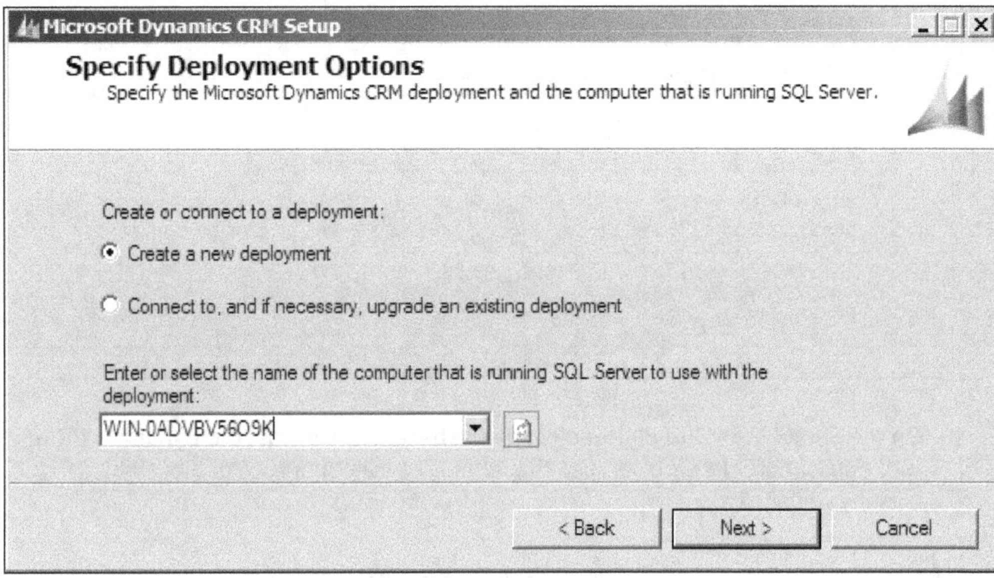

11. On the **Select the Organizational Unit** page, click on **Browse** to display the Active Directory structure. Select the location where the Microsoft Dynamics CRM organizational unit is to be installed, click on **OK**, and then click on **Next**.

    Four Microsoft Dynamics CRM-specific security groups will be created in this organizational unit. To know more about these groups, read the *How it works...* section of this recipe.

12. In the **Specify Service Accounts** page, select the service accounts for the Microsoft Dynamics CRM services and then click on **Next** as shown in the following screenshot:

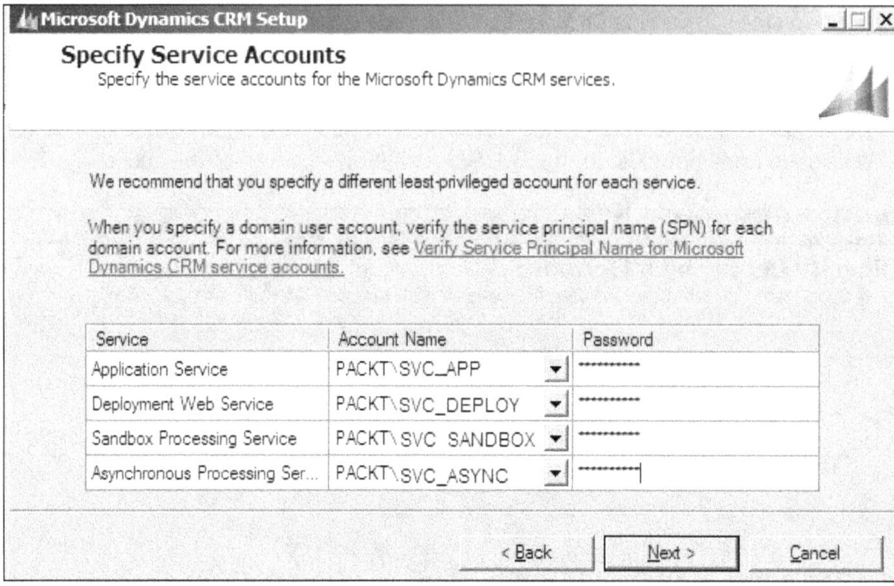

13. On the **Select Web Site** page, select the website that will host the Dynamics CRM web application. Here we can use the default website (port 80) or any other existing websites.

> Unless there is a valid reason for not installing the application in the default website, leave it as it is because among other advantages, it will be much easier for users to access the website as they won't have to remember another port number. If we select a network port other than the default port, we have to ensure that the firewall does not block the port.

If you decide to create a new website, select the **Create new Web site** option; the setup creates a new website for Microsoft Dynamics CRM Server 2011. We can specify the port number by typing the TCP port number that Microsoft Dynamics CRM clients will use to connect to Microsoft Dynamics CRM Server 2011. The default port number is 5555.

14. Click on **Next>** to proceed:

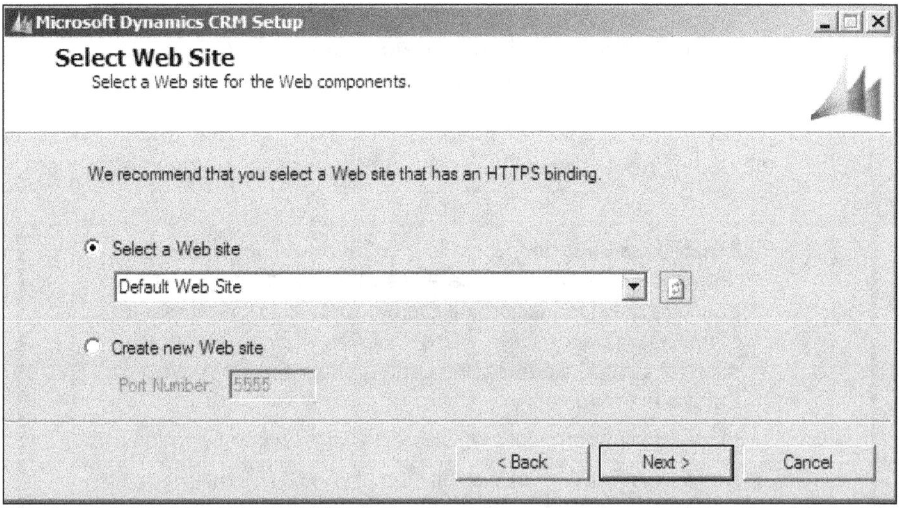

15. On the **Specify E-mail Router Settings** page, specify the name or IP address of the machine where E-mail Router will be installed. If E-mail Router is not to be installed, this information can be left blank. Click on **Next** to proceed.

> We will discuss how to install E-mail Router later in this chapter.

16. On the **Specify Organization Settings** page, we have to specify the following details:
    - Name of the CRM Organization in the **Display Name** textbox. Usually the organization name represents the company name, but the organization name has to be properly thought through as, once deployed, this name cannot be changed.
    - The **Unique Database Name** value will be generated from the organization name specified above it. In most cases, we should proceed with this generated name as it becomes easy in the future to recognize the database linked to a CRM Organization in the database server. But this name can be changed and a new name of up to 30 characters can be provided
    - Under **ISO Currency code**, click on **Browse** and select a base currency.

> Once the CRM Organization is created, the base currency code cannot be updated, though the base currency name and base currency symbol can be changed.
>
> Base currency has been explained in the *There's more...* section of this recipe.

- In the **SQL collation** list, we can leave the default selection or select a different database collation that the organization database will use to sort and compare data characters.

  The default SQL collation changes based on the base language selection of the deployment. The collation settings cannot be changed after installation.

> **SQL Server Collation** refers to a set of rules that is used to determine how character data is sorted and compared. Collation encodes the rules governing the proper use of characters for either a language, such as Greek or Polish, or an alphabet, such as **Latin1_General** (the Latin alphabet used by Western European languages).
>
> More information about SQL Server Collation can be found at:
>
> `http://msdn.microsoft.com/en-IN/library/ms143726.aspx`

After setting these details, click on **Next**.

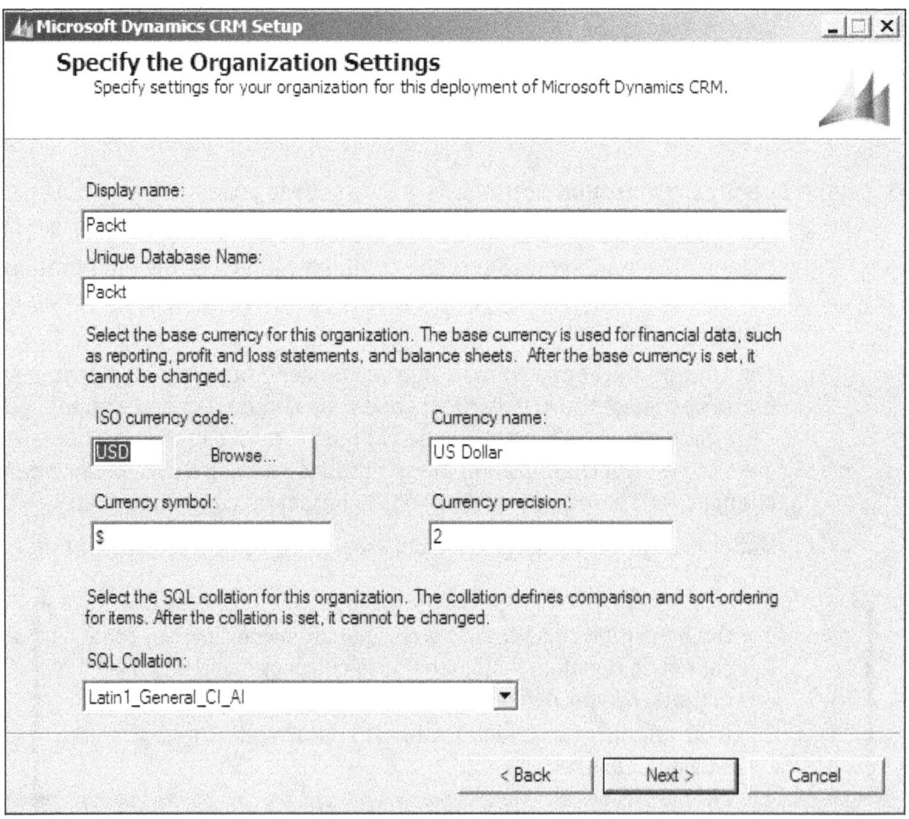

17. On the **Specify Reporting Services Server** page, please type the Reporting Server URL. Please verify the URL in a separate browser window. Please note that the Reporting Server URL should be specified here and not the Reporting Manager URL. Click on **Next** to proceed.
18. On the **Help Us Improve the Customer Experience** page, select whether you want to participate in the Customer Experience Improvement Program, and then click on **Next**.
19. On the **Select Microsoft Update Preference** page, indicate whether to use Microsoft Update to keep CRM Server 2011 updated.

> Automatic rollup update is not recommended, and before applying any update rollup we have to be very sure (by trying the rollup in a test environment) that it does not break existing functionality and that the update rollup itself is not broken.

20. Click on **Next** to proceed.
21. Next is the **System Checks** page, which outlines a summary of all requirements and recommendations for successful installation.

    If there are any errors or warnings, they will be listed here. We have to rectify all errors before proceeding further. Warnings, however, can be ignored, but it is strongly suggested that you rectify the warnings as they may cause issues later on in the system.
22. Click on **Next** to proceed.
23. Next, we have the **Service Disruption Warning** page. This page indicates all services that can be stopped or restarted during installation. Click on **Next** to proceed.
24. Review the **Ready to Install Microsoft Dynamics CRM** page, and click on **Back** to correct any setting to proceed warning free. When we are ready to continue, click on **Install**.
25. If installation completes successfully, the **Microsoft Dynamics CRM Server setup completed** page appears.
26. To install Dynamics CRM, we must click on **Finish** and wait until the server is restarted.

How it works...

In this recipe we have installed Microsoft Dynamics CRM 2011 on a single-server machine. During the process, the installer creates four security groups in Active Directory; these groups are fundamental for Dynamics CRM's functioning. Usually it is left to the installer to create these groups, but these groups can be precreated manually and can be used during the Dynamics CRM installation. If these groups do not already exist in Active Directory, the installation user must have Active Directory rights to create them. The following are the groups that will get created during installation:

Group	Description
`PrivReportingGroup`	This is the privileged Microsoft Dynamics CRM user group for reporting functions. It is configured during the setup of Microsoft Dynamics CRM Reporting Extensions.
`PrivUserGroup`	This is the privileged Microsoft Dynamics CRM user group for special administrative functions, including the `CRMAppPool` identity (domain user or NetworkService).
`SQLAccessGroup`	This group pertains to all server processes / service accounts that require access to SQL Server, including the `CRMAppPool` identity (domain user or NetworkService). Members of this group have the `db_owner` permission on Microsoft Dynamics CRM databases.
`ReportingGroup`	All Microsoft Dynamics CRM users are included in this group. This group is updated automatically as users are added and removed from Microsoft Dynamics CRM. By default, all Microsoft Dynamics CRM Reporting Services reports grant the `Browse` permission to this group.

One more important point to be noted here is that the four service accounts used during installation and the SQL access accounts are part of some or all of the aforementioned Active Directory groups. The following matrix will explain the group membership of these accounts:

Service account	PrivUserGroup	SQLAccessGroup	PrivReportingGroup	ReportingGroup	Performance log users
Application service account	√	√	-	-	√
Deployment Web service account	√	√	-	-	-
Asynchronous Processing service account	√	√	-	-	√
Sandbox Processing service account	-	-	-	-	√
SQL Server service account	-	-	-	-	-
SSRS service account	√	-	√	-	-

> The performance log user group is a local group on each server and not a domain group.

For Dynamics CRM to function properly, these service accounts will have to have the following rights:

- Folder read and write permission on the `Trace` folder, by default located under `\%Program Files%\Microsoft Dynamics CRM\`, and the `%AppData%` folder of the user account on the local computer
- Read and write permission to the `HKEY_LOCAL_MACHINE\SOFTWARE\Microsoft\MSCRM` and `HKEY_LOCAL_MACHINE\SYSTEM\ControlSet001\services\MSCRMSandboxService` subkeys in the Windows Registry
- The Application service account and Deployment Web service account should also be part of the `CRM_WPG` group

Microsoft Dynamics CRM 2011 uses a list of ports, and these ports have to be allowed in the firewall for CRM to function. The following matrix lists all these ports:

Protocol	Port	Description	Explanation
TCP	80	HTTP	The default web application port. The port number may be different if it is changed during Microsoft Dynamics CRM Server setup. For new websites, the default port number is 5555.
TCP	135	MSRPC	RPC endpoint resolution
TCP	139	NETBIOS-SSN	NETBIOS session service
TCP	443	HTTPS	The default HTTP secure port
TCP	445	Microsoft-DS	An Active Directory directory service is required for access and authentication.
UDP	123	NTP	Network Time Protocol
UDP	137	NETBIOS-NS	NETBIOS name service
UDP	138	NetBIOS-dgm	NetBIOS datagram service
UDP	445	Microsoft-DS	Active Directory directory service is required for access and authentication.
UDP	1025	Blackjack	DCOM, used as an RPC listener

Each of these service accounts runs a specific component within the Dynamics CRM 2011 Server infrastructure. The following outlines how these service accounts are used within Dynamics CRM 2011:

- **Application service account**: The installation of Dynamics CRM 2011 creates a separate **application pool** (`CRMAppPool`) in IIS to isolate the CRM application for better security, reliability, availability, and performance and to keep running without impacting other web applications hosted in the same IIS. The Application service account is used by Dynamics CRM 2011 to run the CRM application pool in IIS.
- **Deployment Web service account**: Dynamics CRM 2011 uses this service account to run Deployment Web Service, which is responsible for deployment-related activities such as:
    - Creating, importing, updating, upgrading, enabling, and disabling of CRM Organizations
    - Retrieving Microsoft Dynamics CRM license information for a deployment
    - Adding or removing deployment administrators
    - Enabling, disabling, or deleting servers
    - Updating deployment configuration settings
    - Enumerating and changing the state of servers in the deployment

> The Microsoft Dynamics CRM 2011 deployment service is not backward compatible. Any component, developed using Microsoft Dynamics CRM 4.0 Deployment Web Service has to be upgraded to use the Dynamics CRM 2011 deployment service to work within Dynamics CRM 2011 deployment.

- **Microsoft Dynamics CRM Asynchronous Processing service account**: This service account is used to run the Asynchronous Processing Service, which is responsible for executing long-running operations independent of the main Microsoft Dynamics CRM system process. This results in an improved overall system performance and improved scalability. The asynchronous service features a managed queue for the execution of asynchronous registered plugins, workflows, and operations such as bulk mail, bulk import, and campaign activity propagation. These operations are registered with the asynchronous service and executed later when the service processes its queue.
- **Microsoft Dynamics CRM Sandbox Processing service account**: Dynamics CRM 2011 uses this service account to run Sandbox Processing Service, which enables an isolated environment to allow the execution of custom codes, for example, plugins. Such an isolated environment reduces the possibility of custom code, affecting the operation of the organizations in the production Dynamics CRM 2011 deployment.

> It is worth installing the Sandbox Processing Service role onto a dedicated server on a separate **virtual LAN** (**VLAN**) from other computers that are running Microsoft Dynamics CRM roles. This network isolation strategy can help protect other Microsoft Dynamics CRM 2011 resources from being compromised if there is a malicious plugin running in the sandbox.

Once the installation has completed, its success can be verified by accessing the CRM server URL. The URL would be in the format http://<servername>:<port _ number>/<organization_name>/main.aspx.

Here, we will replace <servername> with the name of the Dynamics CRM 2011 server, <port_number> with the port used by Dynamics CRM 2011 Server, and <organization_name> with the CRM Organization that was created during installation.

If installation is successful, the Dynamics CRM landing page will appear in the browser window as shown in the following screenshot:

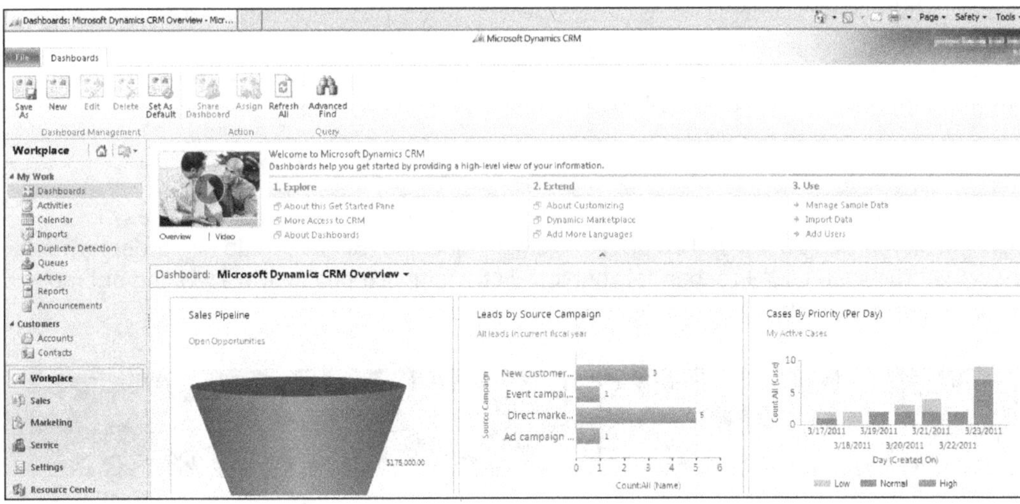

There's more...

Before we end this recipe, let's take look at some information on the use of currency codes in Microsoft Dynamics CRM 2011:

Dynamics CRM 2011 is a multicurrency system that allows a user to perform any financial transaction using their own currency, known as **transaction currency**. During installation, a primary or default currency has to be selected. This currency is the de facto currency for financial transactions within a CRM Organization and known as the **base currency**. After defining a base currency for the organization, we have to define exchange rates to associate the base currency with transaction currencies.

Each currency record has three parts describing the currency:

- The name of the currency
- The symbol that is used to represent the currency, such as $ (dollar), £ (pound), € (euro), or ¥ (yen)
- The exchange rate with the base currency

Any transaction in other currencies will automatically be converted to the base currency, using the exchange rate defined in the record for that currency, in the Microsoft Dynamics CRM database.

The base currency of a CRM Organization has to be selected carefully as:

- The base currency is used as the basis to calculate additional currencies that can be used for transaction-based records. Hence, the native currency of the CRM Organization users is usually chosen as the base currency to avoid too many currency conversions.
- Financial reporting is done based on the base currency.

The supported currency code details can be found at:

`http://msdn.microsoft.com/en-us/library/hh699729.aspx`

We have seen that, in the process of a single-server installation, all the server roles of Dynamics CRM 2011 are installed onto one single machine. But in a multiserver deployment, the server roles are usually separately deployed on multiple machines. We will find out more about multiserver Dynamics CRM deployments in the latter parts of this chapter.

Installing Microsoft Dynamics CRM Reporting Extensions

While Microsoft Dynamics CRM Reporting Extensions is not absolutely required to run Microsoft Dynamics CRM 2011, without Reporting Server installed, certain important functionalities of Dynamics CRM will not function. For example, the reporting functionality will not function and creating a new organization and organization import will be blocked until the extensions are installed and configured.

The Microsoft Dynamics CRM Reporting Extensions setup includes two data processing extensions: **Fetch data processing extension** and **SQL data processing extension**. These extensions are installed by default during Microsoft Dynamics CRM Reporting Extensions setup.

While the Fetch data processing extension is required to create, run, and schedule Fetch-based reports, the SQL data processing extension is required to run and schedule the default (out of box) or SQL-based custom reports in Microsoft Dynamics CRM 2011.

Getting ready

Before we start installing Microsoft Dynamics CRM Reporting Extensions, Microsoft Dynamics CRM Server setup must be complete.

Dynamics CRM Reporting Extensions can only be installed for one instance of SQL Server Reporting Services on a computer. In addition, different deployments of Dynamics CRM 2011 cannot share a single SQL Server Reporting Services server; however, a multitenant CRM deployment can use the same instance of Reporting Services.

The Microsoft Dynamics CRM Reporting Extensions setup must be run on a computer that has Microsoft SQL Server 2012/2008 Reporting Services installed. The user account to be used in order to install Reporting Extensions:

- Must have appropriate rights on the organization databases
- Must be the local machine administrator

The **Microsoft SQL Server Reporting Services** (**SSRS**) should be running under a separate Active Directory service account. This account should be added to two of the Dynamics CRM-specific Active Directory groups, namely, `PrivUserGroup` and `PrivReportingUserGroup`. However, this account should not be part of `SQLAccessGroup`. This account should not be set up as `Local Service` as well.

Reporting Extensions should be installed on that Microsoft SQL Server Reporting Services instance which is being used by the CRM Organization. Otherwise, reports will not function. In addition to that, the base language of CRM Organization and that of CRM Reporting Extensions has to be the same.

How to do it...

Please follow these steps to install Microsoft Dynamics CRM Reporting Extensions:

1. Run the setup utility, or alternatively, navigate to the installation directory for Dynamics CRM 2011 Server located at the route `\Server\amd64\SrsDataConnector\SetupSrsDataConnector.exe`.
2. It is recommended that you run the setup using the **Run as Administrator** option by right-clicking on the `.exe` file.
3. Like the Dynamics CRM 2011 installer, this setup also asks whether we want to check if updates are available for download and apply before proceeding with the installation.

   It is recommended that you assess the impact of the update rollups before applying it because update rollups can break any existing code or the rollup itself can have defects.

4. On the **License Agreement** page, select **I accept this license agreement** and click on **I Accept** to proceed.
5. On the **Install Required Components** page, the installer automatically identifies the components that need to be installed and allows you to install them . This page will not appear if all the required components are already installed. If something is missing, it can be installed by clicking on the **Install** button. When the components are installed, the `Status` column will change from **Missing** to **Installed** and we can click on **Next** to continue.
6. On the **Specify Configuration Database Server** page, please enter the instance of the SQL Server.

   Now if we are using the default instance of the SQL Server, enter the name of the computer that is running SQL Server and contains the Microsoft Dynamics CRM configuration database named `MSCRM_CONFIG`, and if we are using the named instance of SQL Server then enter <machine-name>\<instance-name>:

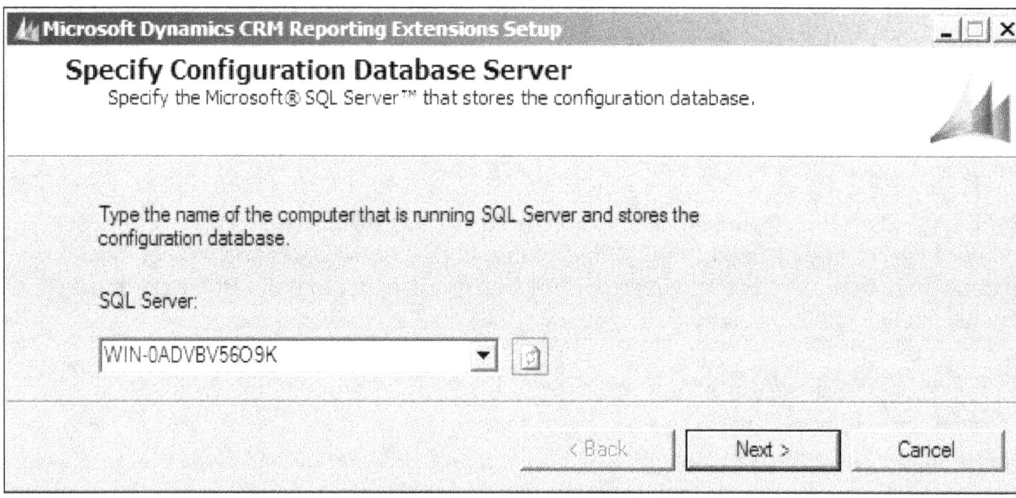

7. On the **Specify SSRS Instance Name** page, select a Microsoft SQL Server Reporting Services instance that will be used for Microsoft Dynamics CRM reporting, and then click on **Next** as shown in the following screenshot:

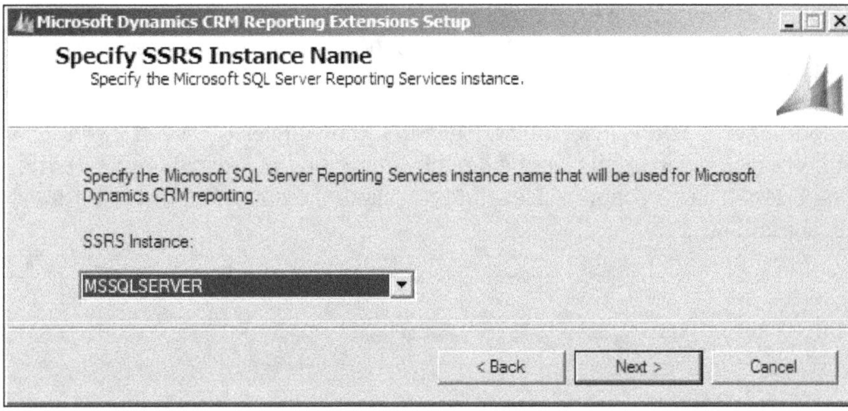

8. On the **Select Microsoft Update Preference** page, select the **Use Microsoft Update when I check for updates** option if updates have to be applied automatically. Proceed by clicking on **Next**.
9. On the **Select Installation Location** page, browse to specify where it will be installed.
10. Then the **System Checks** page appears with a summary of the requirements for a successful CRM Reporting Extensions installation. All errors must be resolved to continue. If no errors and/or only warnings appear, the installation can continue. Click on **Next** to proceed.
11. Then you will see the **Ready to Install Microsoft Dynamics CRM Reporting Extensions** page, which provides us with an overview of the system parameters in order to proceed with it. If you agree, simply click on **Install** to begin the installation.
12. When the setup is completed successfully, the **Microsoft Dynamics CRM Reporting Extensions Setup Completed** page appears. Click on **Finish**. The reports will be published for the default organization.

How it works...

This recipe installs the Fetch and SQL data processing extensions on the Microsoft SQL Server Reporting Services server. It is recommended that the SSRS instance be run on a server separate from the one which has hosted the Dynamics CRM databases.

SQL Server Reporting Services should be running on a service account that is not part of `SQLAccessGroup`; in case it does, the Reporting Extensions installer throws an error message, **A Microsoft Dynamics CRM Server component is using the same account as the instance of SQL Server Reporting Services**. Usually, it happens when the account is used to run the Dynamics CRM 2011 Server components is also used to run the SQL Server Reporting Services. It is recommended that you use a separate account to run the SQL Server Reporting Services to reduce security vulnerability.

With Dynamics CRM Reporting Extensions installed, all the default CRM reports will start working and custom SQL bad Fetch-based reports can now be created, uploaded, and scheduled.

Post the reporting extensions installation, log in to the Dynamics CRM 2011 and run any of the out-of-the-box reports. This can be done by navigating to **Workplace** | **Reports**. If Reporting Extensions has been successfully installed, the out-of-the-box reports will function successfully.

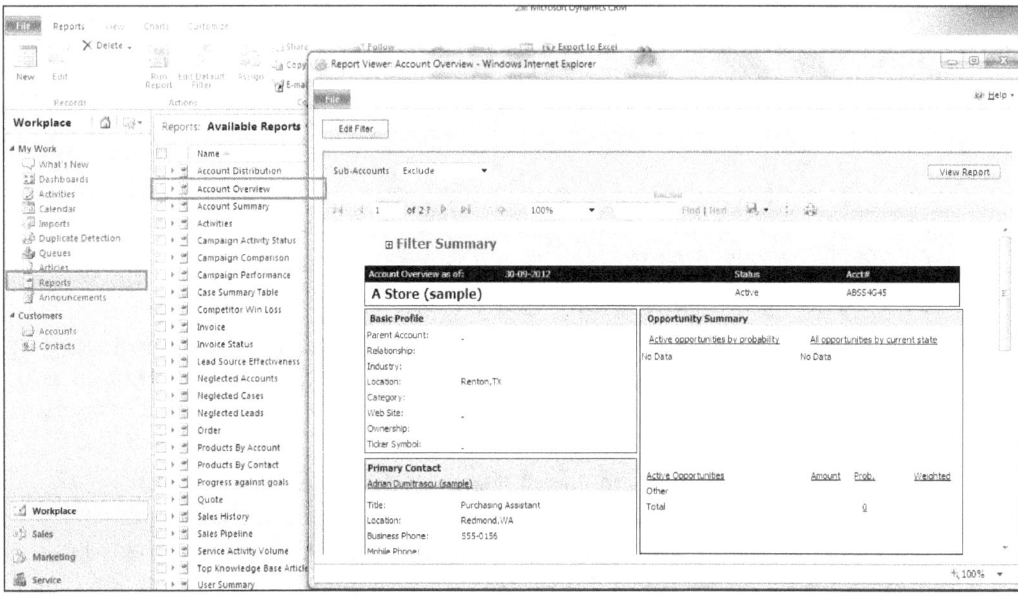

The preceding screenshot of the **Account Overview** report has been generated by using the sample data.

Installing Dynamics CRM for Outlook

Microsoft Dynamics CRM 2011 can also be accessed via a familiar Microsoft Outlook client. To access Dynamics CRM via Outlook, the Dynamics CRM Outlook client has to be installed on the client machine. If a machine is used by multiple users, Microsoft Dynamics CRM for Outlook has to be configured for each user.

Getting ready

Microsoft Dynamics CRM for Outlook can be installed with either the online or offline capability. Offline access enables a user to access Dynamics CRM data even when he or she is not connected to Dynamics CRM Server.

The Microsoft-recommended software and hardware requirements for the machine where Dynamics CRM for Outlook has to be installed are as follows:

Component	Recommended specification
Processor (32-bit)	Multicore 1.8 GHz CPU or higher
Processor (64-bit)	Multicore x64 architecture 2 GHz CPU or higher, such as AMD Opteron or Intel Xeon systems
Memory	4 GB of RAM or more
Hard disk	2 GB of available hard disk space and 7200 RPM or more
Display	Super VGA with a resolution higher than 1024 x 768

> Actual requirements and product functionality may vary based on the system configuration and operating system.

Additionally, Microsoft Dynamics CRM for Outlook using the offline capability increases the need for a higher specification of hardware, which can include processor, memory, hard disk, and network throughput. For a successful network installation, a minimum network bandwidth of 300 kbps or higher is required.

Microsoft-recommended hardware and network specifications for Dynamics CRM 2011 for Outlook can be found at:

`http://msdn.microsoft.com/en-us/library/hh699680.aspx`

To install Microsoft Dynamics CRM for Outlook, any of the following operating environments is required:

- Windows 8 (requires Dynamics CRM 2011 Update Rollup 10 or higher)
- Windows 7 (64- or 32-bit)
- Windows Vista SP2 (64- or 32-bit)
- Windows XP SP3 (32-bit Professional edition or 64-bit Professional edition or Tablet edition)
- Windows Server 2008 or Windows Server 2003 when running with Remote Desktop Services

The other software prerequisites are as follows:

- **Web browser**

  Any one of the following web browsers will suffice for the installation:

  - Internet Explorer 10 (desktop mode only)

   - Internet Explorer 9
   - Internet Explorer 8
   - Internet Explorer 7 (the on-premises version only)
   - Mozilla Firefox (latest publicly released version) running on Windows 8, Windows 7, Windows Vista, or Windows XP
   - Google Chrome (latest publicly released version) running on Windows 8, Windows 7, Windows Vista, or Windows XP
   - Apple Safari (latest publicly released version) running on Mac OS X 10.7 (Lion) or 10.8 (Mountain Lion)

- **Microsoft Office**

  Any one of the following Microsoft Office versions will suffice for the installation:

   - Microsoft Office 2013 (requires Dynamics CRM 2011 Update Rollup 12 or higher for full compatibility)
   - Microsoft Office 2010
   - Microsoft Office 2007 SP2
   - Microsoft Office 2003 SP3

- Indexing service (must be installed and running)
- Before running Microsoft Dynamics CRM for Outlook, the user must have an Outlook profile configured

To install and run the 64-bit version of Microsoft Dynamics CRM for Outlook, a 64-bit version of Office 2010 is required.

> Running Microsoft Dynamics CRM for Outlook on a computer that is running Microsoft Exchange Server is not supported.

Microsoft-recommended software specifications for Dynamics CRM 2011 for Outlook can be found at:

`http://msdn.microsoft.com/en-us/library/hh699818.aspx`

How to do it...

In order to set up Microsoft Dynamics CRM for Outlook for a user, there are three major activities that need to be completed:

- Installing Microsoft Dynamics CRM for Outlook
- Configuring Microsoft Dynamics CRM for Outlook
- Configuring user e-mail settings

During the installation, if a machine restart is requested by the setup, it is recommended that you select the **Restart** option before proceeding further with installation.

- Installing Microsoft Dynamics CRM for Outlook:
    1. Log in to the machine with an account that has local administrative permissions on that computer.
    2. To install Microsoft Dynamics CRM 2011 for Outlook, the installation files can be downloaded from the Microsoft website (`http://www.microsoft.com/en-in/download/details.aspx?id=27821`). If downloading is not permitted on this machine, the files can be downloaded elsewhere and then copied here.

       After downloading the package, start the installation process by double-clicking on the downloaded EXE file. The first step would be to specify the location to which the package content would be unzipped.
    3. Post unzipping, locate the unzipped files and then double-click on the `SetupClient.exe` file. Alternatively, log in to the machine without administrative permissions, right-click on the `SetupClient.exe` file, and select **Run as Administrator** by supplying the administrator password.

       The Microsoft Dynamics CRM 2011 for Microsoft Office Outlook setup wizard will be launched.
    4. On the **License Agreement** page, select **I accept the license agreement**, and then click on **Next**.
    5. On the **Get Recommended Updates** page, indicate whether to obtain updates through Microsoft Update, and then click on **Next**.

       It is recommended that you assess the impact of the update rollups before applying them because update rollups can break any existing code or the rollup itself can have defects.
    6. Next, you will see the **Select the Installation** screen. Here, select the **Install Now** option, if Outlook with online access has to be installed, and **Options**, if Outlook with offline access has to be installed.

7. If **Options** has been selected, select **Offline Capability** on the **Customize Installation** page and then click on **Install Now** as shown in the following screenshot:

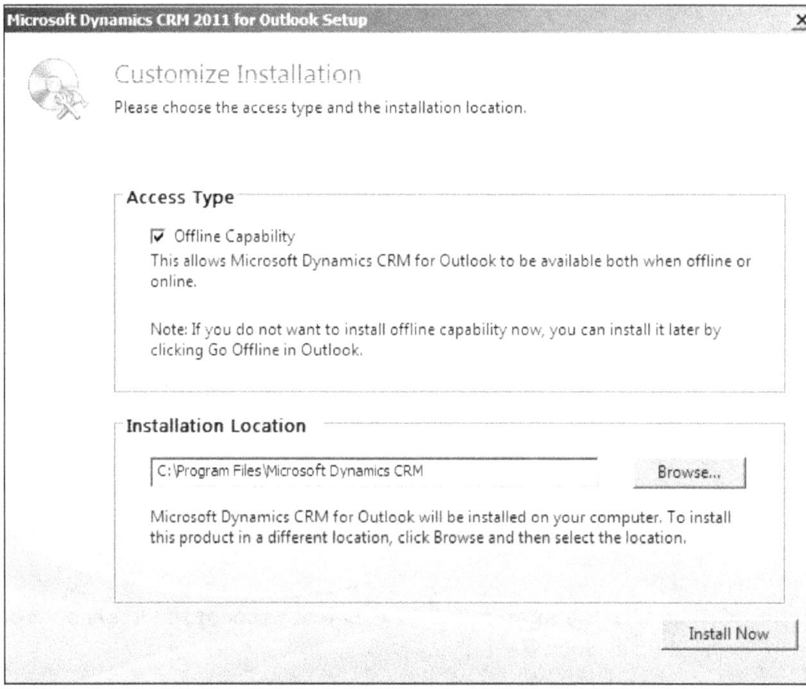

> If the offline capability is not installed at this point, the user will initially have no offline capability. If we choose **Install Now**, the Microsoft Outlook user can add the offline capability later by clicking on **Go Offline** in Microsoft Outlook.

8. On the completion page of the **Microsoft Dynamics CRM 2011 for Microsoft Office Outlook Setup** wizard, click on **Close**.

- Configuring Microsoft Dynamics CRM for Outlook:

  After Microsoft Dynamics CRM for Outlook is installed, it has to be configured for the user. If the machine is used by multiple users, it has to be configured separately for each user.

Please follow these steps to configure Microsoft Dynamics CRM for Outlook:

1. When Outlook is restarted after Microsoft Dynamics CRM for Outlook has been installed, the configuration wizard starts *automatically*.

   If you do not intend to configure Microsoft Dynamics CRM for Outlook immediately after installing it, click on **Cancel** on the **Configure Organization** page of the wizard. A **Configure Microsoft Dynamics CRM for Outlook** button then appears on the Microsoft Outlook toolbar and will remain there until we configure Microsoft Dynamics CRM for Outlook. We also can start the configuration wizard by clicking on the **Configure Microsoft Dynamics CRM for Outlook** button.

   If the configuration wizard does not start automatically, you can manually launch it by clicking on **Start** | **All Programs** | **Microsoft Dynamics CRM 2011** | **Configuration Wizard**.

2. On the **Configure Organization** page, select a value on the Dynamics CRM 2011 **Server URL** drop-down list and then click on **Test Connection**.

   To connect to a Microsoft Dynamics CRM Online organization, click on **CRM Online** in the server URL list.

   Once the connection has been successfully established, select the correct organization from the **Organization** list. If prompted, please provide credentials to connect to CRM and then click on **OK** as shown in the following screenshot:

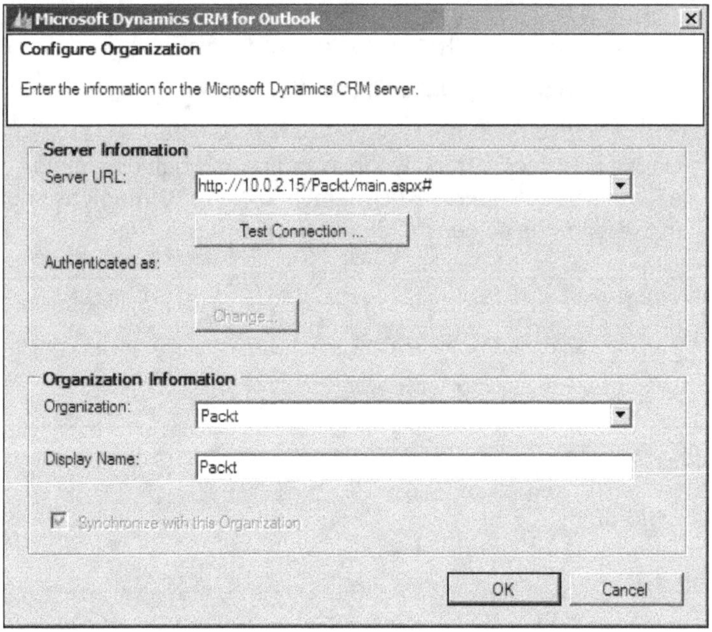

3. Finally, click on the **Close** button on the **Manage Microsoft Dynamics CRM Organizations** page:

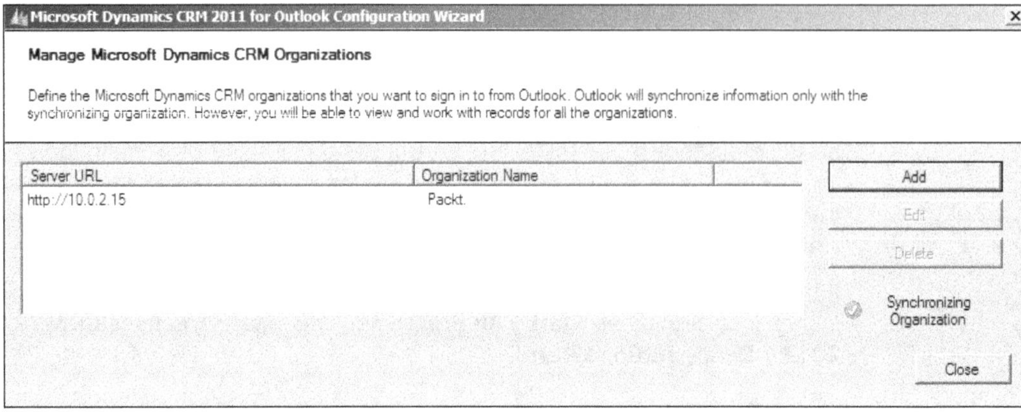

- Configuring user e-mail settings:

  Outlook can be used to send and receive e-mails, and in this case, E-mail Router is not required. By default, the incoming and outgoing e-mail access types are set to **Microsoft Dynamics CRM for Outlook** in Dynamics CRM. If it is changed, Outlook will be unable to send and receive e-mails.

  If the incoming and outgoing e-mail access types have been changed, these can be reset using the following steps:

  1. Log in to Dynamics CRM as a system administrator.
  2. Navigate to **Settings** | **Administration** | **Users**, select the user record, and open it.
  3. On the user record, modify the incoming and outgoing e-mail access types to **Microsoft Dynamics CRM for Outlook** as shown in the following screenshot:

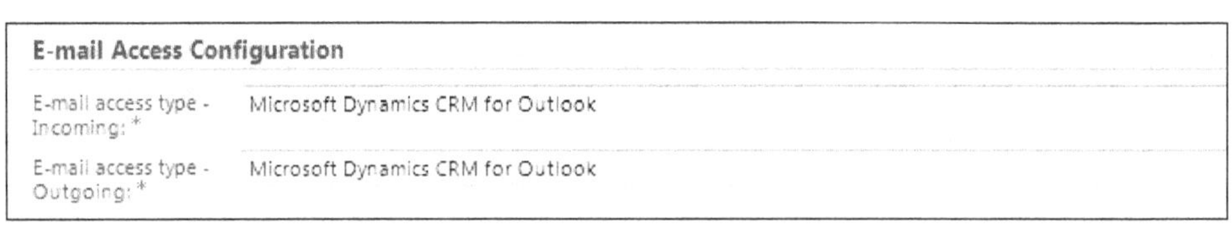

How it works...

Once Microsoft Dynamics CRM for Outlook is installed on a user's computer, Dynamics CRM-related toolbar or ribbon changes will be reflected in the Outlook application. Dynamics CRM 2011 can be accessed by using the Microsoft Outlook shortcut bars, ribbon, and folder navigation. Installing Microsoft Dynamics CRM for Outlook also creates a toolbar in Microsoft Outlook and a folder in the structure of the user's mailbox.

In the following screenshot, we can see how Microsoft Dynamics CRM has been accessed in the Microsoft Outlook 2003 client:

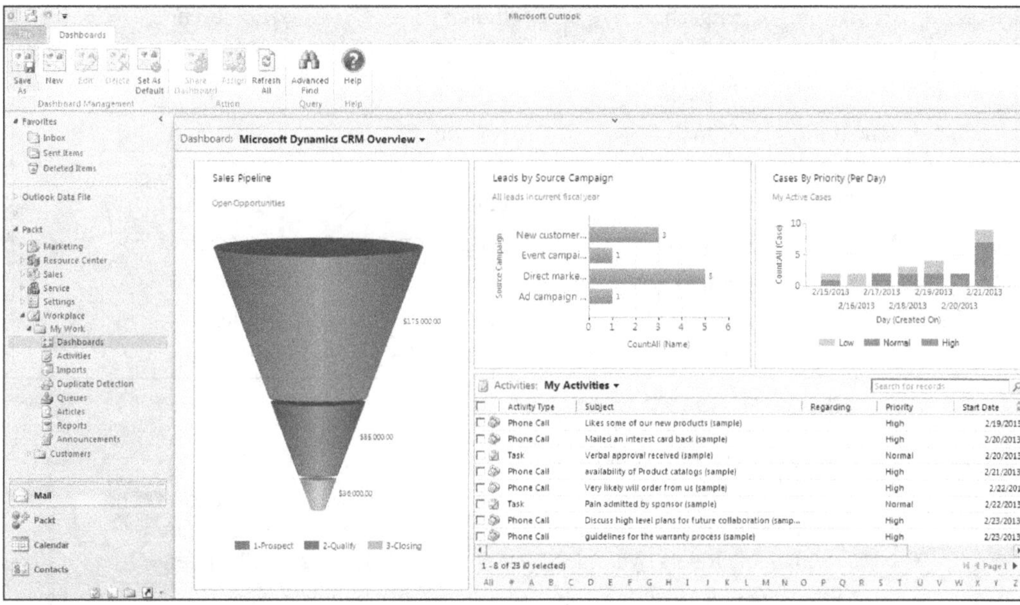

Installing a Dynamics CRM language pack

Dynamics CRM 2011 supports multiple languages. In this recipe, we will discuss how to apply additional language packs after Dynamics CRM 2011 (base language version) has been installed.

Getting ready

The user account that will be used to run the language pack should have local administrative rights on the machine. The language pack for Microsoft Dynamics CRM 2011 enables users to change the CRM user interface language or **Help Text**. It is important to note that the language pack must be installed on both Microsoft Dynamics CRM 2011 Server as well as client machines that are using Microsoft Dynamics CRM for Outlook. The supported languages are as follows:

Arabic	Dutch	Hungarian	Portuguese (Portugal)
Basque	English	Italian	Romanian
Bulgarian	Estonian	Japanese	Russian
Catalan	Finnish	Kazakh	Slovak
Chinese (Hong Kong SAR)	French	Korean	Slovenian
Chinese (Simplified)	Galician	Latvian	Spanish
Chinese (Traditional)	German	Lithuanian	Swedish
Croatian	Greek	Norwegian	Thai
Czech	Hebrew	Polish	Turkish
Danish	Hindi	Portuguese (Brazil)	Ukrainian

> For users who are running Microsoft Dynamics CRM for Microsoft Office Outlook, in addition to installing the language pack on the computer running Microsoft Dynamics CRM Server 2011, the same language pack has to be installed on the computer where Microsoft Dynamics CRM for Outlook is installed.

How to do it...

The language pack deployment has the following two steps:

1. Installing the language pack
2. Provisioning the language pack

The following steps are required to be followed to install the Dynamics CRM language pack:

1. Log on to the computer where Microsoft Dynamics CRM Server 2011 or Microsoft Dynamics CRM for Outlook is installed.

Download Microsoft Dynamics CRM 2011 Language Pack from the Microsoft website (http://www.microsoft.com/en-us/download/details.aspx?id=27819). Before downloading, we should select the correct language in the **Change Language** drop-down list. If download is not permitted on this machine, it can be downloaded elsewhere and then copied onto this machine.

To run the installer, the logged-in user must have administrator privileges on the computer and either full or administrator privileges on Microsoft Dynamics CRM.

2. After downloading the package, start the installation by double-clicking on the downloaded EXE file. The first step would be to specify the location to which the package content will be unzipped.
3. Post unzipping, locate the language pack files and then double-click on the MUISetup_<loc_code>_<proc_type>.msi file, where <loc_ code> is the locale code for the language pack being installed (for example, 1033 for English or 3082 for Spanish), and <proc_type> specifies the type of processor the server is running on (for example, "amd64").
4. On the **End User License Agreement** page, click on **I accept the terms in the license agreement**, and then click on **Install**.
5. Installation continues; once done, please click on **Finish**.

To provision the language pack in the Microsoft Dynamics CRM deployment, perform the following steps:

1. After installation, log in to the Dynamics CRM application with system administrator security privileges. Navigate to **Settings** | **System** | **Administration** | **Languages** as shown in the following screenshot:

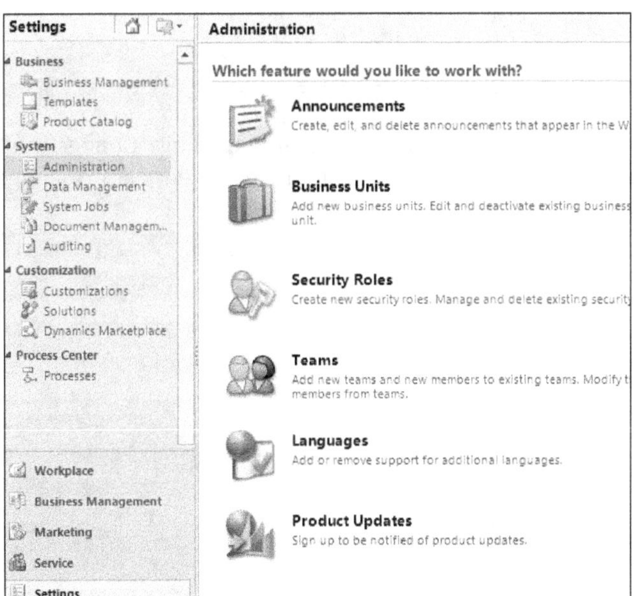

2. This will launch a new web dialog, where the language (in this example, Spanish) can be selected:

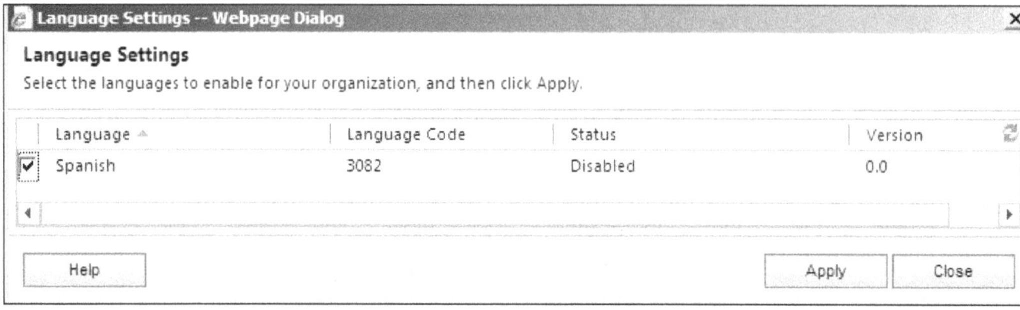

3. Then, click on the **Apply** button to enable the language pack. A confirmation dialog (**Confirm Language Change**) will appear; please click on **OK** and continue.
4. Once done, the language pack's **Status** field must change to **Enabled**.
5. The previous step only enables the language. Now the language change at the user interface level has to be effected. This can be done by navigating to **File** | **Options** for every user login:

6. In the options window, navigate to the **Languages** tab. Change the **User Interface Language** and **Help Language** fields to the newly enabled language (in this case, Spanish):

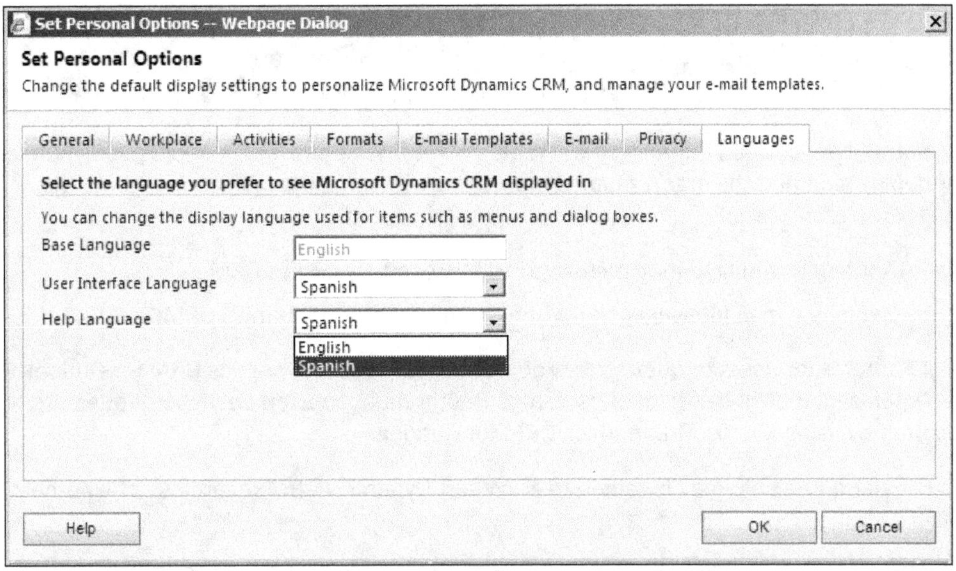

7. Click on the **OK** button to apply the changes.

How it works...

The language pack installs a translation package of the labels, text, and help content of the Dynamics CRM user interface. While the base language defines the default Dynamics CRM UI language, the language packs further installed can provide flexibility to users to select another language of their choice. This is often a very important feature of Dynamics CRM when there is a use case of deploying Dynamics CRM for a multilingual user base.

In Microsoft Dynamics CRM for Outlook, the user language settings only apply to Microsoft Dynamics CRM for Outlook features, such as the user interface display of the CRM menu; they do not affect other areas of Microsoft Office Outlook.

Installing Microsoft Dynamics CRM E-mail Router

Microsoft Dynamics CRM E-mail Router creates an interface between a Microsoft Dynamics CRM deployment and the organization's messaging system. E-mail Router performs the following tasks:

- Routing incoming e-mail messages to Microsoft Dynamics CRM
- Sending e-mail messages generated from Microsoft Dynamics CRM

E-mail Router is for users or queues that do not use Microsoft Dynamics CRM for Outlook. If CRM Organization uses e-mail queues, E-mail Router must be used because queues are not supported by using Microsoft Dynamics CRM for Outlook.

With E-mail Router, an e-mail is routed to Microsoft Dynamics CRM regardless of whether the recipient is logged in.

E-mail Router routes qualified e-mail messages to the Microsoft Dynamics CRM system as e-mail activities and fully integrates with different messaging systems, such as Microsoft Exchange Server, Microsoft Exchange Online, POP3, and SMTP. E-mail Router includes the functionality of sending e-mails through any desired SMTP provider and receiving e-mails from Microsoft Exchange Server or from a POP3 server.

Getting ready

The minimum recommended hardware specifications for the server machine where E-mail Router will be installed are as follows:

- A multi-core 1.8 GHz processor
- 2 GB of RAM or more
- A minimum of 100 MB of available hard disk space

E-mail Router components can be installed on a machine that runs on Windows 7 (32- or 64-bit editions), and on Windows Server 2008 or Windows Server 2008 R2 (x64-bit editions only).

> Running Microsoft Dynamics CRM E-mail Router and the **E-mail Router Configuration Manager** application (32-bit) is not supported on a Windows Server 64-bit operating system in the **Windows on Windows** (**WOW**) mode.

Finally, **Rule Deployment Wizard** requires the Microsoft Exchange Server Messaging API (MAPI) client libraries.

> For Microsoft Exchange Server 2010, MAPI Version 6.5.8147 (or later) is required. If an earlier version is installed, it has to be uninstalled before installing the newer version.
>
> Download the latest MAPI client from:
>
> `http://www.microsoft.com/en-us/download/details.aspx?id=1004`
>
> This package, however, will not be installed on a system on which any version of Microsoft Outlook or Microsoft Exchange Server 2003 or earlier is installed.
>
> Update Rollup 2 (or later) of Microsoft Exchange Server 2010 is also a requirement if **Rule Deployment Wizard** is intended to use Microsoft Exchange Server 2010 as its e-mail server.
>
> Microsoft does not recommend installing E-mail Router on a computer that is running Microsoft Exchange Server.

The minimum permissions required to run E-mail Router are:

- The account that is running E-mail Router must be `LocalSystemAccount`
- The computer where E-mail Router will be installed must be added to the `PrivUserGroup` group

How to do it...

Follow these steps to set up E-mail Router component:

1. Log in to the server machine where E-mail Router has to be installed with local administrative privileges.
2. Download Microsoft Dynamics CRM 2011 E-mail Router from the Microsoft website (`http://www.microsoft.com/en-in/download/details.aspx?id=27818`). If downloading is not permitted on this machine, this can be downloaded elsewhere and then copied onto this machine.
3. After downloading the package, start the installation by double-clicking on the downloaded EXE file. The first step would be to specify the location to which the package content will be unzipped.
4. After unzipping, locate the unzipped files and then double-click on the `SetupEmailRouter.exe` file.
5. If a **Security Warning** page pops up, proceed by clicking on **Run**.
6. Then a **Welcome to Microsoft Dynamics CRM 2011 E-mail Router Setup** page appears. Select **Get Updates for Microsoft Dynamics CRM** if Dynamics CRM update rollups have to be applied; otherwise, select **Do not get updates** and then click on **Next**.

> It is recommended that you assess the impact of the update rollups before applying them because update rollups can break any existing code or the rollup itself can have defects.

7. When the **License Agreement** page appears, select **I accept this license agreement** to accept the license terms and click on **I Accept**.
8. If the required components are missing, the **Download and Install Required Components** page appears. If this page does not appear, all required components are installed and the next step in the installation procedure can be skipped.

   If the required components are listed, they can be installed now. Click on **Install** to launch the installation. After the components are installed, the **Status** column value changes from **Not Installed** to **Installed**. Click on **Next** to continue.

> Some of these components might require an Internet connectivity on the server machine in case the prerequisite binary files are not found on the local machine.

9. On the **Select Router Components** page, select either one or both options and then click on **Next**:
   - The **Microsoft Dynamics CRM E-mail Router Service** option installs the E-mail Router service and the E-mail Router configuration manager
   - The **Rule Deployment Wizard** option installs **Rule Deployment Wizard**. Optionally, this wizard can be installed on any computer in the Active Directory domain of the Exchange Server.

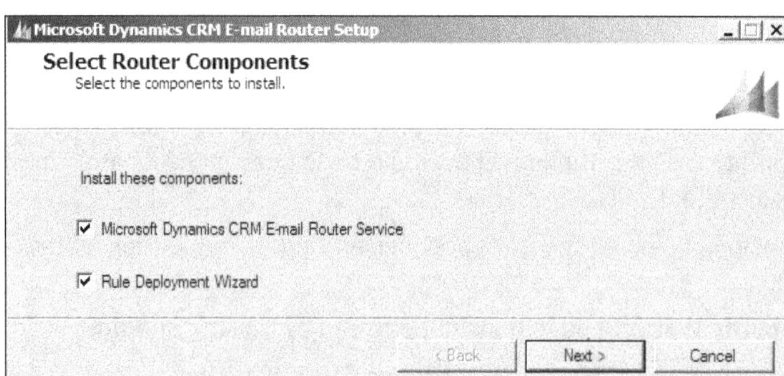

> On the **Select Router Components** page, if we clear the option of a component that has already been installed, that component will be uninstalled.

10. On the **Select Install Location** page, accept either the default file installation directory or browse to indicate a different location, and then click on **Next**.
11. The **System Checks** page appears. This page displays a summary of all system requirements for a successful E-mail Router installation. Any reported error must be corrected before proceeding with installation. If there is a problem that will take time to be solved, setup has to be cancelled at this point; the problem has to be fixed and only then can setup be restarted.

    When no verification errors remain, click on **Next**.
12. The **Ready to Install** page appears. The installation selections made have to be reviewed; click on **Back** to change any selections, or click on **Install** to install now.
13. After the E-mail Router setup has finished installing files, click on **Finish**.

How it works...

The setup for E-mail Router for Microsoft Dynamics CRM 2011 contains two main components:

- E-mail Router (the E-mail Router service and the E-mail Router configuration manager)
- **Rule Deployment Wizard**

Rule Deployment Wizard lets us deploy rules that are used to route e-mail messages to a forward mailbox from the mailbox of a user or queue. **Rule Deployment Wizard** does not work with POP3/SMTP e-mail servers.

Users and queues in CRM can be configured to use E-mail Router for processing of the incoming and outgoing CRM e-mails. To utilize this functionality, users and queues must have a valid e-mail address and must select E-mail Router for the incoming and outgoing E-mail access types. This can be set up by an administrator or by users having the relevant permissions.

There's more...

E-mail Router can also be installed on a multiserver cluster to provide high availability and failover functionality. We will discuss this in the *Installing Microsoft Dynamics CRM E-mail Router on multiple computers* recipe later in this chapter.

After E-mail Router is installed, the E-mail Router configuration manager, an application that is installed during the Microsoft Dynamics CRM E-mail Router setup, must be run. We will discuss this in the next recipe.

Configuring Microsoft Dynamics E-mail Router

After installing E-mail Router, it has to be configured. Certain configuration tasks are mandatory; whereas a few are optional. The configuration tasks can be listed as follows:

- **Task 1** (Mandatory): Setup profiles are (optionally) set up deployments using the E-mail Router configuration manager
- **Task 2** (Mandatory): Dynamics CRM users must have their incoming e-mail access type set to E-mail Router
- **Task 3** (Optional): We can set up the forward mailbox
- **Task 4** (Optional): As part of configuration, inbox rules can also be deployed

E-mail Router has several options, and before running the E-mail Router configuration manager, we need to be certain about the choices to be made here:

- **Incoming configuration**: For incoming e-mail messages, E-mail Router supports the Exchange Server 2003/2007 or POP3 e-mail systems
- **Outgoing configuration**: For outgoing e-mail messages, E-mail Router supports SMTP e-mail systems
- **Mailbox monitoring type**:

  Two types of mailbox monitoring can be configured, they are as follows:

  - **Forward mailbox**: Forward mailbox, also known as *sink mailbox*, allows Dynamics CRM to monitor one central mailbox instead of monitoring the mailbox of each user who needs Microsoft Dynamics CRM e-mail capabilities. CRM Organizations, which has a large number of mailboxes to monitor, can opt for this alternative.
  - E-mail Router: If e-mail messages can be forwarded as attachments but the e-mail system does not allow rules, each user must be configured to use the E-mail Router setting.

> If Exchange Server is used, forward mailbox monitoring is recommended.
>
> To use a forward mailbox with a Microsoft Dynamics CRM deployment that interfaces with a POP3-compliant e-mail system, the e-mail system must be able to forward e-mail messages as attachments.

How to do it...

We will take a look at all the previously mentioned tasks one by one:

Task 1 - Setting up profiles

Please follow the ensuing steps to configure the E-mail Router settings:

1. To start E-mail Router Configuration Manager, click on **Start** | **All Programs** | **Microsoft Dynamics CRM 2011 E-mail Router** | **E-mail Router Configuration Manager**.

   The **E-mail Router Configuration Manager** application will be launched. It has three sections as follows:

   - **Configuration Profiles**: This section contain information about the e-mail server and the authentication methods the E-mail Router will use.

     At least one incoming e-mail profile and one outgoing e-mail profile have to be configured to enable E-mail Router to route e-mails to and from Microsoft Dynamics CRM Organization.

   - **Deployments**: For E-mail Router to use the incoming and outgoing configuration profiles we just created, it has to be linked with a Microsoft Dynamics CRM Deployment.

     We have to select from the following options:

   - **My company**: Select this option if Microsoft Dynamics CRM is deployed on premises
   - **An online service provider**: Select this option if the deployment that E-mail Router will connect to is an online service provider deployment of Microsoft Dynamics CRM
   - **Microsoft Dynamics CRM Online**: Select this option to connect E-mail Router to a Microsoft Dynamics CRM Online organization
   - **Users, Queues, and Forward Mailboxes**: Once the configuration profile and deployment have been completed, we need to manage the users, queues, and forward mailboxes that will be used by E-mail Router.

2. To create a configuration profile, click on **New** in the **Configuration Profile** tab.

3. Provide a profile name and then select the intended values for **Direction** and **E-mail Server Type**. Finally, provide values for **Location** and **Access Credentials** as shown in the following screenshot.

   By repeating steps 2 and 3, multiple incoming and outgoing profiles can be created:

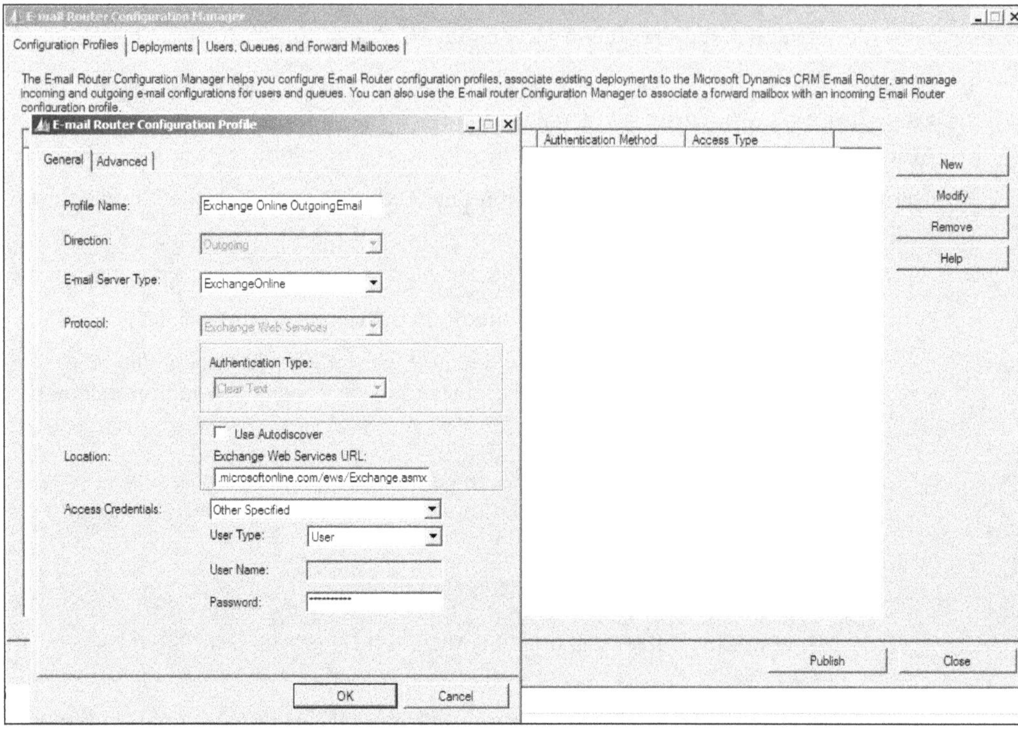

4. To link a Dynamics CRM Deployment, click on **New** in the **Deployment** tab.
5. For **Deployment Type**, select between **My company**, **An online service provider**, and **Microsoft Dynamics CRM Online**.

   In the **Microsoft Dynamics CRM Server** box, please provide the Microsoft Dynamics CRM Discovery service followed by the organization name, which is case-sensitive.

   In the **Access Credentials** section, please specify the credentials that E-mail Router will use to log on to the Microsoft Dynamics CRM Server.

> Use a **Local System** account if the machine account can be used to connect to Microsoft Dynamics CRM Server. In such a case, E-mail Router must be in the same domain as the Microsoft Dynamics CRM Server and the E-mail Router machine account should be added to `PrivUserGroup` in Active Directory.
>
> Alternatively, the **Other Specified** account can be used to specify the credentials of a user of with the system administrator role to connect to Microsoft Dynamics CRM.

In the **Incoming configuration profile** field, select an incoming profile already created, and in the **Outgoing configuration profile** field, select an outgoing profile already created.

Finally, click on **OK** to finish the deployment:

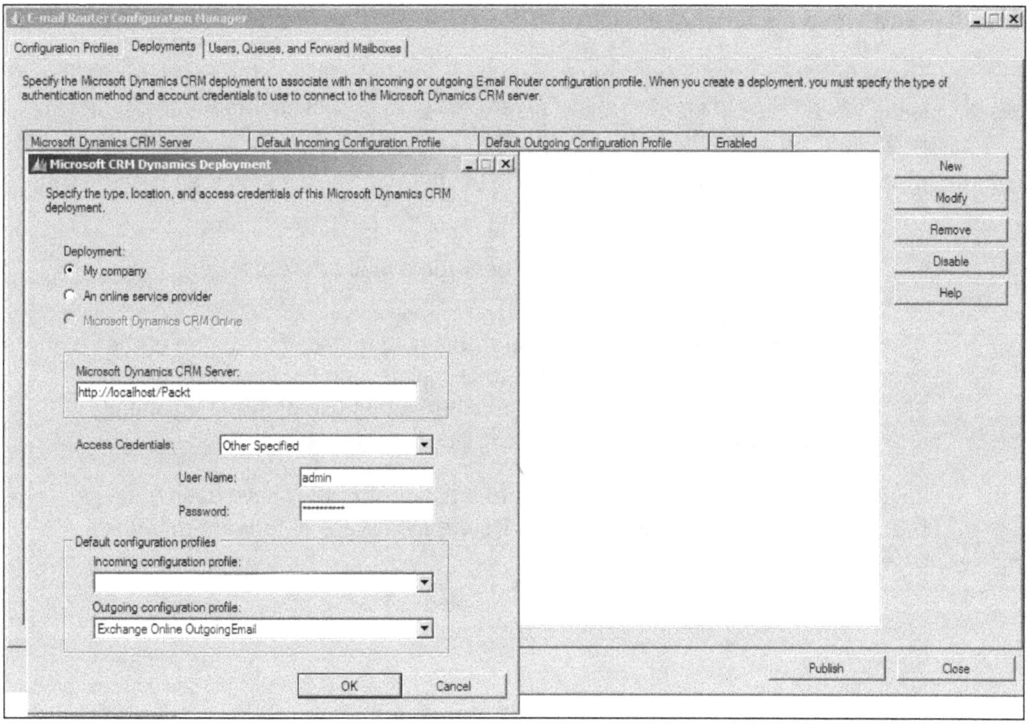

6. The next step would be that of loading the users and mailboxes from CRM Deployment, and this can be done by clicking on the **Load Data** button as shown in the following screenshot:

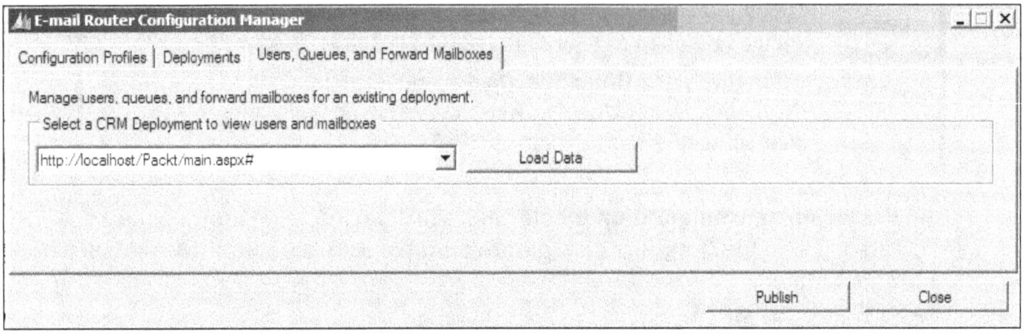

Task 3 – Setting up the forward mailbox

1. To set up forward mailboxes, once the data is loaded, click on the **Forward Mailboxes** tab. Click on **New** to create a new forward mailbox, or click on **Modify** to change an existing forward mailbox.

   In the **Forward Mailbox** dialog box, fill in the following boxes, and then click on **OK**:

   - **Name**: This field will bear the name of the forward mailbox.
   - **E-mail Address**: This field will bear the e-mail address for the forward mailbox.
   - **Incoming Configuration Profile**: This field will bear the name of the incoming configuration profile to associate with the forward mailbox. We can have multiple forward mailboxes that use different incoming configuration profiles.

   To delete e-mail messages in the forward mailbox after they have been processed by E-mail Router, select the **Delete messages in forward mailbox after processing** option.

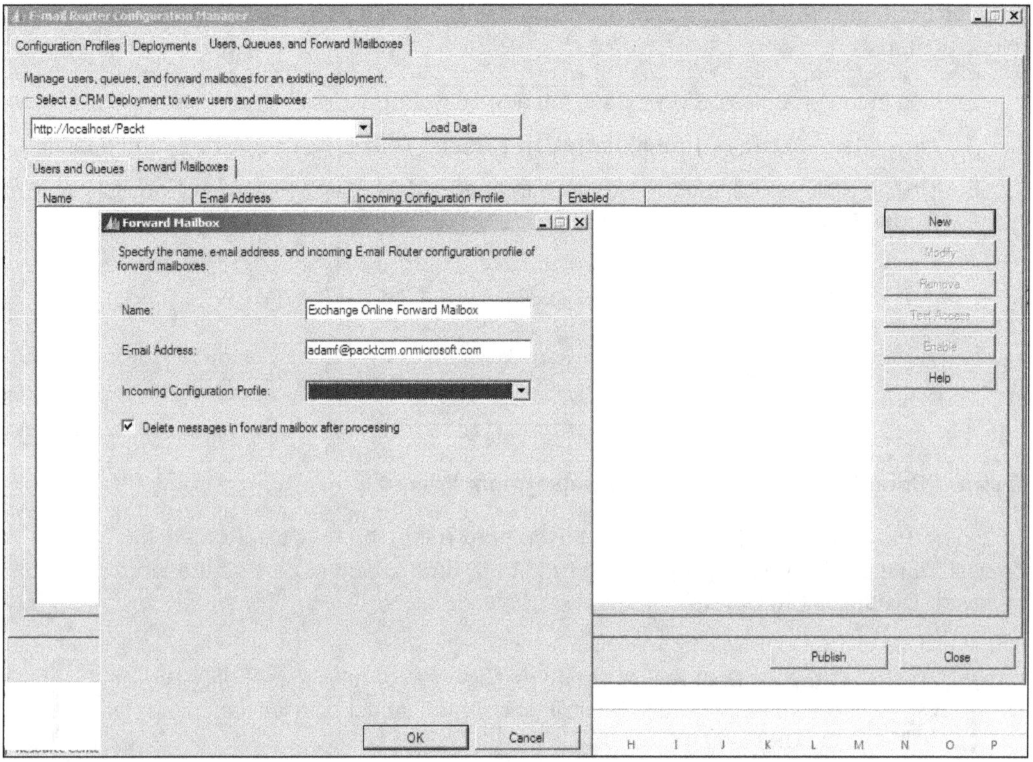

2. Finally, click on **Publish**.
3. Then restart the Microsoft CRM E-mail Router service. To do this, click on **Run**, type `services.msc`, and then press *Enter*. Right-click on the Microsoft CRM E-mail Router service, and then click on **Restart**.

Task 2 – Configuring user e-mail settings

By default, incoming and outgoing e-mail access types in Dynamics CRM are set to **Microsoft Dynamics CRM for Outlook**. Unless this is changed, Outlook will be unable to send and receive e-mails.

To configure E-mail Router for incoming and outgoing e-mail access types, perform the following steps:

1. Log in to Dynamics CRM with system administrator access.
2. Navigate to **Settings** | **Administration** | **Users**, select the user record, and open it.
3. On the user record, modify the incoming and outgoing e-mail access types to **E-mail Router**.

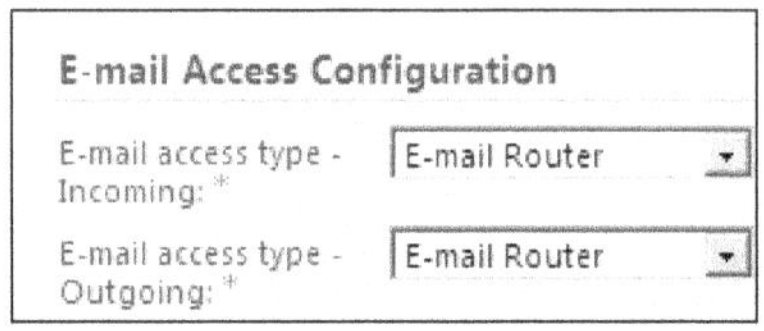

Task 4 – Configuring rules using Rule Deployment Wizard

To deploy these Microsoft Dynamics CRM user inbox rules, the Rule Deployment Wizard can be used. Rule Deployment Wizard can be run at any time to add or change the inbox rules for Microsoft Dynamics CRM users.

> The Rule Deployment Wizard can only deploy rules to Exchange Server mailboxes. The Rule Deployment Wizard cannot be used to deploy rules to POP3 e-mail servers.

To run **Rule Deployment Wizard**, the user must:

- Be logged on as a Microsoft Dynamics CRM user with a security role
- Be a local administrator on the computer on which the wizard is running
- Have Exchange administrative permissions

The following are the steps to run the **Rule Deployment Wizard**:

1. Navigate to **Start** | **All Programs** | **Microsoft Dynamics CRM 2011 E-mail Router** and click on **Rule Deployment Wizard**.
2. Click on **Next** to start the wizard.
3. For **Deployment**, select a Microsoft Dynamics deployment type.

   Enter the URL of the CRM Organization for **Microsoft Dynamics CRM Server**.

   For **Access Credentials**, provide the correct credentials of a system administrator of the Dynamics CRM Organization.

Then click on **Next** to proceed:

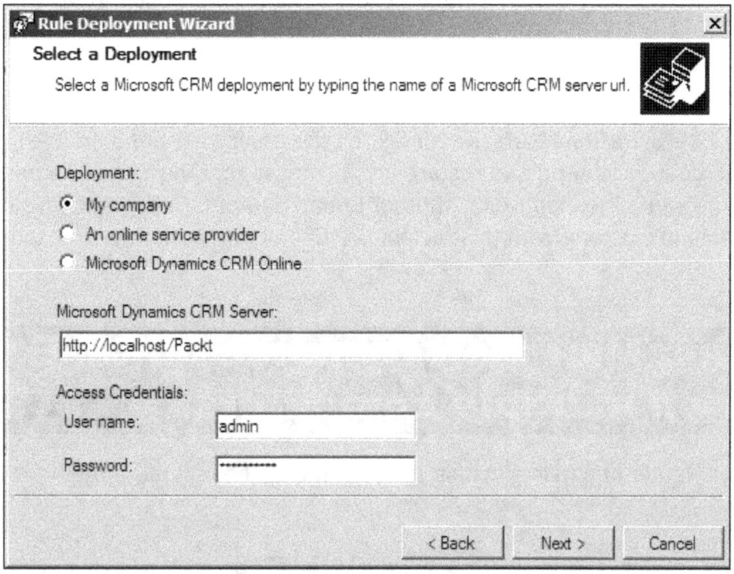

4. Type the e-mail address of the forward mailbox and click on **Next** to proceed.

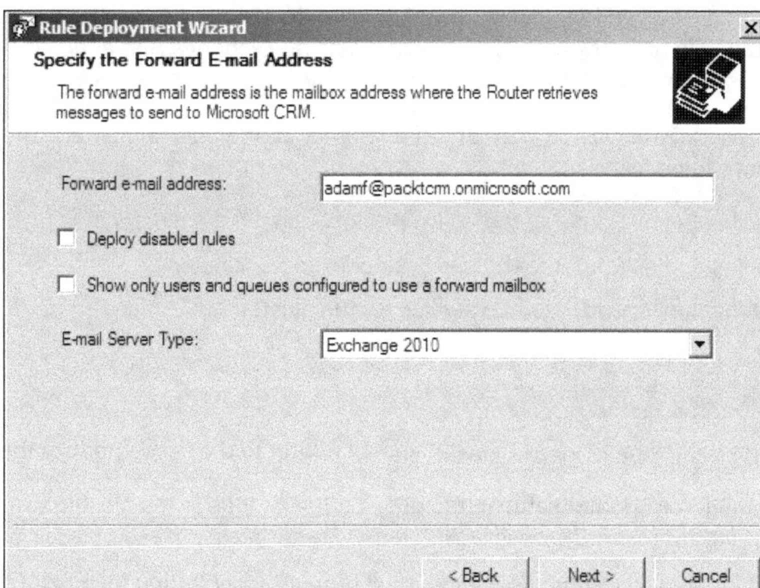

5. Select the Microsoft Dynamics CRM user(s) or queues to whom/which we want to deploy the rule. Then click on **Next**.

6. Click on **Deploy rule to user mailboxes**, and then click on **Next**.
7. After the rules have been deployed, click on **Cancel** to close the wizard.

How it works...

E-mail Router Configuration Manager configures the deployment and enables Dynamics CRM users and queues to send and receive e-mail messages. The E-mail Router configuration steps remain the same irrespective of whether E-mail Router is installed on a single machine or multiple-machine clusters. With this recipe, the E-mail Router installation activities come to a close.

Installing Microsoft Dynamics CRM E-mail Router on multiple computers

To install E-mail Router in a failover cluster environment, the minimum requirements are as follows:

- At least two Windows servers to support clustering
- A common storage I/O technology between the nodes in the cluster, such as **Parallel SCSI** or **Fiber Channel**
- Cluster configured in an active/passive manner; installing E-mail Router on nodes operating in an active/active cluster, such as an Exchange Server active/active cluster, is not supported.

To install Microsoft Dynamics CRM 2011 E-mail Router on multiple computers, the following main steps have to be followed:

- Installing E-mail Router to the active primary node in the cluster
- Installing E-mail Router to the passive nodes in the cluster
- Creating the generic resource service for the cluster

How to do it...

Please perform the following steps to install E-mail Router to the active node in the cluster:

1. Run the E-mail Router setup in the active primary node in the cluster by following the *Installing Microsoft Dynamics CRM E-mail Router* recipe.
2. Configure E-mail Router using the E-mail Router Configuration Manager by following the *Configuring Microsoft Dynamics E-mail Router* recipe. Verify that E-mail Router is routing messages correctly to and from Microsoft Dynamics CRM and the e-mail systems.

3. Create shared storage on a secondary node in the cluster and grant full access to the service account running the E-mail Router service and those administrators who may have to update configuration files manually.

> By default, the E-mail Router files are located in the folder `\%Program Files%\Microsoft CRM Email`.

4. The following files have to be copied manually to the shared storage. This is essential because these files can be moved to a secondary node in the cluster in the event of a failover.
   - `Microsoft.Crm.Tools.EmailAgent.Configuration.bin`
   - `Microsoft.Crm.Tools.EmailAgent.SystemState.xml`
   - `Microsoft.Crm.Tools.EmailAgent.xml`
   - `EncryptionKey.xml` (if it exists)
5. Then update the following registry subkey, so that E-mail Router uses the shared location to load the E-mail Router settings.

   `HKEY_LOCAL_MACHINE\SYSTEM\CurrentControlSet\Services\MSCRMEmail`
6. Finally, restart the Microsoft CRM E-mail Router service.

Next, we will install E-mail Router on each of the passive nodes of the cluster using the following steps:

1. Run the E-mail Router setup in the passive node of the cluster.
2. Update the Windows Registry subkey as mentioned in the previous steps on the primary node.
3. Restart the Microsoft CRM E-mail Router service.

Finally, we will create a generic resource service for the cluster by following these steps:

1. On each node in the cluster, start the Services MMC snap-in. On the list of services, right-click on **Microsoft CRM Email Router**, click on **Properties**, and then set **Startup Type** to **Manual**. Close the Services MMC snap-in.
2. Launch **Active Directory Users and Computers**. Locate the `PrivUserGroup {GUID}` security group for the deployment. Add the computer accounts for each node in the cluster. Close **Active Directory Users and Computers**.

3. If Windows Server 2003 is used here, start **Cluster Administrator**—if Windows Server 2008 is used, start **Failover Cluster Management**—and create a generic resource service. Use the following parameters:
   - **Name**: Create a descriptive name for the generic resource service, for example, `MSCRM E-mail Router`
   - **Resource type**: Enter the generic service
   - **Group**: Enter the cluster group name
   - **Possible owners**: Add all nodes in the cluster
   - **Dependencies**: If Exchange Server is used and E-mail Router has been installed on Exchange Server (not recommended), add **Microsoft Exchange Information Store**
   - **Service Name**: Mention the Microsoft CRM E-mail Router service
   - **Start Parameters**: Leave this field blank
   - **Use Network Name for computer name**: Leave this field unchecked
   - Do not checkpoint any registry keys
4. Bring the resource online. If it is necessary, configure the resource properties, such as the failover policies.
5. Close the **Cluster Administrator/Failover Cluster Management** window.

How it works...

We achieve high availability for the Microsoft Dynamics CRM E-mail Router service by deploying it on multiple computers by using Windows Server's clustering technology. The server cluster has to be configured in an active/passive manner. In case of an active node failover scenario, the passive node becomes the primary node and the common storage or shared disk resources will move from active node 1 to the passive node.

Deploying Microsoft Dynamics CRM on multiple servers

Earlier, in the *Single server versus multiserver* subsection of this chapter's *Introduction* section, we mentioned some of the reasons for and benefits of installing Dynamics CRM 2011 on multiple computers. In this recipe, we will discuss how to deploy Dynamics CRM on a multiserver environment.

Getting ready

In a multiple-server deployment, there are usually two or more server computers running the Dynamics CRM 2011 Full Server installation. But for improved performance, the server roles (Front End Server role, Back End Server role, Deployment Administration Server) can further be deployed across different server machines. When Dynamics CRM 2011 is deployed across multiple servers, **Network Load Balancing** (**NLB**) must be configured to provide load balancing.

In case of deploying various server roles into separate servers, Microsoft's recommendation is to not install the Help Server role on the same server where Front End Server roles are installed. This is to minimize the CRM system's exposure to denial-of-service attacks.

Let us take an example of two server nodes (`CRM001` and `CRM002`), where Microsoft Dynamics CRM 2011 Full Server is configured (or will be installed) as a server cluster (`CRMCluster`) and the CRM installation uses a SQL Cluster environment (`SQLCluster`).

The following network diagram describes our multiserver deployment scenario:

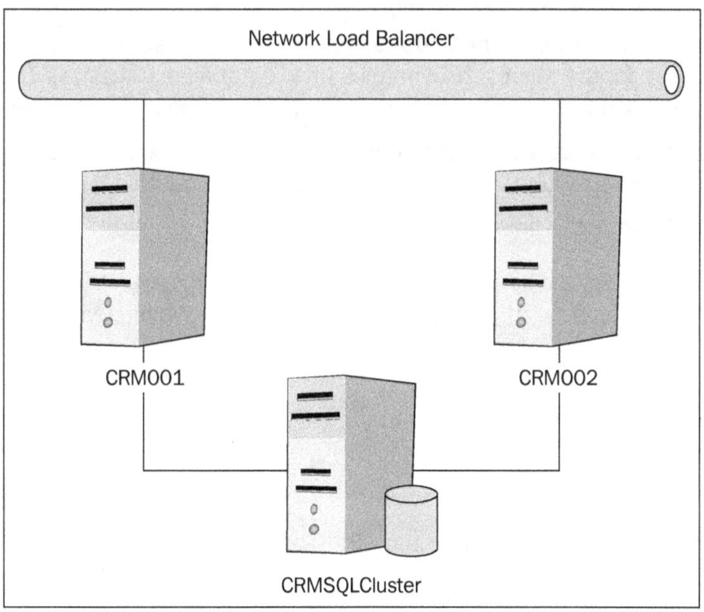

We have to perform the following steps to make this setup work:

- Installing Dynamics CRM 2011 on both the server nodes (`CRM001` and `CRM002`)
- Creating a server cluster (`CRMCluster`)

- Configuring the SPN for the CRM Application Pool service account (`CRMServiceAccount`)
- Configuring NLB

How to do it...

To achieve multi-server deployment in our scenario, we have to complete the following subtasks.

First, we have to install Dynamics CRM 2011 on two server nodes; we will achieve this one at a time. Here, we are assuming that the installation of a Full Server role will be performed for both these server machines. As stated in the earlier sections, installing Microsoft Dynamics CRM Workgroup Server 2011 on multiple servers is not supported.

To install Dynamics CRM 2011 on these two machines, perform the following steps on each of the machines independently:

1. Follow the steps outlined in the *Installing Dynamics CRM 2011 Server* recipe to install Dynamics CRM 2011 server.
2. On the **Specify Deployment Options** page, select the instance of SQL Server that will be used for the Microsoft Dynamics CRM databases (`CRMSQL`). Then, check the **Create a new deployment** option. Click on **Next** and continue the setup.
3. On the **Specify Security Account** page, select a domain user account (`CRMServiceAccount`) that has been created previously.
4. Click on **Continue** to finish the installation.

The next steps are to create a server cluster for servers `CRM001` and `CRM002` and to enable loading balancing between them. The recommended settings while creating the NLB are as follows:

- **Port Range**: `0` to `65535` (the default range)
- **Protocols**: `Both`
- **Affinity**: `Single`

The next step is to configure the SPN for the CRM Application Pool service account.

In this deployment, we are using a domain user account (`CRMServiceAccount`) to run the Dynamics CRM 2011 Application Pool. When IIS 7.0 (or higher) is used on a cluster environment, we need to set up SPN for the Application Pool account. Active Directory uses the SPN for mutual authentication of a service instance, which enables the service instance to correctly authenticate a user who attempts to access resources that are located on other domain-member computers.

Perform the following steps to configure the SPN for the CRM Application Pool Account:

1. Log in to the Active Directory server machines with domain admin credentials.
2. Launch the ADSI Edit console from **All Programs** | **Administrative Tools** | **ADSI Edit**.
3. Expand the domain and the node that starts with `DC=` and then expand `CN=Users`.
4. Right-click on `CRMServiceAccount` and click on **Properties**.
5. From the attribute list, select **servicePrincipalName** and then click on **Edit**.
6. In the **Value to add** textbox, enter `HTTP/CRMNLBName.FQDN` and then click on **Add**.

   Here, `CRMNLBName` is the CRM Server's cluster name (in this case, `CRMCluster`) and `FQDN` is the **Fully Qualified Domain Name** of the cluster, for example, `CRMCluster.MyOrg.com`.
7. In the **Value to add** box, enter `HTTP/CRMNLBName` and then click on **Add**.
8. Click on **OK** the next two times.
9. Close the **ADSI Edit** window.

Now it is time to configure the NLB for this deployment. NLB will be configured using Dynamics CRM 2011 Deployment Manager. Perform the following steps to configure the NLB:

1. Launch the deployment manager. This is usually accessible via the following path:

   Start | **All Programs** | **Microsoft Dynamics CRM** | **Deployment Manager**
2. Right-click on **Microsoft Dynamics CRM**, and then click on **Properties** as shown in the following screenshot:

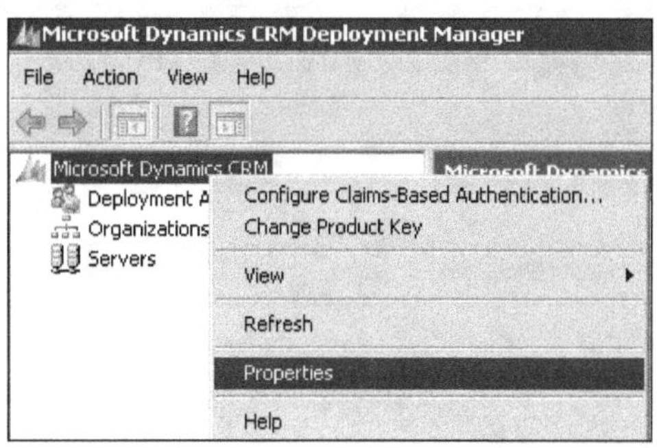

3. Click on the **Web Address** tab and verify that the cluster name (in this example, `CRMCluster`) appears, and then click on **Advanced**:

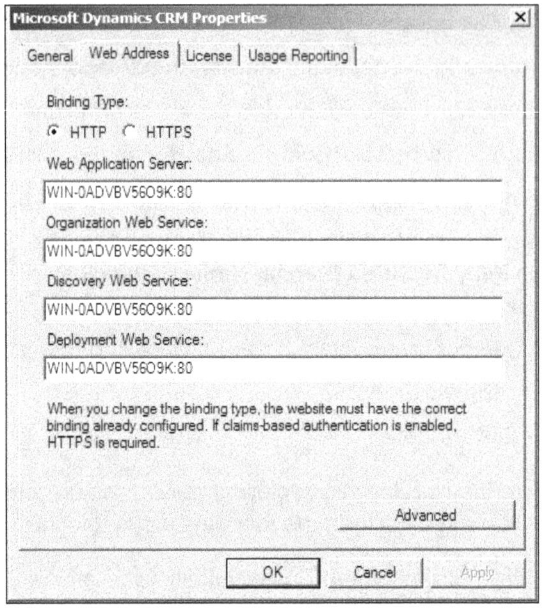

4. Select **The deployment uses an NLB**. Click on **OK** and then close the deployment manager:

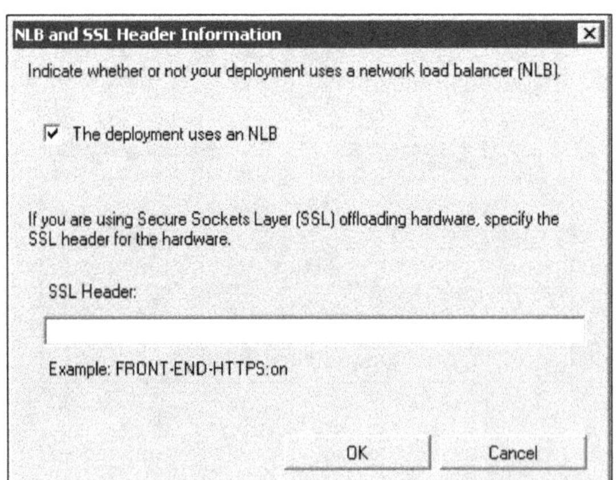

How it works...

Multiserver deployment gives performance benefits and scaling advantages. However, with Microsoft Dynamics CRM Workgroup Server 2011, the Dynamics CRM 2011 server roles cannot be installed on separate computers. Load balanced multiserver deployment, as stated in the recipe, is essentially the most likely deployment paradigm in a production environment.

There's more...

It is common practice to deploy Dynamics CRM 2011 with a SQL Server clustered environment. To achieve this, create a SQL Server cluster, and then during Dynamics CRM 2011 installation, on the **Select SQL Server** page, type the virtual server name that was specified when we created the SQL Server cluster.

The multiserver deployment of Dynamics CRM 2011 can be more complex than what has been discussed in this recipe. One example of a complex deployment can be to deploy all server roles to separate server machines.

The following diagram describes a multiserver CRM 2011 deployment with different server roles deployed on separate server machines.

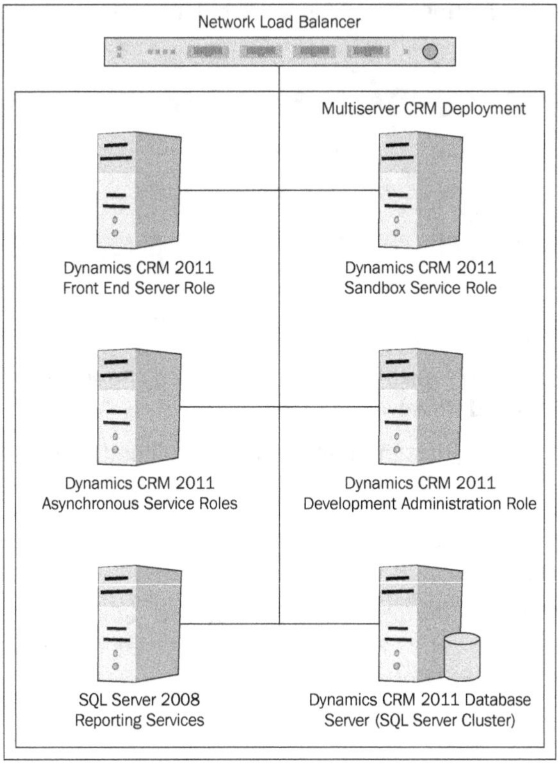

When we select a server role other than Full Server, Microsoft Dynamics CRM Server setup does not create an organization database during the installation. If the deployment does not have an organization database, we must use the deployment manager to create a new organization. The next recipe will guide us with creating a new organization in Dynamics CRM 2011.

Creating a new organization

Microsoft Dynamics CRM 2011 Deployment Manager is a wizard-based application that takes us through all the steps for creating a new organization. For multiserver deployment and while creating a multitenant CRM deployment, multiple organizations can be created for a Dynamics CRM 2011 CRM deployment.

How to do it...

The steps to create a new organization are as follows:

1. Launch the deployment manager. This is usually accessible via at:

   Start | **All Programs** | **Microsoft Dynamics CRM** | **Deployment Manager**

2. Click on the **Organizations** link. This will list all the existing organizations deployed in this CRM environment as shown in the following screenshot:

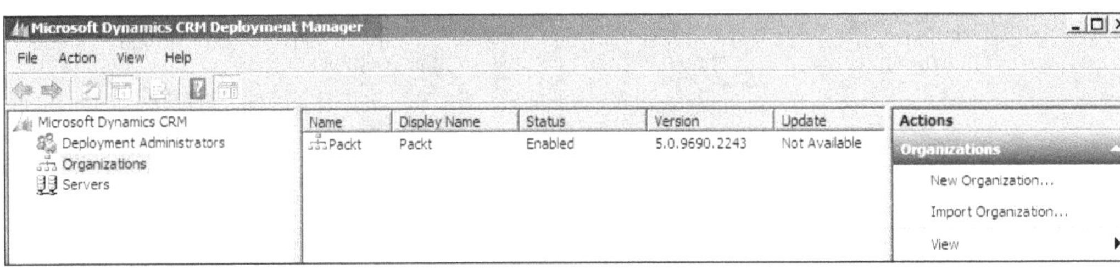

3. Then, right-click on **Organizations** and select **New Organization**. The **New Organization Wizard** window will appear.
4. On the **Specify the Organization Settings** page, enter the following information:
   - **Display Name**: This will contain the name of the CRM Organization.
   - **Unique Database Name**: This will contain the database name for this CRM Organization.
   - **ISO Currency Code**: Click on **Browse** and select a base currency. Setting currencies has been discussed in the *There's more...* section of *the Installing Dynamics CRM Server* recipe.

- **SQL Collation**: In the **SQL collation** list, keep the default selection or select a different database collation that the organization database will use to sort and compare data characters.

5. Click on **Next>** to proceed:

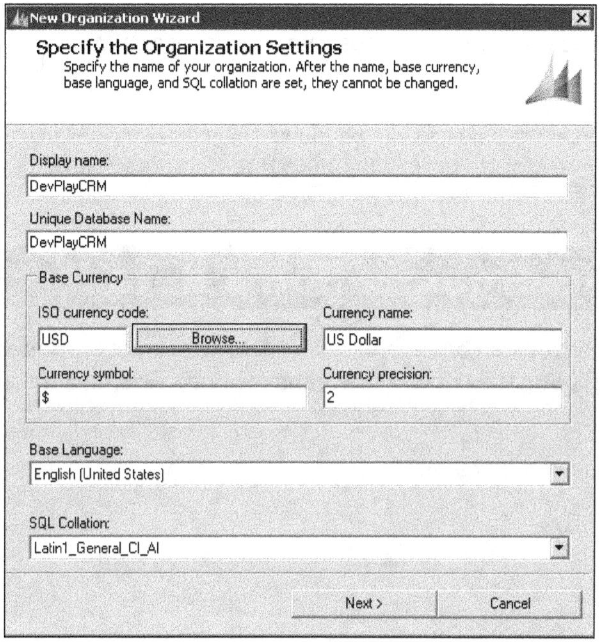

6. On the **Help Us Improve the Customer Experience** page, select whether to participate in the Customer Experience Improvement Program, and then click on **Next**.
7. On the **Select SQL Server** page, specify the SQL Server machine name.

   If we are using the default instance of SQL Server, we need to provide the machine name of the SQL Server, and in case we are using the named instance of SQL Server, we need to enter `<machine-name>\<instance-name>`.

8. On the **Specify Reporting Services Server** page, specify the **Reporting Server URL** value.
9. Next appears the **System Checks** page, which outlines a summary of all requirements and recommendations for a successful installation. If all the previous steps have been followed, everything should be OK. Make sure no errors are reported. If there are errors, they need to be corrected before we can continue. Click on **Next**.
10. Then appears the **Ready to Create** page. Here, review the selections and click on **Create** to create the new organization.

How it works...

Using this recipe, organizations within Dynamics CRM 2011 can be set up. Multiple organizations can be set up by repeating this recipe. An organization within Dynamics CRM 2011 is usually provided a meaningful name from the business standpoint. The organization name appears as part of the Dynamics CRM URL. However, there are some restricted names that cannot be used as organization names within Dynamics CRM.

> These restricted names can be found in the `ReservedName` column of the `ReservedNames` table in the `MSCRM_CONFIG` database.

Editing the organization's details

A organization once set up can be renamed/modified after creation. This is a fairly easy task and can be achieved using the deployment manager. The following details of an organization can be edited:

- Display name of the organization
- SQL Server
- SSRS Server

How to do it....

Please perform the following steps to edit an organization's details:

1. Launch the deployment manager. This is usually accessible via:

   Start Menu | **All Programs** | **Microsoft Dynamics CRM** | **Deployment Manager**

2. Navigate to **Microsoft Dynamics CRM** | **Organizations**, and then right-click on the organization and select **Disable**.
3. Click on the organization name and click on **Edit Organization** from the **Actions** pane as shown in the following screenshot:

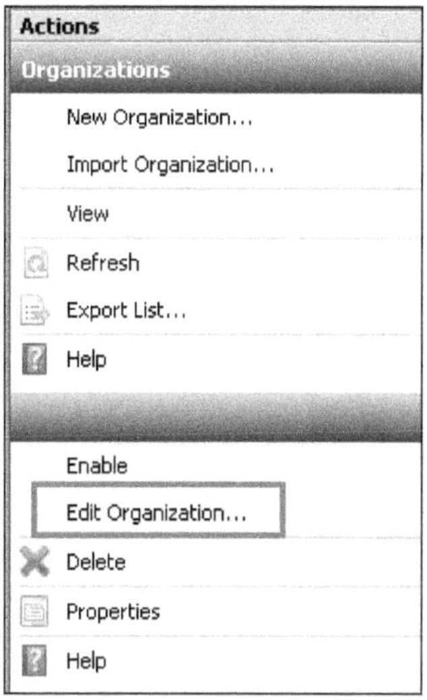

4. On the **Edit Organization** wizard screen, change the required properties and click on **Next** to proceed.
5. On the **System Checks** page, click on **Next**.
6. On the **Ready to Apply Changes** page, click on **Apply**.
7. Finally, click on **Finish** to complete the changes.

How it works...

Once the changes are applied, the organization is updated with the new changes. Unless setup encounters any error, the changes will be published and the changes will be visible in the organization list.

See also

Recipes in this chapter demonstrated how to install various components of Microsoft Dynamics CRM 2011. In the next chapter we would discuss the following recipes:

- Backing up Dynamics CRM 2011 Server
- Recovering Dynamics CRM 2011 Server failure
- Monitoring Dynamics CRM 2011 Server
- Optimizing Dynamics CRM 2011 Server performance

2

Maintaining and Optimizing Microsoft Dynamics CRM 2011 Server

In the previous chapter, we discussed the recipes for installing Microsoft Dynamics CRM 2011 Server on-premises. Post installation, the next important thing to know is how to maintain the health of the servers. In this chapter, we will delve into the recipes for maintaining the health and potential optimization possibilities of Dynamics CRM Server 2011 components. These recipes are intended for Dynamics CRM 2011 on-premises deployment only.

This chapter covers the following recipes:

- Backing up Dynamics CRM 2011 Database Server
- Backing up Dynamics CRM 2011 Server
- Recovering from a Dynamics CRM 2011 Database Server failure
- Recovering from a Dynamics CRM 2011 Server failure
- Enabling server-level tracing
- Enabling deployment-level tracing
- Enabling tracing on a Microsoft Dynamics CRM 2011 E-mail Router machine
- Monitoring Dynamics CRM 2011 Server performance
- Optimizing Dynamics CRM 2011 Database Server performance
- Optimizing Dynamics CRM 2011 Server performance

Introduction

Post the installation of Dynamics CRM 2011 Server, its maintenance, backup, and finally optimization need to be taken care of. The maintenance of Dynamics CRM 2011 requires familiarity with a wide range of servers, networks, mail systems, and so on.

After installation, the best practice is to back up some of the components. The backup would help to restore the server in the case of a failure of one or more components. A comprehensive backup and recovery mechanism should be in place before the Dynamics CRM 2011 solution is rolled out to end users for use.

The following components of the Dynamics CRM 2011 Server infrastructure need to be backed up (as recommended):

- **Database**: The configuration database (`MSCRM_CONFIG`) and the organization databases (`OrganizationName_MSCRM`) should have full database backups and transaction log backups.

  It is also recommended to back up the other databases, such as `master`, `msdb`, `ReportServer`, and `ReportServertempdb`.
- **Dynamics CRM 2011 Server**: The `web.config` file should be backed up in case it is modified post installation. The Windows registry subkeys in `HKEY_LOCAL_MACHINE\SOFTWARE\Microsoft\MSCRM` have to be backed up.
- **Exchange Server**: Backup for Exchange Server is not required from a Dynamics CRM 2011 recovery standpoint. But the Exchange Server backup policy should be in place, in line with the recommended Exchange Server maintenance practices.
- **Domain controller**: A full system state backup of the domain controller should be taken.

Another part of maintenance activities is to enable tracing when the system encounters errors. Dynamics CRM 2011 provides tracing capabilities. Tracing, by default, is disabled when Dynamics CRM 2011 components are installed. In this chapter, we will learn recipes on how to enable them.

We will also delve into the recipes on how to recover from a failure when it occurs. Recovering from a failure is very important, and we will explore how Dynamics CRM 2011 Server and SQL Server for Dynamics CRM 2011 can be recovered from a failure.

The last phase would be to look into the recipes for optimizing Dynamics CRM 2011 Server's performance. Performance optimization is a standard, nonfunctional requirement in any Dynamics CRM 2011 implementation. Though performance optimization greatly depends on the production network and infrastructure, we would explore the standard Dynamics CRM 2011 Server optimization methods.

Backing up Dynamics CRM 2011 Database Server

A database server backup plan is very important for ensuring the ability to recover in case of any disaster. The Dynamics CRM 2011 Database Server backup strategy will usually be of the following two types:

- To back up the Windows Server machine, which is running the Dynamics CRM 2011 Database server
- To back up the Dynamics CRM 2011-related databases using Microsoft SQL Server's in-built backup and recovery feature

Moreover, some level of hardware fault tolerance has to be present for a database server. This can mean the usage of a RAID-5 disk array for the databases and a RAID-1 (mirror) for the transaction logs.

Windows Server backup can be used to create and manage automatic scheduled backups of the database server. More information about Windows Server backup and recovery can be found at the following link:

`http://technet.microsoft.com/en-in/library/dd979562(v=ws.10).aspx`

In this recipe, we will discuss backing up the database server using SQL Server's backup feature. The Dynamics CRM 2011 Database backup plan should include database maintenance and database backups.

Getting ready

Our database backup plan should include each of the Dynamics CRM 2011 databases to make sure of a proper recovery in case one or all databases fail. The backup of `MSCRM_CONFIG` and `OrganizationName_MSCRM` databases should include a full database backup and some number of transaction log backups. For databases that are updated infrequently, such as the `master` and `msdb` databases, we can have the full database backed up.

One important aspect of the database backup strategy is the frequency of the backup, that is, how frequently a database should be backed up. The recommendation here is to make frequent backups, but you need to make sure that the backup process does not impact the availability of the system to the end users to a great extent.

> Frequent, full database backups reduce the number of restores after any database failure.

The other aspect of the database backup strategy depends on how much data loss is acceptable to business users in case of a database failure. For example, if a maximum of an hour's data loss is acceptable, transaction logs should be backed up every one hour and an entire database should be backed up every day to reduce the number of restores.

How to do it...

The following steps will help create a database maintenance plan for the Dynamics CRM 2011 databases:

1. Launch **SQL Server Management Studio** by navigating to **Start** | **All Programs** | **Microsoft SQL Server 2008 R2** | **SQL Server Management Studio**.

    > If the database is running the SQL Server 2012 version, the navigation path will be **Start** | **All Programs** | **Microsoft SQL Server 2012** | **SQL Server Management Studio**.

    SQL Server Management Studio can be installed on a machine that is not running the Dynamics CRM 2011 SQL Server databases.

    Log in to the Dynamics CRM 2011 Database Server with a user having a `sysadmin` role. Then expand the **Management** node in **Object Explorer**.

    > A user having the `sysadmin` role can only create or manage maintenance plans. **Object Explorer** only displays the **Maintenance Plans** node for users who are members of the `sysadmin` fixed server role.

2. Under the **Management** node, right-click on **Maintenance Plans** and select **Maintenance Plan Wizard** as shown in the following screenshot:

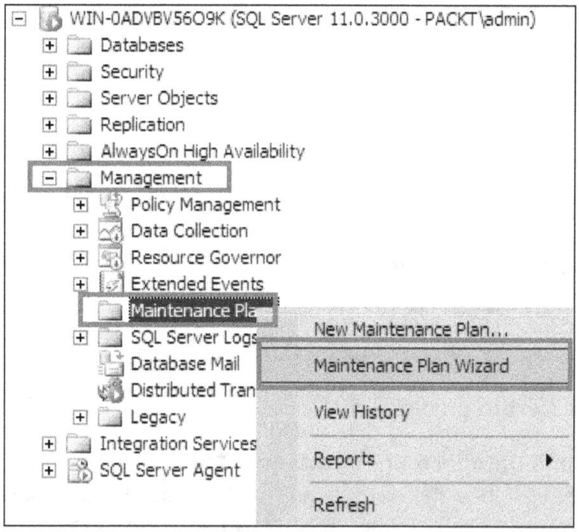

3. On the **SQL Server Maintenance Plan Wizard** page, click on **Next** to continue.
4. On the **Select Plan Properties** page, provide the **Name** and **Description** values for the maintenance plan.

   Then select one of the following schedules:

   - **Separate schedules for each task**: This will create a separate schedule for each task added to the maintenance plan.
   - **Single schedule for the entire plan or no schedule**: This will create one schedule that applies to all tasks added to the maintenance plan.

   In this recipe, select the **Single schedule for the entire plan or no schedule** option as we intend to create only one schedule for our entire maintenance plan. Then click on **Next** to proceed.

   If the database is SQL Server 2012, then under **Run as** select the account that Microsoft SQL Server Agent uses when executing the maintenance plan.

5. On the **Select Maintenance Tasks** page, select one or more maintenance plan tasks. Here the recommendation is to select the following maintenance tasks:

   - **Check Database Integrity**: This maintenance task, by executing the `DBCC CHECKDB` T-SQL statement, would check the allocation and structural integrity of user and system tables and indexes to ensure that any integrity problems with the database are reported.
   - **Back Up Database (Full)**: This maintenance task, by executing the `BACKUP DATABASE` T-SQL statement, would back up the whole database.

- **Back Up Database (Transaction Log)**: This maintenance task, by executing the `BACKUP LOG` T-SQL statement, would back up the transaction logs of the database.

  Then click on **Next** to proceed.

6. On the **Select Maintenance Task Order** page, select the following order (usually the proposed order):
    1. **Check Database Integrity**
    2. **Back Up Database (Full)**
    3. **Back Up Database (Transaction Log)**

   Then click on **Next** to proceed.

7. Then the **Define Database Check Integrity Task** page is shown, and on this page we need to define the databases that the **Check Database Integrity** task has to be associated with. Click on the **Databases** drop-down list and select the **These databases** option. Thereafter, select the following databases by ticking the checkboxes associated with each of them:
    - **master**
    - **msdb**
    - **MSCRM_CONFIG**
    - **<OrganizationName>_MSCRM**

    > There can be more than one organization database, so select all of them.

    - **ReportServer**
    - **ReportServerTempDB**

Click on **OK** to confirm the selection and then click on **Next** to proceed as shown in the following screenshot:

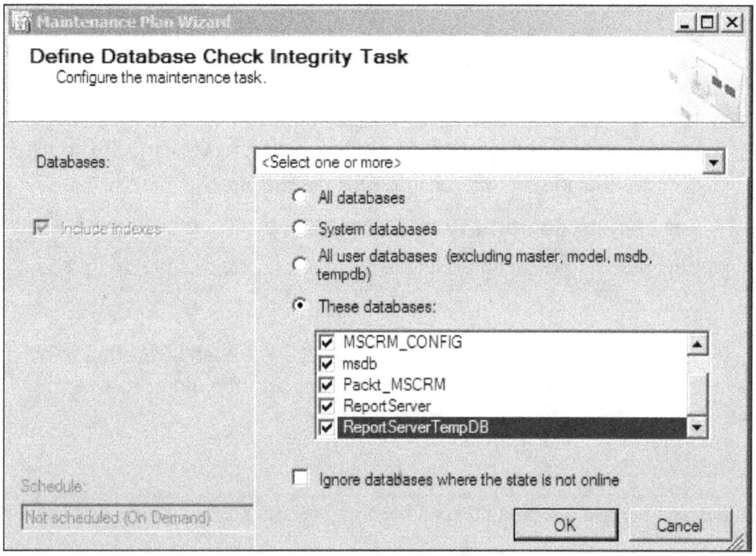

8. Then the **Define Back Up Database (Full) Task** page is shown, and on this page we need to define the databases that the full backup task has to be associated with. Click on the **Databases** drop-down list and select the **These databases** option. Thereafter, select the following databases by ticking the checkboxes associated with each of them:
    - **master**
    - **msdb**
    - **MSCRM_CONFIG**
    - **<OrganizationName>_MSCRM**

    > There can be more than one organization database, so select all of them.

    - **ReportServer**
    - **ReportServerTempDB**

Here select the **Create a backup file for every database** option, and then we can also modify the following options:

- **Backup files location**: We can choose a file location (different from the default one) to store the backup files using a file browser associated with it and can define the backup file extension as well
- **Backup file extension**: The default extension is `.bak`
- **Verify backup integrity**: Check this option to verify that the backup set is complete and that all volumes are readable
- **Set backup compression**: Select from the list whether we want to compress the database backup or not

> By default, compression significantly increases CPU usage and the additional CPU consumed by the compression process might adversely affect concurrent operations.

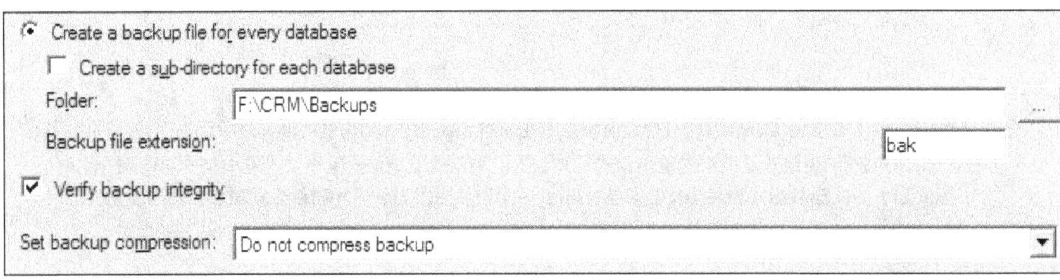

Then, click on **OK** to confirm the selection and finally click on **Next** to proceed.

9. Next, we will see the **Define Back Up Database (Transaction Log) Task** page, and on this page you need to define the databases the transaction log backup task will be associated with.

   Click on the **Databases** drop-down list and select the **These databases** option. Here, do not select databases, such as `master` and `msdb`, as these databases are updated infrequently.

   Apply the same choices defined in the previous step for backup location, backup file extension, and backup file compression choices.

   After making the selections, click on **OK** to confirm and then click on **Next** to proceed.

10. Next, we will see the **Select Report Options** page. Here a file location other than the default one can be provided in the **Folder location:** field of the **Write a report to a text file** option. This location is used to save a report of the maintenance plan actions, and this report can be e-mailed by selecting the **Email report** option and providing an e-mail address under the **To** option.

11. Next, we will see the **Complete the Wizard** page; click on **Finish** to complete the maintenance plan.
12. On the **Maintenance Wizard Progress** page, monitor the status information of the actions of the **Maintenance Plan Wizard**, and once all the task statuses end on **Success**, click on **Close** to close the wizard.

After creating the maintenance task, we will now schedule it to run automatically at a scheduled time by performing the following steps:

1. In **Object Explorer**, expand the **SQL Server Agent** node and then expand the **Jobs** node under it.
2. Select the job that has the name in the <MaintenancePlan_Name>.Subplan_1 format. Then right-click on this task and select **Rename**. Modify the **Job Name** field to a better, self-explanatory name.
3. Again, right-click on the job name and select **Properties** from the context menu.
4. This will launch the **Job Properties** page. Then, click on the **Schedules** page under the **Select a page** list.
5. Click on **New** from the task pane at the bottom. This will open the **New Job Schedule** window. Provide the following details, such as the name, schedule type, frequency, daily frequency, and duration in their respective fields. Then click on **OK** to save the details:

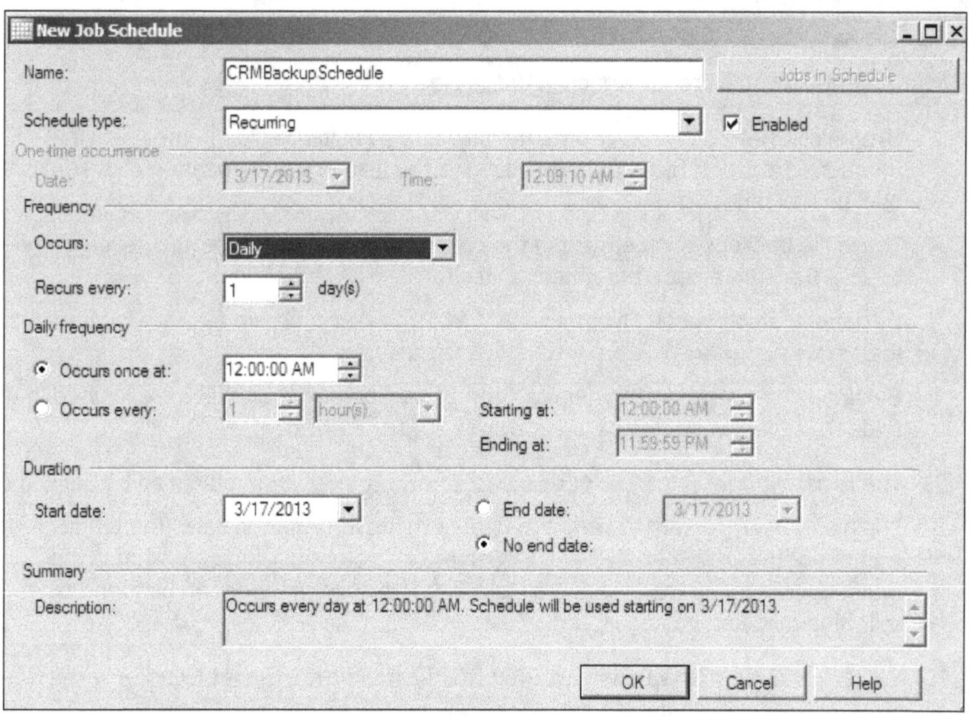

6. Again, click on **OK** to save the scheduled job.

How it works...

The maintenance plan created in this recipe includes checking database integrity and taking the full and transactional backups of Dynamics CRM 2011 databases. Once the maintenance plan is created, it can be executed manually as well by right-clicking on the maintenance plan and then selecting **Execute**. The maintenance plan created can also be modified in the future. This can be done by right-clicking on the maintenance plan name and then selecting **Modify**.

Backing up Dynamics CRM 2011 Server

Backing up Microsoft Dynamics CRM 2011 Server would include backing up its databases, program files, and website files. Now the database backup has already been discussed in the previous recipe. In this recipe, we will explore backing up program files and website files.

In addition to these files, if any update rollups have been applied, the versions of these update rollups have to also be noted so that in case of failure recovery, these update rollups can also be reapplied.

The registry should also be backed up so that it can be restored in the case of a failure.

How to do it...

The following steps would create a backup of the files:

1. Dynamics CRM 2011 Server program files and websites reside in the following mentioned location by default. Please save the files in a safe location on a separate backup machine.

   These file backups can be used in the case of any failure. Hence, it is recommended to save them on a separate machine itself.

   By default, all Microsoft Dynamics CRM 2011 Server program files are located in the folder `C:\Program Files\Microsoft CRM\`.

   By default, the Microsoft Dynamics CRM 2011 Server website files are located in the folder `C:\Program Files\Microsoft CRM\CRMWeb`.

2. The registry under `HKLM\Software\Microsoft\MSCRM` should also be backed up.
3. It is also very important to keep the update rollup information safe. The build number of the Dynamics CRM 2011 Server can potentially indicate what is the latest update rollup that has to be installed. The build number can be found by following these steps:

   1. Browse to the Dynamics CRM 2011 URL in the Internet Explorer window.
   2. Then go to **File** | **Help** | **About Microsoft Dynamics CRM**.

3. This will show the build number of the Dynamics CRM 2011 Server as shown below.

How it works...

In this recipe, we have taken backup copies of the `web.config` and registry files. The backups become very important in case changes have been made to them post the installation of Dynamics CRM 2011. In any case, keeping a backup copy is always recommended. This backup copy can be restored when a failure occurs.

The build number of the Dynamics CRM 2011 Server will confirm that the latest update rollup was installed on the environment. The RTM version of Dynamics CRM 2011 has a build number of **5.0.9688.583**, and then with every update rollup release the build number changes. The following table shows the build numbers of the update rollups available till this book was written:

Update rollup version	Build number	Update rollup version	Build number
Update Rollup 1	5.0.9688.1045	Update Rollup 7	05.00.9690.2165
Update Rollup 2	05.00.9688.1155	Update Rollup 8	05.00.9690.2243
Update Rollup 3	05.00.9688.1244	Update Rollup 10	05.00.9690.2740
Update Rollup 4	05.00.9688.1450	Update Rollup 11	05.00.9690.2835
Update Rollup 5	05.00.9688.1533	Update Rollup 12	05.00.9690.3236
Update Rollup 6	05.00.9690.1992	Update Rollup 13	05.00.9690.3448

Recovering from a Dynamics CRM 2011 Database Server failure

In the case of a Dynamics CRM 2011 Database Server failure, the database must be restored from the backup and reassociated with Dynamics CRM 2011.

How to do it...

Perform the following steps to recover from a SQL Server failure:

1. In the case of a Full Server machine crash or failure, we might need to reinstall the operating environment of the server machine. Hence, we have to install the Windows Server version and make sure that the machine is joined to the same domain where Microsoft CRM Server is joined. Thereafter, we have to install the SQL Server version.

   > We have to use the same database name and disk structure. If we changed the database name, additional steps would be needed to associate it back with Dynamics CRM 2011 Server.

2. Log in to **SQL Server Management Studio** using Windows Authentication with a user credential, having **CREATE DATABASE** permissions on the instance of the SQL Server.
3. On the recovery path, the first step would be to recover the master database, provided we have a backup of this database. To recover any system database, the database has to be started in single user mode.

   More information about starting a SQL Server instance in single user mode can be found at the following link:

   http://msdn.microsoft.com/en-IN/library/ms188236.aspx

   Then to restore the full backup of the master database, type the following T-SQL statement:

   ```
   RESTORE DATABASE master FROM <backup_device> WITH REPLACE
   ```

   Replace <backup_device> with the file location in a backup device, for example, T:\MS_CRM_Master_DB_Backup\master.bak.

   > If changes are made after the database has been backed up, these changes will be lost once the backup is restored. After the master database is restored, the instance of SQL Server may stop automatically. Please restart the SQL Server instance if required.

4. Post the master database restoration, the msdb database has to be restored. Before restoring msdb, stop the **SQL Server Agent** instance. Then, use the following T-SQL command to restore the msdb database:

   ```
   RESTORE DATABASE msdb FROM <backup_device> WITH REPLACE
   ```

   Replace <backup_device> with the file location in a backup device, for example, T:\MS_CRM_Master_DB_Backup\msdb.bak.

> It is necessary to restore msdb once the master database has been restored. The msdb database contains scheduling and other data used by the system. If msdb is not restored, and is not accessible, **SQL Server Agent** cannot access or initiate any previously scheduled tasks.

5. Next, restore the MSCRM_CONFIG database and then all the organization databases. Execute the following T-SQL command to restore these databases:

   ```
   RESTORE DATABASE MSCRM_CONFIG FROM <backup_device> WITH REPLACE

   RESTORE DATABASE <Organization_MSCRM> FROM <backup_device> WITH
   REPLACE
   ```

   Replace <backup_device> with the file location in a backup device, for example, T:\MS_CRM_Master_DB_Backup\MSCRM_CONFIG.bak.

6. In case SQL Server Reporting Services and Microsoft Dynamics CRM 2011 Connector for Microsoft SQL Server Reporting Services are also installed on the same machine, ReportingServer and ReportingServertempDB are also required to be restored using the RESTORE DATABASE command as shown in the following T-SQL commands:

   ```
   RESTORE DATABASE ReportingServer FROM <backup_device> WITH REPLACE

   RESTORE DATABASE ReportingServertempDB FROM <backup_device> WITH
   REPLACE
   ```

   Replace <backup_device> with the file location in a backup device, for example, T:\MS_CRM_Master_DB_Backup\ReportingServer.bak.

7. Finally, we need to run the Microsoft Dynamics CRM 2011 Server setup as stated in the *Installing Dynamics CRM Server* recipe of *Chapter 1, Installing Dynamics CRM 2011*. But in this case, in the **Specify Deployment Options** page, we have to select the **Connect to existing databases** option.

> This step should only be tried in case the MSCRM_CONFIG database has been restored. If this database has not been restored (because it was not required), then we can reconnect to this database using the deployment manager. Please follow the *Editing the organization's details* recipe as stated in *Chapter 1, Installing Dynamics CRM 2011*, and change the SQL Server value.

How it works...

In this recipe, we have recovered all the databases required to make Dynamics CRM 2011 function step by step. The discussed scenario was a case of a Full Server failure. In case of a partial failure, we might need to restore a specific database. If the `MSCRM_CONFIG` database is not restored, it has only to be reconnected to Dynamics CRM 2011 Server as stated in step 7 of this recipe.

Recovering from a Dynamics CRM 2011 Server failure

In this recipe, we will see how to recover from a Dynamics CRM 2011 Server failure.

How to do it...

Perform the following steps to recover from a Dynamics CRM 2011 Server failure:

1. In the case of a Full Server machine crash or failure, we might need to reinstall the operating environment of the server machine. Install the Windows Server version on the server, and join the machine to the same active directory where SQL Server for Dynamics CRM 2011 is already linked.
2. Install Microsoft Dynamics CRM 2011 Server by following the *Installing Dynamics CRM Server* recipe from *Chapter 1, Installing Dynamics CRM 2011*. During the installation, select **Connect to, and if necessary, upgrade an existing deployment** from the **Specify Deployment Options** page.
3. Apply the appropriate update rollups if they were installed before failure.
4. Once the installation is complete, replace the `ISV.config` and `web.config` files from their backups in case changes were made in these files from their default settings.
5. Restore the registry keys from the backups in case changes were made in the registry from their default settings.
6. In case the **Microsoft Dynamics CRM 2011 Connector for Microsoft SQL Server Reporting Services** component was also installed in the machine that failed, this component will have to be reinstalled.

How it works...

This recipe completes the restoration of Dynamic CRM 2011 Server in the case of a complete server failure. In the case of only a Dynamics CRM 2011 website failure, we only need to restore `ISV.Config` and `web.config` other than restoring the registry keys and importing and publishing any custom solution component.

In the case of a multiserver deployment, where different server roles are deployed separately, if any server machine encounters failure, upon recovery of that server we might need to repair Dynamics CRM 2011 on other servers as well.

Enabling server-level tracing

This recipe guides us through the tracing feature while providing the method to enable server-level tracing.

Getting ready

Tracing is a helpful feature for capturing valuable information while debugging or fixing any errors or warnings within the Dynamics CRM 2011 servers.

> Tracing is not available for the Microsoft Dynamics CRM Online version.

Enabling tracing, however, has performance implications. Because of its resource-intensive nature, tracing slows down the performance of the server. Another warning on tracing is that it might log sensitive information and should be handled very carefully.

> Tracing is disabled by default and the standard recommendation is to keep it disabled unless some error or warning debugging activity has to be performed.

There are two methods of enabling tracing in Microsoft Dynamics CRM 2011 Server. These are as follows:

- **Server-level tracing**: By enabling server-level tracing, only the current server machine where tracing is enabled can be monitored. Server-level tracing does not require any specific server role to be running in the computer, and it can provide a greater degree of control, where we can set specific trace values such as which Microsoft Dynamics CRM 2011 features to trace or the maximum trace file size.

  Server-level tracing has to be manually set in the Windows registry on the computer where one or more Microsoft Dynamics CRM 2011 server roles are running.

- **Deployment-level tracing**: By enabling deployment-level tracing, all the machines that are running various Dynamics CRM 2011 server roles and services would be monitored regardless of the server roles installed on the local computer where tracing is enabled.

With deployment-level tracing enabled, all the server roles, such as Asynchronous Service, Sandbox Processing Service, Unzip Service, the web application (w3wp), and deployment tools (mmc-Tools), are monitored. Corresponding trace files are created.

Deployment-level tracing is enabled using the Windows PowerShell command and is maintained in the `MSCRM_CONFIG` database.

> Deployment-level tracing can only be enabled from a computer that has the Microsoft Dynamics CRM 2011 Deployment Tools server role.
>
> If both deployment-level and server-level tracing are enabled on the same computer, only server-level tracing will be used.

To enable server-level tracing, certain registry changes have to be made on the Dynamics CRM 2011 server computer. Now the recommended practice is to back up the registry before any changes are performed. So before enabling tracing, back up the registry and save it in a safe location so that we can restore it if required.

How to do it...

To enable server-level tracing, perform the following steps:

1. Log in to the Dynamics CRM 2011 Server machine as a local machine administrator.
2. Launch the **Registry Editor** application by going to the Start menu and clicking on **Run**. Then, type `regedit` and click on **OK**.
3. Navigate to `HKEY_LOCAL_MACHINE\SOFTWARE\Microsoft\MSCRM` in the registry.

   Create the following *mandatory registry keys* for enabling tracing.

4. Right-click and select **New** | **DWORD (32-bit) Value**.
5. Enter the key name as `TraceEnabled` and value as `1` as shown in the following screenshot:

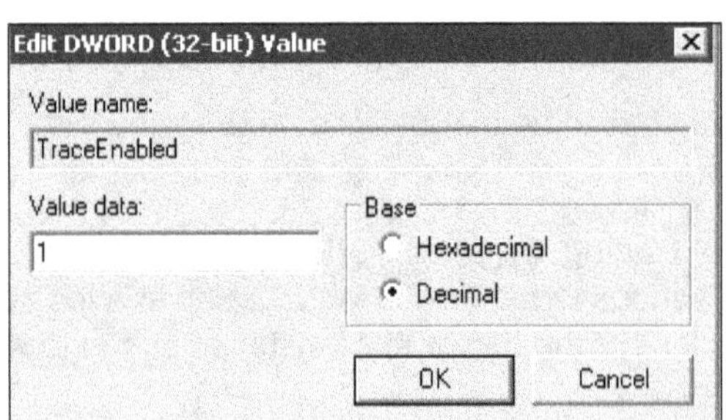

6. Right-click and select **New | DWORD (32-bit) Value**. Then enter the key name as **TraceRefresh** with a value between zero 0 and 99. Actually, the data value does not matter; the act of changing the value of this registry subkey will trigger a trace setting change in the system:

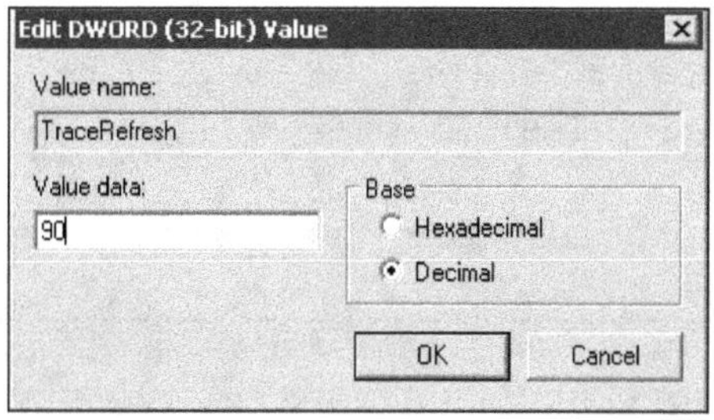

Now, there are a few **optional registry keys** that can be added.

7. Add a **String or Multi-String** value with the name `TraceCategories` and the value in the format `Category.Feature:TraceLevel`. You should know that `TraceCategories` is a combination of category, feature, and trace levels.

   One of the examples of the value would be `Application.*.Error`; it is going to capture the error logs for all the application features. Another example could be `Platform.Sql.Verbose` that would capture verbose logs of interactions with SQL Server.

8. Add a DWORD with the name `TraceCallStack` and decimal value of either `0` or `1`.

   A value of `1` would mean the call stack would be included in the trace log and a value of `0` would mean the call stack would not be included.

9. Add a DWORD with the name `TraceFileSizeLimit` and decimal value between `1` and `100`. This value will specify the maximum size of the trace files. New files will be created in case the maximum size is reached.

How it works...

These registry keys have to be created with the values previously specified. If the registry keys have been created with default values, tracing will not be enabled.

For the `TraceEnabled` mandatory registry key, a value of `0` means tracing is disabled and a value of `1` means it is enabled.

If the optional registry keys have not been created, the default values for these keys will be used by tracing. The default values for the optional registry keys are:

Optional registry keys	Default values
`TraceCategories`	`*:Error`
`TraceCallStack`	`0`
`TraceFileSizeLimit`	`5`

The complete list of category values for `TraceCategories` is as follows:

ADUtility	Live.Provisioning	Platform.Async	Sandbox.StartStop
Application	Live.Support	Platform.ImportExportPublish	Sandbox.Performance
Application.Outlook	Live.SyncDaemon	Platform.Import	Sandbox.Monitoring
DataMigration	Monitoring	Platform.Metadata	SchedulingEngine
Deployment	NewOrgUtility	Platform.Sdk	ServiceBus
Deployment.Provisioning	ObjectModel	Platform.Soap	Shared
Deployment.Sdk	ParameterFilter	Platform.Sql	SharePointCollaboration
Exception	Platform	Platform.Workflow	Solutions
Etm	Platform.Async	Reports	Unmanaged.Outlook
Live	Platform.ImportExportPublish	Sandbox	Unmanaged.Platform
Live.AggregationDataExport	Platform.Import	Sandbox.AssemblyCache	Unmanaged.Sql
Live.PartnerInteraction	Platform.Metadata	Sandbox.LoadBalancer	Visualizations
Live.Platform	ParameterFilter	Sandbox.CallReturn	
Live.Portal	Platform	Sandbox.EnterExit	

[Unless changed, the tracing files are located at `C:\Program Files\Microsoft Dynamics CRM\Trace`.]

Enabling deployment-level tracing

Deployment-level tracing would enable tracing for all the server roles. However, this tracing can only be configured from a machine that has the Deployment Tool role installed.

Deployment-level tracing can only be configured using Windows PowerShell commands.

How to do it...

By following this recipe, we can enable deployment-level tracing on the machine that is running the Deployment Tool server role.

We need to perform the following steps to achieve this:

1. Log in to the machine as a local administrator and launch Windows PowerShell by clicking on **Start** | **All Programs** | **Accessories** | **Windows PowerShell** | **Windows PowerShell**.
2. In the PowerShell window, type the following command:

   ```
   Add-PSSnapin Microsoft.Crm.PowerShell
   ```

3. To turn on the deployment-wide tracing, type the following commands:

   ```
   $Setting = Get-CrmSetting TraceSettings
   $Setting.Enabled = $True
   Set-CrmSetting $setting
   ```

4. To turn off the deployment-wide tracing, type the following commands:

   ```
   $Setting = Get-CrmSetting TraceSettings
   $Setting.Enabled = $False
   Set-CrmSetting $setting
   ```

5. To check the current status of the deployment-wide tracing, type the following command:

   ```
   Get-CrmSetting TraceSettings
   ```

> The trace files are located at `C:\crmdrop\logs`.

How it works...

Deployment-level tracing provides deployment-wide tracing information. This setting should be carefully enabled as this would log tracing from every server where the Dynamics CRM 2011 server roles are running.

The deployment-level trace setting is stored in the `MSCRM_CONFIG` database. Use the following T-SQL command to find the deployment tracing setting in the database:

```
SELECT [ColumnName], [IntColumn], [BitColumn], [NVarCharColumn]
FROM [MSCRM_CONFIG].[dbo].[DeploymentProperties]
WHERE ColumnName LIKE'Trace%'
```

The default values will be as shown in the following screenshot:

	ColumnName	IntColumn	BitColumn	NVarCharColumn
1	TraceCallStack	NULL	1	NULL
2	TraceCategories	NULL	NULL	*:Error
3	TraceDirectory	NULL	NULL	c:\crmdrop\logs
4	TraceEnabled	NULL	0	NULL
5	TraceFileSize	10	NULL	NULL

Enabling tracing on the Microsoft Dynamics CRM 2011 E-mail Router machine

In this recipe, we will explore the steps to enable tracing for the Dynamics CRM 2011 E-mail router service.

How to do it...

Follow the next steps to enable tracing on the Dynamics CRM 2011 E-mail Router machine:

1. Log in to the server where Microsoft Dynamics CRM 2011 E-mail Router is installed with the local machine administrative permission.
2. Launch **Registry Editor** by going to the Start menu and clicking on **Run**. Then type `regedit` and click on **OK**.
3. Navigate to the `HKEY_LOCAL_MACHINE\SYSTEM\CurrentControlSet\Services\MSCRMEmail` subkey in the registry.
4. Right-click on the subkey and select **Modify**. Change the decimal value to `3` from the default value of `1`.
5. Thereafter, locate the `Microsoft.Crm.Tools.EmailAgent.xml` file in the machine. By default, the file is located at `SystemDrive:\Program Files\Microsoft CRM Email\Service`.
6. Open the file in a text editor such as Notepad. Then, change the `<LogLevel>` value from `1` to `3` shown as follows:

   ```
   <LogLevel>3</LogLevel>
   ```

7. Save the file.
8. And finally, restart E-mail Router.

How it works...

This recipe enables tracing for the E-mail Router machine. Tracing specific to E-mail Router is enabled by modifying the registry entries specific to E-mail Router in the machine where the E-mail Router component is installed.

Monitoring Dynamics CRM 2011 Server performance

Consistently monitoring a system's performance is very important to assess its health. Constant monitoring would assist to identify any potential issue in advance. Microsoft Windows comes with a performance-monitoring tool called **Performance Monitor**. This tool can be used to assess the performance of Dynamics CRM 2011 Server components.

There are many **performance objects** built into the operating system to monitor systems' performance. Dynamics CRM 2011 also adds to these performance objects to better monitor Dynamics CRM 2011 Server components. Dynamics CRM 2011 provides additional **performance counters** that are to be added. We can configure Windows Performance Monitor to obtain and display performance data as system components run on a Microsoft Dynamics CRM 2011 Deployment.

How to do it...

Perform the following steps to add Dynamics CRM 2011 performance counters:

1. Log in to the Dynamics CRM 2011 Server machine(s) with local administrative privileges.
2. Launch the **Performance Monitor** tool by going to the Start menu and clicking on **Run**, and then type `perfmon.msc` in the box and press *Enter*.
3. Select **Performance Monitor** under **Monitoring Tools** as shown in the following screenshot:

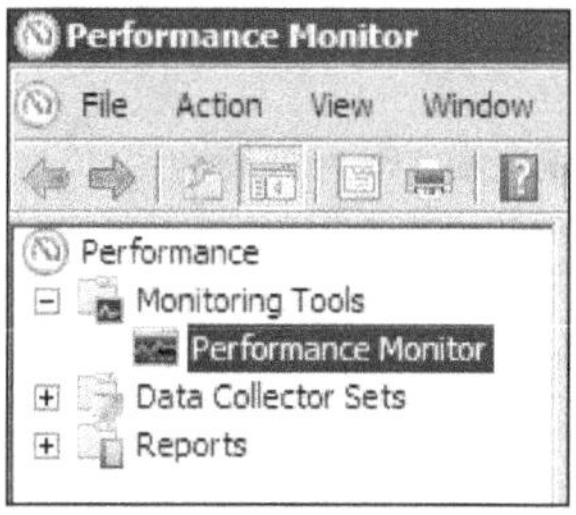

4. Then, click on the add (plus sign) toolbar icon in the right pane to open the **Add Counters** dialog box:

5. From the list of available counters, select the counters specific to Dynamics CRM 2011 and then click on the **Add** button below as shown in the following screenshot:

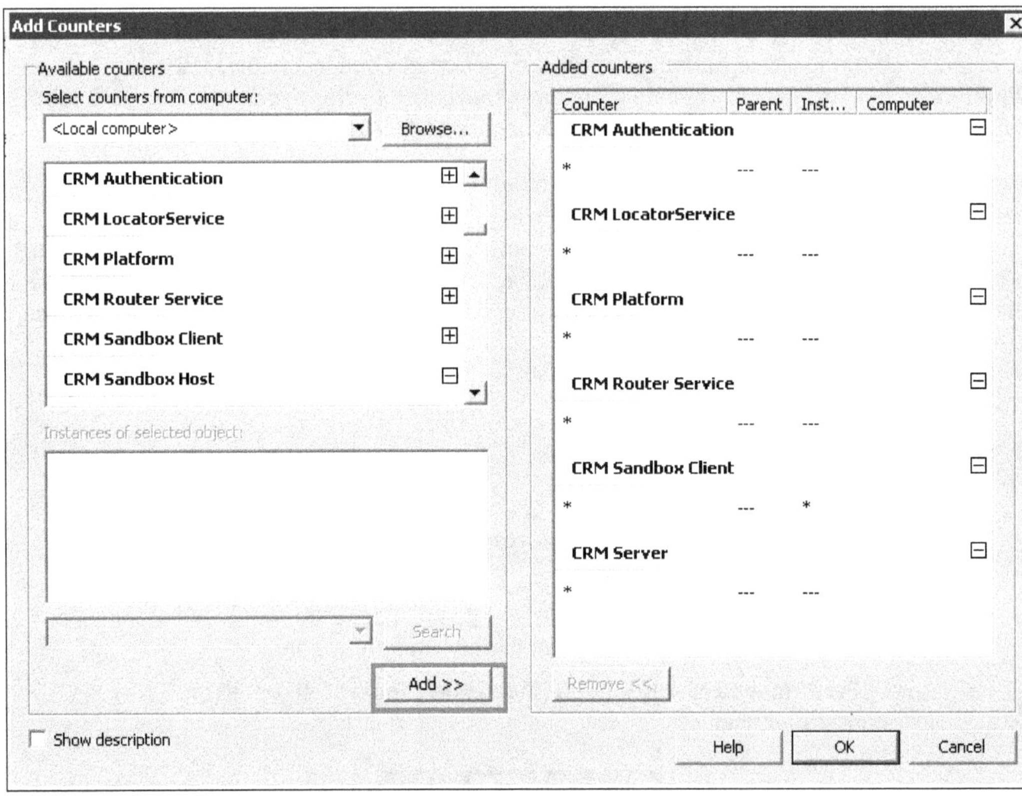

6. Finally, click on **OK**. The selected counters are added to the list of active counters and the data that they generate is shown in the dynamic graph.

How it works...

Microsoft Dynamics CRM 2011 offers the following performance counters that we need to monitor:

- Microsoft Dynamics CRM Client counters
- Microsoft Dynamics CRM Server counters
- Microsoft Dynamics CRM Authentication counters
- Microsoft Dynamics CRM Outlook Sync counters
- Microsoft Dynamics CRM Discovery counters
- Microsoft Dynamics CRM LocatorService counters
- Microsoft Dynamics CRM Platform counters
- Microsoft Dynamics CRM Service counters
- Microsoft Dynamics CRM Sandbox Client counters
- Microsoft Dynamics CRM Sandbox Host counters
- Microsoft Dynamics CRM Async Service counters
- Microsoft Dynamics CRM E-mail Router counters

The necessary performance counters have to be chosen based on the server roles installed on the machine. More detailed information about these performance counters can be downloaded from the following Microsoft website link:

`http://www.microsoft.com/en-us/download/details.aspx?id=27119`

Usually, the performance counters are used only for a specified time to check or diagnose any performance issues. Therefore, adding them to the base Performance Monitors is easy and serves the purpose too. In this recipe, the performance counters are directly added to the existing set. Alternatively, a separate data collector set can also be created and then the Dynamics CRM 2011 performance counter can be added to the set. More information on creating a data collector set can be found at `http://technet.microsoft.com/en-us/library/cc722414.aspx`.

Optimizing Dynamics CRM 2011 Database Server performance

Microsoft Dynamics CRM 2011 is a resource-intensive, web-based application. Certain parameters of the system have to be tuned for optimum performance. Dynamics CRM 2011 Server performance tuning can happen mainly in two components: the Dynamics CRM 2011 Database level and the Dynamics CRM 2011 Server component level. In this recipe, we will delve into how the Dynamics CRM 2011 database can be tuned for better performance.

Getting ready

Microsoft Dynamics CRM 2011 uses SQL Server. For better performance tuning on SQL Server, we need to identify the performance bottlenecks in the database server. SQL Server performance monitoring tools such as **Activity Monitor** (part of SQL Server 2008 Management Studio) should be used to check the performance of SQL Server.

Accurate performance tuning steps should be taken by analyzing the performance bottlenecks. Here we will explore a few common performance-tuning techniques for the Dynamics CRM 2011 database.

> Before applying these performance optimization techniques in a live environment, they should first be verified in a test environment that approximately matches the complexity, data volume, and integration points of the production environment.

How to do it...

The following points explain how to performance tune your Dynamics CRM 2011 database:

1. **Store datafiles and logfiles on separate physical disks**: Keeping both data and log files on the same drive can cause contention for that device and result in poor performance. Storing the files on separate drives allows I/O activity to occur at the same time for both the data and log files. This is a very important consideration for organization databases as the data growth is very frequent and usually very high too.

   During a database `CREATE` operation, specify separate physical drive locations for the data and log files. In case the database has already been created, move the files by performing the following steps:

   1. **Take a backup of the database and then take the database offline**: The database can be backed up by right-clicking on the database name in the **Object Explorer** pane within **SQL Server Management Studio** and then selecting **Tasks** | **Back Up...** as shown in the following screenshot:

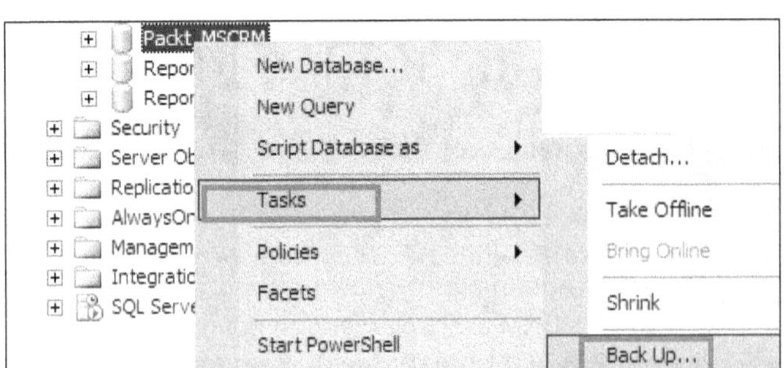

2. This will open a **Back Up Database** screen; enter a value for **Backup type** and the location information, and click on **OK** to back up. Wait until a backup successful message appears.
3. Thereafter, to take the database offline, right-click on the database name inside **SQL Server Management Studio** and then select **Tasks** | **Take Offline**.

2. **Restore the database from the backup**: Right-click on the **Databases** node inside **SQL Server Management Studio** and then select the **Restore Database...** option as shown in the following screenshot:

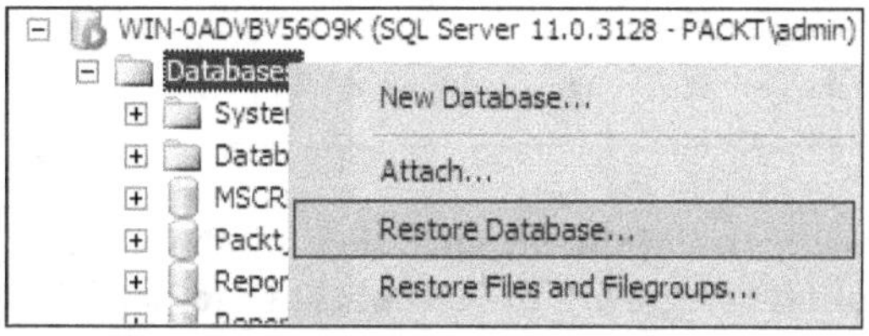

This will launch the **Restore Database** page. Here select the **Device** option under the **Source** details in the **Generals** node and then click on the associated File Explorer beside it. This will launch the **Select Backup Devices** page. Choose **Backup media type** as **File** and click on the **Add** button to select the database backup file(s). Then, click on **OK** to save the selections.

The next step would be to specify separate locations for data and log files. Click on the **Files** node on the **Restore Database** page. In this page, check the **Relocate all files to folder** option and then use the folder browser to change the **Data file folder** and **Log file folder** values. Finally, click on **OK** to start the database restore operation and wait until it is successful.

Finally, restart the SQL Server instance.

3. **Set the right database file size for the organization databases**: Organization databases contain data that changes more frequently, and the arrival of new data is also more frequent. If the database file size is small, it will attract incremental growth of the file. There is a little overhead in frequent increments in the database file. Hence, it is recommended to specify a reasonable amount considering the data growth for the next three to six months.

   To change the initial database file size using **SQL Server Management Studio**, please follow these steps:

   1. Right-click on the organization database and then select **Properties** | **Files**.
   2. On the **Files** page, modify the **Initial Size** column values (as shown in the following screenshot).

3. Restart the SQL Server service:

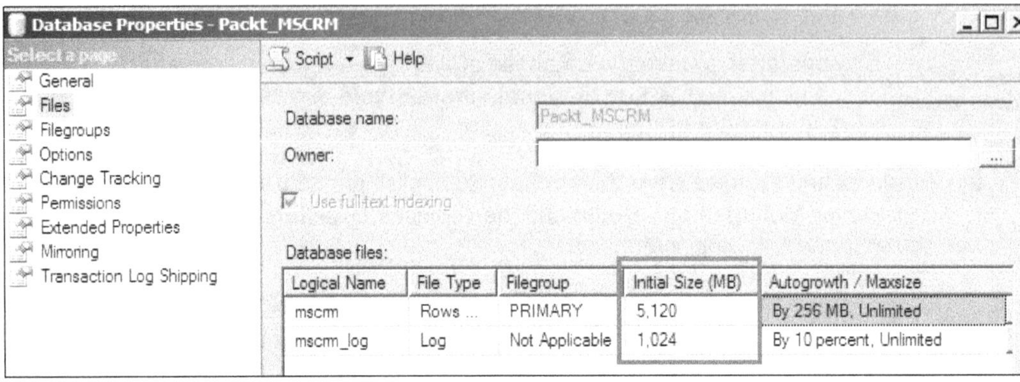

4. **Set the Autogrowth size of the organization databases** (`OrganizationName_MSCRM`) **considering the growth of the database for a period of three to six months**: If the autogrowth size is not managed properly, the database might experience many autogrow events, or very few. Every time an autogrowth event is fired, SQL Server holds up the database processing until the autogrowth event is complete. This equates to a slower response time for those SQL commands that are being processed against the database that is growing.

   The autogrowth size of a database can be modified by right-clicking on the database name, then going to **Properties** | **Files**. Then, click on the button associated under the **Autogrowth** column; then in the pop-up window, autogrowth-related settings can be modified.

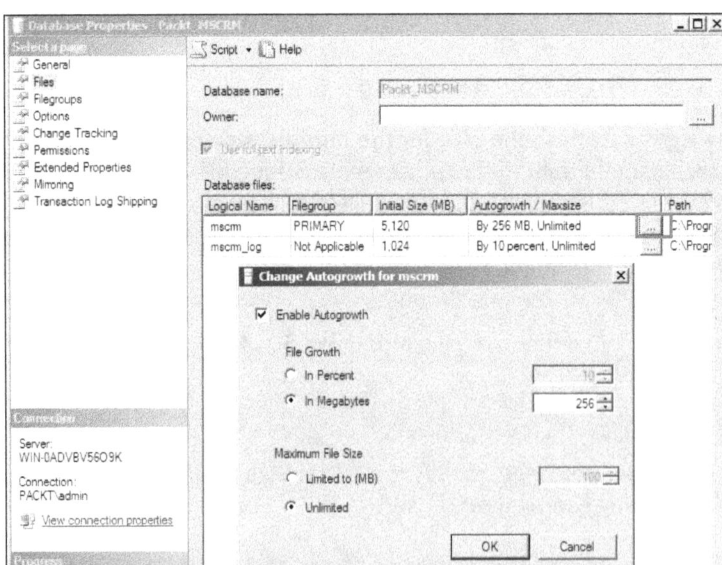

5. **Increase the Initial Size value and the Autogrowth size of the tempdb database**: This database is used by SQL Server, and it increments as its usage increases. By default, the initial size of `tempdb` is 8 MB; this means that every time `tempdb` crosses the 8 MB size, an autogrowth event would fire. In addition to this, every time a SQL Server service is restarted, `tempdb` would be set back to its initial size, which is 8 MB, by default. Frequent `tempdb` file size growth slows down the performance of SQL Server. Hence, its initial size has to be increased to a larger value.

> The `FileGrowth` property of `tempdb` has to be adjusted based on the speed of the I/O subsystem on which the `tempdb` files are located. It is recommended that we put the `tempdb` database on a fast I/O subsystem and on disks that differ from those that are used by Dynamics CRM 2011 databases.

The best way to estimate the size and the reasonable `FileGrowth` size of `tempdb` is to run the workload in a test environment. Once we have a good estimate of the size of `tempdb`, set its size with a safety factor that is appropriate. Autogrow should be used as a last resort but not as a strategy. Moreover, to avoid any potential latch timeouts, it is usually recommended to limit the autogrow operation to approximately 2 minutes.

Another general guideline about `tempdb` is to create one data file for each CPU or core on the server (accounting for any affinity mask settings) and then adjust the number of files up or down as appropriate.

Using multiple files reduces the `tempdb` storage contention and yields significantly better scalability. Make each data file the same size; this allows for optimal proportional-fill performance.

To change the `tempdb` database file sizes using **SQL Server Management Studio**, please follow these steps:

1. Right-click on the `tempdb` database and then go to **Properties** | **Files**.
2. On the **Files** page, modify the **Initial Size** and **Autogrowth** size field to an appropriate size.
3. Click on the **Add** button to add additional data files to the `tempdb` database. When additional data files are added, we should specify the following properties of the data file:
    - **Logical Name**
    - **Initial Size**
    - **Autogrowth** size
    - **Path**
    - **File Name**
4. Then restart the SQL Server service.

We will also see how to allocate sufficient memory to SQL Server. By default, SQL Server can change its memory requirements dynamically based on the maximum resources available. The default setting for maximum server memory in SQL Server 2008 R2 or the 2012 edition is 2147483647 MB. Maximizing the allocation of maximum server memory might assist in getting a better performance. But if more memory is provided to SQL Server, the other applications will perform slowly on the same machine.

To change the maximum server memory size of SQL Server, follow these steps:

1. Inside **SQL Server Management Studio**, on the **Object Explorer** pane, right-click on the server and select **Properties**.
2. Then, navigate to the **Memory** node and under **Server memory options**, enter the **Maximum server memory** value as shown in the following screenshot:

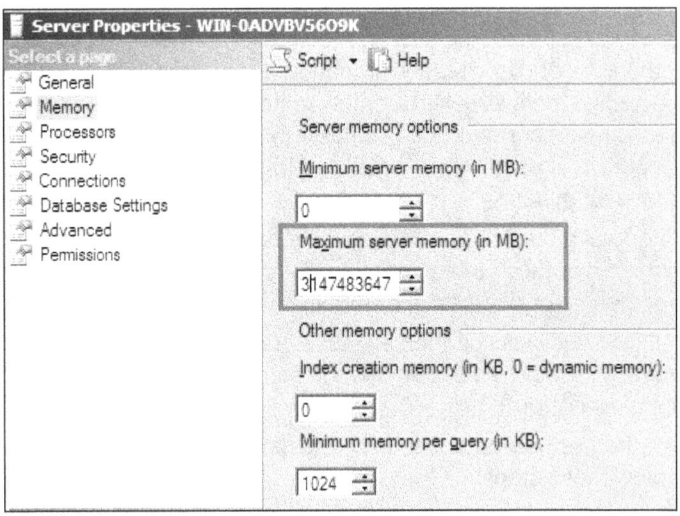

More information on SQL Server memory configuration options can be found at the following link:

`http://msdn.microsoft.com/en-us/library/ms178067.aspx`

6. **Create indexes for the Extension and custom entity tables**: Dynamics CRM 2011 creates the `<EntityName>_Extension` table for storing the custom attributes of a system entity, and custom entities are stored in custom tables in the organization databases. Monitor slow performing queries for these tables and then create a custom index for the `Extension` and custom entity tables. This would assist in improving performance.

   If the Quick Find View and Lookup View features contain many custom fields, it can have an adverse impact on the performance of these lookup queries. Either use very limited custom fields in these views or create a non-clustered index that includes these custom fields.

   > The application of any update rollup might delete existing custom indexes on Dynamics CRM 2011 database tables.

   Use the `CREATE INDEX` query to create indexes in the Dynamics CRM 2011 tables.

7. **Set maximum degree of parallelism (MAXDOP) to 1**: When SQL Server runs on a multicore machine, the number of processors that can be used to run a single statement for each parallel execution plan can be specified. This is called **maximum degree of parallelism**. When the default value of MAXDOP is `0`, it means that SQL Server determines the maximum degree of parallelism.

   When we set the MAXDOP value to `1`, the parallel plan generation will be suppressed. It is often observed that with the MAXDOP value of `1`, SQL Server performs better.

The MAXDOP value can be set inside **SQL Server Management Studio** by following these steps:

1. Right-click on the server name and then go to **Properties** | **Advanced**.
2. In the advanced settings page, we can set the **Max Degree of Parallelism** field as shown in the following screenshot:

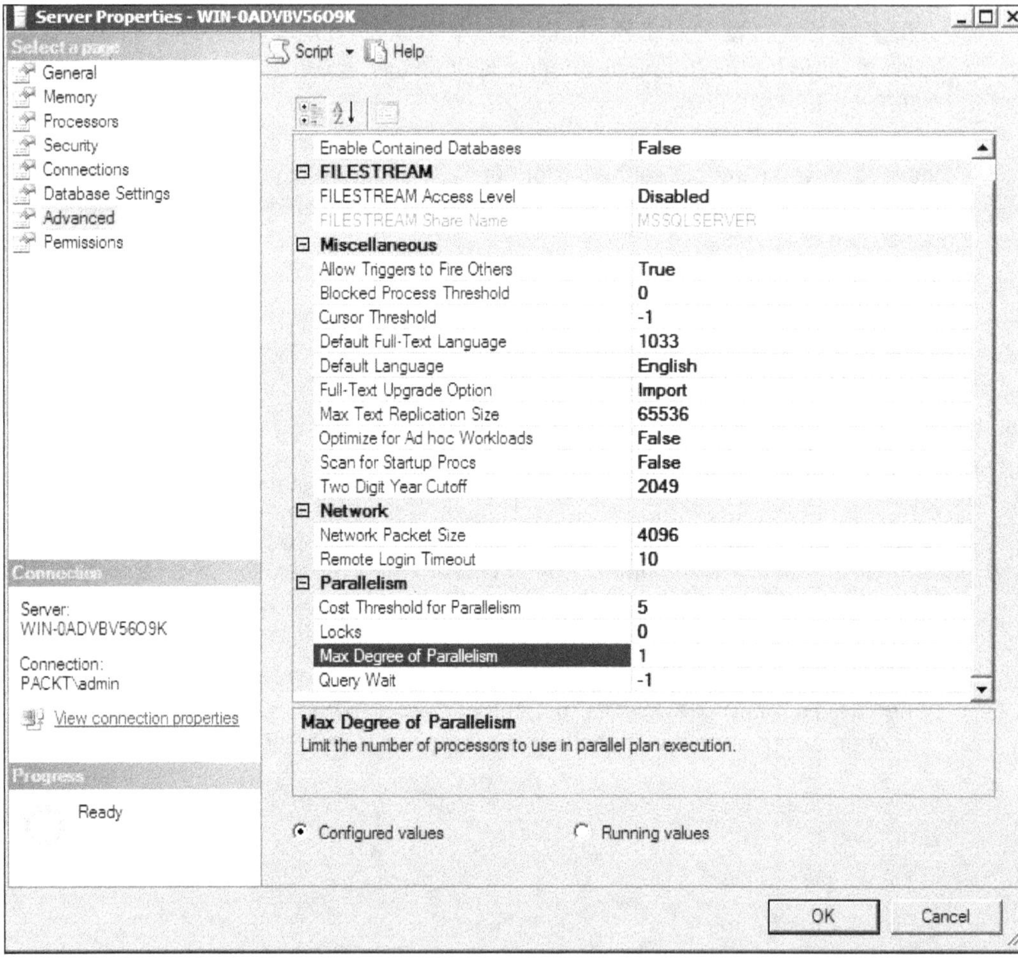

8. **Modify certain deployment properties' parameters**: Updating a few deployment properties in the Dynamics CRM 2011 database provides fixes around certain database-level issues and exceptions.
   - `SQLCommandTimeout`: It has been observed that a large size file import fails inside Dynamics CRM 2011 throwing SQL Server-level timeout errors. `SQLCommandTimeout` is a field with a default value of `30` that is present in the `MSCRM_CONFIG` database.

Increase the value of the `SQLCOmmandTimeout` parameter to a larger value. Use the following SQL command to modify the value:

```
USE MSCRM_CONFIG
GO
UPDATE DeploymentProperties SET IntColumn=9000 WHERE
ColumnName='SqlCommandTimeout'
```

- `AggregateQueryRecordLimit`: This deployment setting controls the maximum number of records that are returned by aggregate queries (used in charts). Sometimes the default value of 50000 does not suffice and exceptions such as `AggregateQueryRecordLimit exceeded` are thrown.

  Increase the value of the `AggregateQueryRecordLimit` parameter to a larger value. Use the following SQL command to modify the value:

```
USE MSCRM_CONFIG
GO
UPDATE DeploymentProperties SET IntColumn=100000 WHERE Colum
nName='AggregateQueryRecordLimit '
```

9. **Control the growth of the PrincipleObjectAccess (POA) table**: As almost every access to the Dynamics CRM 2011 data interacts with the POA table of the `<OrganizationName>_MSCRM` database, a large-size POA table would significantly slow down the SQL queries' performance. Until Update Rollup 6 for Dynamics CRM 2011, when a record was deleted from the Dynamics CRM 2011 system, corresponding POA entries were not getting deleted. This was causing a significant growth of the POA table and slowness in SQL query execution.

   Update Rollup 6 applies control over the growth of the **PrincipleObjectAccess** (**POA**) table by deleting entries when a Dynamics CRM 2011 record gets deleted from the system. However after installing Update Rollup 6, there is a SQL query that is required to be executed on the Dynamics CRM 2011 database only once. The SQL query can be found at the following link:

   `http://support.microsoft.com/kb/2664150`

10. **Control the growth of the AsyncOperationBase table**: The `AsyncOperationBase` table of Dynamics CRM 2011's organization database grows to be very large in no time if the organization executes asynchronous operations such as workflows. Unless controlled, the growth of this table can affect performance adversely.

    A regular cleanup of the `AsyncOperationBase` table is recommended, although it will delete all the entries for every job run in a period. If completed system job entries have some business value and have to be stored for a longer period, cleaning up this table regularly is not possible.

The SQL script to delete the `AsyncOperationsBase` table can be found at `http://support.microsoft.com/kb/968520`.

- **Rescheduling Dynamics CRM 2011 maintenance jobs**:

  By default, Dynamics CRM 2011 creates and runs a few maintenance jobs on a daily basis. These jobs are actually executed by **Microsoft Dynamics CRM Asynchronous Processing Service** (maintenance). This service schedules these jobs based on when the organization has been created. Therefore, these jobs can very well run when there is a pick user load on the system and will not slow down the system's performance or cause timeouts. Hence, it is recommended to reschedule these jobs when we expect very little of the user in the system. In the *How it works...* section of this recipe, we shall discuss a little more about these jobs.

  Dynamics CRM stores scheduling information about these jobs in the `ScaleGroupOrganizationMaintenanceJobs` table of the `MSCRM_CONFIG` database. However, there is a GUI tool available to modify the settings of these jobs. The GUI tool is known as **CRM 2011 Maintenance Job Editor** and is available at the following link for download:

  `http://crmjobeditor.codeplex.com/`

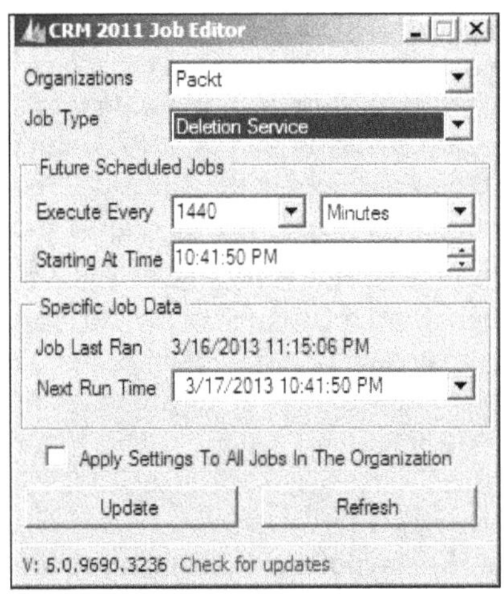

If you want to disable a job, please specify a future date (for example, 12/31/3000) under **Next Run Time** for that job.

How it works...

This recipe discusses the common performance tuning techniques performed on the Dynamics CRM 2011 database. These tuning techniques should be applied in conjunction with the specific performance bottlenecks identified in the Dynamics CRM 2011 environment.

In this recipe, we have first tried to check the firing of the autogrowth event. Frequent autogrowth event fire would significantly impact performance. Indexing data, which does not use indexes, is important to improve the performance of SQL queries. MAXDOP should be set to `1` for performance improvement. Additionally, the best practices around `temdb` are also recommended.

Finally, control the growth of the `PrincipleObjectAccess` and `AsyncOperationBase` tables along with adjusting the timings for the Dynamics CRM 2011 maintenance tasks. A list of maintenance jobs run by Asynchronous Processing Service (maintenance) is as follows:

Maintenance job name	Operation code	Frequency	Purpose
Deletion Service	14	Daily	Performs a cleanup of records associated with deleted entity data, which include `MatchCode`, POA records, and so on. *With Update Rollup 12*, it now cleans up the subscription-tracking records for deleted metadata objects as they expire.
Indexing Management	15	Daily	Validates the system-managed indexes for all entities and even recreates indexes if any system-defined index is missing.
Reindex All	30	Daily	Rebuilds fragmented indexes. This job will perform a `DBCC SHRINKDATABASE` command to release unused space for both database and transaction logs. *With Update Rollup 12*, this job no longer performs the shrink database command.
Cleanup Workflows	31	Daily	Finds custom workflow assemblies that are no longer referenced in any workflow rules or in-process jobs, and these unreferenced assemblies are then deleted.
Create Audit Partition	41	Monthly	Responsible for altering the partitioning scheme of the `auditbase` table. This feature is available only for SQL Enterprise editions.

Maintenance job name	Operation code	Frequency	Purpose
Check for MUI Updates	42	Daily	Detects any upgrade to the installed language (MUI) packs and schedules additional async operations to perform individual language provisioning.
Refresh Entity Row Counts	46	Daily	Refreshes the record count snapshot statistics leveraged in UR10's enhanced query plans. This maintenance task is available from *Update Rollup 10* onwards.
Refresh Sharing Counts	47	Daily	Refreshes the POA read snapshot statistics leveraged in UR10's enhanced query plans. This maintenance task is available from *Update Rollup 10* onwards.

Optimizing Dynamics CRM 2011 Server performance

In this recipe, we will try to figure out the different performance-boosting techniques we can adopt in the Dynamics CRM 2011 Server environment. Performance tuning is a continuous balancing act between design decision, available resources, hardware, cost, and so on. Additionally, identifying the performance issues in the Dynamics CRM 2011 system is also very important to conduct a tuning.

How to do it...

The following steps explore a few high-level methods of performance tuning:

1. While considering multiserver deployment of Dynamics CRM 2011, separating the server roles and using network load balancers would significantly improve the performance of the system. In a multiserver deployment, consider deploying the following in dedicated servers:
    - The Dynamics CRM 2011 Front End Server role
    - The Dynamics CRM 2011 Back End Server role
    - The Dynamics CRM 2011 Deployment Server role
    - Dynamics CRM 2011 Database Server
    - Reporting Server for Dynamics CRM 2011
    - Microsoft Dynamics CRM 2011 E-mail Router or Microsoft Exchange Server
    - Active Directory Domain Controller

    Another important consideration of deployment would be federated architecture. If Dynamics CRM 2011 is accessible from different geographies, you should deploy the Dynamics CRM 2011 infrastructure in a federated manner instead of deploying it in a centralized location. The deployment of the Dynamics CRM 2011 servers in the close proximity of the user's access location would assist in reducing the effect of network latency and travel time.

2. Using HTTP Compression in the IIS7 or any higher versions enables both **static** and **dynamics** compression of the Dynamics CRM 2011 web servers in the IIS.

    Perform the following steps to configure HTTP Compression in a web server:

    1. In the Dynamics CRM 2011 web server, go to the Start menu and click on **Run**, and type `inetmgr` and press *Enter*. This will launch the **Internet Information Services (IIS) Manager** administrative interface.
    2. Double-click on **Compression** on the **Features View** tab of the interface.

3. Click on the **Enable dynamic content compression** checkbox to enable dynamic compression.
4. Then, click on the **Enable static content compression** checkbox to enable static compression.

> If static compression is enabled, in the **Only compress files larger than (in bytes)** textbox type the minimum file size that we want IIS to compress.
>
> Browse to select a cache directory and leave the default value.
>
> Click on the **Per application pool disk space limit (in MB)** checkbox and type the maximum amount of space per application pool that IIS uses when it compresses static content.
>
> Click on the **Apply** button on the **Actions** pane to apply these changes.

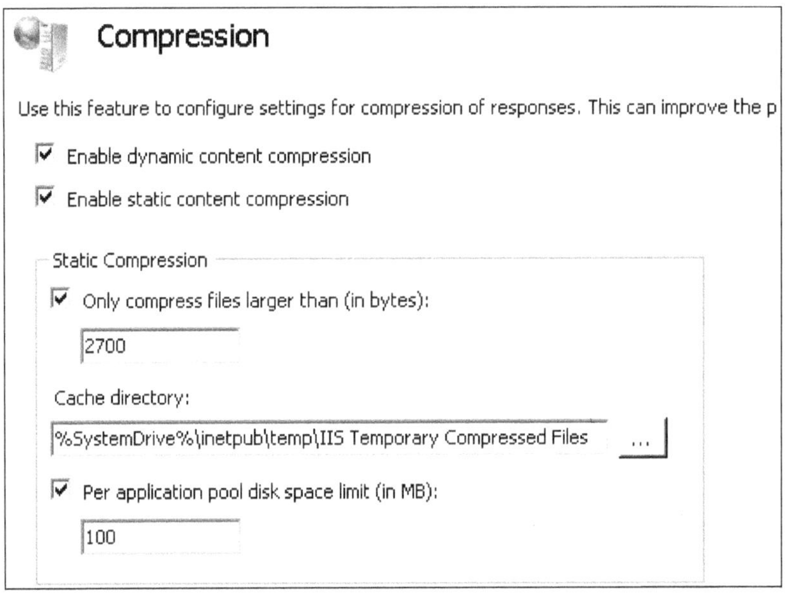

3. This step will help you change the `MaxConcurrentRequestsPerCPU` setting. By default, IIS7.5 (with .NET Framework 4.0) is limited to handling 5000 concurrent requests per CPU and will queue requests above this limit. 5000 is also the value we should use in ASP.NET Versions 2.0 and 3.5, which have a default of 12. Although most web applications usually work fine with the value of 5000, to achieve a better concurrency this value can be altered. This parameter should first be altered and tested for performance in a test environment before moving on to a production system.

Perform the following steps to modify the `MaxConcurrentRequestsPerCPU` setting in IIS7.5:

1. Log in to Windows Server where Microsoft Dynamics CRM 2011 is installed with local machine administrative permission.
2. Launch **Registry Editor** by going to the Start menu and clicking on **Run**. Then type `regedit` and click on **OK**.
3. Navigate to the following location and check whether a DWORD by the name of `MaxConcurrentReqeustsPerCPU` exists or not.
   - For ASP.NET 4.0:

     ```
     HKEY_LOCAL_MACHINE\SOFTWARE\Microsoft\
     ASP.NET\4.0.30319.0
     ```

   - For ASP.NET 2.0:

     ```
     HKEY_LOCAL_MACHINE\SOFTWARE\Microsoft\
     ASP.NET\2.0.50727.0
     ```

   If the DWORD does not exist, create a new DWORD with the name `MaxConcurrentReqeustsPerCPU` and specify the value as a higher number.

   If the DWORD already exists, modify the value to a higher number. This is shown in the following screenshot:

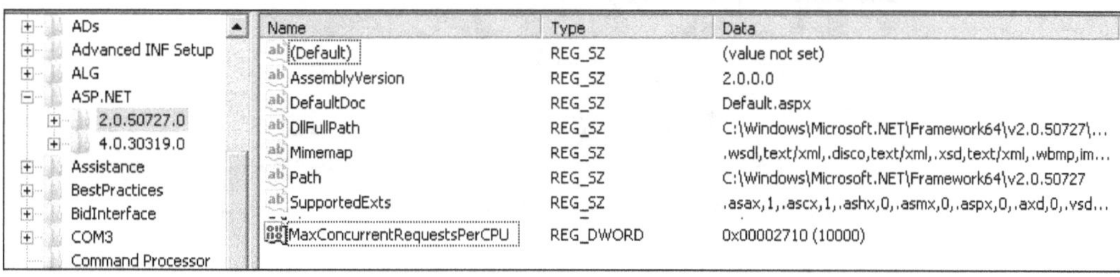

4. Output caching will cache a frequently used object into memory so that it can be delivered quickly on subsequent requests. Add output caching around images files and script files. Perform the following steps to configure output caching:
   1. In the Dynamics CRM 2011 web server, go to the Start menu and click on **Run**. Type `inetmgr` and press *Enter*. This will launch the **Internet Information Services (IIS) Manager** administrative interface.
   2. Double-click on **Output Caching** on **Features View** of IIS.
   3. Then, click on **Add** in the **Actions** pane. The **Edit Cache Rule** page will be launched.

4. Provide the output caching rule definition by providing the **File name extension** value, for example, `.js`.
5. Select the **User-mode caching** option.
6. In the **File Cache Monitoring** section, select the **At time intervals (hh:mm:ss)** option and provide a time interval.
7. Finally, click on the **OK** button to add the output caching rule as shown in the following screenshot:

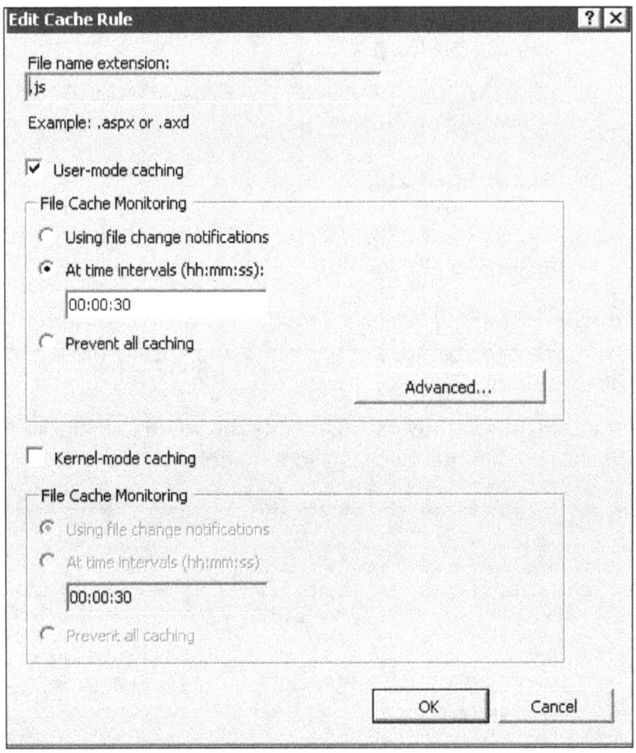

5. Set the Dynamics CRM 2011 Application Pool Recycling interval to an hour or so. Follow the ensuing steps to achieve this:
   1. Launch the **Internet Information Services (IIS) Manager** interface as a local system administrator.
   2. Click on the **Application Pools** node in the **Object Explorer** pane.
   3. Then, right-click on the **CRMAppPool** node and select **Recycling...**.
   4. The **Edit Application Pool Recycling Settings** page will appear. Set the **Regular time intervals (in minutes)** settings to an appropriate time interval, say 60 minutes, and click on **Next** to proceed.
   5. Click on **Finish** to save the setting.

6. To change the timeout values, that is, to add/modify the `OLEDBTimeout` and `ExtendedTimeout` registry settings in the web server, follow the ensuing steps:
    1. Go to the Start menu and click on **Run**, and then type `regedit` and press *Enter*.
    2. Navigate to `HKEY_LCAL_MACHINE\Software\Microsoft\MSCRM` in the registry.
    3. Add a DWORD with the name `OLEDBTimeout` and a value of `86400`, if not already present.
    4. Add another DWORD with the name `ExtendedTimeout` and a value of `1000000`, if not already present.

> Note that configuring these settings via the web server registry will apply the configuration to all organizations that use the web servers.

7. Configuring the **EnableRetrieveMultipleOptimization** (**ERMO**) setting to the default value of `0` should take place when Update Rollup 10 or higher is installed. Otherwise, Dynamics CRM 2011 will not be able to automatically optimize the performance of the queries against large data sets. With Update Rollup 10, two new statistical settings have been introduced to optimize the `RetrieveMultiple` queries. These statistical settings are as follows:
    - `RecordCountLimitToSwitchToCteSecuritySql` (default value of `75000`): This specifies the number of records below which Microsoft Dynamics CRM 2011 will default to a query based on the `OR` operator using joins. We will try to keep this value as high as possible because a lower value will have an impact on SQL Server memory use.
    - `RetrieveMultipleSharingCountThreshold` (default value of `1000`): This specifies the number of shared records that are associated with a user directly or with the teams to which the user belongs. We should consider increasing its value in case a user with an above average number of shared records for any entity is experiencing slow performance with that entity. It is recommended to increase its value in small (100 or 200) increments.

The value of these two parameters can be modified using the `OrgDBOrgSettings` tool offered by Microsoft. This tool can be downloaded from `http://support.microsoft.com/kb/2691237`. There are many more settings that can be modified using this tool. The lists of these settings can be found at the aforementioned link. However, it is advisable to measure the performance benefit as a result of any such modification in a test environment before its application to any live system.

If these settings do not provide the desired performance, we can consider adjusting the value for the EnableRetrieveMultipleOptimization setting. This specific setting can also be configured with Dynamics CRM 2011 using Update Rollup 2 or higher. Please perform the following steps to configure this setting in the web server:

1. Go to the Start menu and click on **Run**, and then type regedit and press *Enter*.
2. Navigate to HKEY_LCAL_MACHINE\Software\Microsoft\MSCRM in the registry.
3. Add a DWORD with the name EnableRetrieveMultipleOptimization and a value of 2, if not already present.

> Adding a preferred domain controller setting in the Dynamics CRM 2011 application server will speed up the Active Directory checks. Please follow the ensuing steps to configure this setting in the web server:
>
> Go to the Start menu and click on **Run**, and then type regedit and press *Enter*.
>
> Navigate to HKEY_LCAL_MACHINE\Software\Microsoft\MSCRM in the registry.
>
> Add a string value with the name PreferredDC and the value <DC_Name>, if not already present.

How it works...

In this recipe, we have discussed scaling the deployment to improve performance. Thereafter, we have applied IIS-level optimizations offered by IIS7 or higher versions. Though Microsoft Dynamics CRM 2011 is configured to compress web responses that are sent to browser clients by default, HTTP response compression is an IIS-level setting and has to be enabled from IIS. But, compression setting is an IIS-wide setting and cannot be enabled/disabled only for specific websites.

The Dynamics CRM 2011 level settings changes are done to optimize the performance of queries involving large data sets, and the timeout setting is configured so that such queries do not throw timeout errors.

See also

In this chapter, we have discussed various maintenance and optimization recipes. In the next chapter, we will discuss the recipes for administering Dynamics CRM 2011. Some interesting recipes are as follows:

- Securing Dynamics CRM 2011 deployment with SSL/HTTPS
- Configuring Internet-facing Deployment
- Creating a new deployment administrator
- Creating a Custom Administrator Security role
- Configuring system-wide settings

3

Administering Microsoft Dynamics CRM 2011

After successful installation of Dynamics CRM 2011 Server, we looked at recipes in the previous chapter for backing up and restoring Dynamics CRM 2011 Server components. In this chapter, we will delve into recipes for configuring the Dynamics CRM 2011 system to make it ready for customization work. As part of administration, we will find out how Dynamics CRM 2011 deployment can be secured with SSL and then how to configure AD FS-based authentication, and finally how to deploy Internet-facing Dynamics CRM 2011. In addition, we will delve into recipes for configuring system-wide settings. These recipes will have system-wide impact; hence, before implementing any of these recipes, careful thought should be put into assessing the impact on Dynamics CRM 2011 Server.

The chapter will include the following recipes:

- Securing Dynamics CRM 2011 deployment with SSL/HTTPS
- Configuring Claims-based authentication (AD FS) for Microsoft Dynamics CRM 2011
- Configuring Internet-facing Deployment (IFD)
- Creating a new deployment administrator
- Creating a new system administrator
- Creating a new business unit
- Configuring a security role
- Creating a custom administrator security role
- Creating a field-level security profile
- Adding a new user account in the Dynamics CRM 2011 system
- Adding multiple users in the Dynamics CRM 2011 system
- Creating a new team in the Dynamics CRM 2011 system

- Configuring autonumbering formats
- Configuring system-wide settings
- Configuring fiscal year settings
- Configuring error notification preferences

Securing Dynamics CRM 2011 deployment with SSL/HTTPS

Configuring systems for SSL/HTTPS is a more secure way to transfer data. But the activity of configuring Dynamics CRM 2011 for HTTPS causes disruption in CRM usage. Hence this activity should be carried out at a time at which it will cause minimal possible disruptions to users.

How to do it...

We can secure Dynamics CRM 2011 by following these steps:

1. Log in to the machine where **Microsoft Dynamics CRM 2011 Deployment Manager** is running. Launch the Deployment Manager console by navigating to **Start** | **All Programs** | **Microsoft Dynamics CRM 2011**.
2. Disable the servers where frontend server roles (the web application server, organization web service, discovery web service, and deployment web service roles) are running by right-clicking on each frontend server and selecting **Disable**.

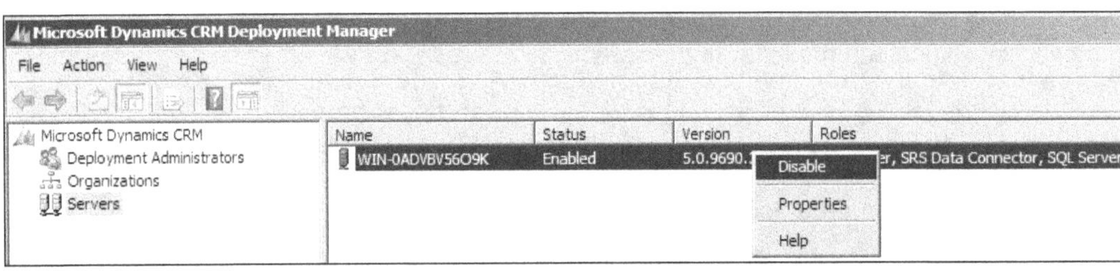

3. The next step will be to configure the Dynamics CRM 2011 website to use HTTPS. To start with, we must obtain an appropriate **certificate**. After the certificate has been obtained, install the certificate on the same server to complete the certificate request process. The certificate is now complete and ready for use. Now, secure it with a password.

> Certificates can be obtained at IIS level. Internet server certificates are issued by public **certification authorities** (**CAs**). The following link describes how to request an IIS certificate:
>
> `http://technet.microsoft.com/en-us/library/cc732906(v=ws.10).aspx`

4. Once the certificate is obtained, configure the server(s) to use HTTPS where the Web Application Server role is installed.
5. Log in to the machine where the Application Server role is installed and launch the **Internet Information Services (IIS) Manager** console. Then, right-click on the Microsoft Dynamics CRM website and select **Edit Bindings**. Finally, click on the **Add...** button.
6. The **Add Site Binding** page will appear. Here, we need to specify the values for the **Type**, **IP address**, and **Port** fields and pick the value for **SSL certificate**.

> In case of a multi-server deployment, repeat this step in every frontend server where Web Application Server role is deployed.

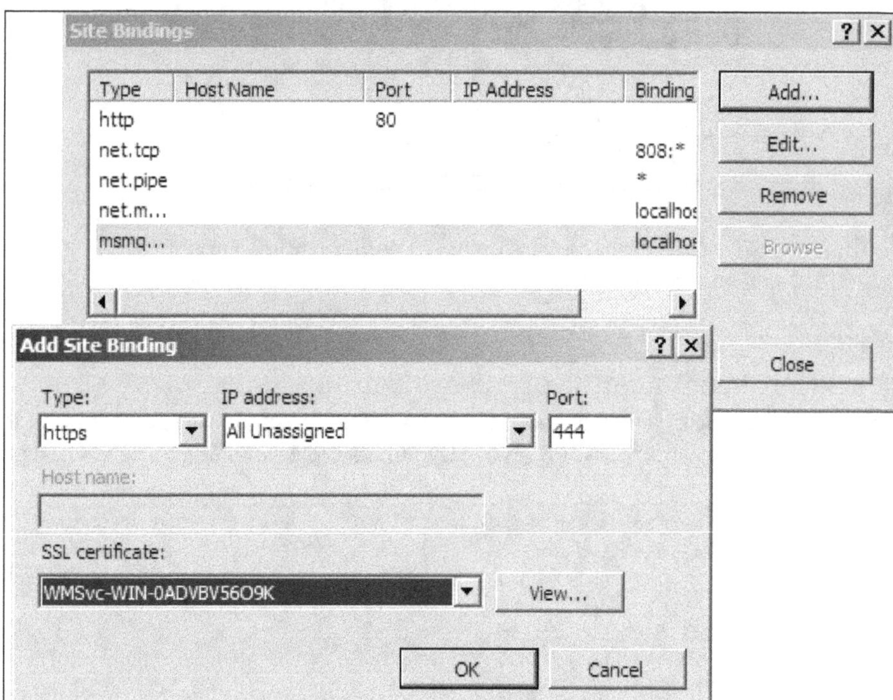

7. Restart the IIS for all of the preceding servers.
8. Launch Microsoft Dynamics CRM 2011 Deployment Manager and click on the **Microsoft Dynamics CRM** node in the **Object Explorer** window. Then, in the **Actions** pane, click on **Properties** | **Web Address** tab. Under **Binding Type**, select **HTTPS**. Verify that the web addresses are valid for the SSL certificate and the SSL port bound to the Microsoft Dynamics CRM Server 2011 website. Finally, click on the **OK** button to apply the changes.

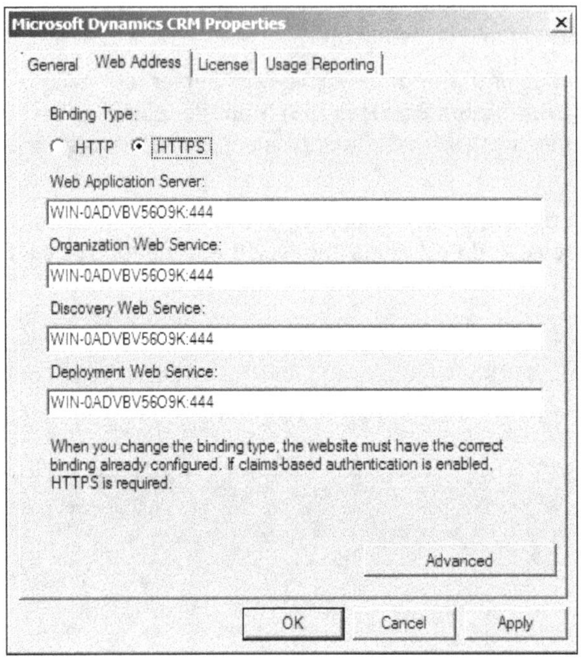

9. Then enable the frontend servers disabled earlier using Microsoft Dynamics CRM 2011 Deployment Manager.

How it works...

Secure Socket Layer (**SSL**) provides secure data transfer across the wire. By following this recipe, we will be able to enable HTTPS on our Dynamics CRM website and hence can ensure secure data transfer.

Configuring Claims-based authentication (AD FS) for Microsoft Dynamics CRM 2011

Active Directory Federation Services (**AD FS**) provides web-based single sign-on to authenticate a user to use multiple web applications during the lifetime of a single online session. AD FS achieves this by securely sharing the digital identity and entitlement rights, or "claims" across security and enterprise boundaries.

AD FS can help in authenticating Dynamics CRM 2011 users located in completely different networks or organizations.

Getting ready

When we want to deploy Dynamics CRM 2011 using **Internet-Facing Deployment**, Dynamics CRM 2011 has to be configured to use a **Secure Token Service** (**STS**) such as AD FS. Both CRM and AD FS have to be secured with SSL, that is, users will connect to them using HTTPS.

There are usually two ways to deploy a CRM and AD FS solution:

- **Installing CRM (frontend roles) and AD FS on the same server**: It is preferable to run the AD FS service on the default website with default port bindings (port 80 and 443). Hence, Dynamics CRM 2011 has to be configured to use different ports (for example, port 5555 for HTTP and port 444 for HTTPS).

  It is even possible to run both AD FS and CRM on the same port, 443, using different IP addresses. Usually, such a deployment strategy is avoided because of deployment issues encountered.

- **Install CRM (Frontend roles) and AD FS in separate servers**: In this type of deployment, both CRM and AD FS can be deployed using HTTPS on port 443. But we have to make sure both these servers are highly available.

How to do it...

In this recipe, we will discuss the first alternative of deploying AD FS on the same server as that of CRM frontend roles using separate ports, that is, AD FS on Port 443 and Dynamics CRM 2011 on Port 444, both using HTTPS.

1. Log in to the server machine on which AD FS is installed with local administrative permissions. As a first step, we have to secure the AD FS website, that is, the default website using a Wildcard certificate.

2. Launch the IIS Manager console. Then right-click on the default website and select **Edit Bindings**. Then, click on the **Add...** button. The **Add Site Binding** page will appear. Here, we need to specify the values for **Type** (**https**), **IP address**, and **Port** (`443`) and pick the value for **SSL certificate**.

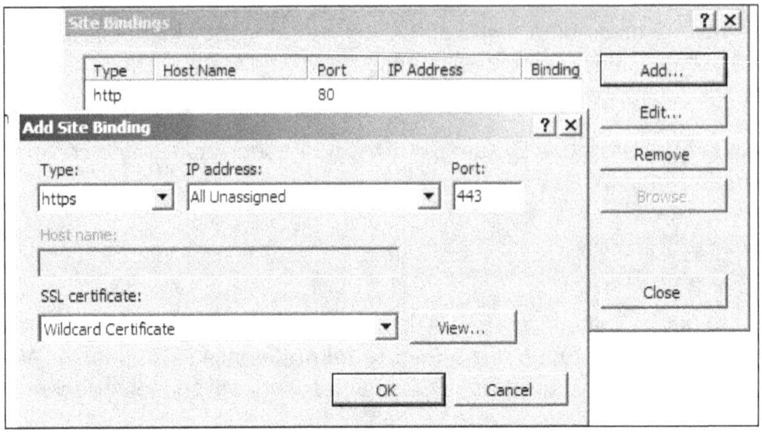

3. The next step will be to bind the Wildcard certificate with the Microsoft Dynamics CRM 2011 website. To achieve this, follow the *Securing Dynamics CRM 2011 deployment with SSL/HTTPS* recipe in this chapter.
4. Then, we have to create DNS entries for AD FS and CRM.
5. In this case, we will configure our AD FS and CRM to be on the `packt.com` domain. AD FS will be using `adfs.packt.com`, and Dynamics CRM 2011 will be using `crm.packt.com`, as URLs.
6. Thereafter, AD FS is required to be configured. Navigate to **Start** | **All Programs** | **Administrative Tools** | **AD FS 2.0 Management**. This will bring up the AD FD 2.0 Management console. Then, click on the **AD FS 2.0 Federation Server Configuration Wizard** button on the **Actions** pane. This will bring up the **AD FS 2.0 Federation Server Configuration Wizard** page. Select **Create a new Federation Service** here and click on the **Next** button.

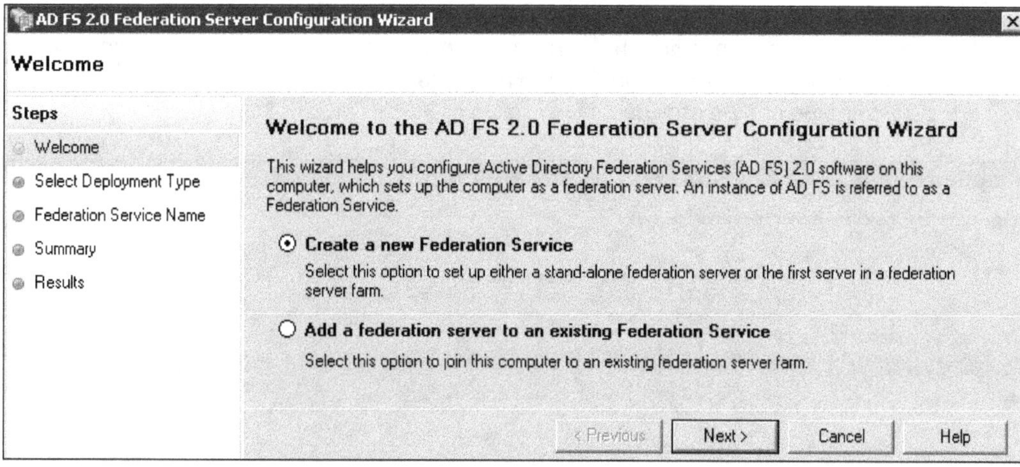

7. The **Select Stand-Alone or Farm Deployment** page appears. Here, we have to select an appropriate deployment option between **New Federation server farm** and **Stand-alone federation server**.

   A federation server farm is used when we have to scale with increasing demand and is the recommended option for live deployments. Stand-alone federation servers are recommended for development and testing purposes. Though in-depth discussion of federation server farms is beyond the scope of this recipe, expanding a federation server is always optional.

8. We will choose **Stand–alone Federation Server** here and proceed. Once the deployment choice has been made, please click on **Next**.
9. Next, the **Specify the Federation Service Name** page appears. On this page, provide values for **SSL certificate**, **Port**, and **Federation Service name**, and proceed by clicking on **Next**.

10. By default, the wizard will retrieve the SSL certificate configured in IIS and will use the subject name specified there. However, in case of any ambiguity regarding the subject name, the **Federation Service name** combo box will be enabled and a valid service name can be provided.

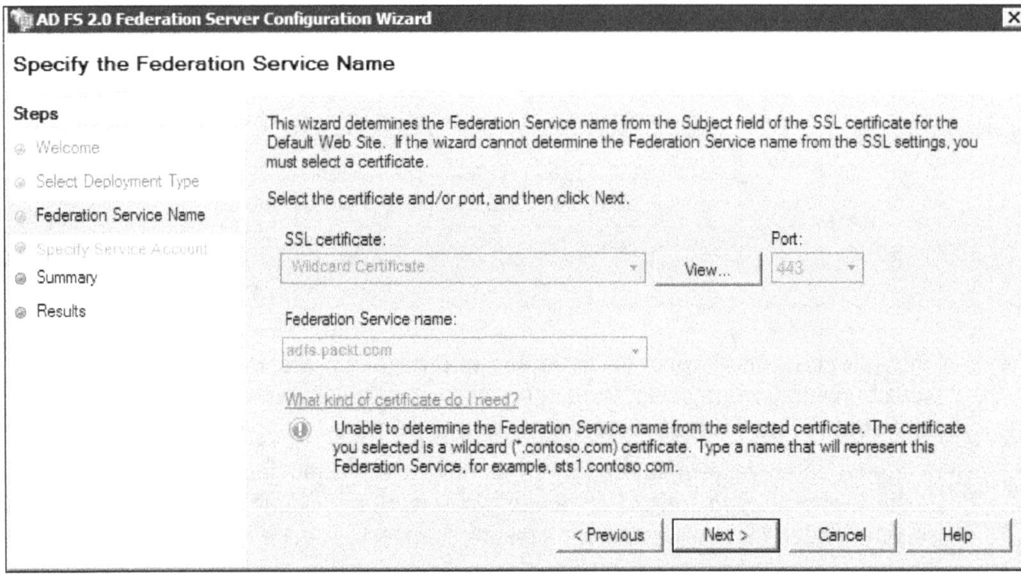

11. On the **Specify Service Account** page, we have to select an account under which the service will run. The recommendation is to use a specific service account for this purpose. The service account will be granted `SeServiceLogonRight` and `SeAuditPrivilege` by the configuration wizard. Use the **Browse** button to select the service account, enter the password for the account, and then click on **Next** to proceed.

    Detailed information about configuring service accounts for Federation Farm can be found at `http://technet.microsoft.com/en-us/library/dd807078(WS.10).aspx`.

12. The **Ready to Apply Settings** page appears. Click on **Next** to proceed.
13. Finally comes the **Configuration Results** page; click on **Close** to complete the AD FS configurations.
14. After finishing the AD FS configuration, we need to configure Dynamics CRM 2011 for Claims-based authentication. Log in to the machine where Microsoft Dynamics CRM 2011 Deployment Manager is installed and launch the console with the credentials of a Deployment Administrator account.
15. Then, click on the **Microsoft Dynamics CRM** node in the **Object Explorer** window; in the **Actions** pane, click on **Configure Claims-Based Authentication** and then click on **Next**.
16. On the next page, specify the value for **Federation metadata URL** and click on **Next**.

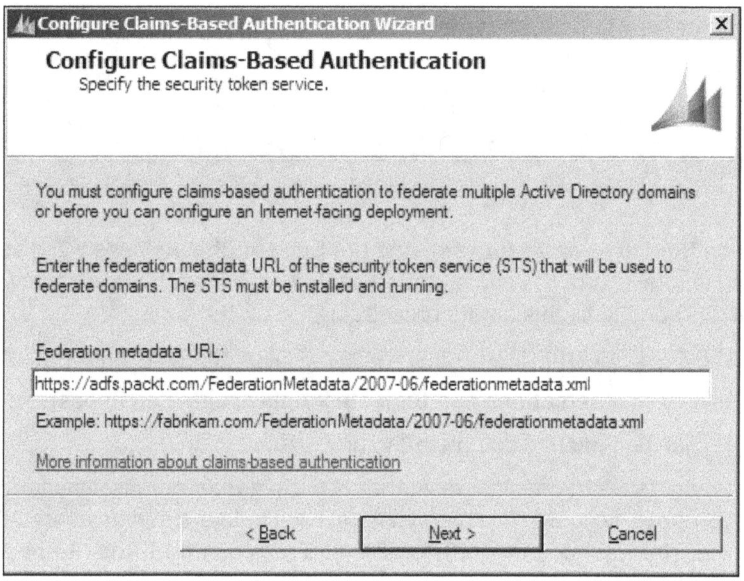

17. On the next screen, select the Wildcard certificate that has been associated with the AD FS default web site and then click on **Next**.

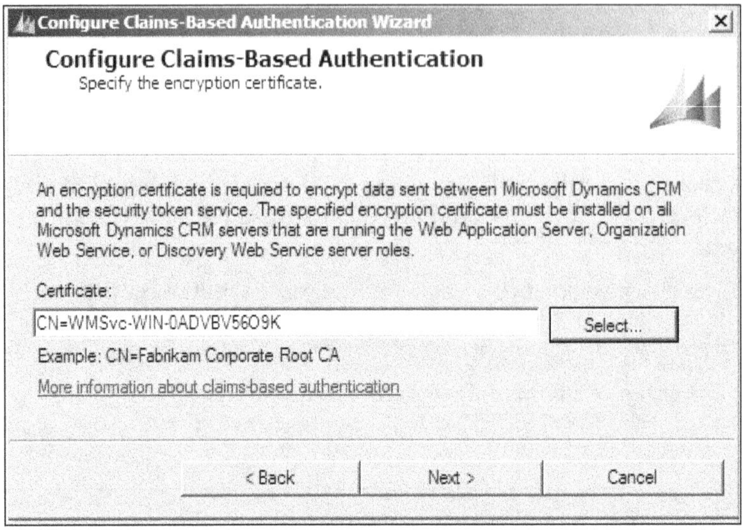

18. Click on **Next** to navigate forward, and the **System Checks** page will display the verification results of the configuration settings provided. If any error or warning is listed, we need to fix this before proceeding.
19. Unless there is an error or warning, we can click on the **Next** button to proceed.
20. The **Review your selections and then click Apply** page then appears. Click on **Apply**.
21. Finally, click on **Finish** to complete the process.
22. Now we are left with one final task, that of setting **read** permissions for the `ADFSAppPool` account. To accomplish this, log in to the server where AD FS is installed. Then launch the MMC console and click on **File** | **Add/Remove Snap-in...**.

23. This will launch the **Add or Remove Snap-ins** console; select **Certificates** from the **Available snap-ins** section and click on **Add** to add this to the **Selected snap-ins** list.

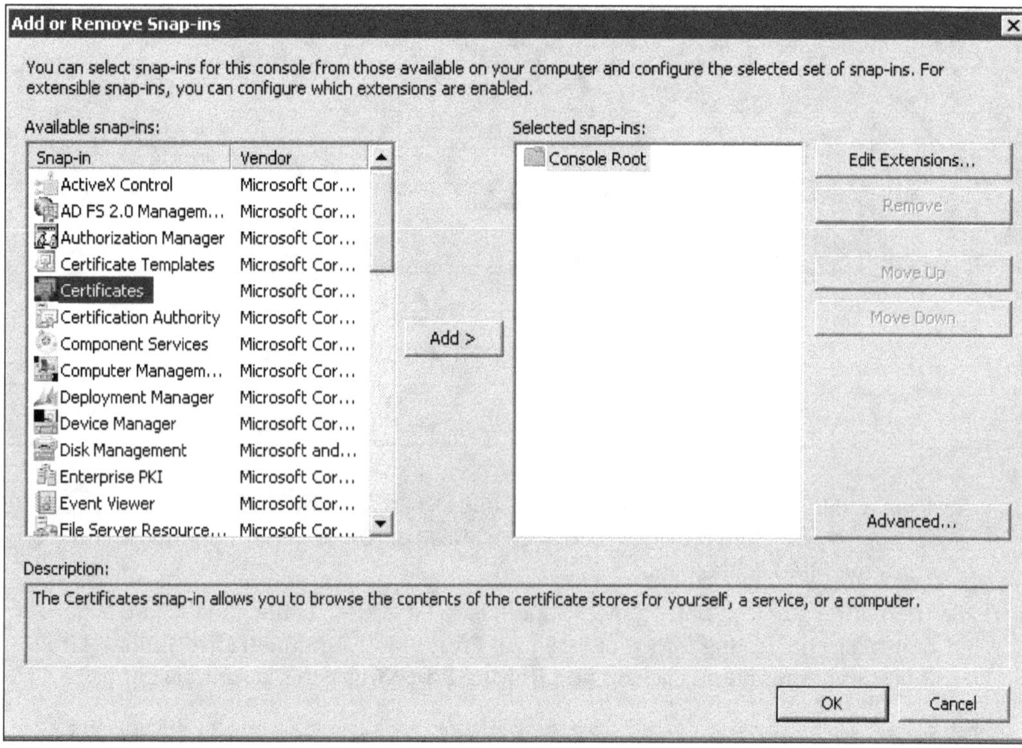

24. The **Certificates Snap-in page** appears. Select **Computer Account** and click on **Next** on the screen. Click on **Finish** on the next window.

25. Click on **OK** to close the **Add or Remove Snap-ins** dialog.

26. Then expand the **Certificates** node and navigate to **Personal** | **Certificates**. Right-click on the AD FS certificate and select the **Manage Private Keys...** option under **All Tasks**.

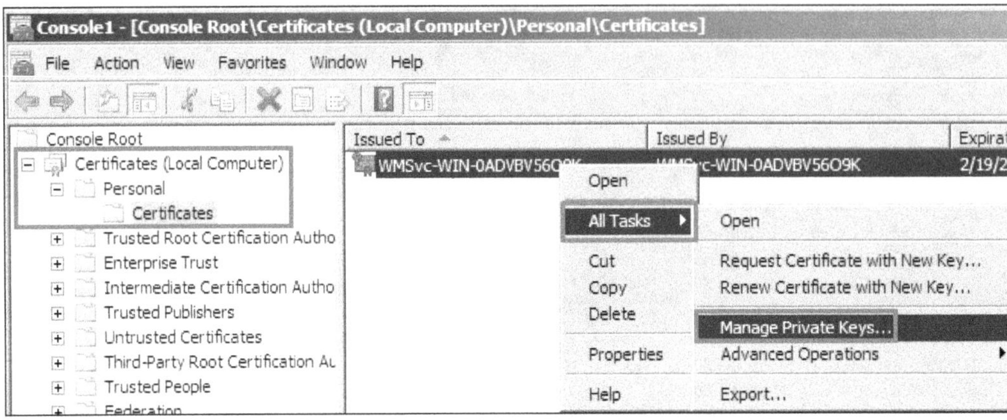

27. Then add Identity/User Account, which runs Dynamics CRM 2011 Application Pool (`CRMAppPool`), and provides read access. Click on **OK** to close the window and then close the MMC console too.

28. Thereafter, a relying party to AD FS 2.0 has to be added. Launch the **AD FS 2.0** console by navigating through **Start** | **All Programs** | **Administrative Tools** | **AD FS 2.0 Management** and click on **Add Relying Party Trust** on the **Actions** pane.

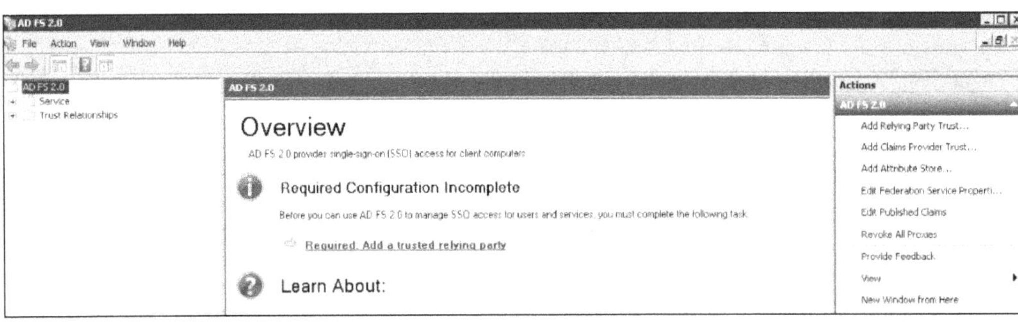

29. On the **Welcome** page, click on the **Start** button.

30. When the **Select Data Source** page appears, click on the imported data about the relying party published online or on a local network, and then type the URL to locate the `federationmetadata.xml` file. Then, click on **Next**.

31. On the next **Select Display Name** page, provide a display name and then click on **Next**.

32. On the **Choose Issuance Authorization Rules** page, click on **Permit all users to access this relying party**, and then click on **Next**.

33. On the **Ready to Add Trust** page, in the **Identifiers** tab, verify that the **Relying party** identifier has a single identifier, such as `https://crm.packt.com:444`.

    If the identifier differs from the Dynamics CRM 2011 URL, click on **Previous** in the **Add Relying Party Trust Wizard** window and check the Federation metadata address.

34. Click on **Next**, and then click on **Close**.
35. If the **Rules Editor** page appears, click on **Add Rule**. Otherwise, in the **Relying Party Trusts** list, right-click the relying party object that just got created, click on **Edit Claims Rules**, and then click on **Add Rule**.

    The following three rules have to be added:

    - **User Principle Name** (**UPN**)
    - Primary SID
    - Windows account name

36. Create the UPN rule by adding the following values:
    - **Claim Rule Template**: **Pass Through or Filter an Incoming Claim**
    - **Claim rule name**: **Pass through UPN**
    - Add the following mappings:

      Incoming claim type: **UPN**

      Select the radio button **Pass through all claim values**

    Click on **Finish**.

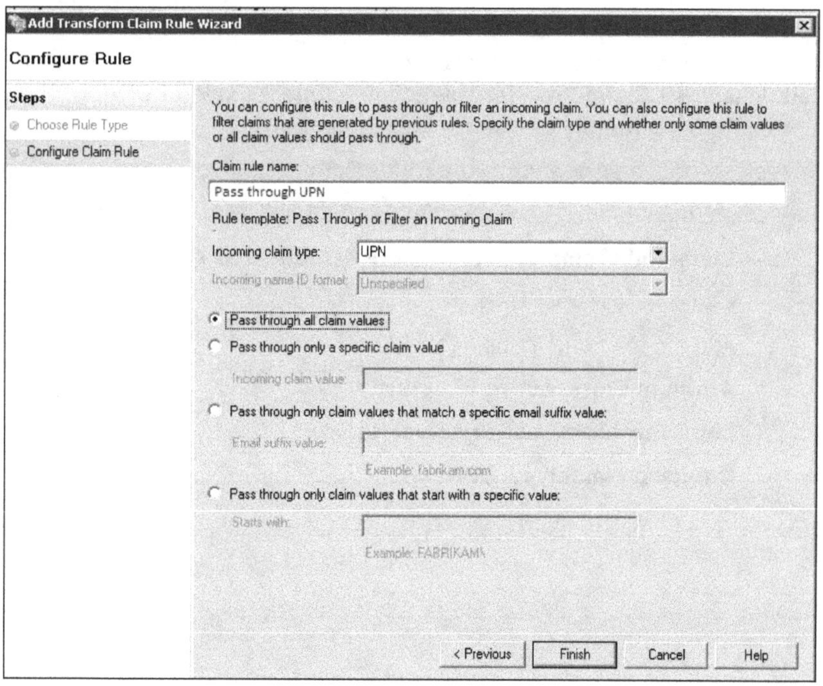

37. Then, in the **Rules Editor** page, click on **Add Rule**.

    Now create the Primary SID rule in a similar way to that stated before for UPN.

    - **Claim Rule Template**: **Pass Through or Filter an Incoming Claim**
    - **Claim rule name**: **Pass through Primary SID**
    - Add the following mappings:

      Incoming claim type: **Primary SID**

      Select the radio button **Pass through all claim values**

    Click on **Finish**.

38. Thereafter, click on **Add Rule** again in the **Rules Editor**. Now create the Windows account name with the following settings:

    - **Claim Rule Template**: **Transform an Incoming Claim**
    - **Claim Rule Name**: **Transform Windows Account Name to Name**
    - Add the following mappings:

      Incoming claim type: **Windows Account Name**

      Outgoing claim type: **Name or * Name**

      Select the radio button **Pass through all claim values**

    Click on **Finish**.

39. When the three rules get created, click on **OK** in the **Rules Editor**.
40. Now it is time to edit the rules for Active Directory. Navigate to **AD FS 2.0** | **Trusted Relationships** | **Claim Provider Trusts** in the **Object Explorer** window. Then, right-click on **Active Directory** and select **Edit Claim Rule**.
41. Thereafter, click on **Add Rule** in the **Rules Editor**.

    Now, create the Windows account name with the following settings:

    - **Claim Rule Template**: **Send LDAP Attributes as Claims**
    - **Claim Rule Name**: **UPN**
    - Add the following mappings:

      Attribute Store: **Active Directory**

      LADP Attribute: **User-Principal-Name**

      Outgoing claim type: **UPN**

Click on **Finish**.

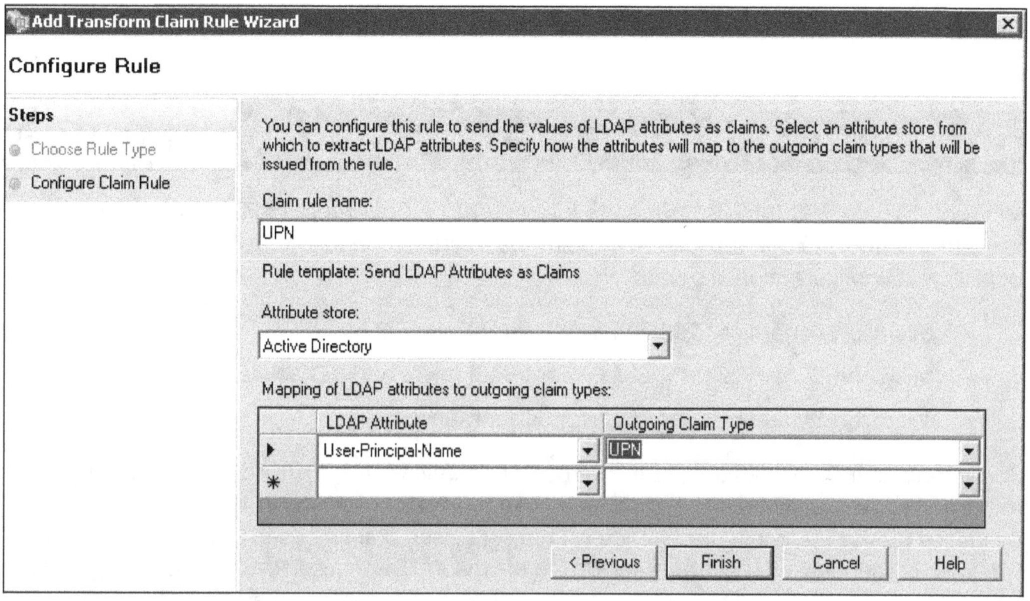

42. Thereafter, perform an IIS Reset on the Dynamics CRM 2011 server.

How it works...

Microsoft Dynamics CRM 2011 replaces form-based authentication with Claims-based authentication to enable Internet access for external users not accessing CRM via VPN. Claims-based authentication is built on **Windows Identity Foundation** (**WIF**). One of the common scenarios where Claims-based authentication finds use is when Dynamics CRM 2011 has to be deployed as an Internet-facing application.

Another deployment scenario is where the user of a domain tries to access an instance of Dynamics CRM 2011 that is installed on another domain and there exists no trust between these two domains. In such a case, Claims-based authentication helps Dynamics CRM 2011 to authenticate users from a non-trusted domain.

When Dynamics CRM 2011 is configured to use AD FS, every user's sign-on request is redirected to a sign-in page where the user is expected to enter his or her credentials. Behind the scenes, the sign-in page checks all of the directories (called **identity providers**) that it trusts to verify whether the user's credentials are valid. If the user's credentials are found valid, the sign-in page provides the user with a token, and it is this token that the Dynamics CRM 2011 application (called **relying party**) accepts as authentication.

> A more detailed description of Active Directory Federation Services can be found at `http://technet.microsoft.com/en-us/library/cc772593(v=ws.10).aspx`.

Configuring Internet-facing Deployment (IFD)

Microsoft Dynamics CRM 2011 supports Internet-facing Deployment (IFD) so that remote users can connect to the application through the Internet. The following Internet-facing Deployment configurations are supported:

- Microsoft Dynamics CRM 2011 for internal users only
- Microsoft Dynamics CRM 2011 for internal users and IFD access
- Microsoft Dynamics CRM 2011 for IFD-only access

Configuring an IFD enables access to Microsoft Dynamics CRM 2011 from the Internet outside the company firewall without the need for a **virtual private network** (**VPN**) solution. Microsoft Dynamics CRM 2011 configured for Internet access uses Claims-based authentication to verify the credentials of external users. When Microsoft Dynamics CRM 2011 is configured for Internet access, integrated Windows authentication must remain in place for internal users.

To let users access the application over the Internet, the server that is IIS and where the Microsoft Dynamics CRM 2011 application is installed must be available over the Internet.

One prerequisite for this is having AD FS2.0 installed on the default website in any machine within the domain. Dynamics CRM 2011 cannot be operated from port 80 if AD FS is being installed on the same machine where Dynamics CRM 2011 is installed.

Before you start configuring Dynamics CRM 2011 for Internet-facing Deployment you need to have completed the *Configuring Claims-based authentication (AD FS) for Microsoft Dynamics CRM 2011* recipe.

How to do it...

Please follow the ensuing steps to configure Internet-facing Deployment:

1. Log in to the machine where Microsoft Dynamics CRM 2011 Deployment Manager is installed.
2. Launch Microsoft Dynamics CRM Deployment Manager using a Deployment Administrator account. This is usually present in **Start** | **All Programs** | **Microsoft Dynamics CRM 2011** | **Deployment Manager**.

3. Select the **Microsoft Dynamics CRM** node in the **Object Explorer** window, and then click on the **Configure Internet-Facing Deployment** option in the **Actions** pane.

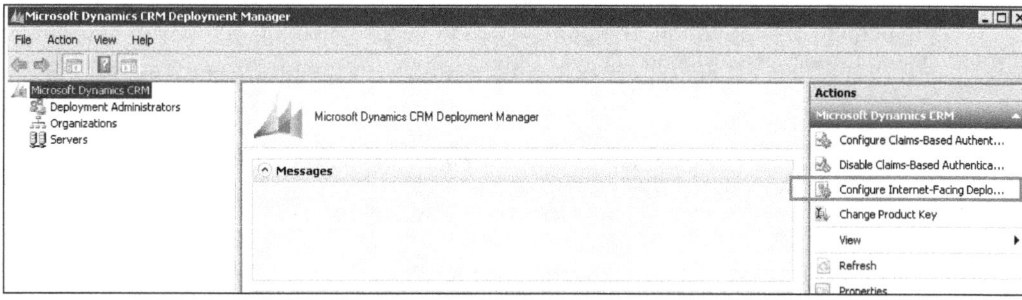

4. On the **Configure Internet-Facing Deployment** page, click on the **Next** button to proceed.
5. On the next screen, provide the URLs for **Web Application Server Domain**, **Organization Server Domain**, and **Discovery Web Service Domain**.

   In our case, as the Dynamics CRM 2011 Server roles are installed on the same server, the URLs in **Web Application Server Domain**, **Organization Web Service Domain**, and **Discovery Web Service Domain** will be the same.

   Domain names must use the SSL Port.

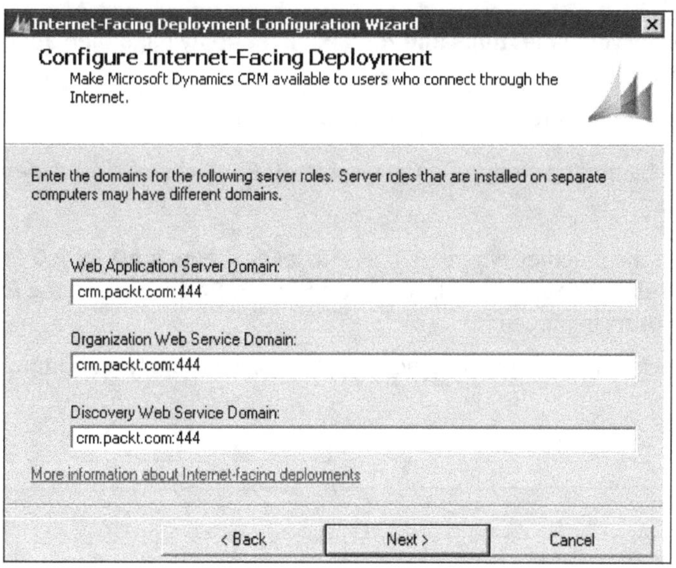

6. On the next screen, enter the external domain where your Internet-facing servers are located and click on the **Next** button.
7. We have to configure the Internet to our Dynamics CRM 2011 server located outside the domain of information. The domain has to be a subdomain of the Web Application Server domain. The default value would be `auth.<Web Application Server Domain>`.

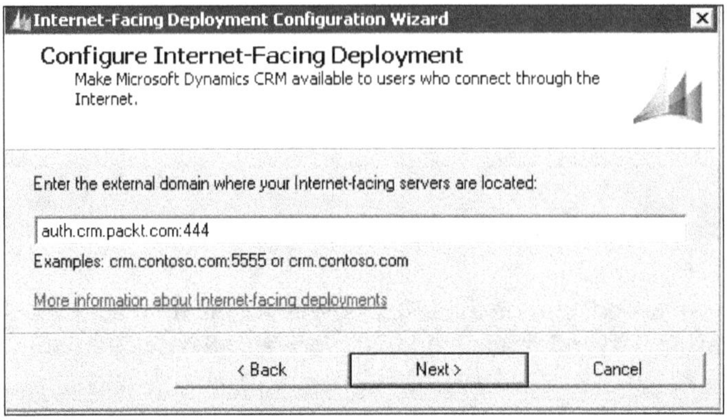

8. On the **System Checks** page, check for warnings or errors. All warnings and errors have to be fixed before proceeding. If there are no warnings or errors, click on **Next** to proceed.
9. The **Review your selections and then click on Apply** page then appears; here, click on **Apply**.
10. Finally, click on **Finish** to complete the task.

The next step will be adding a relying party trust in AD FS. Please follow the ensuing steps to achieve this:

1. Log on to the machine where AD FS is installed. Launch **AD FS 2.0 Federation Server Configuration Wizard**, and click on **Add Relying Party Trust** on the **Actions** pane. Click on **Start** to proceed.
2. Enter the federation metadata address and click on the **Next** button.

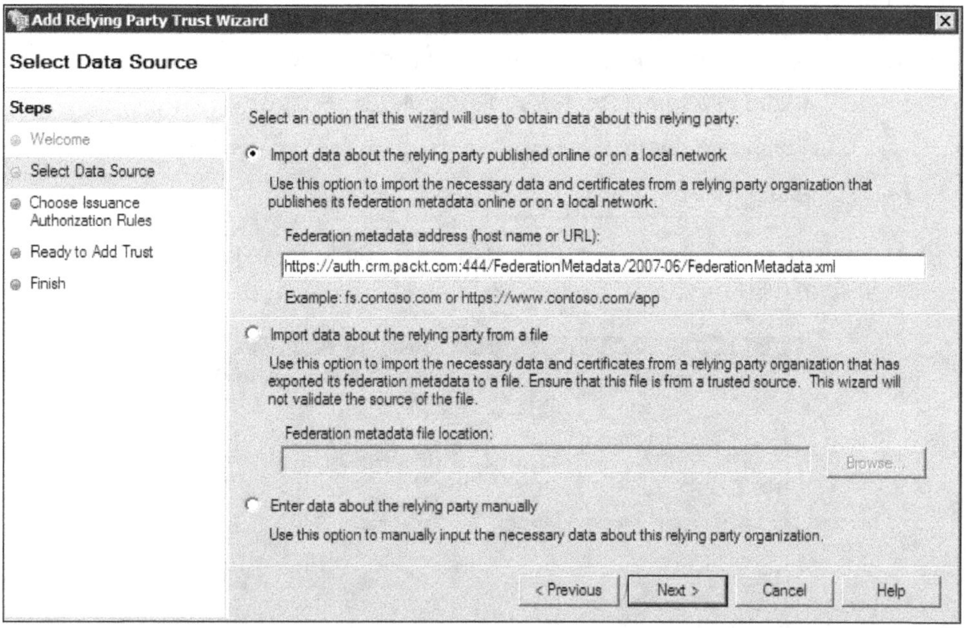

3. On the **Specify Display** page, enter a value for **Display Name** (such as `CRM IFD Relying Party`) and click on the **Next** button.
4. On the **Choose Issuance Authorization Rules** page, choose **Permit all users to access this relying party** and click on **Next** to proceed.
5. On the **Ready to Add Trust** page, check the trust details and click on **Next**.
6. Then select the relying party that just got created and click on **Edit Claim Rules** on the **Actions** pane.
7. Thereafter, click on the **Add Rule** button in **Rules Editor**.

   Now create the User Principal Name by adding the following values:

   - **Claim rule template**: `Pass Through or Filter an Incoming Claim`
   - **Claim rule name**: `UPN`

   Click on **Finish**.

8. Thereafter, click again on **Add Rule** in **Rules Editor**.

   Now create the Primary SID by adding the following values:

   - **Claim rule template**: `Pass Through or Filter an Incoming Claim`
   - **Claim rule name**: `Primary SID`

   Click on **Finish**.

9. Thereafter, click again on **Add Rule** in **Rules Editor**.

   Now create a Windows account name by adding the following values:

   - **Claim rule template**: `Pass Through or Filter an Incoming Claim`
   - **Claim rule name**: `Windows Account name to name`

   Click on **Finish**.

10. Once these three rules have been added, there will be three issuance transform rules.

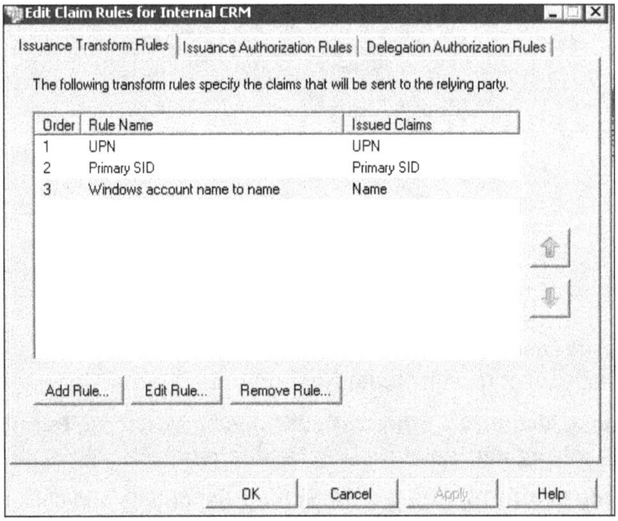

11. Finally perform an IIS Reset.

How it works...

Internet-facing Deployment enables users to access Dynamics CRM 2011 over the Internet from outside the company's network and without VPN. Dynamics CRM 2011 takes advantage of Active Directory Federation Services (AD FS), a standards-based technology for controlling security access to Internet services while Internet-facing Deployment is configured.

Without having Claims-based authentication enabled, Internet-facing Deployment cannot be configured.

Creating a new deployment administrator

In the Dynamics CRM 2011 system, there are two separate types of administrators: **deployment administrators** and **system administrators**. A deployment administrator is a deployment-level administrator and manages deployment properties and activities. A system administrator is an organization-level administrator and administers the Dynamics CRM 2011 system settings. In this recipe, we will discuss how to create new deployment administrators in the Dynamics CRM 2011 system.

Getting ready

The deployment administrator role is a role very important to administering Dynamics CRM 2011 Server. With the installation of the Dynamics CRM 2011 Server component, an MMC snap-in called Deployment Manager gets installed. Deployment administrators have complete and unrestricted access to perform deployment manager tasks on all organizations and servers in a Microsoft Dynamics CRM 2011 deployment. The deployment administrator is expected to carry out the following activities on the system:

- Creating organizations
- Managing organizations
- Importing organizations
- Disabling organizations

The installation user is added as the deployment administrator to the Dynamics CRM 2011 system by default, but it is always advisable to add backup deployment administrators.

How to do it...

Proceed with the following steps to create a new deployment administrator in the Dynamics CRM 2011 system. These steps should be performed on the Active Directory Federation Services machine:

1. Create a new Active Directory Group for deployment administrators.
2. Create a new Active Directory user account for backup administrators if it does not already exist. Then add the user account to the newly created deployment administrator security group.
3. Add this deployment administrator domain group to the following Dynamics CRM 2011 specific Active Directory Groups:
    - `ReportingGroup`
    - `PrivUserGroup`
    - `SQLAccessGroup`

4. The deployment administrators group should have the following types of access to the preceding security groups:

Permissions	▶ Read ▶ Write ▶ Add/remove self as member
Advanced permissions	▶ List contents ▶ Read all properties ▶ Write all properties ▶ Read permissions ▶ Modify permissions ▶ All validated writes ▶ Add/remove self as member

Perform these steps in the Dynamics CRM 2011 Server machine(s):

1. Add the deployment administrator domain group to all the Dynamics CRM 2011 servers' local administrator groups, if not already added.
2. Log on to the Dynamics CRM 2011 server machine on which the Deployment Tools role is installed as the user who has installed the Dynamics CRM 2011 Server or as a user who is already a deployment administrator.
3. Then click on **Start** | **All Programs** | **Microsoft Dynamics CRM 2011** | **Deployment Manager**.
4. Right-click on **Deployment Administrator** and select **New Deployment Administrator**.

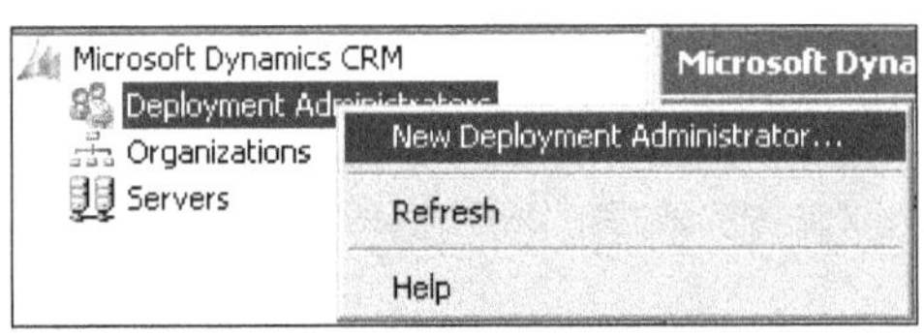

5. Add the backup deployment administrator user account, and then click on **OK**.

Perform the following steps on the SQL server machine:

1. Log on to the SQL server machine as the user who has installed Dynamics CRM 2011 Server or as a user who is already a deployment administrator.
2. Add the deployment administrator domain group to the local administrators' group, if not already added.
3. Launch SQL Server Management Studio and connect to the server.
4. Then expand **Security**, right-click on **Logins**, and then select **New Login**.

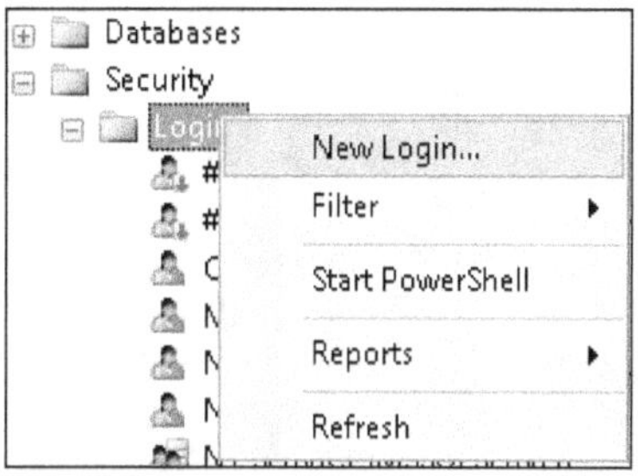

5. The **Login - New** page will appear. Click on the **Search** button beside the **Login name** textbox.
6. In the **Select User or Group** dialog box, click on **Object Types** and enable the **Groups** type; then, click on **OK**.

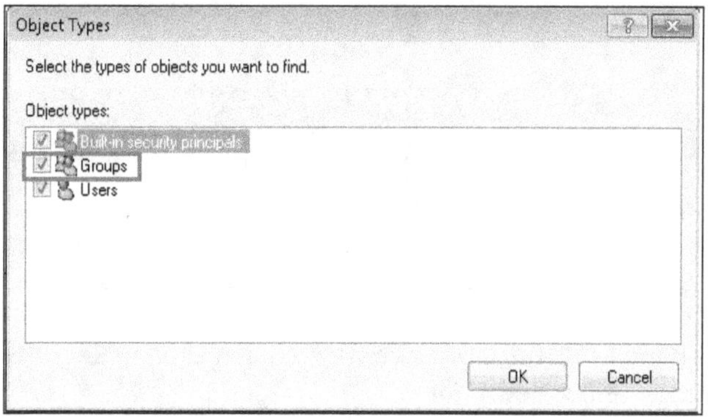

7. Click on **Locations**, select **Entire Directory**, and then click on **OK**.

8. In the **Enter the object name to select** textbox, type the deployment administrator domain group name, click on the **Check Names** button, and then click on **OK**.
9. In the **Default database** drop-down menu, select **MSCRM_CONFIG**.

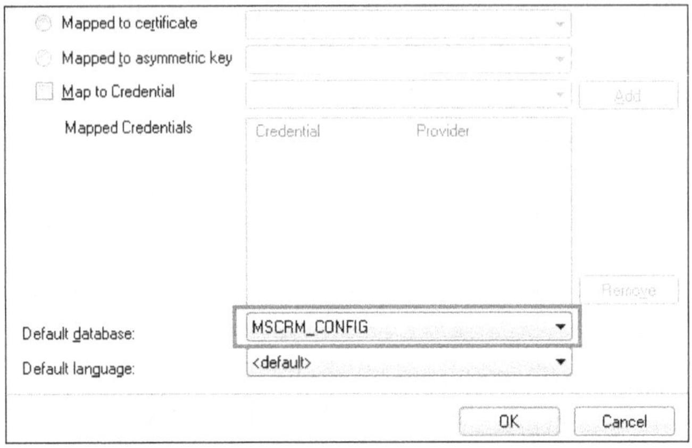

10. From the left-hand navigation of the **Login – New** page, select **Server Roles** and then enable the `sysadmin` role. Click on the **OK** button.

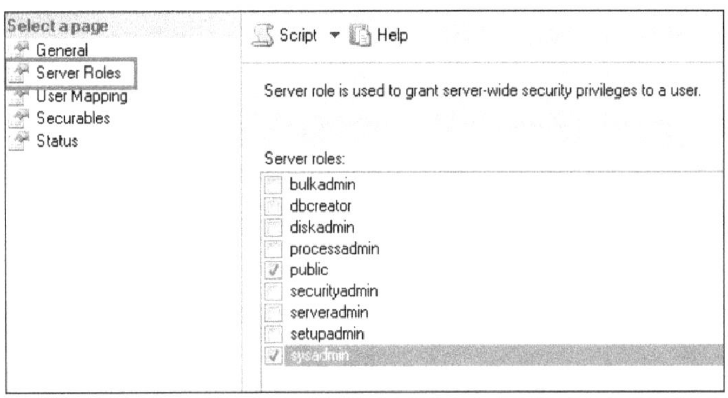

11. Then expand the **MSCRM_CONFIG** database and expand **Security**. Right-click on **Users** and then select **New User**.

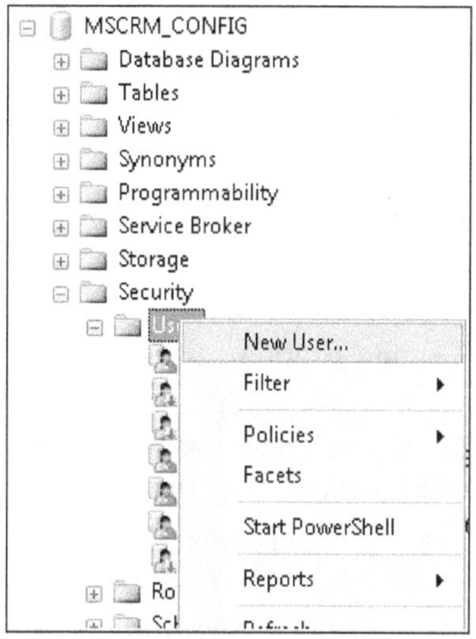

12. In the **User Name** textbox, type the backup administrator's domain login name (in the format `domain\username`).
13. In the **Database role membership** section, check the **db_owner** checkbox and then click on **OK**.
14. Close SQL Server Management Studio.

How it works...

The user who is the deployment administrator is not automatically added to the existing organization. However, the user can be added to an existing organization as a user in Microsoft Dynamics CRM 2011.

The deployment administrator is the system administrator of any organization that the deployment administrator creates or imports. Additionally, the deployment administrator has access to the organization in Microsoft Dynamics CRM 2011.

Creating a new system administrator

A system administrator is a Dynamics CRM 2011 organization-level administrator, and by default, the installation user is added as a user in the system with the system administrator security role assigned. Any user assigned the system administrator security role is known as a system administrator within the Dynamics CRM 2011 system. This user will have all possible access within that organization.

How to do it...

Follow these steps to create a new system administrator in any Dynamics CRM 2011 organization:

1. Log in to the Dynamics CRM 2011 system with a user account that was used to install Dynamics CRM 2011 or as a user who is already a system administrator in the Dynamics CRM 2011 system.
2. Navigate to **Settings** | **Administration** | **User**. Then click on the **New** button on the top ribbon.
3. In the **User New** page, enter the username in for the new system administrator into the **User Name** field in the format `domain\username`.
4. The **User Information** section will automatically be populated with details pulled from Active Directory. We can modify these details here.
5. In the **Client Access License (CAL) Information** section, select **Access Mode** as **Administrative**.
6. Then click on the **Save** button on the top ribbon.
7. Once the record is saved, click on the **Manage Roles** button on the top ribbon.
8. On the **Manage User Roles** page, check the **System Administrator** checkbox and then click on **OK**.
9. If you wish to modify the business unit of the user, click on the **Change Business Unit** button on the top ribbon.
10. Select the right business unit from the business unit lookup and then click on **OK**.

How it works...

The system administrator will have the highest level of access to the Dynamics CRM 2011 entities within the organization. When any custom entity is created, all the system administrators, by default, get full access to these entities. We will use a system administrator user to administer the Dynamics CRM 2011 system settings.

Creating a new business unit

Business units are security containers in the Dynamics CRM 2011 system. Business units contain users and teams inside a Dynamics CRM 2011 organization and are created to separate users and teams with different security requirements. Business units might (but not necessarily) correspond to an organization's departments or divisions.

A business unit can be the parent of another business unit, and the first business unit created inside a Dynamics CRM 2011 organization is known as the **parent business unit**. One or more business units can be created under it; these are known as **child business units**.

A **root business unit** is automatically created by Dynamics CRM 2011 when a Dynamics CRM organization is created. This business unit cannot be renamed, disabled, or deleted and does not have any parent business unit.

Business units can also own records. If an entity ownership type is set to **Business Owned**, the business unit alone can own records for that entity.

In this recipe we will discuss how to create new child business units.

How to do it...

Please follow these steps to create a child business unit:

1. Log in to the Dynamics CRM 2011 organization with a system administrator or equivalent security role.
2. Navigate to **Settings** | **Administration** | **Business Units**. Then click on the **New** button on the top ribbon.
3. In the **Business Unit: New** form, provide the following details:
    - **Name**: Name of the business unit. The name has to be unique.
    - **Parent Business**: Provide a parent business unit. Use the Lookup button to select the parent business unit.

    We can also (optionally) provide the phone numbers, e-mail address, and address details.

4. Then, click on **Save and Close** to create the new business unit.

How it works...

After creating a business unit, users and teams can be assigned to it. Security roles are defined at the business unit level, and a child business unit inherits all the security roles defined in its parent business unit. When we create a business unit, a team with the same name gets created and every user that is added to the business unit gets automatically added to that team.

The parent of a business unit can be changed. When a business unit is reassigned to a new parent business unit, all its child business units move with it, along with their users, teams, and so on.

> A circular relationship is not permitted within a business unit hierarchy. If business unit A is parent of business unit B and business unit B is parent of business unit C, business unit C cannot be parent of business unit A.

Business units (except root business units) can be *disabled*. This can be done by selecting the business unit and then clicking on **More Actions** | **Disable** from the toolbar. There are certain important considerations for disabling a business unit:

- Disabling a business unit will also disable all its child business units.
- Users of a disabled business unit are not disabled but they cannot log in to the Dynamics CRM 2011 system. Hence, the user licenses of such users are not withdrawn.
- Users, teams, or child business units cannot be assigned to a disabled business unit.
- Users who relied on membership of teams for access to certain resources will not be able to access those resources if the business unit is disabled.

A disabled business unit can be *enabled* at any time. Select the **Inactive Business Units** view and then select the business unit to be enabled. Click on **More Actions** | **Enable** from the toolbar to enable a business unit. When a business unit is enabled, all the child business units are also enabled automatically.

Finally, business units (except root business units) can also be *deleted*. To delete a business unit, it first has to be disabled. Only disabled business units can be deleted. To delete a business unit, select the **Inactive Business Units** view and then select the business unit to be deleted. Click on **More Actions** | **Delete** on the toolbar. A few important considerations when deleting a business unit are:

- A business unit with child business units cannot be deleted. Hence, before deleting any business unit all its child business units have to be deleted or reparented.
- For a business unit with teams (except the default team), users cannot be deleted unless these teams and users are not reassigned.
- Business unit deletion cannot be undone.

Configuring a security role

Microsoft Dynamics CRM 2011 provides a security model that ensures **data integrity** and **privacy**. The security model has the following levels:

- **Role-based security**: Groups a set of privileges for a user in a security role. A security role can be assigned to a user or a team and determines what the user or team members can and cannot do in a Dynamics CRM 2011 organization.

- **Field-level security**: Restricts access to fields in an entity only to specified users or teams.

Security roles are core to the role-based security model. The security role has two main concepts: **privileges** and **access levels**. Combined, these two concepts define a security role. The privileges associated with a security role are groups in various tabs in the UI of the security role. These are the privilege grouping tabs for any security role: **Core Records**, **Marketing**, **Sales**, **Service**, **Business Management**, **Service Management**, **Customization**, and **Custom Entities**.

The Dynamics CRM 2011 system will already have a few security roles configured by default. These are known as system-defined security roles or standard security roles. Except for the system administrator security role. the other roles can be customized to fit in with the functional security model. New security roles can also be created under any business unit.

In this recipe, we will discuss how to customize an existing security role and how to create a custom security role.

How to do it...

To customize an existing security role, follow these steps to customize an existing security role:

1. Log in to the Dynamics CRM 2011 system as a user who has the system administrator security role.
2. Navigate to the **Settings** | **Administration** | **Security Role** section.

> If we intend to customize any default or standard security roles offered by Dynamics CRM 2011, the best practice is to copy the security role with a different name and then customize the newly created security role.

3. Then, select the security role to be customized and double-click on the security role name to open its settings.
4. The next step is to customize the security role:
    - **Change the security role name**: Navigate to the **Details** tab and modify the **Role Name** field.
    - **Customize entity-level access rights**: Navigate to the security role UI tab where the specific entity is present. Then set the access level for various access rights of the entity.

- **Customize the miscellaneous privileges**: There is a set of privileges that is not linked to any entity; rather, they are tasks that can be performed within the Dynamics CRM 2011 system. To customize any such privilege, navigate to the tab where the privilege is listed and then set the access level.

5. Finally, click on the **Save and Close** button on the top ribbon.

Creating a custom security role can be achieved in two ways:

- Copying an existing security role and then modifying it; this can be done as follows:
    1. Log in to the Dynamics CRM 2011 system as a user that has the system administrator security role.
    2. Navigate to the **Settings** | **Administration** | **Security Role** section.
    3. Select the security role to be copied, click on **More Actions** in the toolbar, and select **Copy Role**.
    4. The **Copy Security Role** pop-up will appear. Provide the name for the new role and click on the **OK** button.

    > When a security role is created by copying an existing security role, the new security role will be created under the same business unit of the existing security role that was copied and the business unit cannot be modified.

    5. Then, modify the required access levels for various access rights of the available entities and miscellaneous privileges according to the functional need.
    6. Finally, click on the **Save and Close** button on the top ribbon.
- Creating a new security role; this can be done with the following steps:
    1. Log in to the Dynamics CRM 2011 system as a user that has the system administrator security role.
    2. Navigate to the **Settings** | **Administration** | **Security Role** section.
    3. Click on **New** in the toolbar.
    4. The **Security Role: New** page appears. On this page, provide the role name and business unit information.
    5. Then, set the required access levels for the various access rights of the available entities and miscellaneous privileges according to the functional need.

> When a custom security role is created, organization-level **read** access is provided for the following entities by default: **Plug-in Assembly**, **Plug-in Type**, **SDK Message**, **SDK Message Processing Step**, and **SDK Message Processing Step Image**. These entities can be found under the **Customization** tab of the security role.

6. Finally, click on the **Save and Close** button on the top ribbon.

How it works...

The security role is a three-dimensional model in Dynamics CRM 2011. These three dimensions in combination decide what a user or a member of a team can access within the system. The three dimensions are:

- Entity
- Privileges
- Access Level

Entities are the units within the Dynamics CRM 2011 Security Role model to which an access level is applied for every privilege.

The security role **privileges** define the access rights granted to a user for a particular entity instance. The access rights are as follows:

Access Right	Description
Read	This access right controls whether the user can read the entity instance.
Write	This access right controls whether the user can update the entity instance.
Assign	This access right controls whether the user can assign the entity instance to another user.
Append	This access right controls whether the user can attach another entity instance to the specified entity instance.
Append To	This access right controls whether the user can attach the entity instance in question to another entity instance.
Share	This access right controls whether the user can share the entity instance with another user or team.
Delete	This access right controls whether the user can delete the entity instance.

The **Append** and **Append To** access rights work in combination with one another. Every time a user wants to attach an entity instance to another entity instance, the user must have both rights. For example, when a user wants to attach a note to a case, the user must have the Append access right on the note and the Append To access right on the case for the operation to work.

Most of the preceding access rights have dependencies on other access roles for proper functioning. For example, a user may have the Create access right to an entity, but unless the user has read access to the same entity, he cannot create an instance of the entity and be the owner at the same time. The following table describes the access right dependencies for the actions specified:

Action	Access rights required
To create a record of an entity and be the owner of the record	Create, Read
To share a record of an entity	Share, Read
To assign a record of an entity	Assign, Write, Read
To append to an entity record	Read, Append To
To append an entity record	Read, Append

The security role access level determines the depth of access. The following are the access levels:

Access Level name	Notation	Description
None		No access is granted
User		Access is granted to the entity instances owned by the user or shared with the user or shared with a team of which the user is a member.
Business unit		Access is granted on the entity instances owned by someone within the user's own business unit.
Parent-child business unit		Access is granted on the entity instances owned by someone within the user's own business unit or within a child business unit of the user.
Organization		Access is granted to the entity instances owned by anyone within the user's organization.

If a custom entity is created in the system, all security roles except for system administrator have to be configured to provide relevant access to this entity.

There's more...

There is something more with security roles:

- If we decide to create a new child business unit for a parent business unit, all the security roles of the parent business unit will be copied to the child business unit as an inherited role. Inherited security roles can neither be modified nor deleted.
- If we want to customize any security role, it can only be done in the business unit that the security role was created in.
- If we change any security role, the changes made will cascade down to all the child business units as well.
- If we wish to create a security role that is available to the whole organization, we have to create it under the root business unit.
- Security roles are very tightly coupled with business units. Hence a user who wishes to create a new security role has to be a member of that business unit or any parent business unit.
- It is technically possible to create security roles with the same name under different business units. However, best practice recommends assigning such security roles to the parent business unit.

Creating a custom administrator security role

The Dynamics CRM 2011 system has an out-of-the-box system administrator security role. But, at times, we want to create custom administrator security roles to provide some restrictive administrative tasks to a set of users. For example, we want to provide the right to create users, teams, queues, goals, currencies and so on, but restrict access to solution management, entity customization, and so on. In this recipe, we will explore the best way to create such a custom administrator security role.

How to do it...

Please follow the ensuing steps to create a custom administrator security role:

1. Log in to the Dynamics CRM 2011 system as a user that has the system administrator security role.
2. Navigate to the **Settings** | **Administration** | **Security Role** section.

3. Then, select the **System Administrator** security role, click on **More Actions** in the toolbar, and then select **Copy Role**.

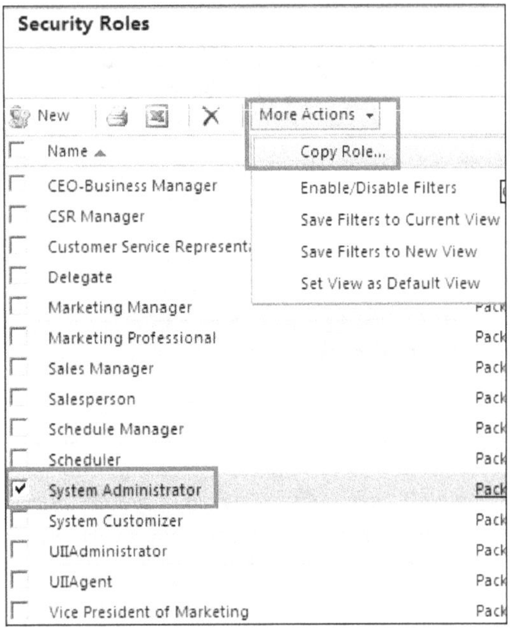

4. In the **Copy Security Role** web pop-up, provide a new role name and then click on **OK**.
5. The custom administrator security role page opens. Customize the new security role as per the functional need. Then, click on the **Save and Close** button on the top ribbon.

How it works...

We have created a custom administrator security role in this recipe. After that, we have to assign this security role to the custom administrator users. Custom administrator users should have both **Access Mode** and **License Type** set to **Administrative**.

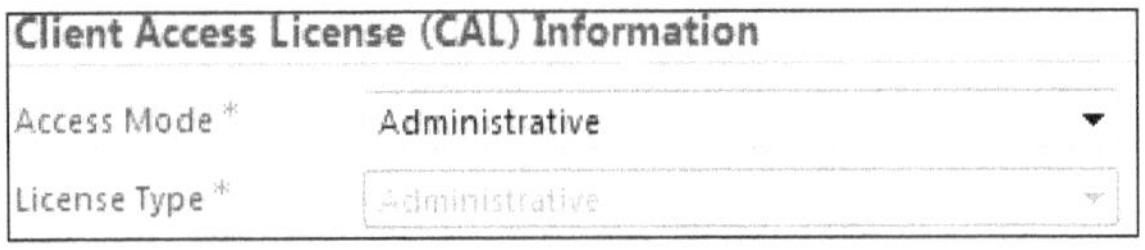

This user can perform administrative functions and assign all roles (except the system administrator role) to other users but cannot work with Sales, Marketing, and Service (except view the knowledge base).

One more important fact for Dynamics CRM 2011 is that, until the release of **Update Rollup 10**, if there are custom entities, the custom administrator cannot assign a security role—which has more privileges than the custom administrator role—to any user. Update Rollup 10 for Dynamics CRM 2011 has enabled the `AllowRoleAssignInAdminMode` option for users in the administrative mode. This is a registry subkey to be added under `HKEY_LOCAL_MACHINE\SOFTWARE\Microsoft\MSCRM` with the value `1`.

The custom administrative security role should have the following rights to be able to assign security roles to another user:

- Organization-level read access to the User, User Settings, and Security Role entities
- Append and Append To permissions to the User entity

Creating a field-level security profile

Using field-level security, access to certain fields can be restricted to some specific users or teams. However, field-level security cannot be applied to all fields. Field-level security can be applied to:

- Only custom fields for system entities
- All fields for any custom entity

Field-level security is applied by creating field-level security profiles. Fields with field-level security enabled can be added to these profiles. Finally, a user or team is associated with every field-level security profile. The field-level security rules will be applicable to these users or members of the teams.

How to do it...

Follow these steps to configure a field-level security profile:

1. Set the **Field Security** field to **Enable** for all those fields to be included in the field-level security profile.
2. Publish the entity by clicking on **Publish**.
3. Create a field-level security profile. This can be done by navigating to **Settings** | **Administration** | **Field Security Profiles** and then clicking on the **New** button on the ribbon to create a new field-level security profile.
4. Provide a name and description for the profile and then click on the **Save** button on the ribbon.
5. Then click on **Members** | **Teams** under the **Related** section. Add teams to this profile by clicking on the **Add** button under the **Team Associated View**. If no team is required to be added to this field-level security profile, this step can be skipped.

6. Finally, configure the field-level security access rights by navigating to **Field Permissions** under the **Common** section. This section will list all the fields for which field-level security has been configured.
7. Now, click on the field name and then select **Edit** in the top area of the section. This will bring up the **Edit Field Security** page. Set the access mode for **Read**, **Update**, and **Create** for this specific field.
8. Repeat the preceding step for all the fields listed in this profile.
9. Finally, click on the **Save and Close** button on the top ribbon.

How it works...

Field-level security restricts the access to a field for a set of users. When a user opens up a record form, unless the user has read access to a field for which field-level security has been enabled, the user will not be able to see the value for the field. When a user wants to share a record with someone else, the user can provide access only to those secure fields to which the user has access.

Enabling field-level security has other implications as well inside the Dynamics CRM 2011 system. In the `Retrieve` and `RetrieveMultiple` queries, if a secure field is used in the column set, the column will not have any value returned unless the caller (or impersonated user) has read access to the secure field.

If a secure field is used in the filter condition of the query, the condition involving the secure field will be replaced by `null` during the condition evaluation unless the caller (or impersonated user) has read access to the secure field.

If the secure field is used to order the result set, the order by condition at SQL level will consider the value to be `null` for the secure field.

Adding a new user account in the Dynamics CRM 2011 system

A user is any individual who is associated with the business unit and uses the Dynamics CRM 2011 system. Any user can only be associated with only *one* business unit. Let us first delve into the recipe for adding a single user at a time in the Dynamics CRM 2011 system.

How to do it...

Follow these steps to add a user in Dynamics CRM 2011:

1. Log in to the Dynamics CRM 2011 system as a user with the system administrator or equivalent security role.

2. Navigate to the **Settings** | **Administration** | **Users** section.
3. Click on the **New** button on the ribbon.

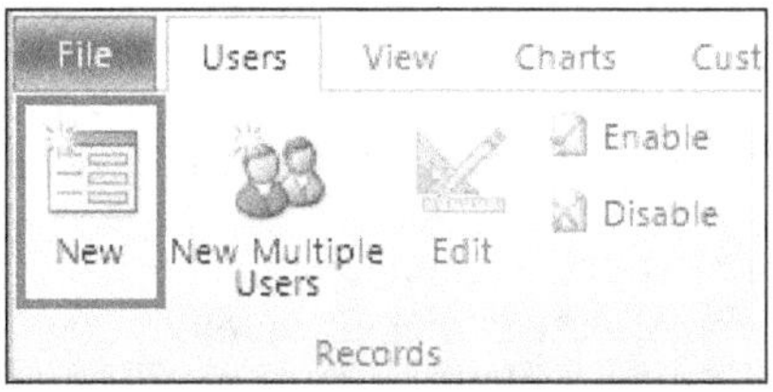

4. In the **New User** form, enter a value in the **User Name** field in the format of `Domain Name\Logon Name`. Then, press *Tab* or click on any other field in the form. This will fetch user information about the user from Active Directory.
5. We can modify the user information values fetched from Active Directory.
6. Then, we can enter information for these sections: **Organization Information**, **E-mail Access Configuration**, **Addresses**, and **Default Queue**.
7. Then, enter the values in the **Client Access License (CAL) Information** form.

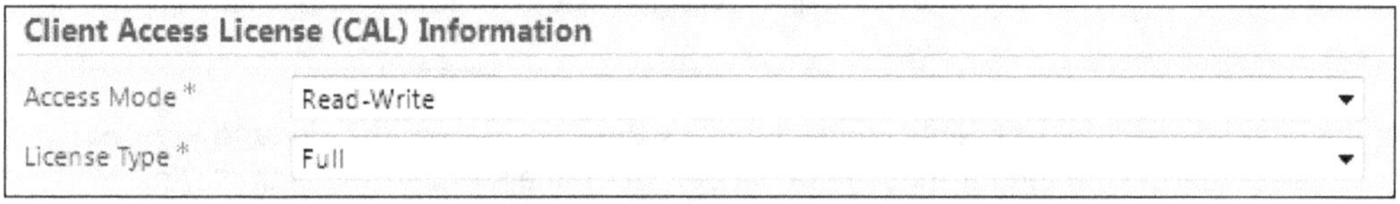

8. Click on the **Save** button on the top ribbon.
9. Once the user record is created, click on the **Manage Roles** button on the top ribbon to set the security role for the user. In the **Manage User Roles** pop-up, select the security roles to be assigned to the user and then select **OK**.
10. If the user has to be added to some teams, click on the **Join Teams** button on the top ribbon. When the **Teams Lookup** pop up appears, select the teams the user should be part of and then click on the **OK** button.
11. The **Change Business Unit** button can be used if the business unit of the user has to be modified.
12. The **Change Manager** button can be used if the manager of the user is to be modified.

How it works...

Adding users is pretty simple in the Dynamics CRM 2011 system. It mainly involves information about the user's login details, account information, and demographic information. One important piece of information entered here is the **client access information**. This section has two important attributes of a system user entity: Access Mode and License Type.

Access Mode: The Access Mode specifies the type of access the user has on the Dynamics CRM 2011 system. The following are the possible values for the field:

Access mode	Description
`Administrative`	If we set the access mode to Administrative for a user, the user can access the **Settings** section but cannot access the **Sales**, **Marketing**, and **Services** sections in the system.
`Non-interactive`	Such types of users can only access the system via Dynamics CRM Web Service not via the user interface.
`Read`	The user will have only read access to the system.
`Read-Write`	The user will have both read and write access
`Support User`	Such users are created by the Microsoft Dynamics Support team.

The default form for the User entity does not show the `Non-interactive` and `Support User` options. It is scripted for these to be hidden. To make them visible in the form, customize the form to add the Access Mode attribute again. When we add a new field in the UI for Access Mode, all the preceding options will be visible in the drop-down list. Another way would be to set the Access Mode using Dynamics CRM 2011 SDK.

> Non-interactive users are usually used in Service-to-Service code because such users do not use a license. Dynamics CRM 2011 Online supports only five free non-interactive users.

License Type: This field specifies the **Client Access License** (**CAL**) type. The following values are available to choose from:

License Type	Description
`Administrative`	The user will have administrative rights.
`Device Full`	The user who is using the device running Dynamics CRM 2011 will have both read and write access.
`Device Limited`	The user who is using the device running Dynamics CRM 2011 will have only read access.
`Full`	The user has both read and write access.
`Limited`	The user only has read access.

When a user leaves the organization, reassign all the active records owned by this user to another active user and deactivate the current user. The deactivated user does not use up licenses, and this way, we can regain a license for a user who no longer belongs to the organization.

> When we create a user, we must assign the user at least one security role. Even if the user is part of a team that has assigned roles, the user should be assigned a role.

There's more...

Dynamics CRM 2011 includes more security settings for approving e-mail addresses of the user before they can be used by the e-mail router. To update the security settings, navigate to the **Settings** | **Administration** | **System Settings** | **E-mail** tab and deselect the checkbox next to **Process e-mails only for approved users**.

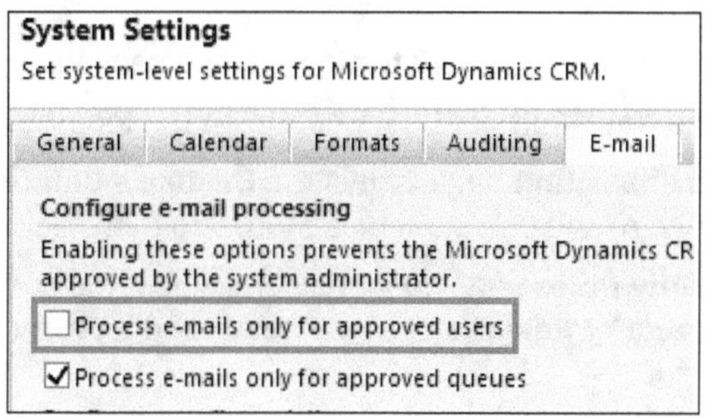

As a result of this change, each user's e-mail address has to be approved before e-mails can be processed by the e-mail router. This can be achieved by launching each individual user's records and then by clicking on the **Approve E-mail** button on the ribbon.

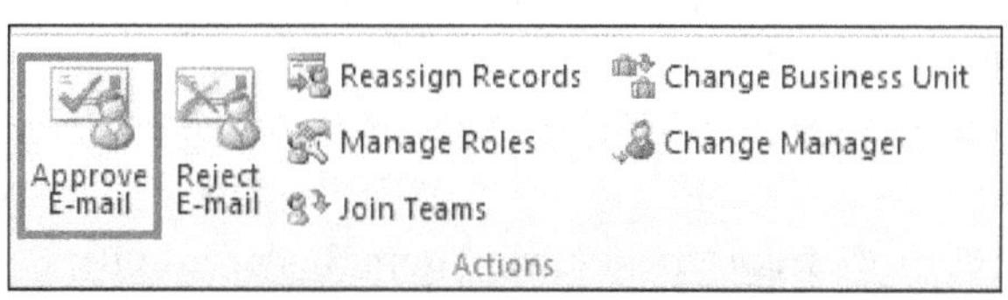

In the **Confirm Primary E-mail Approval** pop up, click on **OK** to approve and close the window. The e-mail address can be rejected by clicking on the **Reject E-mail** button on the ribbon.

Adding multiple users in the Dynamics CRM 2011 system

In this recipe we will find out how to add multiple users in the system at a time. The process of adding multiple users is slightly different from the *Adding a new user account in Dynamic CRM 2011* recipe. When a single user is added at a time, we assign the security role of the user after adding the user in the system. When we add multiple users using the multiple user addition wizard, we select the security role first and then add the users; hence, users with the same security roles are usually added together.

How to do it...

Follow these steps to add multiple users in the system at a time:

1. Log in to the Dynamics CRM 2011 system as a user with the system administrator or an equivalent security role.
2. Navigate to the **Settings** | **Administration** | **Users** section.
3. Then, click on the **New Multiple Users** button on the top ribbon.
4. In the **Select Business Unit** page, select the **Business Unit** from the drop-down, under which all the users will be added, and then click on **Next** to continue.
5. The **Select Security Roles** page appears; here, select the correct security roles from the **Security Roles** list that will be applied to all the users to be added. Then click on **Next**.
6. On the **Select Access and License Type** page, select the appropriate values for **Access Type**, **License Type**, and **E-mail Access Configuration**. The selected Access Mode and License Type will be applied to all the users to be added here. Then click on **Next** to proceed.
7. Then the **Select Domain or Group** page appears; here, select one of the following options:
    1. **Select users from all trusted domains or groups**: Choose this option if users to be added are spread across different domains or groups
    2. **Select users from the following domains or groups**: Choose this option is users to be added are part of one common domain or group.

    After the selection, please click on **Next** to proceed.
8. On the **Select Users** page, please specify the usernames in the `domainName\logonName` format, delimited by semicolons between usernames. Then, click on the Lookup (lens) button on the right-hand side. Once all the user names are resolved, click on the **Create New Users** button to create all the users in the system.

9. Finally, on the **Summary** page, click on **Close** if you want to finish. If you intend to add more users, click on the **Add More Users** button and follow the current recipe from step 1 again.
10. Some information about the users, such as address information, can only be added by opening each of the added users and then entering the data.
11. To assign a manager to these users, please open each of the users, click on the **Change Manager** button on the top ribbon, and set the manager.
12. If these users have to be added to some teams, launch each of the user's records and then click on the **Join Teams** button on the top ribbon. When the **Teams Lookup** pop up appears, select the teams the user should be part of and then click on the **OK** button.

How it works...

Multiple user addition helps us to add users of the same type, who share the same security roles, access type, license type, and e-mail configuration, in the Dynamics CRM 2011 system at one go.

There is another way to add multiple users at a time and that is by using the Dynamics CRM 2011 system's Import Data wizard. This wizard can be accessed by navigating to the **Workplace** | **My Work** | **Imports** section and then clicking on the **Import Data** button on the top ribbon. The Import Data Wizard will be discussed in *Chapter 4, Data Management*. But one important point about importing user data is that only the attributes of the User entity can be specified in the Import Data wizard. The security role of the user cannot be specified during user import.

> The Dynamics CRM 2011 system will assign the `Salesperson` security role to all the users imported using the Import Data wizard. If the `Salesperson` role is deleted from the system, the Import Data wizard cannot create users during an import.

There's more...

Users added to the Dynamics CRM 2011 system cannot be deleted but can be disabled. To disable users, navigate to **System** | **Administration** | **Users** and then select the users to be disabled. Finally, click on the **Disable** button in the top ribbon to disable them.

Once a user record is disabled inside the Dynamics CRM 2011 system, the following will happen:

- The user cannot log on to the Dynamics CRM 2011 system
- The user stops consuming Client Access Licenses (CALs)
- Published workflows or dialogs owned by the user stop working
- Records can no longer be assigned to this user

A disabled user can be enabled at any time by clicking the **Enable** button on the User entity's top ribbon. When a disabled user is re-enabled, the user will consume a Client Access License.

Creating a new team in the Dynamics CRM 2011 system

A team is a group of users and allows groups of users to share information in an organization. In this recipe we will delve into how to create a team in the Dynamics CRM 2011 system.

How to do it...

Follow this recipe to create a team in the Dynamics CRM 2011 system:

1. Log in to the Dynamics CRM 2011 system as a user with the system administrator or an equivalent security role.
2. Navigate to the **Settings** | **Administration** | **Teams** section.
3. Click on the **New** button on the top ribbon.
4. In the **Team New** page, please enter the following information:
    - **Team Name**: Enter a unique name for the team that describes the team's purpose, business focus, location, or other meaningful characteristics.
    - **Business Unit**: The business unit to which the team belongs. One team can only be part of one business unit. This is a mandatory field.
    - **Administrator**: Select a user from the lookup. This user will be the administrator of the team. This is a mandatory field.
    - **Default Queue**: Select the team's queue from the lookup.
    - **Description**: Enter a description for the team, if any.

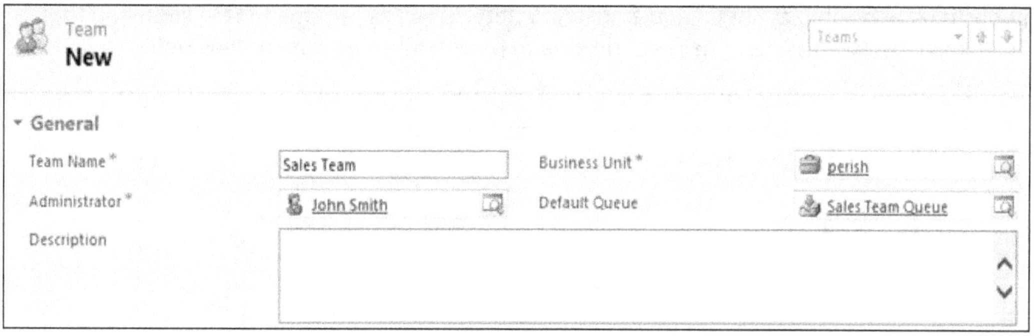

5. Then click on the **Save** button on the top ribbon.
6. Click on the **Manage Roles** button on the top ribbon to assign security roles to the team.
7. Then, navigate to the **Related** | **Common** | **Members** section. Then click on the **Add Members** button on the ribbon.
8. To remove users from a team, select the members and then click on the **Remove** button on the ribbon.
9. In the **User Lookup** pop up, select team members and then click on the **Add** button. Click on the **OK** button to close the pop up.

How it works...

A team is an important construct in Dynamics CRM 2011 system. Each team must be assigned a security role and must have an administrator.

After creation of the team, we add members to it. Though a team belongs to only one business unit, users from multiple business units can be added as team members. When team members are reassigned to different business units within the organization, we can remove them from one team and add them to another. We can also remove team members when they leave the organization.

When we assign a security role to a team, the security role is also assigned to all the users based on the business unit of the team. When a user is assigned a team, the user can perform any task on behalf of the team; however, the user does not necessarily *inherit* the access rights of the team.

Let us take an example. Let us add a custom entity `Subscription` in the system and then customize the `Sales Manager` security role to provide the following access rights to this entity:

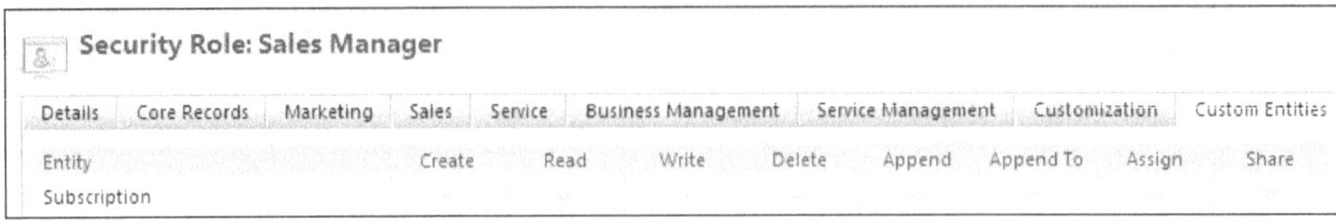

Now create a new team with the name `Sales Team` and assign the `Sales Manager` security role to this team. Thereafter, assume we have a user `John Smith` in the system with the security role `Salesperson` assigned. The `Salesperson` security role has no access rights to the `Subscription` entity. The user `John Smith` is added to `Sales Team`. Now log in to Dynamics CRM as `John Smith` and try to create a subscription record. During the record save, the system will throw the **Access is denied** error. Now if `John Smith` had inherited the access rights of the team's security role, that is, `Sales Manager`, `John Smith` would have been able to save the record. Now change the owner of the record to the team `Sales Team` and save the record. This save attempt will be successful. Here, `John Smith` was able to impersonate his team and was able to create the record.

A team, too, can own records and can provide access by sharing those records with the team members. Sharing a record with a team essentially shares it with all the members of the team irrespective of their business units.

Configuring autonumbering formats

Some entities within the Dynamics CRM 2011 system use an automatic incremental numbering system to uniquely identity individual records. This automatic numbering system comes with a default configuration. In this recipe we will find out how to update these default settings.

How to do it...

Follow these steps to configure the autonumbering formats:

1. Log in to the Dynamics CRM 2011 system as a user with the system administrator or an equivalent security role.
2. Navigate to the **Settings** | **Administration** section and click on **Auto-Numbering**.
3. Set the **Auto-Numbering** value in the web pop-up that is launched. This page will have multiple tabs listing the entities that use autonumbering in the system.

4. Click on the tabs and modify the value in the **Prefix** field and/or the **Suffix Length** field of the **Auto-Number** page as follows:
    - **Prefix**: We can enter up to three characters, symbols, or numbers
    - **Suffix Length**: We can select a value of **4**, **5**, or **6** from the drop-down list

> **Articles** does not have a **Suffix Length** option.

5. Finally, click on the **OK** button to save and close the changes.

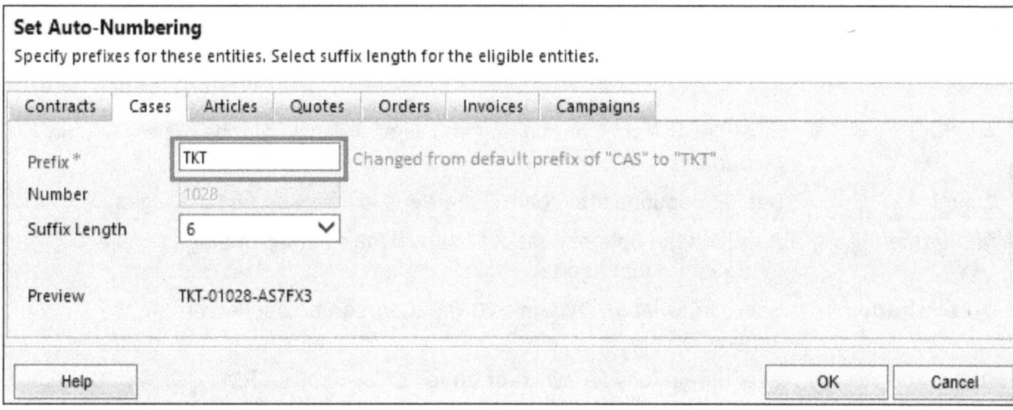

How it works...

Any autonumber has three parts: a fixed prefix, an incremental number, and a changing suffix.

Prefixes have a maximum length of three and are used for all system-generated numbers for the selected record type. If we change the prefix for a record type, it will not change the prefix of numbers that have already been assigned.

For every entity other than Article, we can specify the length of the automatically generated alphanumeric suffix of the autonumber. The suffix is used for records that are created while the user is offline and for which the number cannot be guaranteed to be unique.

Configuring system-wide settings

The system settings in the Dynamics CRM 2011 is the largest group of settings and each of them affects the whole system as such. These are configurable settings and might need modifications to meet business requirements. System settings are grouped into the following 10 headers depending on their nature:

Tab/group name	Description
General	Specifies the name format, currency display options, how records are shared, and whether attachments are allowed
Calendar	Sets the maximum length of an appointment
Formats	Specifies the regional display format for number, currency, time, and date
Auditing	Specifies the start of auditing and what areas within the system should be audited
E-mail	Sets the options that control how e-mail is tracked and managed
Marketing	Specifies the options that control how marketing campaign e-mail features are managed
Customization	Specifies whether Dynamics CRM 2011 can be opened in application mode
Outlook	Sets the options for synchronization of Dynamics CRM 2011 with Outlook
Reporting	Specifies the report categories
Goals	Sets the roll-up frequency and expiry time

In this recipe we will find out how to modify the default settings and will dive deep into a few very important settings.

How to do it...

The following steps tell you how to carry out the changes in the **System Settings** section:

1. Log in to the Dynamics CRM 2011 system as the system administrator or an equivalent role.
2. Navigate to the **Settings** | **Administration** | **System Settings** section. Double-click to launch the **System Settings** dialog.
3. After the settings are modified, click on the **OK** button to save the modified settings and close the dialog.
4. To modify a specific type of setting, click on the tab or group where the setting is present and then modify its value.
5. After all the modifications are done, click on **OK** to save the changes.

How it works...

The **System Settings** section contains a few very important configurations regarding the Dynamics CRM 2011 system. Let's see what they are.

The **General** setting has the following options:

- **Show Get Started panes on all lists for all users**: This setting determines whether or not to display the **Get Started** pane.
- **Enable presence for the system**: This setting determines whether instant messaging will display the current status for users, contacts, opportunities, or leads.
- **Name Format**: This setting determines the format in which the full name of the users and contacts will be displayed in the system. Changing the name format does not affect the existing entries. It only affects the new entries to be added post **Name Format** change.
- **Pricing Decimal Precision**: This setting determines how many decimal points to use for currency.
- **Share reassigned records with the original owner**: Select whether or not a record is shared with the original owner of the record or is completely reassigned to another user.
- **Set blocked file extensions for attachments**: Prevent users from attaching files with specific file name extensions.
- **Display currency by using**: Select how currency is to be displayed.
- **Enable Quick Find records limit**: **Update Rollup 10** of Dynamics CRM 2011 has introduced Quick Find Optimization. By default, this setting is enabled but can be disabled using the UI option. If Quick Find Optimization is enabled, any quick find query returning more than 10,000 records will result in the following error:

  Quick find limit exceeded. Please use a more selective search value, or use Advanced Find for your search

  Disabling this setting will result in slow performance of quick find queries.

The **Calendar** setting will have the following options:

- **Maximum duration of an appointment in days**: Sets the maximum duration for an appointment record

The **Formats** setting will have the following options:

- **Format**: This setting determines the language and locale that corresponds to the format that we want to use as the default format for the organization. If you want to customize number, currency, time, and date formats for the organization, click on **Customize** and modify the default formats, and then click on **OK** to save the values.

The **Audit** setting will have the following options:

- **Start Auditing**: Turn on this setting to begin auditing the system.
- **Audit user access**: Turn on this setting to audit user access to the system. This feature logs the following information about user access:
    - When a user logged in to the CRM system
    - Which of these locations the access originates from: Microsoft Dynamics CRM 2011 web application, Microsoft Dynamics CRM 2011 for Outlook, or SDK calls to the web services

  Auditing is discussed in detail in the next chapter under the *Enabling Auditing* recipe.

The **E-mail** setting will have the following options:

- **Configure Email Processing**: Select this option to prevent Dynamics CRM 2011 e-mail router from processing unapproved email addresses.
- **User Tracking Token**: Select the checkbox to use tracking tokens and to configure how Dynamics CRM 2011 will display the subject line of an e-mail message. Use tracking tokens to more accurately determine if a new record is related to an existing, tracked record. When we change the e-mail prefix, up to 256 characters are saved as history. Long prefixes or too many prefix changes may cause lost data in history.
- **Set tracking options for e-mails between CRM users**: This option determines whether to create two e-mail activities between Microsoft Dynamics CRM 2011 users, one for the sender and one for the recipient.
- **Set E-mail form options**: Select these options for e-mail forms.
- **Set file size limit for attachments**: Using this option, increase or decrease the allowed size of files that can be attached to records. The file size limit that we specify for attachments also limits the size of web resources that can be uploaded in the Microsoft Dynamics CRM 2011 systems.

The **Marketing** setting will have the following options:

- **Enable Direct E-mail via Mail Merge**: This option enables users to send e-mail messages as a campaign activity using the mail merge feature. To enable this option, the security role (a defined set of privileges) assigned to users for whom we want to enable mail merge must also include the mail merge privilege. The security role assigned to a user determines which tasks the user can perform and which parts of the user interface the user can view. All users must be assigned at least one security role in order to access the system.
- **Create campaign responses for incoming e-mail**: This option enables the Dynamics CRM 2011 system to create a campaign response automatically when an e-mail message is received in response to a specific marketing campaign.

- **Set the auto-unsubscribe options**: This setting defines how to handle accounts, contacts, or leads who do not want to receive marketing communications.

The **Customization** setting will have the following options:

- **Application Mode**: Enables the user to set whether Dynamics CRM 2011 can be opened in a browser window without menu, navigation, and command bars. Once we enable application mode, there is little difference in using the URL. To launch Dynamics CRM 2011 in Application Mode after enabling this setting, we need to use the `http://servername:portnumber/orgname` URL format.
- **Form Mode**: Form mode defines different presentations of the form of an entity. We can choose from the following alternatives:
    - **Edit**: This is the default **From Mode** option. In this mode, the form can behave in different ways depending on the state of the record, user permissions, and the action that is being performed. The **Edit** mode also has a subtype called read only, which is used when a user does not have access to modify the data in the form. The read-only form is just an **Edit** form with disabled fields.
    - **Read-Optimized**: This mode of the form is optimized to load the data quickly. The **Read-Optimized** option shortens the time required to load a form by stripping the form down to its bare essentials. This type of form:

      Displays all fields, notes, IFrames, and subgrids that are visible by default

      Honors all form- and field-level security configurations

      Does not display the ribbon or allow editing a record

      Does not display form navigation

      Does not display embedded web resources

      Does not execute form scripts

The **Outlook** setting will have the following options:

- **E-mail promotion options**: Determines whether incoming e-mails have to be tracked and the tracking frequency.
    - **Perform checks as new e-mail is received**: Determines whether incoming e-mails have to be tracked. If it is set to **yes**, the following two options drive the frequency of the tracking.
    - **Promote incoming e-mail every**: Determines how often the incoming e-mails are polled or reviewed.
    - **Send pending CRM e-mail every**: Determines how often to send e-mail from the CRM web client.

- **Whether user can schedule synchronization**: Determines whether a user can schedule synchronization with the Dynamics CRM 2011 and Outlook system along with the frequency of the synchronization
- **User can update their local data in the background**: Determines whether users can update the data that is stored on their computers to use when offline, and how often
- **Address book synchronization**: Determines how often the address book is synchronized
- **User sees the "Get the Outlook client" message**: Determines whether the **Get CRM for Outlook** button is displayed in Microsoft Dynamics CRM 2011

The **Reporting** setting will have the following options: Determines the categories of the reports and the default category

The **Goals** setting will have the following options:

- **Days after the goal end date when the rollup will stop**: The system will recalculate goal attainment regularly during the goal period and for a specified period of time after the end of the goal period
- **Roll-up recurrence frequency**: This setting is used to specify how often goal attainment should be recalculated

Configuring fiscal-year settings

Fiscal year settings are organizational settings that can be modified to suit organizational needs. These settings can be modified any time in an organization.

How to do it...

Please perform the following steps to configure the fiscal year settings in the CRM system:

1. Log in to the Dynamics CRM 2011 system with the system administrator or an equivalent role.
2. Navigate to the **Settings** | **Business Management** | **Fiscal Year Settings** section. Double-click to launch the **Fiscal Year Settings** dialog.
3. In the **Fiscal Year Settings** web pop up, modify a setting and then click on **OK** to save the setting and close the pop up.

How it works...

The fiscal year options affect the way in which an organization's data is stored in the Microsoft Dynamics CRM 2011 database. Therefore, we can set the fiscal year options only once. We cannot change these settings after we have set them.

The fiscal period and display-related settings are available to configure here.

- **Start Date**: Determines the start date of the fiscal year.
- **Fiscal Period Template**: The template for how the fiscal year is divided. Possible options are **Annually**, **Semiannually**, **Quarterly**, **Monthly**, and **4-Week period**. Once the start date and period type are defined, the system can calculate the start and end dates of fiscal periods for various fiscal years.

There are other display options to be configured as shown in the following screenshot:

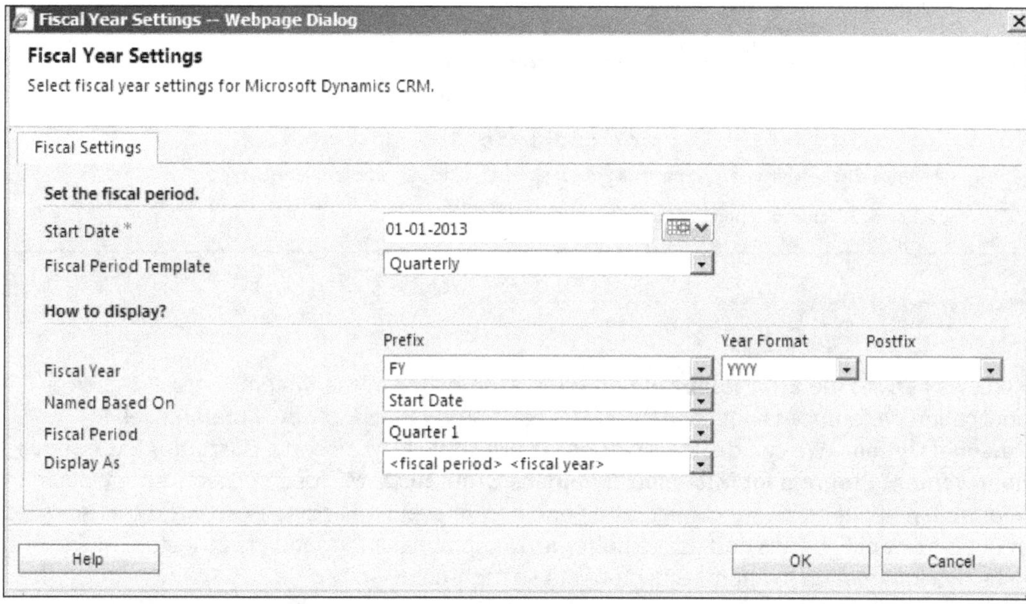

Configuring error-notification preferences

How to do it...

Please perform the following steps to configure error notification preferences in the system:

1. Log in to the Dynamics CRM 2011 system with the system administrator or an equivalent role.
2. Navigate to the **Settings** | **Administration** | **Privacy Preferences** section. Double-click to launch the **Privacy Preferences** dialog.

3. Modify the error notification preferences and then click on the **OK** button to save the changes and to close the dialog.

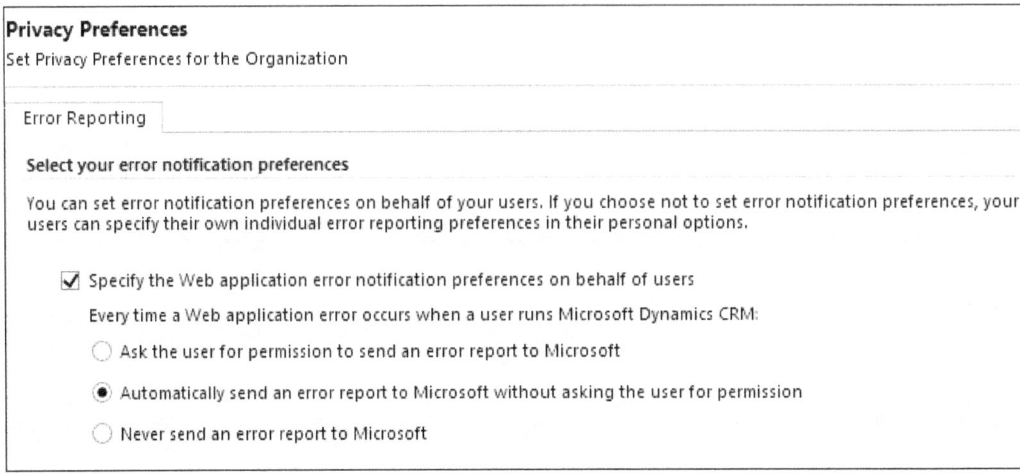

How it works...

Here, we can set the **Error Reporting** preference on behalf of the system users. If the error notification preference is not set here, users can specify their individual preferences in **Personal Options**. We can decide whether to participate in Microsoft's **Customer Experience Improvement Program for Microsoft Dynamics CRM 2011**. Microsoft collects anonymous information about hardware configuration and how users use Microsoft hardware and services in order to identify trends and usage patterns. No personal information is collected. Microsoft uses this information to improve its products and features.

See also

This chapter outlined the recipes that help us to administer Dynamics CRM 2011 system. In the next chapter, we will delve into recipes for data management within the Dynamics CRM 2011 system. A few very important recipes to look for in the next chapter are:

- *Importing data in Dynamics CRM 2011*
- *Cleaning data using Bulk Deletion Wizard*
- *Creating duplicate detection rules*
- *Scheduling duplicate detection jobs*

4
Data Management

Data management is a very important feature for any CRM system. No matter how flexible and feature rich the system is, unless there is relevant data within the CRM system the end users will not find it useful. Data import and export functionality along with duplicate detection and audit management are a significant part of data management in the Dynamics CRM 2011 system. In this chapter, we will discuss the main pillars of data management inside the Dynamics CRM 2011 system: **Import Data Wizard**, **Bulk Deletion Wizard**, **duplicate detection**, and **Audit management**.

The following recipes will be discussed in this chapter in detail:

- Importing data into Dynamics CRM 2011 with Import Data Wizard
- Exporting Dynamics CRM 2011 data to Microsoft Excel
- Cleaning data using Bulk Deletion Wizard
- Creating duplicate detection rules
- Scheduling duplicate detection jobs
- Enabling auditing in the Dynamics CRM 2011 system
- Viewing and cleaning audit records

Introduction to data import

Data can be imported in two ways within Dynamics CRM 2011 system. These are explained as follows:

Using Import Wizard: Dynamics CRM 2011 provides Import Data Wizard for quick and easy data import. Import Data Wizard can import data from any of the following supported file types:

- XML Spreadsheet 2003 (XMLSS) file (`.xml`) format
- CSV

- TXT with columns separated by commas
- ZIP (A `.zip` file can include multiple files of the `.csv`, `.xml`, or `.txt` formats. All files in a single compressed file must be of the same format)

> Each file's size can be up to 8 MB and if multiple files are zipped together then the size limit goes up to 32 MB of data when Data Import Wizard is used. For zipped files, the total size of the extracted files must not exceed 200 MB. The zipped files get unzipped in the Dynamics CRM 2011 server before import and hence each individual extracted file size cannot exceed 8 MB as well.

This import file size is stored in the `ImportMaxAllowedFileSizeInMB` column of the `ServerSettingsProperties` table of the `MSCRM_CONFIG` database. It is *not supported* to update this value in the database. It is also *not recommended* to increase this size limit, because sending a large file to Dynamics CRM 2011 Server for upload may clog bandwidth as well as increase load on the asynchronous service. Other asynchronous operations waiting for asynchronous service will starve and might result in errors.

When importing a `.zip` file, all files contained in the `.zip` file must use the same field and data delimiters. It is not supported to import non-printable characters such as carriage returns and line feeds and these must be stripped out of things like any description text before importing.

Import Data Wizard uses an XML file, called `Data Map`, to associate the data to be imported with correct entities and attributes within the Dynamics CRM 2011 system. Dynamics CRM 2011 offers a list of data maps out of the box. These data maps can be used during data import via Import Wizard. New data maps can be created to facilitate the data import process as well.

Using Dynamics CRM 2011 SDK: Dynamics CRM 2011 SDK provides programmatic ways of importing data into the Dynamics CRM 2011 system. Large volumes of data, especially from legacy systems, are imported into Dynamics CRM 2011 in a programmatic way.

Importing data into Dynamics CRM 2011 with Import Data Wizard

In this recipe, we will discuss how to import data using Import Wizard. During the data import process we will also create a custom data map and use it during the import process.

How to do it...

Please perform the following steps to import data within the Dynamics CRM 2011 system:

1. Log in to the Dynamics CRM 2011 system with system administrator or relevant security role.
2. Navigate to **Settings** | **System** | **Data Management** | **Imports** or alternatively to **Workplace** | **My Work** | **Imports**.
3. Click on the **Import Data** button in the top ribbon.
4. In the **Upload Data File** web pop-up, browse to a file that we intend to upload using the new data map to be created. After selecting the file, click on **Next** to proceed.
5. In the **Review File Upload Summary** page expand the **Delimiter Settings** section and verify the following delimiter settings before clicking on **Next** to continue:
    - **Field delimiter**: This delimiter is used to separate fields in the import file. The possible delimiters are **Comma (,)**, **Colon (:)**, **Semicolon (;)**, and **Tab (\t)**.
    - **Data delimiter**: This delimiter is used to keep the field value intact in case the field delimiter character itself is used as part of the field value. The possible delimiters are **Quotation Mark (")**, **Single Quotation Mark (')**, and **None**.
    - **First row contains column headings**: Tick this checkbox if the first row in the data file contains the field names or column headings.

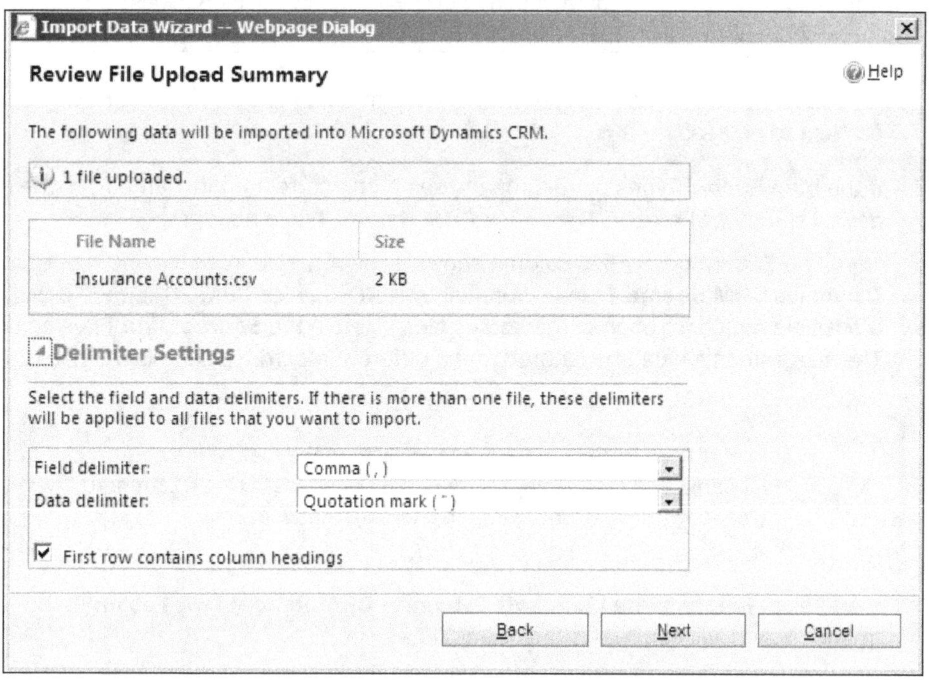

Then the **Select Data Map** page appears. Some generic data maps are already made available by the Dynamics CRM 2011 system. The following table describes the generic data maps and when to use them as well:

Data map name	When to use
Default (Automatic Mapping)	Use this data map to let Import Data Wizard automatically map the files and columns. The import wizard will allow us to map any fields it doesn't automatically resolve in further steps.
Generic Map for Contact and Account	Choose when the source files contain records for Contact and Account entities where Contact is the primary record type.
For Full Data Export	Select this data map if the source data is exported using the `Full Data Export` feature of `Salesforce.com`.
For Report Export	Select this data map if the source data is exported using the `Report Export` feature of `Salesforce.com`.
For Contact and Account Report Export	Select this data map when the source files contain records for Contact and Account entity exported from `Salesforce.com` where Contact is the primary record type.
Microsoft Outlook Business Contact Manager 2010 Map	Select this data map where the source files contain data obtained from Microsoft Outlook Business Contact Manager 2010.

Alternatively, we also can choose from a custom data map if available. Finally, click on **Next** to proceed.

6. If the **Map Record Types** page appears, select the correct entity name from the drop-down list under **Microsoft Dynamics CRM Record Types** header.

   Here, the **Source Data Files** column shows a list of the source files and the **Microsoft Dynamics CRM Record Types** column shows a Dynamics CRM 2011 record type as a possible match for each of the source files listed in the **Source Data Files** column. The suggested type can be ignored and a different record type can be selected.

   > Import Data Wizard can automatically map the files, if the source filename and the display name of the Dynamics CRM 2011 record type to which we want to import the data match exactly.

   If we select **Ignore** in the **Microsoft Dynamics CRM Record Types** column, the Import Wizard will ignore this file during data import.

If we want to create a new custom entity in the system during data import, navigate to **Actions** | **Create New** under **Microsoft Dynamics CRM Record Types**. We can mention the entity name, its plural name, and the primary field name here.

> If the entity name specified already exists, Dynamics CRM 2011 will prompt again to specify a new name.
>
> Also, importing a user can create a new record type only if the user has the privileges to create and publish custom record types in the Dynamics CRM 2011 system.

Then click on **Next** to proceed.

7. In the **Map Fields** page, create the source fields to target fields mapping for those fields marked as **Not Mapped** under both **Source Fields** and **Target Fields**.
   - **Option Sets**: If we choose to map a column of the source file with an `Option Set` type field, the Import Wizard will allow us to map with the values present in the import file with the `Option Set` values.

If the import data file contains a value for an Option Set column that is not part of the Option Set values, we can add the new values to the Option Set using the Import Wizard. Import Wizard, thus can create up to 400 Option Set values.

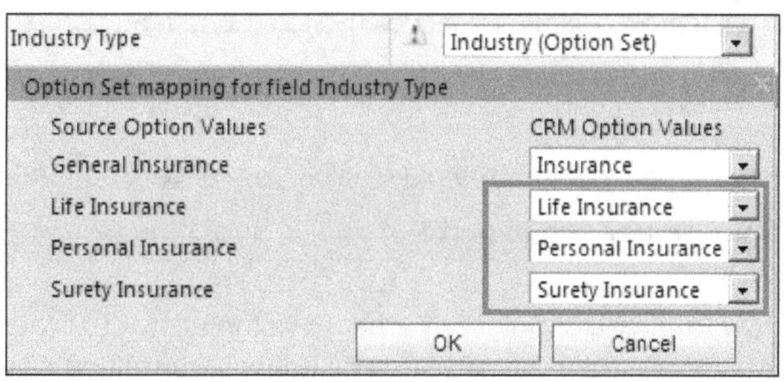

   - **Lookups**: If we choose to map a column of the source file with a Lookup type field, the Import Wizard will allow us to map with the correct relationship type.

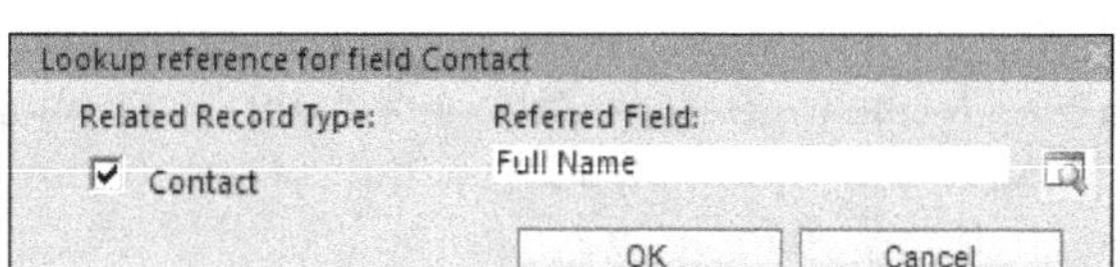

- **Custom field**: If data file contains columns for which there exists no matching field in the entity, then we can create a new field by choosing **Create New Field** during mapping. We can specify the name and data type of the field. The following screenshot is an example of a custom Option Set to be created during data import:

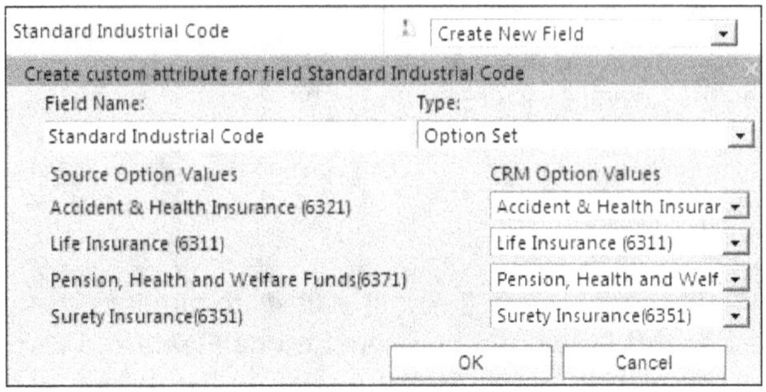

> The newly created attribute does not get automatically added to the entity forms or any other views. Moreover, additional field-level settings such as **Requirement Level**, **Searchable**, **Field Security**, and **Auditing** would be set to the default value of the respective fields. In case the custom column header exceeds 160 characters, then Import Wizard fails to create the new custom field within Dynamics CRM 2011 system.

Then click on **Next** to continue.

8. In the **Review Mapping Summary** page, click on the **Next** button to continue.
9. In the **Review Settings and Import Data** page, select the following options before proceeding:
   - **Allow Duplicates**: Select whether or not to allow duplicate records during data import. The duplicate records will be determined based on the duplicate detection settings. If the **Allow Duplicate** setting is set to **Yes**, the system will not allow duplicate entries to be inserted.
   - **Select Owner for Imported Records**: Select a user or team who will be owning the imported records in the system. By default, the current user is selected.
   - **Data Map Name (optional)**: Optionally enter a data map name under the **Data Map Name (optional)** section. If this is not entered, the data map would not be saved for future use. The logged in user must have create privilege on the Data Map entity if a custom data map is to be created.

Then click on the **Submit** button.

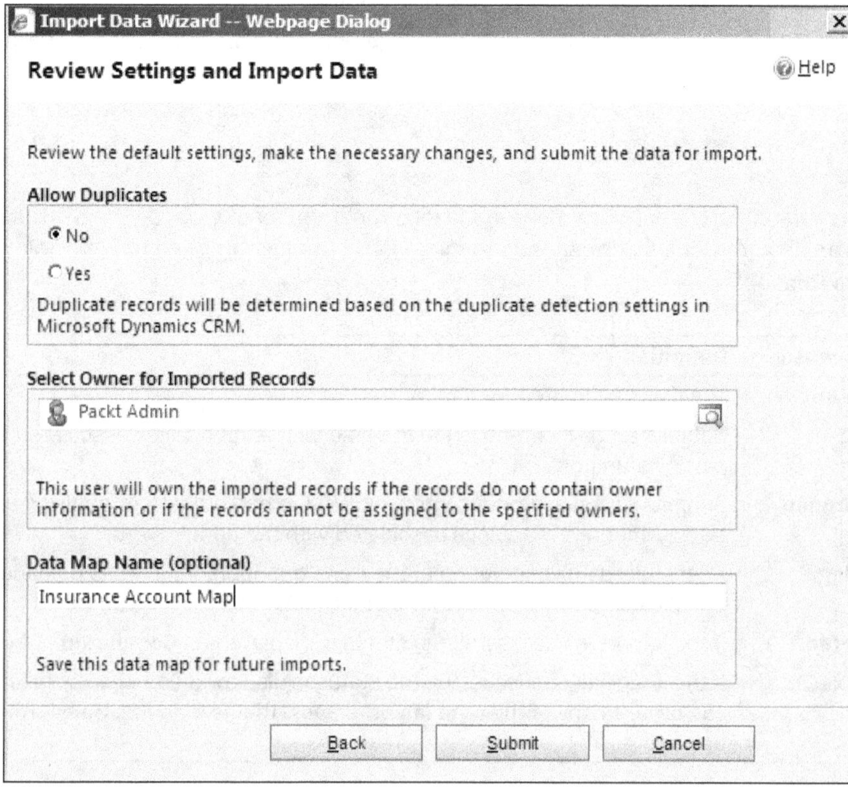

10. In the **Data Submitted for Import** page, click on the **Finish** button to close the wizard.
11. Once the Data Import Wizard closes, navigate to **Settings** | **System** | **Data Management** | **Imports** or alternatively to **Workplace** | **My Work** | **Imports**. The current import file should be present under the **My Imports** view.
12. Check the value of the **Status Reason** column for the imported file. A periodic refresh is required to view the current status reason as the data grid does not refresh automatically. The import is considered successful if **Status Reason** shows **Completed**.

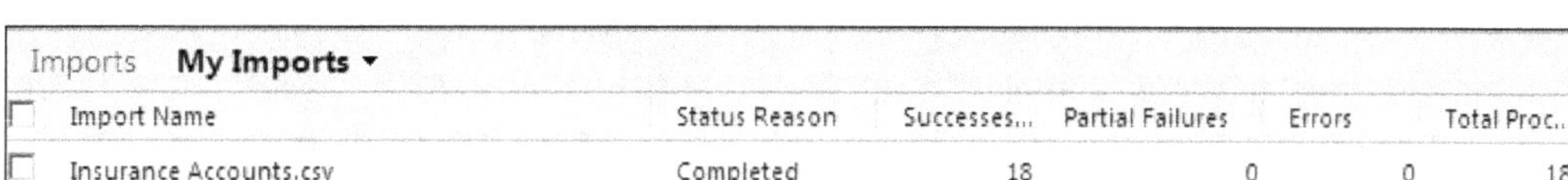

13. To check more details (failures and so on) open the **Import Job** window by double-clicking on the job name.

14. Then navigate to **Settings** | **Data Management** | **Data Maps**.
15. The created data map should be visible in the list.
16. This data map can then also be exported using the **Export** button in the data map's tool bar.

How it works...

To run the data import, a set of asynchronous jobs run in the background. The **Status Reason** value of the data import file corresponds to these jobs. The following are the possible values for **Status Reason**:

Status Reason	Definition
Submitted	The file is submitted for import.
Parsing	Submits an asynchronous job to parse all the import files associated with a particular import.
Transforming	Submits an asynchronous job to modify the parsed data by applying all the transformations mappings associated with the data import.
Importing	After successful completion of the transformation, the data is uploaded into the Microsoft Dynamics CRM 2011 system.
Completed	If the import is successful, the status is displayed as **Completed**.
Failed	If the import is unsuccessful, the status is displayed as **Failed**. A failure can occur in any of the data import stages, that is, parsing, transforming, or uploading.

For any reason, if we want to roll back the import we can achieve this within the Dynamics CRM 2011 system. We can remove the imported records by deleting the imported job that has created the records. Navigate to **Settings** | **System** | **Data Management** | **Imports**, then select the imported job, and click on the **Delete** button in the top ribbon. The **Delete** button allows the user to select from the following three options:

- **Delete the Import Source File**: This removes the uploaded import job along with the source file and mapping information, but not the imported data.
- **All Records Imported to this Entity During this Import**: This will remove all records imported during a data import.

  This is an entity level rollback feature. During import, if a `.zip` file having multiple individual files (for example, `Lead1.csv` and `Lead2.csv`) for a specific entity (Lead) has been used, then selecting this deletion option even for one of these files (say `Lead1.csv`) will actually delete all successfully imported records of the entity (Lead) from all the import files (both `Lead1.csv` and `Lead2.csv`) contained within the `.zip` file. But records of other entities contained within the same `.zip` file would not be deleted.

- **All Imported Records from the .zip File**: This will remove all records that were imported from a `.zip` file during an import.

A data map is a complex XML file used for mapping source data with Dynamics CRM 2011 entities and fields. In this recipe, we have discussed generic data maps and how to create a custom data map using Import Wizard.

But in some scenarios data transformation is complex and data maps are required to be edited manually to include the transformation mappings and then import the data map in the Dynamics CRM 2011 system. A data map can be exported from the Dynamics CRM 2011 system, edited in any XML editor, and then imported back into Dynamics CRM 2011 system.

To export a data map, navigate to **Settings** | **System** | **Data Management** | **Data Maps** and then select the data map and click on the **Export** button in the toolbar.

Data transformation mappings help to modify the data on the fly before importing into the Dynamics CRM 2011 system. The transformed data must be compatible with the entity attribute type and precision. The following table lists the available transformation mappings in Dynamics CRM 2011 system:

Field	Value	Description
`AddToCurrentDate`	`Microsoft.Crm.Transformations.AddToCurrentDate`	Adds a specified number of days, months, and years to the current date and sets the specified date.
`AddToDate`	`Microsoft.Crm.Transformations.AddToDate`	Adds a specified number of days, months, and years to a date.
`AdvancedAddToCurrentDate`	`Microsoft.Crm.Transformations.AdvancedAddToCurrentDate`	Adds a specified number of days, months, and years to the current date. It can also be specified whether offsets are relative to the current date or absolute values. The offsets can only be integer numbers.
`AssignValue`	`Microsoft.Crm.Transformations.AssignValue`	Replaces all values with a specified value.
`Concatenate`	`Microsoft.Crm.Transformations.Concatenate`	Concatenates strings and separates them with a delimiter.
`Replace`	`Microsoft.Crm.Transformations.Replace`	Replaces all occurrences of a specified string with another specified string.
`Split`	`Microsoft.Crm.Transformations.Split`	Separates a string that includes a delimiter into substrings. There can be up to 10 substrings.
`Substring`	`Microsoft.Crm.Transformations.Substring`	Returns a substring of a specified length, starting at a specified point in the string.

While importing a data map XML file in the Dynamics CRM 2011 system, the system validates the following properties of the data map file:

- Uniqueness of the data map filename
- Data map XML is well formed

> The XML definition of the data map can be found in the following location: `C:\Program Files\Microsoft Dynamics CRM\CRMWeb\_Resources\ImportMapSchema.xsd`.

The fundamental differences between creating a data map using Import Data Wizard and manually editing a data map are as follows:

Task	Import Data Wizard	Manual editing of data map
Map existing files, columns, and users.	All mapping will be preserved	All mapping will be preserved.
Create new record types, fields, or users as part of the migration process.	Import Data Wizard can customize the system	Data map will not be imported if target record type and attribute names do not exist in Dynamics CRM 2011.
Use transformations (Types of mappings used to modify data before migrating it. Transformations include concatenation, split, replace, substring, assignment, and date modifications.)	No	Yes
Use the display name for target record types and fields.	Yes	No. Uses the logical name instead. (The logical name is the name that is used in the Microsoft Dynamics CRM Online database schema. To identify schema names for record types and attributes, use the Customization area of Microsoft Dynamics CRM Online.)

Manually edited data maps can be imported into the system by following the ensuing steps:

1. Navigate to **Settings** | **System** | **Data Management** | **Data Maps**.
2. On the **Actions** menu, click on **Import**.
3. In the **Select File to Import** dialog box, click on **Browse**, locate the file, and then click on **OK**.

There's more...

In this recipe, we have discussed how to import data of a specific record type using a data map. Dynamics CRM 2011 also supports importing a single data file into multiple entities. For example, a single CSV file having data for both Lead and Competitor entities as shown in the following table:

Lead record fields						**Competitor record fields**			
Topic	First name	Last name	Company name	E-mail	Phone	Competitor name	Key product	Website	Ticker symbol

If we want to import data for multiple entities using one data map, we have to create a data map capable of mapping data to multiple entities. We can create a multi-entity data map using any XML editor. The following code snippet is an example of such a data map:

```
<Map Name="Lead and Competitor Data Maps" Source="Import">
  <Description> Lead and Competitor Data maps</Description>
  <EntitiesPerFile>Multiple</EntitiesPerFile>
  <EntityMaps>
    <EntityMap TargetEntityName="lead"
               SourceEntityName="Lead"
               Dedupe="Ignore"
               ProcessCode="Process">
    </EntityMap>
    <EntityMap TargetEntityName="competitor"
               SourceEntityName="Competitor"
               Dedupe="Eliminate"
               ProcessCode="Process">
    </EntityMap>
  </EntityMaps>
</Map>
```

Then this custom data map has to be imported in the Dynamics CRM 2011 system. Navigate to **Settings** | **System** | **Data Management** | **Data Maps**. On the **Actions** menu, click on **Import**. In the **Import Data Map** dialog box, click on **Browse**, locate the multi-entity Map XML file, and then click on **OK**.

Thereafter, start the data file import process. Select the newly imported custom multi-entity data map during the data import. In the **Map Fields** page, all the entities will be listed under **CRM Record Types**. Map the entity record fields with correct column headers from the import file.

> Use **Ignore** for those fields in the source file that should not be linked with a field of a specific entity.

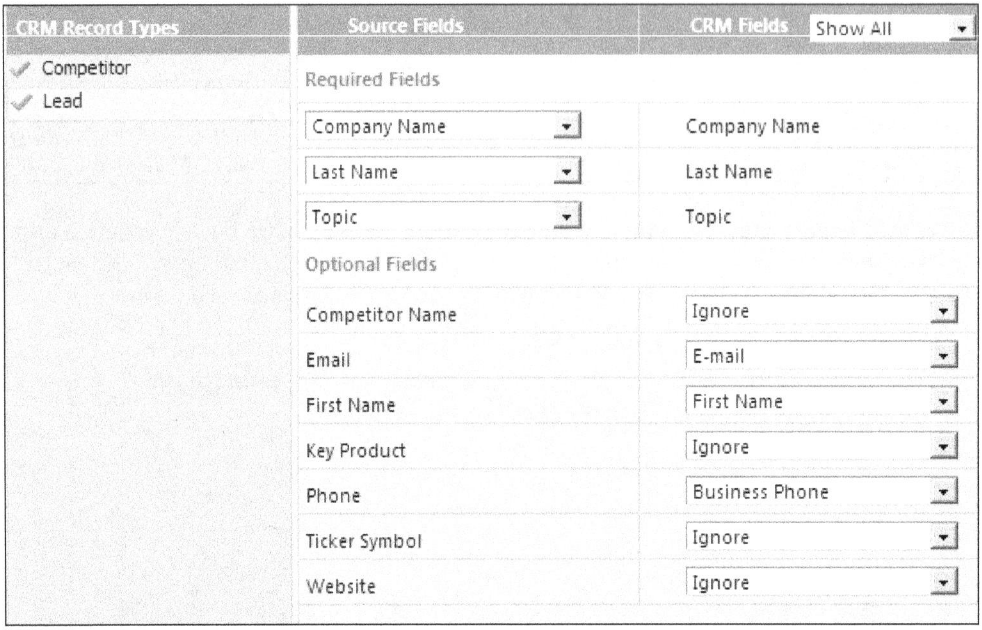

The **Review Mapping Summary** page will also list multiple files, one for each entity.

Exporting Dynamics CRM 2011 data to Microsoft Excel

Dynamics CRM 2011 allows you to export Dynamics CRM data using the Microsoft Excel tool. In this recipe, we will discuss how to export data from the Dynamics CRM 2011 system.

How to do it...

Please follow the ensuing steps to export data from the Dynamics CRM 2011 system to Microsoft Excel:

1. Log in to the Dynamics CRM 2011 system as a user with rights to export data.
2. Navigate to **System View** or **Saved View** or **Advanced Find View** of an entity from which data has to be exported.
3. Then click on the **Export to Excel** button in the ribbon.

4. This will bring up the **Export Data to Excel** web pop-up. Select in what type of Excel worksheet the data is to be exported from the following options:
    - **Static worksheet with records from this page**
    - **Static worksheet with records from all pages in the current view** (this option is not available in **Advanced Find View**)
    - **Dynamics PivotTable**
    - **Dynamics worksheet**

> If the **Static Worksheet** option has been selected then we can tick the **Mark this data available for re-importing by including required column headings** option as well. This option is useful when we intend to modify the exported data and want to re-import to Dynamics CRM 2011 later.

5. Finally click on the **Export** button to export and save the data.

How it works...

If the **Dynamic PivotTable** worksheet type is selected, we can specify which fields from the entity we want to export. By default, the fields used in the current view will be selected. But we can modify the column selection by clicking on the **Select Columns** button, which will be enabled once the **Dynamic PivotTable** option is selected. We need to use Microsoft Excel 2007 or higher versions to export a list to a PivotTable.

If the **Dynamic worksheet** option is selected, we can specify which fields from the entity we want to export. By default, the fields used in the current view will be selected. But we can modify the column selection by clicking on the **Edit Columns** button, which will be enabled once the **Dynamic worksheet** option is selected. In addition, we can also select the sorting order of the exported records.

If we only want to export the data displayed in the current page, select the **Static worksheet with records from this page** option and in case we intend to export all the records from the current view, then select **Static worksheet with records from all pages in the current view**. Data exported to static worksheets can be modified in Microsoft Excel and can be re-imported back into the Dynamics CRM 2011 system. If we intend to do this, we have to select the **Mark this data available for re-importing by including required column headings** option during export. But if we have selected this setting during data export, there are certain considerations for data modification before re-importing it:

- Deleting a row does not delete the corresponding record in Dynamics CRM 2011 after re-import
- We cannot modify or specify values for those fields that have a value **Not Valid for Update** such as the **Created By** field

- Value for `Full Name` attribute should be entered following the `Name Format` setting under **System Settings** of the Dynamics CRM 2011 system.
- The **Party List type** fields are not supported for data import.
- If the entity has more than one field with the same display name and the exported Excel worksheet contains one or more of these fields, this Excel cannot be re-imported.
- Field data cannot be modified or inserted if field-level security does not permit the logged-in user.

The **Money** field's value is exported to Microsoft Excel as numbers, not as currency. Such field values can be converted to currency using Microsoft Excel features.

There's more...

By default, Microsoft Dynamics CRM allows you to export a list of 10,000 records at a time to a **static** (a file that does not change when data changes in Microsoft Dynamics CRM Online) Excel worksheet. This limit can be increased by updating the `MaxRecordsForExportToExcel` attribute in organization database. This can be done by using the following CRM SDK call:

```
Organization organization = new Organization();
organization.Id = orgId; //GUID of the Organization
organization.MaxRecordsForExportToExcel = 50000; //Increases the limit
to 50,000
service.Update(organization);
```

This value is stored in the `MaxRecordsForExportToExcel` column in the `OrganizationBase` table of the `<OrganizationName>_MSCRM` database. But updating the value in the database directly is unsupported.

It is *not recommended* to update these settings to a very high value as this can peg the server resources.

Cleaning data using Bulk Deletion Wizard

Bulk record deletion is a very useful feature in Dynamics CRM 2011. Using this feature, unwanted or stale records can be deleted in bulk. In this recipe, we will delve into how to bulk delete records in Dynamics CRM 2011.

How to do it...

Please follow the ensuing steps to bulk delete data from Dynamics CRM 2011 system:

1. Log in to the Dynamics CRM 2011 system as a user having bulk delete permission.

2. Navigate to the entity (whose records have to be deleted) by clicking on the entity link in the navigation pane.
3. On the top ribbon, click on **Delete** and then select the **Bulk Delete** option.

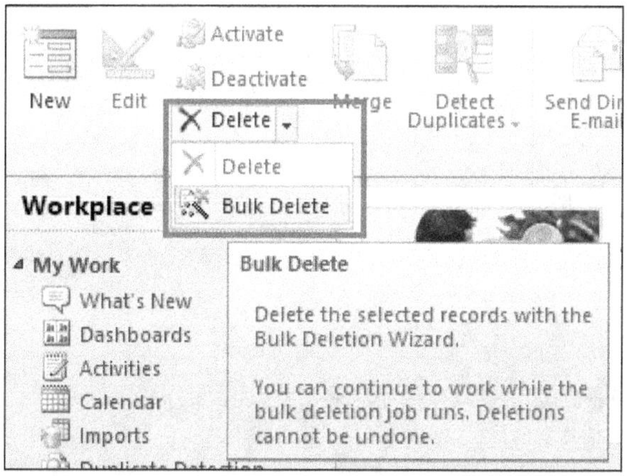

4. **Bulk Deletion Wizard** will pop-up. On the **Define Search Criteria** page, define the criteria based on which data has to be retrieved for bulk deletion.

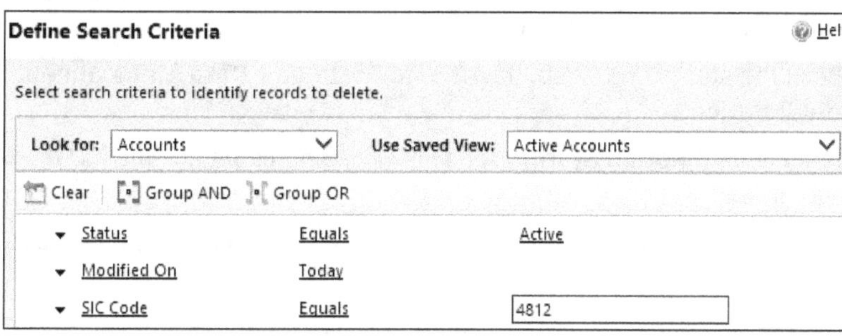

5. Post the search query formation, then click on the **Preview Records** button to preview the records satisfying the search criteria. If we want to modify the query criteria, we can click on **Back to Query** to modify the query and then once again preview the records to be deleted.
6. Thereafter, click on the **Next** button. The selected **Options** page appears. On this page, provide the following details:
    - **Name** is the name for the bulk deletion job
    - **Bulk deletion job start time** is the bulk deletion job start time
    - **Run this job after every** allows you to choose whether this job needs to occur once or on a recurring basis

- Option to have an e-mail sent to the current user as well as other users when the job is completed

7. Then click on the **Next** button. The **Review Bulk Deletion Details** page will appear. Click on **Submit** to submit the bulk deletion job.
8. To check the status of the job, navigate to **Settings** | **Data Management** | **Bulk Record Deletion**.
9. In the **All Bulk Deletion System Jobs** view, we should be able to find the bulk deletion job submitted.
10. Once the **Status Reason** of the job is displayed as **Succeeded**, the records are deleted from the system.
11. We can double-click and open the job details to find any failures during deletion.

How it works...

Microsoft Dynamics CRM 2011 provides bulk data deletion feature, which can be used to clean the following data to manage system storage and maintain data quality:

- Stale data
- Sample or test data
- Data incorrectly imported into the system

If a bulk delete job fails or ends prematurely, any records that were deleted before the failure or ending of the job will not be rolled back and remain deleted. Bulk delete job deletes the records according to cascading rules based on the relationships between entities in the Dynamics CRM 2011 system.

If a workflow or plug-in is configured to be triggered when an entity record is deleted, such workflows or plug-ins will trigger when the entity record is deleted by the bulk delete job.

Creating duplicate detection rules

In Microsoft Dynamics CRM 2011, duplicate detection allows us to set duplicate detection policies and detect duplicate records. These rules can be applied across different record types. For example, we can define a duplicate detection rule that a lead is a duplicate of a contact, if they have the same name and e-mail. Duplicate detection is possible only when duplicate detection rules exist in the system. To maintain data quality duplicate detection is very important for the Dynamics CRM 2011 system and in this recipe we will delve into creation steps of the duplicate detection rule.

How to do it...

Please follow the ensuing steps to create duplication detection rules in the Dynamics CRM 2011 system:

1. Log in to the Dynamics CRM 2011 system as a user having access rights to create duplicate detection rules.
2. Navigate to **Settings** | **System** | **Data Management** | **Duplication Detection Rules**.
3. Click on the **New** button in the **Actions** menu. The **Duplicate Detection Rule: New** page appears. Please provide the appropriate values for the **Name** and **Description** fields for the duplicate detection rule.

   Then we have to provide the value for **Duplicate Detection Rule Criteria**. Select the value **Base Record Type** (the entity to which this rule applies) and **Matching Record Type** (the entity records to which the base record type will be matched).

   If we do not want the duplicate detection rule to be applied to inactive records, check the **Exclude inactive matching records** box. Similarly check the **Case-sensitive** box if the rule needs to be case sensitive.

Finally, we have to define the duplicate detection rule. Check the **Ignore Blank Values** box if we do not want the rule to detect blank fields (null values) as equal while identifying duplicates.

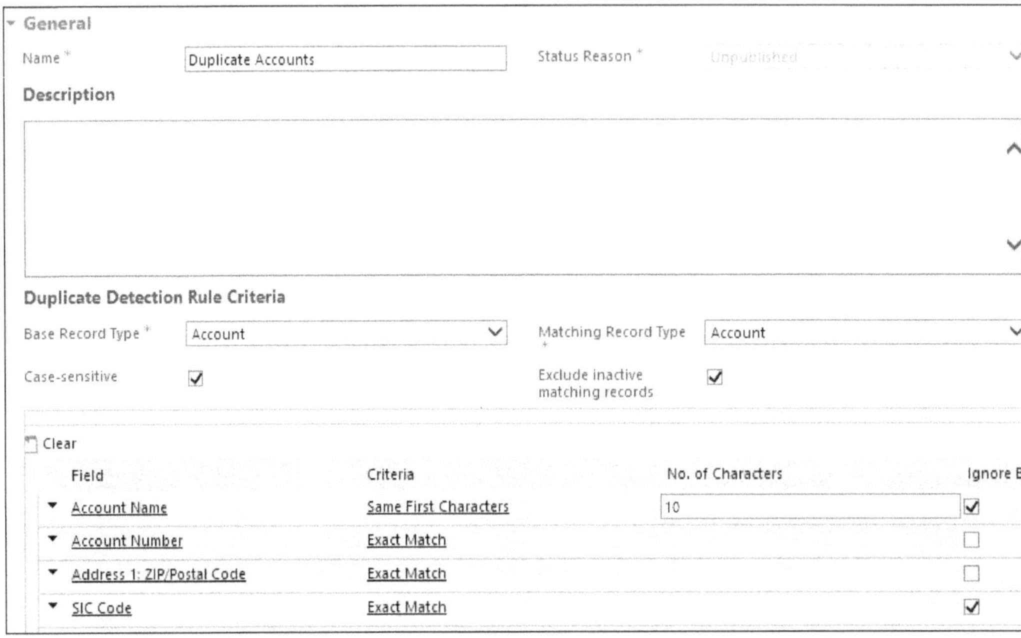

4. Then click on the **Save and Close** button in the top ribbon to save and close the duplicate detection rule.
5. Then in the **All Duplicate Detection Rules** view, select the duplicate detection rule created and click on **Publish** in the **Actions** menu.
6. In the **Publish Rule** web pop-up, click on the **OK** button. This activity will publish the duplicate detection rule created. The value for **Status Reason** of this rule will be updated to **Published**. This confirms that the duplicate detection rule is published in the system.

How it works...

Duplicate detection rules allow organizations to set duplicate detection policies for various entity records. Microsoft Dynamics CRM 2011 uses duplicate detection rules to determine whether a record is a potential duplicate or not. Duplicate detection rule can be created for an entity if the entity allows a duplicate detection rule to be set. To check this navigate to the entity's **General** settings page in the **Customizations** section and check whether **Duplicate detection** is selected or not.

> Multiple duplicate detection rules, with a maximum limit of five, can be created per base record type.

A duplicate detection rule will ignore null values, whether or not **Ignore Null Values** is selected, if the duplicate detection rule contains only one condition. That is, null values in the selected fields will not be considered equal during duplicate detection.

> A duplicate detection rule can have one or more conditions and these conditions are combined by the system in logical **AND** operation.

The number of criteria that we can select is limited by the number of characters that can be stored in the **matchcode** for the record. A matchcode is created for every record that a duplicate detection rule might apply to, used as part of the process of detecting duplicates. Check the **Current matchcode length** value shown at the bottom-left of the duplicate detection rule area.

> After the publishing of the duplicate detection rule, if we increase the length of the fields used in the duplicate detection rule, the matchcode goes undetected. The field length could exceed the matchcode length limit and not be verified. This may result in duplicates not being detected. Hence if the length of any field, which is used in duplicate detection criteria, needs to be increased, good practice is to **Unpublish** the duplicate detection rule and re-publish it again.

Two types of duplicate detection rules can be set up in Dynamics CRM 2011 system:

- **Single entity duplicate detection rule**: In this type, duplicate detection criteria are defined within a single entity. For example, account records are duplicates of each other if they have the same account name, post code, and SIC code.
- **Cross entity duplicate detection rule**: In this type, duplicate detection criteria are defined across two entities. For example, contact records are duplicate to lead records if they have the same first name, last name, post code, and e-mail address.

> If an entity's metadata changes, all duplicate detection rules associated with the entity will be automatically unpublished. Hence, every time there is a change in the entity metadata when a new solution is imported, we have to re-publish the duplicate detection rules for that entity.

Duplicate Detection Settings determine whether and when duplicates will be detected in the system. To set the system-wide duplicate detection settings, navigate to **Settings** | **System** | **Data Management** | **Duplicate Detection Settings**. Double-click to launch the **Duplicate Detection Settings** web pop-up. Here we can enable duplicate detection in the system and also decide when duplicates will be detected.

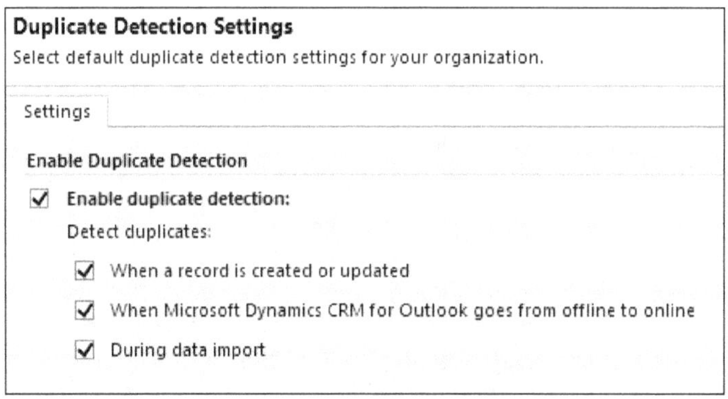

The following are the effective system-wide duplicate detection settings:

- **When a record is created or updated**: Duplicates will be detected if records are created or updated from the Dynamics CRM 2011 Web UI or Dynamics CRM 2011 for Outlook client. Dynamics CRM 2011 prompts the user before saving or importing potential duplicate records.

  Duplicates cannot be detected when a user merges two records, converts a lead, or saves activities as completed. Duplicate detection is also not available when the status of a record changes such as with activation and deactivation of a record.

- **When Microsoft Dynamics CRM for Outlook goes from offline to online**: Duplicates will be detected if Microsoft Dynamics CRM 2011 for Outlook is going from offline mode to online mode.
- **During data import**: Duplicates can be detected when data is imported using the Import Data Wizard.

However, if data is entered or modified using Dynamics CRM 2011 SDK, by default the Dynamics CRM 2011 system will not detect duplicates in the system. The duplicate detection rules have to be manually invoked using the following code:

```
// create operation by using duplicate detection
CreateRequest createRequest = new CreateRequest();
createRequest.Target = contact;

// Duplicate detection is activated.
createRequest.Parameters.Add("SuppressDuplicateDetection", false);

// Update operation by using duplicate detection
UpdateRequest updateRequest = new UpdateRequest();
updateRequest.Target = retrievedAccount;

// Duplicate detection is activated.
updateRequest["SuppressDuplicateDetection"] = false;
```

There's more...

As duplicate detection rules cannot be exported as part of the managed or unmanaged solution and even cannot be exported like data export, duplicate detection rules can only be migrated from one organization to another using manual creation activity or creating them programmatically using Dynamics CRM 2011 SDK.

If there are quite a large number of duplicate detection rules to be migrated from development to test to production environment, programmatic creation of a duplicate detection rule is a better alternative. With this approach, the rule creation can be repeated every time with new organizations with not much manual activity:

```
//Create Duplicate Detection Rule
DuplicateRule duplicateRule = new DuplicateRule();
duplicateRule.BaseEntityName = "account";
duplicateRule.MatchingEntityName = "account";
duplicateRule.Name = "Accounts having same Account Number";
duplicateRule.IsCaseSensitive = true;
duplicateRule.ExcludeInactiveRecords = true;

//Create Duplicate Rule Conditions
DuplicateRuleCondition duplicateRuleCondition = new
                    DuplicateRuleCondition();

duplicateRuleCondition.OperatorCode = new
 Microsoft.Xrm.Sdk.OptionSetValue(0);
duplicateRuleCondition.IgnoreBlankValues = true;
```

```
duplicateRuleCondition.BaseAttributeName = "accountnumber";
duplicateRuleCondition.MatchingAttributeName = "accountnumber";
DuplicateRuleCondition.OperatorParam = null;

DuplicateRuleCondition[] duplicateRuleConditions = new
DuplicateRuleCondition[] {duplicateRuleCondition };

//Create Duplicate Detection Rule with conditions in one go
TargetCompoundDuplicateRule target = new
                    TargetCompoundDuplicateRule();
target.DuplicateRule = duplicateRule;
target.DuplicateRuleConditions = duplicateRuleConditions;
CompoundCreateRequest request = new CompoundCreateRequest();
request.Target = target;
CompoundCreateResponse response = (CompoundCreateResponse)crmService.
Execute(request);
```

Scheduling duplicate detection jobs

In the previous recipe, we discussed how to create duplicate detection rules. After creating these rules, we can periodically detect duplicates in the system and take corrective action for maintaining data quality in the system. In this recipe, we will delve into the creation of periodic duplicate detection jobs in Dynamics CRM 2011 system.

How to do it...

Perform the following steps to configure duplicate detection jobs:

1. Log in to the Dynamics CRM 2011 system as a user having relevant permission.
2. Navigate to **Settings** | **System** | **Data Management** | **Duplicate Detection Jobs** or to **Workplace** | **My Work** | **Duplicate Detection**.
3. Click on the **New** button in the **Actions** menu.
4. The **Welcome to the Duplicate Detection Wizard** page will launch. Click on **Next** to proceed.
5. In the **Select Records** page, select the entity against which the duplicate detection job has to be configured from the **Look for** drop-down list. Entities against which duplicate detection rules are published will only be listed in the drop-down list. Then, select an existing view from the **Use Saved View** list or create an **Advanced Find View**. Then click on **Next** to proceed.

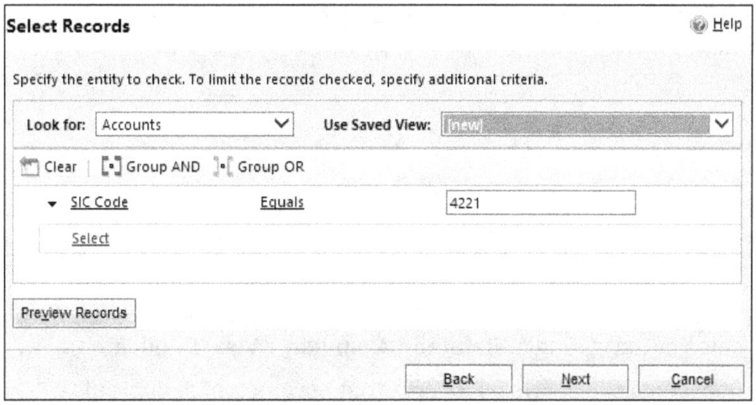

6. In the **Select Options** page, provide the following details and then click on **Next** to continue:
    - **Name** is the name for the duplicate detection job
    - **Start time** is the duplicate detection job start time
    - **Run this job after every** allows you to choose whether this job needs to occur one time or on a recurring basis
    - Option to have an e-mail sent to the current user as well as other users when the job is completed

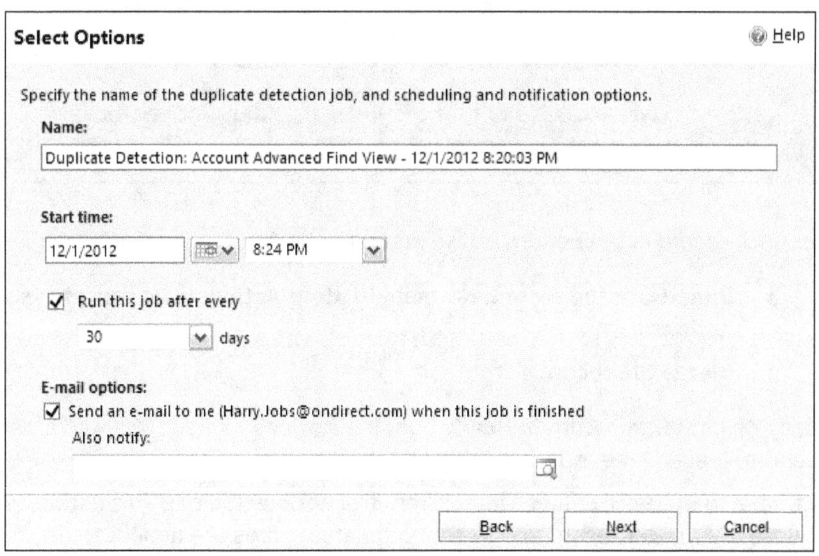

7. In the **Start Duplicate Detection Job** page, click on **Submit** to submit the job. This will also close the wizard.

8. Then we can find the duplicate detection job listed in the **My Duplicate Detection Jobs** view.

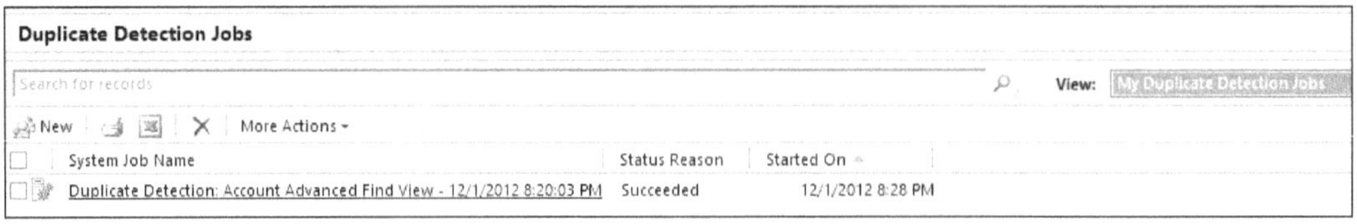

9. Double-click on the duplicate detection job to open the job details. We can find the duplicates by navigating to **Related** | **Common** | **View Duplicates** view.
10. The preceding list displays all records that have potential duplicates. When we select a record in the preceding list, the following list shows all the potential duplicates for that record.

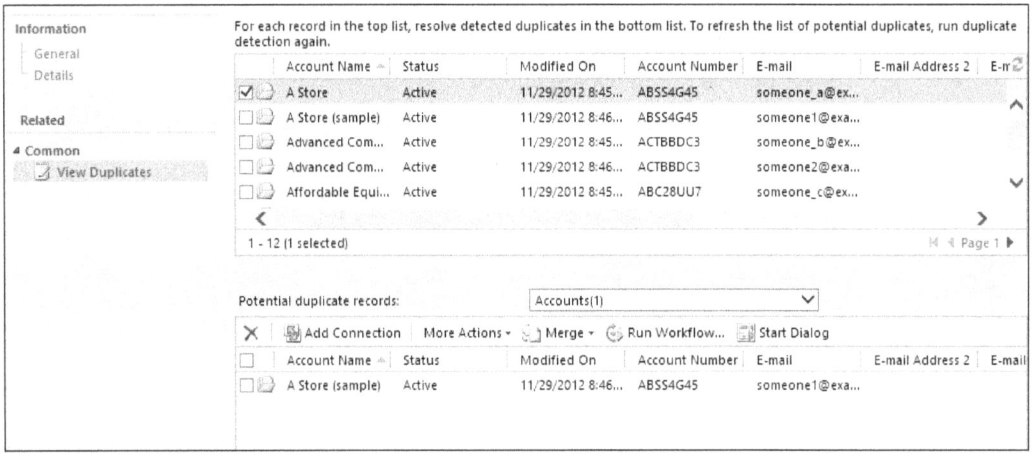

11. For each record in the bottom list we can take the following actions:
    - **Deactivate the record**: Navigate to **More Actions** | **Deactivate** from the **Actions** menu.
    - **Merge the record**:

Navigate to **Merge** | **Automatically** from the **Actions** toolbar. This will merge the records selecting the top record as Master record.

Navigate to **Merge** | **Select Master** from the **Actions** toolbar. This allows us to choose the master record and the subordinate records are deactivated.

- **Delete the record**: Select **Delete** from the **Actions** toolbar.

How it works...

Duplicate detection jobs can run periodically to identify duplicates in the system. Once potential duplicates are identified, the corrective actions such as de-activating the duplicate, merging the duplicate, or even deleting the duplicate can be taken.

Enabling auditing in the Dynamics CRM 2011 system

Auditing is a very important feature offered by Dynamics CRM 2011. Auditing helps administrators to figure how the system is being used. In this recipe, we will discuss how to enable auditing inside the Dynamics CRM 2011 system.

How to do it...

Perform the following steps to enable Global Audit settings:

1. Log in to the Dynamics CRM 2011 system as a user having rights to view audit summary.
2. Navigate to **Settings** | **System** | **Administration** | **System Settings** | **Audit**.

   Select the following options:

   - Select the **Start Auditing** checkbox to enable auditing at the system level
   - Select the **Audit user access** checkbox to start user access auditing. Auditing user access captures the following information only:

     When the user has logged in

     Where the access originated—from the Microsoft Dynamics CRM 2011 web application, Microsoft Dynamics CRM 2011 for Outlook, or SDK calls to the web services.
   - Select **Common Entities** to start auditing for common entities around Sales, Marketing, and Services module. These entities include Account, Contact, Lead, Product, Sales Literature, Marketing List, Quick Campaign, Goal, Goal Metric, and Rollup Query.
   - Select **Sales Entities** to start auditing for the Sales module-related entities. These entities include Opportunity, Order, Competitor, Quote, and Invoice.
   - Select **Marketing Entities** to start auditing for Marketing module-related entities. These entities include Campaign.

- Select **Customer Service Entities** to start auditing for Customer Service module-related entities. These entities include Case, Service, and Contract.

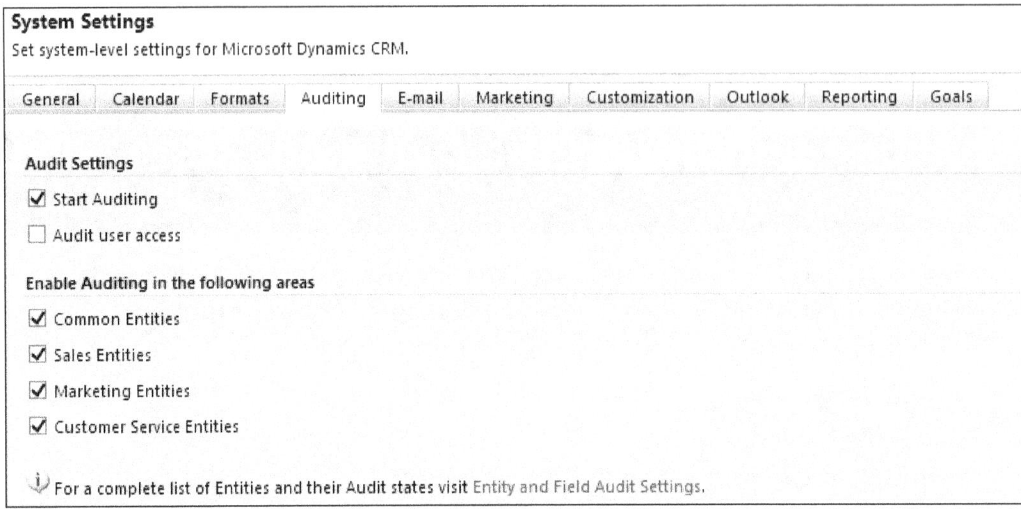

3. Then click on **OK** to save and close the settings.

After enabling auditing at the global level, the next step would be to enable auditing at entity and field level. Follow the next steps to enable entity- and field-level auditing:

1. Navigate to **Settings** | **System** | **Auditing** | **Entity and Field Level Settings**. This will bring up the Default Solution web dialog.

   Alternatively, we can select an unmanaged solution by navigating to **Settings** | **Customization** | **Solutions** and then double-clicking to open the specific solution web dialog.

2. Now extend the **Entities** section and then click on the entity for which auditing has to be enabled. Then select the **Auditing** option under the **Data Services** header.

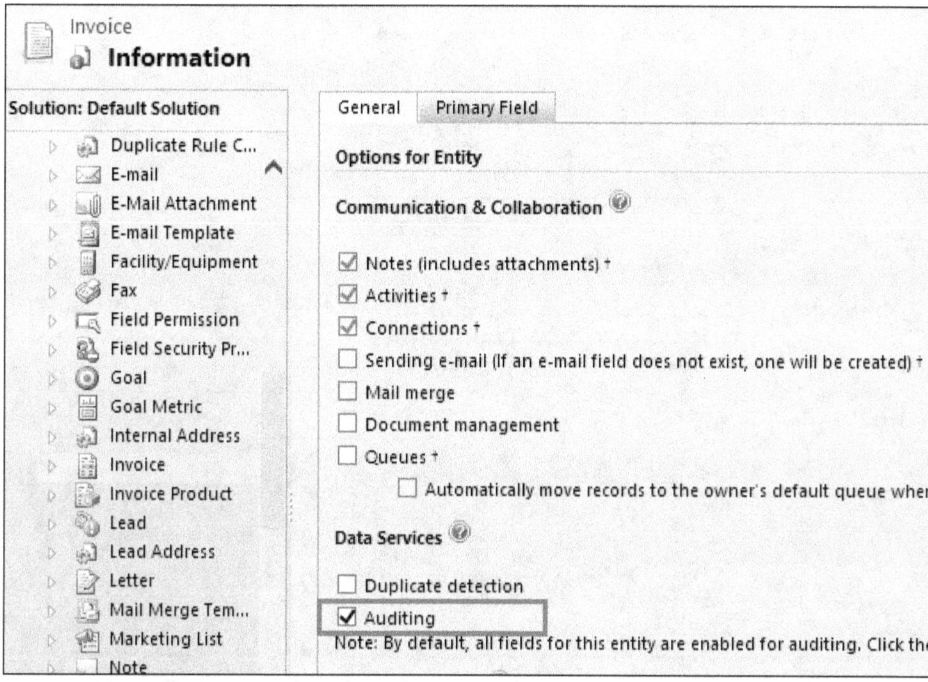

3. To enable field-level auditing, extend the **Entity** section and then select **Fields**. This will display all the fields of the entity. Then select the field against which auditing has to be enabled and double-click to open its properties.

4. Now select **Enable** against **Auditing** and then select **Save and Close** from the top to close the dialog.

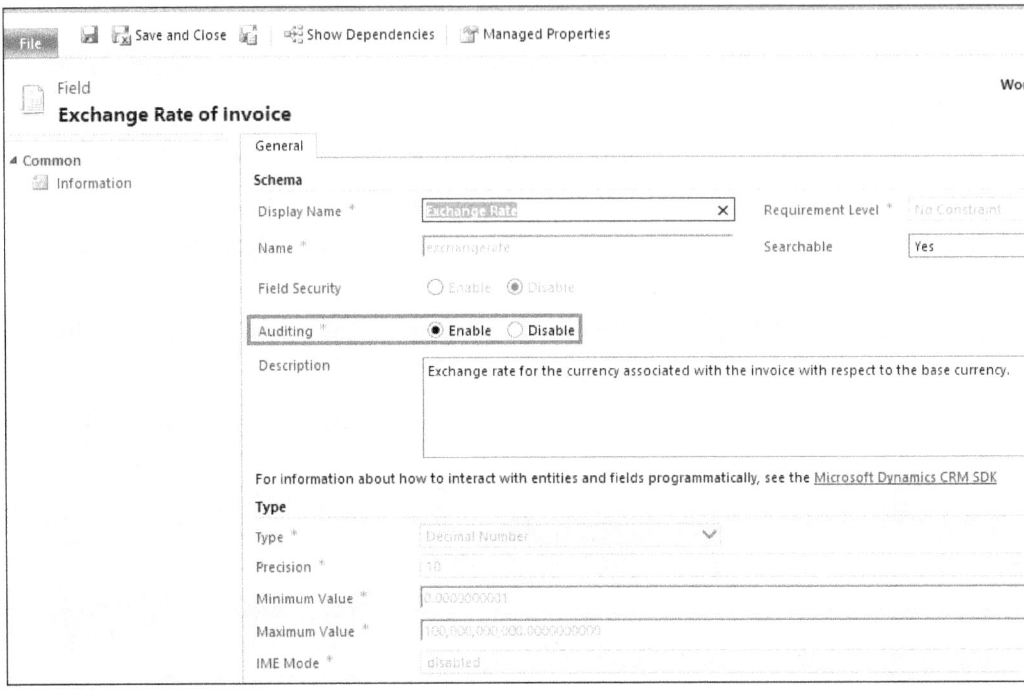

5. Finally publish the entity to publish the auditing changes. To publish the changes, click on the entity name again and then select the **Publish** button from the top menu.

How it works...

Microsoft Dynamics CRM 2011 supports an auditing capability where entity and attribute data changes within an organization can be recorded over time for use in analysis and reporting purposes. Auditing is supported on all custom and most customizable entities and attributes. The following actions cannot be audited:

- Read operations
- Metadata changes
- Text blobs, notes, and attachments
- Export to Excel operations
- Reporting
- Querying with Advanced Find
- Customization changes such as creating, modifying, or deleting Solution components

Auditing can be enabled at the organization, entity and attribute levels. If auditing is not enabled at the organization level, auditing of entities and attributes, even if it is enabled, does not occur. By default, auditing is enabled on all auditable entity attributes but is disabled at the entity and organization level. When turning on auditing for an entity, all fields are automatically set to be audited. This can affect performance during saving of a record as each field will need to be read and interpreted then saved to the database.

> The best practice is to enable auditing only for those fields the organization would like to audit. Limiting auditing to only the fields and entities that are needed will improve the performance and efficiency of the Microsoft Dynamics CRM 2011 system.

For a user to modify (enable or disable) organization level audit setting, the user must have the following access rights within Dynamics CRM 2011 system:

Audit settings Task	Required Privilege
Modify global auditing	Read and write access on Organization entity
Modify entity-level auditing	Read and write access on the entity
Modify user access auditing	Read and write access on Organization entity
View audit summary	**Audit Summary View** access
View audit history of entity records	Read access at entity level and View Audit History right
Manage audit logs	View Audit Partitions right and Delete Audit Partitions right

Global audit settings cannot be exported using a Dynamics CRM 2011 solution. Only entity and field-level audit settings can be exported via Dynamics CRM 2011 solution.

Viewing and cleaning audit records

After enabling auditing, Dynamics CRM 2011 will start auditing according to the settings. The next step will be to view and if necessary clean the audit log in the Dynamics CRM 2011 system. In this recipe, we will discuss how to perform these operations.

How to do it...

Perform the following steps to view audit summary records:

1. Log in to the Dynamics CRM 2011 system with system administrator or relevant security role.
2. Navigate to **Settings** | **System** | **Auditing** | **Audit Summary View**.
3. Auditing records can be viewed here. The records can be filtered using the **Enable/Disable Filters** option.

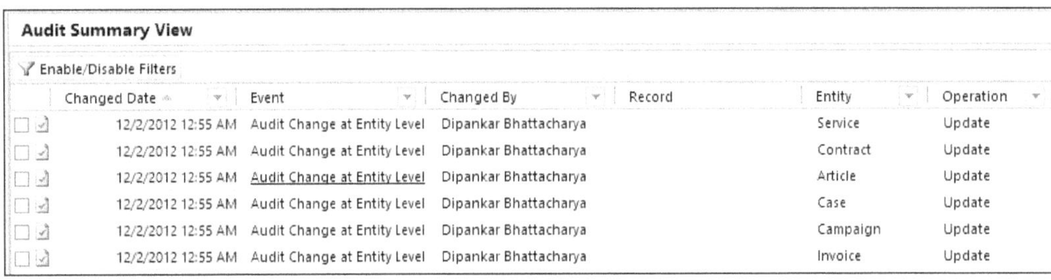

Perform the following steps to clean the Audit Summary logs:

1. Navigate to **Settings** | **Auditing** | **Audit Log Management**.
2. All the audit logs will be visible there.
3. To delete a specific audit log, select the audit log entry and then click on the **Delete Logs** option from the **Actions** menu.

How it works...

Audit Summary View displays the list of audit records. No Advanced Find or Workflow capability exists on Audit entity. Audit records also cannot be exported. No charts or views can be configured on audit records.

Once auditing is enabled, an audit log file is automatically created. This log file is created automatically by the Dynamics CRM 2011 system and is not configurable. This log gets created on a quarterly basis of the calendar year. The previous version of audit logs can be deleted. Once the audit log file is deleted, the audit history for the related record in that time period is no longer available.

Audit logs use disk space, hence clean audit logs periodically. The oldest audit log has to be deleted before deleting the latest one.

See also

In this chapter, we have discussed various recipes stating how data can be imported, exported, and managed within the Dynamics CRM 2011 system. In the next chapter, we will discuss Dynamics CRM 2011 solutions. Solutions are the first step in customization of the system. The following are some of the interesting recipes discussed in the next chapter:

- *Creating a solution publisher*
- *Creating an unmanaged solution*
- *Exporting and importing a solution*
- *Uninstalling or deleting a solution*
- *Exporting or importing Translations*

5
Solution Management

Dynamics CRM 2011 is a flexible system and offers the opportunity to customize the system to meet the business needs. Dynamics CRM 2011 introduced Solution Framework—a container to store multiple customizations in an easy-to-manage package. Solutions make it easy to store customizations and move them from one organization to another. It is important to understand the solution management within Dynamics CRM 2011 for those who want to customize and develop Dynamics CRM 2011-based business solutions. In this chapter, we will delve into the recipes of Solution Management.

The following recipes will be discussed in this chapter:

- Creating a solution publisher
- Creating a new unmanaged solution
- Adding an item in the unmanaged solution
- Removing/deleting an item from the unmanaged solution
- Exporting a solution
- Importing a solution
- Updating a managed solution
- Deleting components from a managed solution
- Uninstalling or deleting a solution
- Exporting translations from an unmanaged solution
- Importing translations to an unmanaged solution

Introduction to solution management

Solutions are the container where customizers and developers author and maintain customizations within a Dynamics CRM 2011 system. Solutions created in one organization can be moved to another organization without creating any installer. Solutions are created by using the customization tools or APIs included in Microsoft Dynamics CRM 2011 and are fully hosted in the application. The following table outlines what a solution can contain:

Schema	User Interface	Analytics
Entities	Ribbon	Dashboards
Attributes	SiteMap	Reports
Relationships	Forms	Visualizations
Global Option Sets	Web Resources	

Process	Templates	Security
Dialogs	Mail-Merge	Security Roles
Workflows	E-mail	Field level Security
Plugins	Contract	Profile
	Article	

Solutions are additive in nature. They can only add new components or override existing components, but cannot delete existing components.

If the customization also contains external components, which are not part of Microsoft Dynamics CRM 2011 solution components, we have to create a custom installer to install these components together.

There are two types of solutions as follows:

- **Unmanaged solution**: Similar to writing the source code of a program, unmanaged solution is the only choice during development. From an unmanaged solution, we can add, remove, and update any of the components of the solution. An unmanaged solution helps in a multiple developer scenario, as every developer can work on the same unmanaged solution and once the development completes, the complete solution can be exported as a managed solution.
- **Managed solution**: When our unmanaged solution is ready for deployment, we can export it as a managed solution. This is similar to compiled code. From managed solutions, we cannot add or remove components of the solution. We can only update those components of the managed solution that are not restricted for customization.

In contrast to unmanaged and managed solutions, a **default solution**, comprises out of the box customizations with the standard Microsoft Dynamics CRM 2011 software. Without any managed solutions or customizations, the system solution defines the default application behavior.

Each solution requires a **solution publisher**. One default publisher is created when a Dynamics CRM 2011 organization is created. The default solution is published using the default publisher. Any custom unmanaged or managed solution can be published using either this default publisher or any custom publisher.

Creating a solution publisher

It is a recommended practice to create custom solution publishers before creating any unmanaged or managed solution. This helps in identifying the solutions created by different solution publishers. In this recipe, we will discuss how to create a solution publisher in Dynamics CRM 2011.

How to do it...

Perform the following steps to create a solution publisher:

1. Log in to the Dynamics CRM 2011 system as system administrator or a user having customization access rights.
2. Navigate to **Settings** | **Customization** | **Customizations** | **Publishers**.
3. Click on **New** in the actions menu. Provide the following information on the **Publisher: New Information** page:

Settings	**Description**
General section	
Display Name	The name that needs to be displayed in the publisher lookup field in the solution.
Name	Dynamics CRM 2011 generated a unique name based on the Display Name value.
Description	Description and additional details about the publisher.
Prefix name for custom entities and fields	
Prefix	The customization prefix helps us identify which solution components are added by a solution created by this publisher. The prefix must be between two and eight characters long, and can contain only alphanumeric characters. It cannot start with "mscrm".

Settings	Description
Option Value Prefix	This value helps us to identify the option sets added by a solution created by this publisher. The value must be between 10,000 and 99,999
Contact details	
	Contact details of the publisher.

These settings are illustrated in the following screenshot:

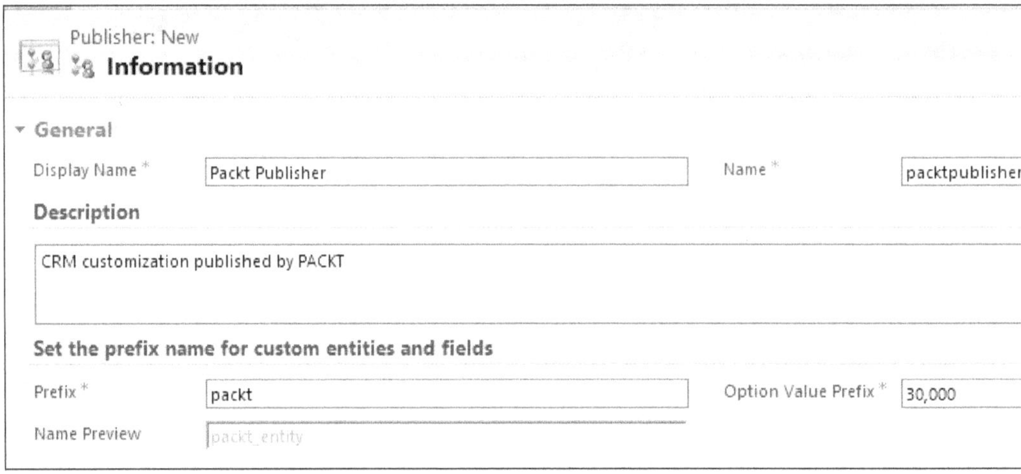

4. Then, click on the **Save and Close** button in the top ribbon to save and close the publisher information.

How it works...

Each solution requires a solution publisher. The unique **Name** field is used to uniquely identify the publishers. The solution publisher controls how managed solutions can be updated. Managed solutions that share the same publisher can update each other. Many solutions can be associated with a single solution publisher. Each organization will have a solution publisher called **Default Publisher for <OrganizationUniqueName>**. We can associate our solutions with the default publisher as well.

Creating a new unmanaged solution

After the creation of a new solution publisher, the next customization step is to create an unmanaged solution to contain the customizations. In this recipe, we will discuss how to create an unmanaged solution.

How to do it...

Perform the following steps to create an unmanaged solution:

1. Log in to the Dynamics CRM 2011 system as a system administrator or a user having customization access rights.
2. Navigate to **Settings** | **Customization** | **Solutions**.
3. Click on **New** in the actions menu.
4. The **Solution: New** page will pop up. Provide the following details on this page:

Settings	Description
Display Name	The name of the solution.
Name	Microsoft Dynamics CRM 2011 generates a unique name based on the **Display Name** value. We can edit this name, but the name can only contain alphanumeric characters and underscores.
Publisher	We can associate a publisher with the solution. Use the lookup button to search for a publisher.
Configuration Page	The solution configuration page provides a canvas that can be used to display information or enable customers to perform actions in the context of our solution. Set the configuration page by using the **Configuration Page** lookup field to select a web page (HTML) web resource included in the solution.
Version	Specify a version in the following format: `major.minor.build.revision`
Description	Add details about the solution.

These settings are illustrated in the following screenshot:

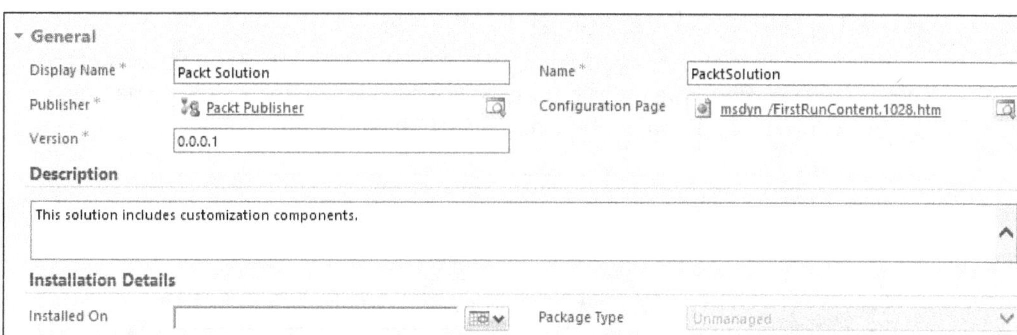

5. Then, click on the **Save and Close** button on the top ribbon to save and close the solution.

How it works...

An unmanaged solution is usually created for development purposes and not intended for distribution. However, this is not a rule, rather a practice. If we do not need a managed solution, then we may not need to create an unmanaged solution; customizations can be done in the default solution also. But when we have to export the solution to another organization, then we need to create an unmanaged solution. Managed solutions are also created from an unmanaged solution.

When a solution is unmanaged, we can perform the following actions:

- Add components
- Remove components
- Delete components that allow for deletion
- Export and import the unmanaged solution
- Export the solution as a managed solution

Adding an item in the unmanaged solution

After creating an unmanaged solution, the next logical step is to add customized items in the solution. In this recipe we will discuss how to add an item in the unmanaged solution.

How to do it...

Perform the following steps to add an item in the unmanaged solution:

1. Log in to the Dynamics CRM 2011 system as a system administrator or a user having customization access rights.
2. Navigate to **Settings** | **Customization** | **Solutions**.
3. Change the view to **Unmanaged Solutions** using the view selector. Then select the unmanaged solution from the list. Double-click on the solution name to open the solution contents as shown in the following screenshot:

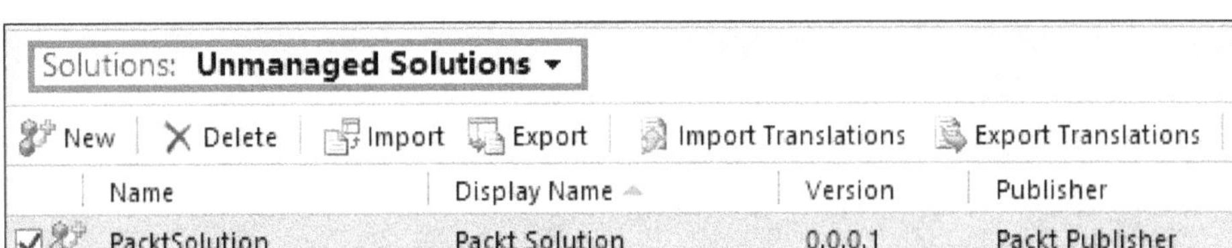

4. We can add the following types of items in the unmanaged solution:
    - **Entities**
    - **Option Sets**
    - **Client Extensions**
    - **Web Resources**
    - **Processes**
    - **Plug-in Assemblies**
    - **Sdk Message Processing Steps**
    - **Service Endpoints**
    - **Dashboards**
    - **Reports**
    - **Connection Roles**
    - **Article Templates**
    - **Contract Templates**
    - **Email Templates**
    - **Mail Merge Templates**
    - **Security Roles**
    - **Field Security Profiles**
5. To add any of the aforementioned components, click on the component name. For example, if we want to add an entity, click on the **Entities** component.
6. Thereafter, if we wish to add an existing component to the solution, click on **Add Existing** in the actions menu. If we wish to add a new component, click on **New** in the actions menu:

Only a few components allow to add existing items, for example, **Client Extensions** allows us to add existing **Ribbon** or **SiteMap** components. Similarly, **Plug-ins Assemblies** and **Sdk Message Processing Steps** also allow us only to add from the existing registered plugins.

7. After components are added, click on the **Save and Close** button in the top ribbon to save the changes and close the web pop up.

How it works...

An unmanaged solution allows us to add an existing or any new item in the solution. We can create multiple unmanaged solutions to store different components of the entire customization. For example, one unmanaged solution can contain only the plugin assemblies and SDK messaging steps; another can only contain the ribbon customization and the last one can contain other components of the overall customization.

Any component we add to the unmanaged solution is included in the customizable solution components for the system. Any unmanaged solution component can be added to multiple unmanaged solutions and changes made to any of these shared components in any unmanaged solution will also be applied to all other unmanaged solutions sharing the component.

When we add components to any unmanaged solution, we need to be careful about the exported size of the solution.

> For Microsoft Dynamics CRM 2011 Online, the maximum size of the solution is 29.296 MB whereas, for on-premises, the default maximum size is 6 MB. If our solution file's size is bigger than the specified size, we will not be able to import them in another organization.

The maximum size of the solution in an on-premises deployment can be increased by editing the `<httpRuntime>` element in the `web.config` file for the application. Edit the `executionTimeout` and `maxRequestLength` attributes to allow for the necessary size. After we finish installing the solution, we can reset it to the default size of 6 MB.

Removing/deleting an item from the unmanaged solution

During customization, we may want to exclude a few customizations from our unmanaged solution after we have added them. In this recipe, we will discuss how to remove or delete an item from the unmanaged solution.

How to do it...

Perform the following steps to remove/delete an item from the unmanaged solution:

1. Log in to the Dynamics CRM 2011 system as a system administrator or a user having customization access rights.
2. Navigate to **Settings** | **Customization** | **Solutions**.

3. Change the view to **Unmanaged Solutions** using the view selector. Then select the unmanaged solution from the list. Double-click on the solution name to open the solution contents as shown in the following screenshot:

4. In the **Unmanaged Solutions** view, select the component type of the item to be removed/deleted. Then navigate to the item we want to remove/delete.

   For example, if we want to delete a custom workflow from the solution, we first have to navigate to **Processes** and then select the workflow to be removed/deleted. For items of the **Processes** (Workflows and Dialogs) and **Sdk Message Processing Type** (Plug-in Steps) type, if the item is in activate mode then we need to deactivate it before we can delete the item. For removing any item from the solution, there is no need to deactivate any active item:

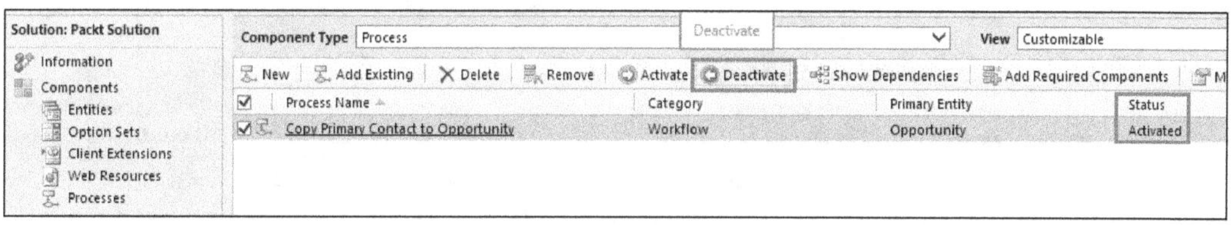

   To remove an item from the solution, select the item and then click on **Remove** in the actions menu. To delete an item, select the item and then click on **Delete** in the actions menu.

5. Once the item is successfully removed/deleted, click on **Save and Close** in the top ribbon. This will save the changes and close the page.

How it works...

An unmanaged solution allows us to remove and delete components from it. But there is a big difference between these two actions. The remove action only removes the item from the current unmanaged solution. If this item is included in any other unmanaged solution, it does not get automatically removed from that solution.

The delete action deletes the item from the system itself. Hence, this item would be deleted from all the solutions. The delete option is required to be exercised with utmost care. The delete action cannot be undone. If any item is accidentally deleted, we have to re-create it.

Hence, we should use "remove" instead of "delete" if we just want to remove a solution component from an unmanaged solution.

Exporting a solution

After making the customization, the customizations within an unmanaged solution are required to be exported from the environment so that they can be applied in other environments. In this recipe, we will discuss how to export a solution from the Dynamics CRM 2011 system.

How to do it...

Perform the following steps to export a solution:

1. Log in to the Dynamics CRM 2011 system as a system administrator or a user having customization access rights.
2. Navigate to **Settings** | **Customization** | **Solutions**.
3. Change the view to **Unmanaged Solutions** using the view selector. Then select the unmanaged solution from the list as shown in the following screenshot:

4. Then click on **Export** on the actions menu. The **Export Solution** web dialog will pop up.
5. On the **Publish Customizations** page, click on **Publish All Customizations** in case all the customizations of this unmanaged solution have not been published in the current organization. Otherwise, we can directly click on the **Next** button to proceed as shown in the following screenshot:

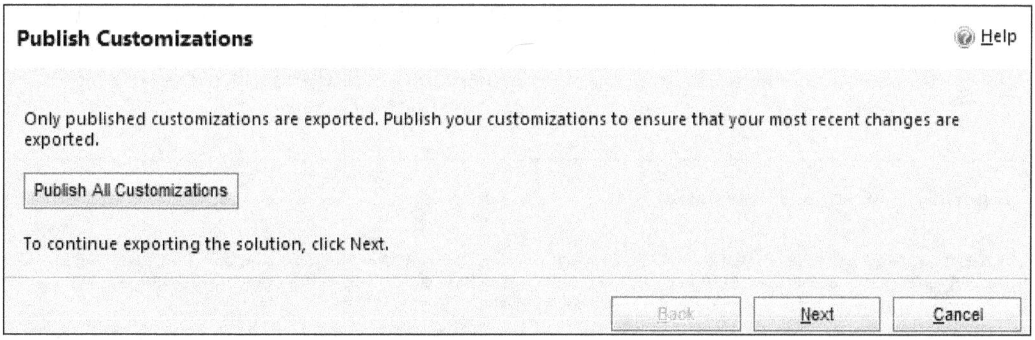

6. If there are any required components that are missing in the unmanaged solution, the **Missing Required Components** page appears.

   This page will list a set of components on which the components included in the current solution are linked. If we know that these required missing components will be present in the target organization where the exported solution will be imported, we can skip adding these components in the solution. But if any one of the required components is found to be missing in the target organization, the import of the exported solution will fail.

   If some/all of the missing required components have to be added to this unmanaged solution, click on the **Cancel** button to cancel the export activity. Edit the solution to add these required components and then restart the export activity as mentioned in this recipe.

   Otherwise, click on the **Next** button to proceed.

7. Next, you will see that the **Export System Settings (Advanced)** page appears. We can include any of the listed system settings from this environment to be exported with this solution, which will be applied on the organization where this exported solution will be imported. After the selection, click on **Next** to proceed:

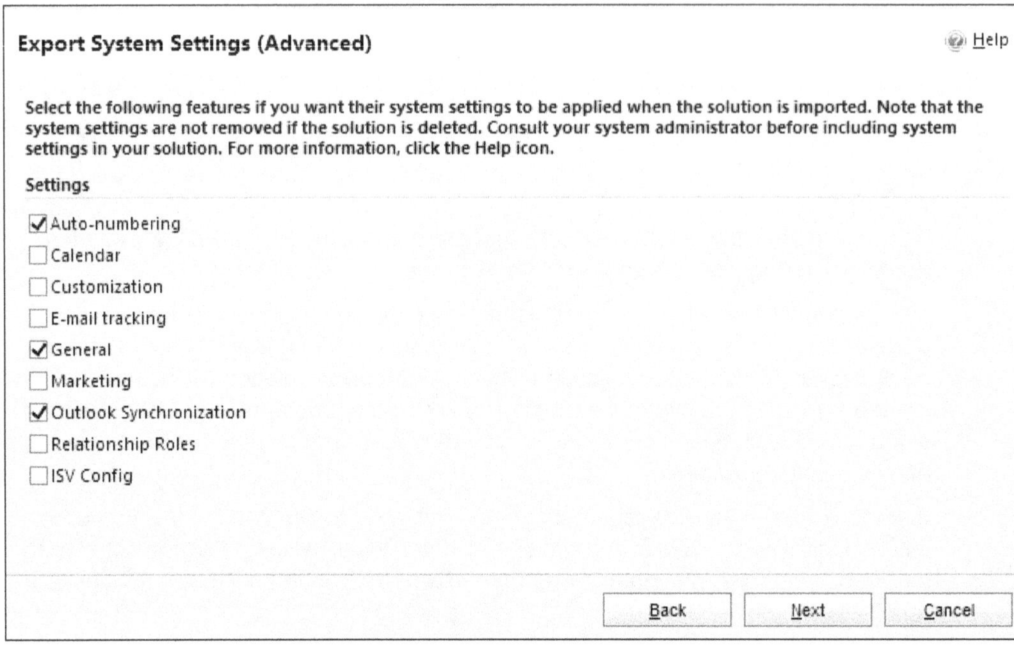

8. Then, the **Package Type** page appears. In this page, we have to decide whether we want to export this unmanaged solution as an unmanaged or managed solution. Once the selection is done, click on the **Export** button to export the solution as shown in the following screenshot:

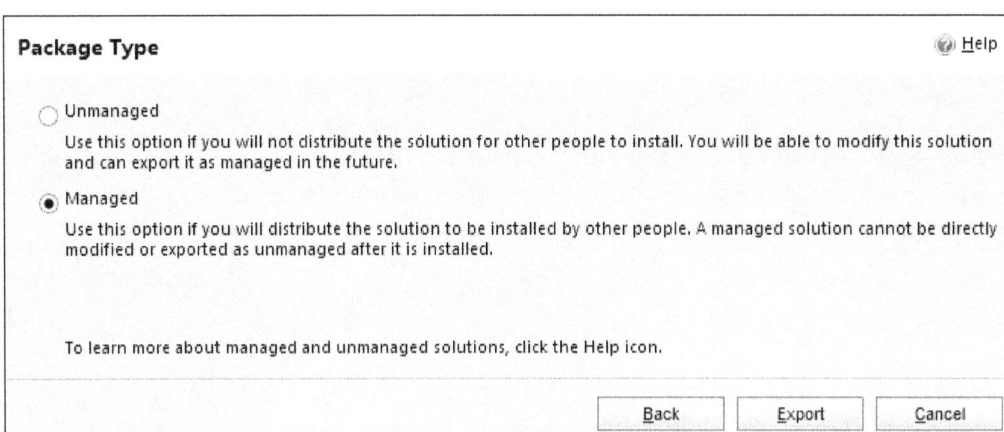

9. Thereafter, a file download prompt will appear. Click on **Save/Save As** to save the file in the disk; we can rename the solution file before saving. The solution file can even be renamed after saving it to the disk.

How it works...

Only an unmanaged solution can be exported. An unmanaged solution can be exported as an unmanaged or managed solution. The exported solution can then be imported into another organization. This is how customizations are migrated from the development organization to the test or production systems. Managed solutions, however, cannot be exported.

Importing a solution

It is necessary to apply exported customizations to another environment by importing them. In this recipe, we will discuss how to import a solution with Dynamics CRM 2011 system.

How to do it...

Perform the following steps to import a solution:

1. Log in to the Dynamics CRM 2011 system as a system administrator or a user having customization access rights.
2. Navigate to **Settings** | **Customization** | **Solutions**.
3. Click on the **Import** button to import a solution.
4. The **Import Solution** web dialog will pop up. On the **Select Solution Package** page, click on the **Browse** button to browse the solution file from the disk. Then click on **Next** to proceed:

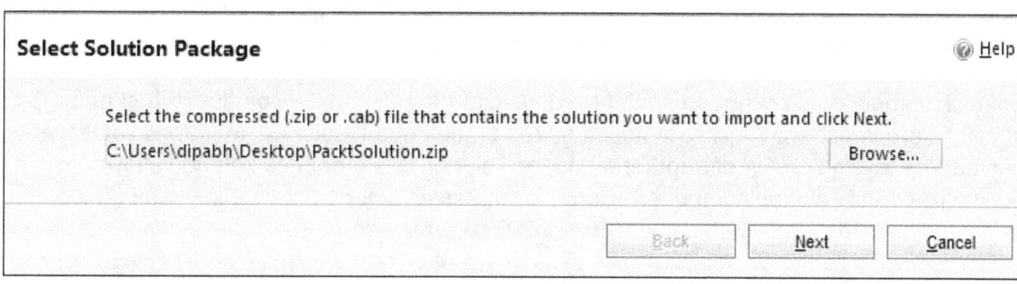

5. Next, the **Solution Information** page will appear. Click on **Next** to proceed.

6. If there are any process type components (workflows or dialogs) or plugins existing in the solution, the **Import Options** page will appear. Here, tick the **Activate any processes and enable any SDK message processing steps included in the solution** checkbox if you want to activate the processes or SDK message processing steps automatically by this import process.
7. Then click on **Next** to proceed:

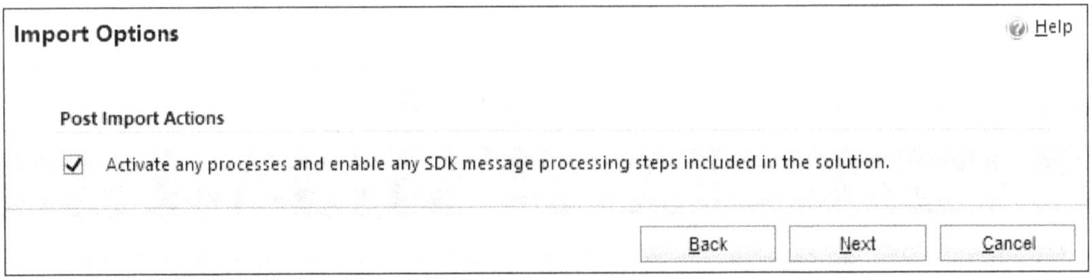

8. Then the solution import will begin. Once the import successfully completes, click on **Close** to close the **Import** dialog.
9. If an error occurs during the import, then we can click on **Download Log File** to download the solution import log file to find more about the error.

How it works...

The solution import will fail if all the required components are either not included in the solution or they do not exist in the target organization. When managed solutions are imported, all the required components should be of the managed type only. A component in a managed solution can only depend on another managed component.

We cannot import a managed solution into the Dynamics CRM 2011 organization that contains the unmanaged solution, which was used to create the managed solution. Managed solutions can only be installed in a different organization from the one it was generated.

Solution components cannot be added or removed from a managed solution. When managed solutions are imported, they are installed on top of the default solution. Managed solutions can also be layered on top of another managed solution. If a managed solution allows for customization of solution components, another managed solution can be installed on top of it that can also modify the customizable solution components.

When two or more solutions define a single component differently, Microsoft Dynamics CRM 2011 has to solve the conflict and it uses two strategies to resolve conflicts: **merge** and **top wins**. The conflict resolution mechanism stack ranks the layers created by the solutions imported within the organization. All unmanaged solutions are at the same layer. Hence, any unmanaged customization carried out in the system will only override the existing one. But managed solutions have the capability of keeping separate layers within the system. Conflicts involving managed solutions are resolved using the merge and top wins strategy. Managed solutions can be cleanly uninstalled because they maintain separate layers. If a managed solution is uninstalled, the system falls back to the other managed solutions installed in the organization.

Versioning of managed solutions is built-in and a managed solution having the same name but different version numbers is considered to be two different solution layers within the system.

- **Merge**: The UI elements such as Ribbon, Forms, and SiteMap are merged, which means that the solution component would be recalculated from the lowest (oldest) to the highest (newest) so that the organization's unmanaged customization are the last to be applied. The following diagram will clarify the merge stack:

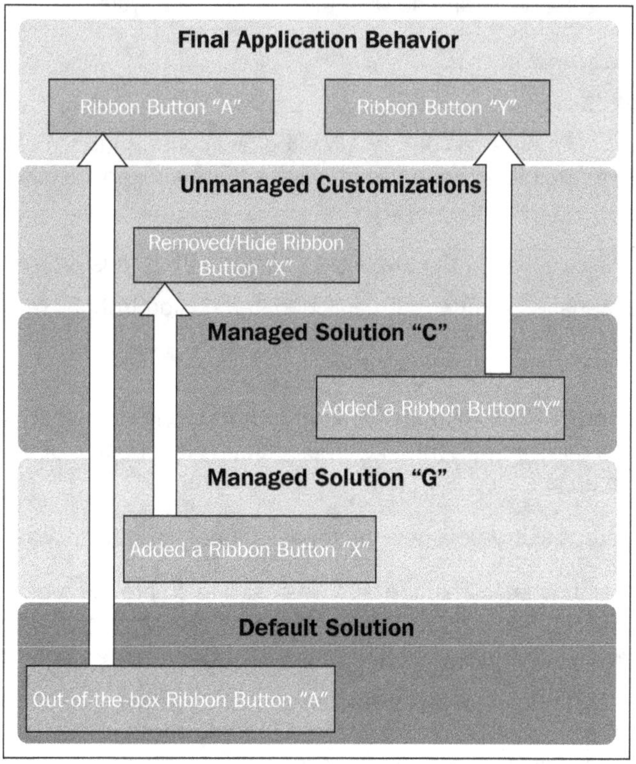

- **Top wins**: For any other solution components, the last managed solution installed wins. However, any unmanaged customizations is considered "above" any managed solutions while resolving conflicts. Hence, sometimes changes applied to a managed solution may not be visible because of unmanaged customizations. When conflicts are detected while importing any managed solution with an existing unmanaged customization, the Dynamics CRM 2011 system provides us with the following options:
    - **Maintain customizations** (recommended): This option makes sure that the unmanaged customizations prevail.
    - **Overwrite customizations**: This option makes sure that any unmanaged customization performed earlier in the solution are overwritten by the current solution components.

Updating a managed solution

Usually it is a very common requirement to update customizations of an already installed managed solution in an organization. In this recipe, we will delve into the steps of updating a managed solution within the Dynamics CRM 2011 system.

How to do it...

Managed solution components can only be updated by another managed solution from the same publisher. There are two approaches to update the managed customizations by another managed solution:

- Release a new version of the managed solution with all customizations (a full release)
- Release a managed solution with only updated customizations (a delta release)

In this recipe, we will discuss both the approaches.

A **full release** will contain all the updated customizations along with other non-edited customizations. A full release will contain all the solution components of the managed solution it intends to update plus any additional component.

Follow the ensuing steps to create a new managed solution for a full release:

1. Update the unmanaged solution that was used to create the previous version of the managed solution, with an incremental version number. Navigate to **Settings** | **Customization** | **Solutions section and select Unmanaged Solutions**.
2. Double-click on the unmanaged solution to open it. Then click on the **Information** section of the unmanaged solution. Once the **Information** page appears, update the **Version** number as shown in the following screenshot:

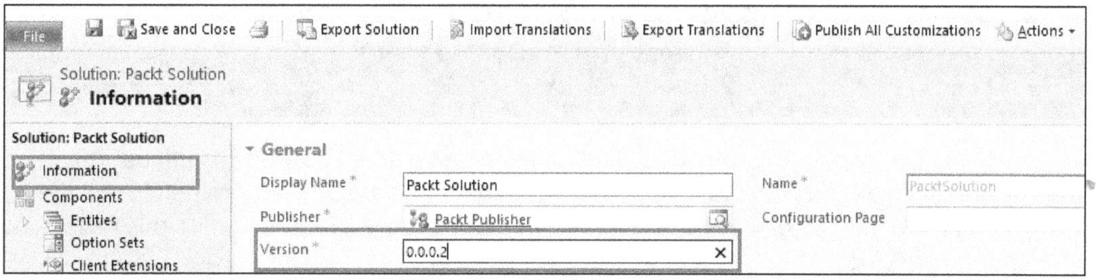

3. Next, click on the save icon [ ] in the top ribbon to save the changes.
4. Thereafter, make the necessary updates of the solution components.
5. Once the updates are completed, export the solution as a managed solution following the *Exporting a solution* recipe in this chapter.

A **delta release** will contain only the updated customizations of the managed solution previously installed.

Perform the following steps to create a delta release:

1. Create a new unmanaged solution by following the *Creating a new unmanaged solution* recipe in this chapter. Select the same publisher as that of the managed solution to be updated and use an incremental version number.
2. Thereafter, make the necessary updates of the solution components.
3. Once the updates are completed, export the solution as a managed solution following the *Exporting a solution* recipe.

How it works...

When we have to release an update to a managed solution, the preferred method is to provide a full release. Then the new managed solution of the full release will be installed in the organization, and the customizations will be upgraded to include the new changes. In case any conflicts arise, they will be resolved using either the merge or top wins strategy as discussed in the *Importing a solution* recipe. If we want to go back to the earlier version of the solution, we just have to reinstall the previous version of the managed solution. This overwrites any solution components with definitions from the previous version, but does not remove solution components added in the newer version. Those newer solution components remain in the system but have no effect because the older solution component definitions will not use them.

When a small subset of the customizations is updated, a delta release would be preferred. When the update solution is installed in an organization where the original solution was installed, the changes included in the update will be applied to the organization. If an organization needs to "roll back" to the original version, it can simply uninstall the update.

Deleting components from a managed solution

A customized component of a managed solution cannot be deleted by any solutions. The only way to remove customizable components from a managed solution is to delete solution components of a managed solution using the **Customize the System** option. In this recipe we will discuss how to do it.

How to do it...

Perform the following steps to customize managed solution components:

1. Log in to the Dynamics CRM 2011 system as a system administrator or a user having customization access rights.
2. Navigate to **Settings** | **Customization** | **Customizations** | **Customize the System**.
3. This will launch the default solution of the organization.
4. We can navigate to any solution component. The default solution will allow us to customize any customizable component in the system.
5. Once the customizations are done, click on the save icon [ ] on the top ribbon.
6. Thereafter, click on the **Publish All Customizations** button on the top ribbon.
7. Finally, click on the **Save and Close** button on the top ribbon to close the page.

How it works

Using managed properties, the creator of a managed solution can decide if a solution component is customizable and if yes, which specific parts of it can be customized. Managed properties can be set in the unmanaged solution. Once the customization is packaged as a managed solution, managed properties settings will take effect. The exact managed properties available depend on the type of solution component.

The following screenshot displays the managed properties of the **Account** entity:

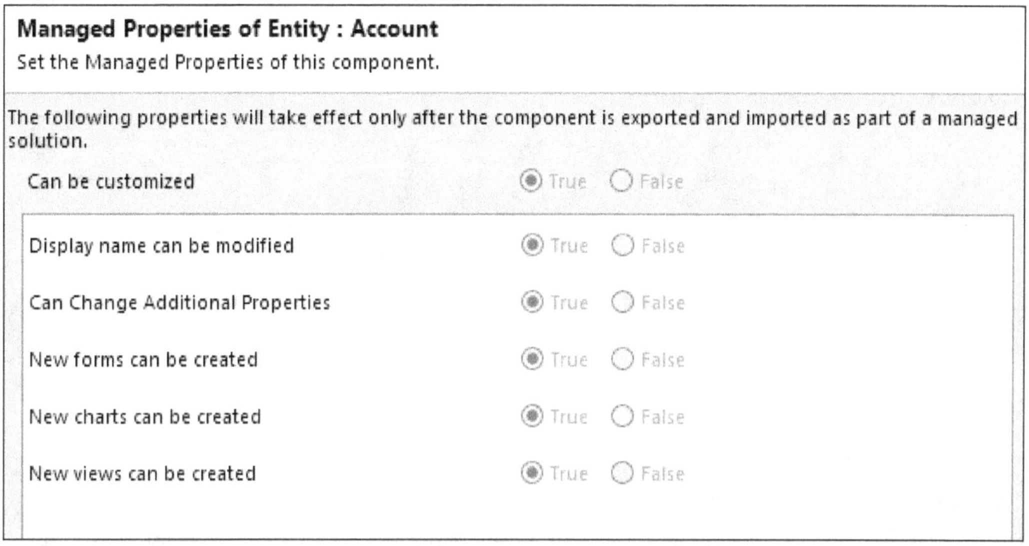

Managed solution components cannot be deleted from any organization, they can only be customized if the managed properties permit. If we intend to delete a component from a managed solution, we need to uninstall the entire solution and reinstall a new version of the managed solution without that solution component. But customizable managed components can be deleted using this recipe.

Uninstalling or deleting a solution

After importing a solution, at times we may want to uninstall or delete it from the environment. Though both managed and unmanaged solutions support different behavior, both these solution types can be uninstalled or deleted post the import. In this recipe, we will discuss how to do this within the Dynamics CRM 2011 system.

How to do it...

Perform the following steps to uninstall or delete a solution:

1. Log in to the Dynamics CRM 2011 system as a system administrator or a user having customization access rights.
2. Navigate to **Settings** | **Customization** | **Solutions**.
3. Select the solution to be deleted from the list.
4. Next, click on the **Delete** button in the actions menu.

5. The **Confirm Deletion** page will appear. On this page, click on **OK** to uninstall or delete the solution as shown in the following screenshot:

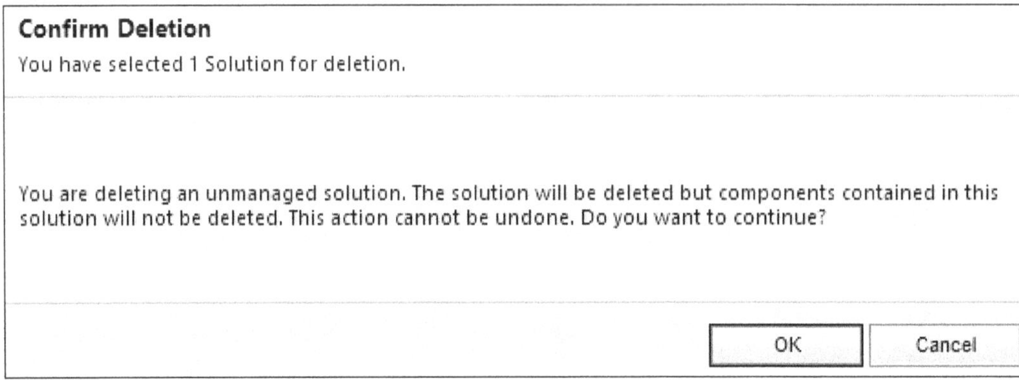

How it works...

Uninstallation/deletion of managed and unmanaged solutions has a different effect on the Dynamics CRM 2011 system.

When an unmanaged solution is deleted it just deletes the solution container but does not delete the solution components the unmanaged solution contained. The solution components remain in the system, but are no longer associated with the unmanaged solution. Hence, unmanaged solution uninstallation actually uninstalls nothing from the system.

Deleting or uninstalling a managed solution will uninstall all the solution components within it.

Exporting translations from an unmanaged solution

Translations are XML documents that define the display names and descriptions for entities, fields, navigation items, and so on, for a solution. Translations can be exported, modified, and reimported into Dynamics CRM 2011 to support localization. In this recipe, we will discuss how to export translations from an unmanaged solution.

How to do it...

Perform the following steps to export the translations from a solution:

1. Log in to the Dynamics CRM 2011 system as a system administrator or a user having customization access rights.
2. Navigate to **Settings** | **Customization** | **Unmanaged Solutions**.

3. Select the solution from the list.
4. Next, click on the **Export Translations** button in the actions menu:

5. When prompted, save the translation file to the disk.
6. After saving the translation file, we can edit the translations outside the Dynamics CRM 2011 environment. Extract the ZIP file and open the `CrmTranslations.xml` file in Microsoft Excel.
7. Once the editing is complete, again zip the contents into a translation ZIP file.

How it works...

Translations can only be exported from unmanaged solutions. Managed solutions do not allow to export or import translations.

Translations help us in modifying system messages and text literals. We usually change the translations in a multilanguage deployment. A translation file contains translated text for all types of text displayed within the system against the language code. For English, the language code is 1033.

The following screenshot is a sample of translation file contents when opened using Microsoft Excel:

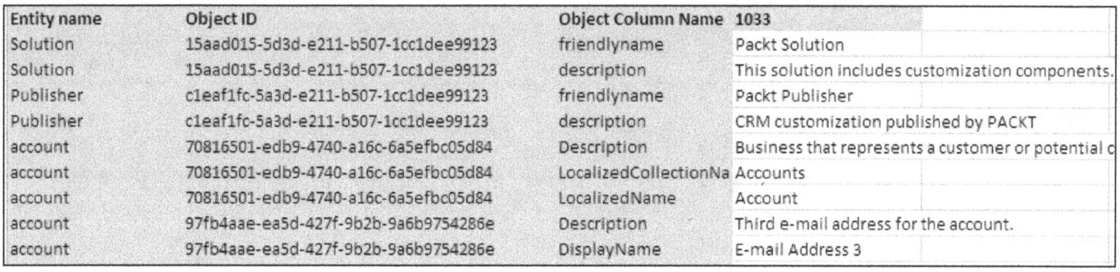

Entity name	Object ID	Object Column Name	1033
Solution	15aad015-5d3d-e211-b507-1cc1dee99123	friendlyname	Packt Solution
Solution	15aad015-5d3d-e211-b507-1cc1dee99123	description	This solution includes customization components.
Publisher	c1eaf1fc-5a3d-e211-b507-1cc1dee99123	friendlyname	Packt Publisher
Publisher	c1eaf1fc-5a3d-e211-b507-1cc1dee99123	description	CRM customization published by PACKT
account	70816501-edb9-4740-a16c-6a5efbc05d84	Description	Business that represents a customer or potential c
account	70816501-edb9-4740-a16c-6a5efbc05d84	LocalizedCollectionNa	Accounts
account	70816501-edb9-4740-a16c-6a5efbc05d84	LocalizedName	Account
account	97fb4aae-ea5d-427f-9b2b-9a6b9754286e	Description	Third e-mail address for the account.
account	97fb4aae-ea5d-427f-9b2b-9a6b9754286e	DisplayName	E-mail Address 3

We are allowed to modify only the language columns of the file (in the preceding screenshot, texts under the 1033 column only). If we modify the schema columns, the import of the translations will fail.

Importing translations to an unmanaged solution

Translations are usually exported for making any change to the entity labels, navigation text, and so on. Post modifications, the translations will be imported back to an environment. In this recipe, we will discuss how to import translations into an unmanaged solution.

How to do it...

Perform the following steps to export the translations from a solution:

1. Log in to the Dynamics CRM 2011 system as a system administrator or a user having customization access rights.
2. Navigate to **Settings** | **Customization** | **Solutions**.
3. Select the solution from the list.
4. Next, click on the **Import Translations** button in the actions menu as shown in the following screenshot:

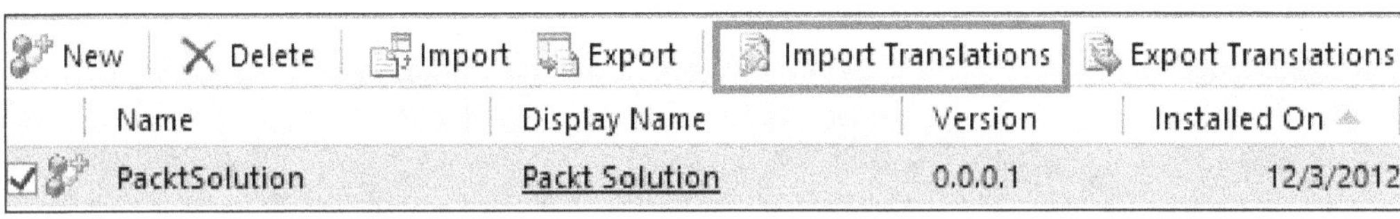

5. The **Import Translated Text** web dialog will appear. Use the **Browse** button to browse the translations file to be imported in the disk. Then, click on the **Import** button to import the translations to the solution.

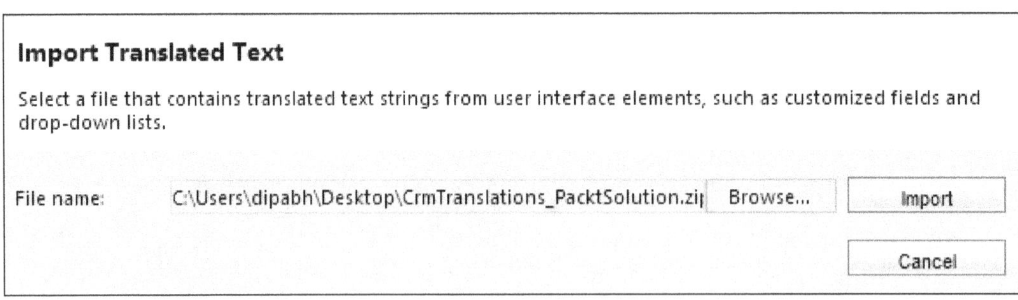

6. Next, you will see the **Translations successfully imported** message. Click on the **Close** button to complete the import:

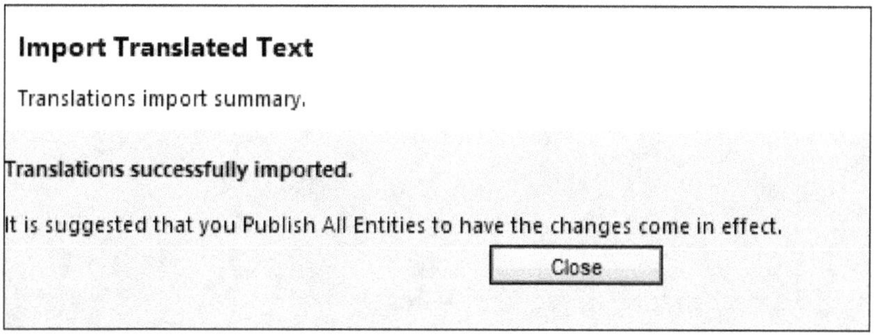

How it works...

We can modify the translations outside the Dynamics CRM 2011 environment using editing tools such as Microsoft Excel and then the modified translations file can be imported into an unmanaged solution. Managed solutions are locked down and do not allow modification of the translation files.

See also

In this chapter, we have discussed solution management in Dynamics CRM 2011. In the next chapter, we would explore entity customization in detail. A few important recipes in the next chapter will be as follows:

- Creating a custom entity
- Creating a new attribute for an entity
- Creating a new one-to-many (1:N) or many-to-one (N:1) relationship
- Creating a new many-to-many (N:N) relationship
- Creating a global option set

6
Entity Customizations

Entities constitute the core of the Dynamics CRM 2011 system. Entities are used to model and manage the business data. Dynamics CRM 2011 provides a set of entities to store data related to sales, marketing, and services functions. These existing entities can be customized and we can also create new entities in the system to support the business process. In this chapter, we will discuss the recipes for creating a new entity and customizing existing entities. In addition, we will also discuss the relationship behavior between two entities. The following recipes will be covered in this chapter:

- Creating a custom entity
- Updating the icon of an entity
- Creating a custom field for an entity
- Creating a global option set
- Creating a new one-to-many (1:N) or many-to-one (N:1) relationship
- Creating a new many-to-many (N:N) relationship
- Customizing a relationship field mapping

Introduction to entities

Entities are basic building blocks of the Dynamics CRM 2011 system. Entities contain data, form, views, relationships, and charts, which are associated with presenting information to users. There are three main types of entities inside the Dynamics CRM 2011 system: system entities, business entities, and custom entities.

- **System entities**: Entities that are used internally by the Dynamics CRM 2011 system are known as system entities. For example, workflows, system jobs, solutions, and so on. are system entities. System entities cannot be customized or deleted.

- **Business entities**: Business entities are entities other than system entities present after the installation of Dynamics CRM. Business entities store business data for the sales, marketing, and services modules. Account, Contact, Lead, Opportunity, Campaign, and Case are a few examples of business entities. Business entities can be customized but cannot be deleted.
- **Custom entities**: After the installation of Dynamics CRM, we can create additional custom entities to fulfill the needs of the business process. Custom entities can be deleted as well. Custom entities can be marked as either "customizable" or "noncustomizable" during publishing. Noncustomizable entities cannot be customized in future.

Entities are similar to tables in any relational database and entity attributes are like columns in that table. But within the Dynamics CRM system, entity data are not necessarily stored in one database table.

There are two specific types of business entities, which are worth a mention here:

- **Customer**: This is a composite entity and comprises Account and Contact. In Dynamics CRM 2011, an account represents a business or company and a contact usually represents an individual. Both Account and Contact manage a customer.
- **Activity**: This is a special type of business entity. These types of entities represent any activity or task that is performed or needs to be performed. Activity type entities are Phone Call, E-mail, Task, Letter, Fax, Appointment, and Recurring Appointment. Activity entities are associated with other business entities such as Account, Contact, Case, Lead, and Opportunity.

  The following diagram shows how an activity is linked with other entities within Dynamics CRM:

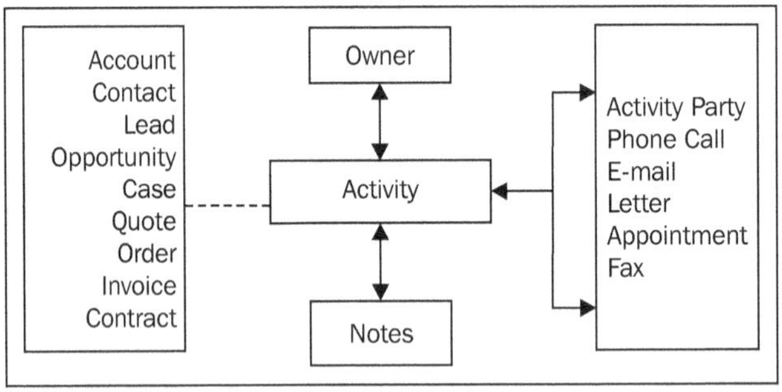

  Activities involve one or more participants, called **activity parties** in Microsoft Dynamics CRM 2011. For an Appointment activity, the participants are those contacts or users attending the meeting and for an E-mail activity, the participants are the sender and the recipients of the e-mail.

Activity entities are synced with Microsoft Outlook. Custom activities can also be created for supporting activities such as **instant messaging** (**IM**) or **Short Message Service** (**SMS**). But custom activities do not synchronize with Microsoft Outlook.

Entity ownership

Entities within the Dynamics CRM 2011 system can be owned by the organization or the business unit or "by a user or a team" or by none. Here, let us discuss the ownership in detail with the help of the following table:

Entity ownership type	Description	Can we create custom entities of this type?	Security and access-level depth
Organization	Entity data is viewable within the whole organization. Such entity records cannot be assigned or shared. For example, Product, Article, Discount List, and so on, are organization-owned entities.	Organization-owned custom entities can be created.	Organization-owned entities provide loose security permissions around its data. The security access levels around such an entity are only Global or None.
Business unit	Entity data is viewable within the business unit. User, Team, and so on, are business unit-owned entities. Custom entities can also be business unit-owned.	Business unit-owned custom entities cannot be created.	Such an entity provides little stricter security permission compared to organization-owned entities around its data. The access levels around such an entity are Global, Deep, Local, and None.
User or team	Entity data is viewable only by the user or team who has created it. Most of the entities such as Account, Contact, Lead, Opportunity, Campaign, and so on, are user- or team-owned entities. Custom entities can also be user- or team-owned.	User- or team-owned custom entities can be created.	User- or team-owned entities provide stricter security permissions around the data. Entity records for such entities can be shared with another user or team using Assign or Share. The access levels around such an entity are Global, Deep, Local, Basic, and None.
None	Such an entity does not have an owner. Their owner is usually driven by the parent entity owner. For example, the Price List Item entity does not have an owner and its ownership is driven by the parent entity Price List.	Custom entities cannot be created with "None" as the owner.	Security privilege cannot be set against such an entity. There are no access levels for this type of entity.

Creating a custom entity

Custom entities are entities created by a system administrator or customizer for fulfilling a business need that is not satisfied with out of the box entities. In this recipe, we will discuss how to create a custom entity in Dynamics CRM 2011 system.

How to do it...

Perform the following steps to create a custom entity:

1. Log in to the Dynamics CRM 2011 system as a system administrator or with a relevant security role.
2. Navigate to **Settings** | **Customizations** | **Solutions** and change the view to **Unmanaged Solutions**, if not already selected.

> Custom entities can be created in the default solution, but in that case the prefix for the entity and its attributes would be `new_`. To apply the solution publisher's prefix for custom entities and fields, create them using an unmanaged solution only.

3. Then, double-click on the unmanaged solution to open it.
4. In the expanded solution page, click on **Entities** under the **Components** section. After the page refreshes, click on the **New** button in the actions menu as shown in the following screenshot:

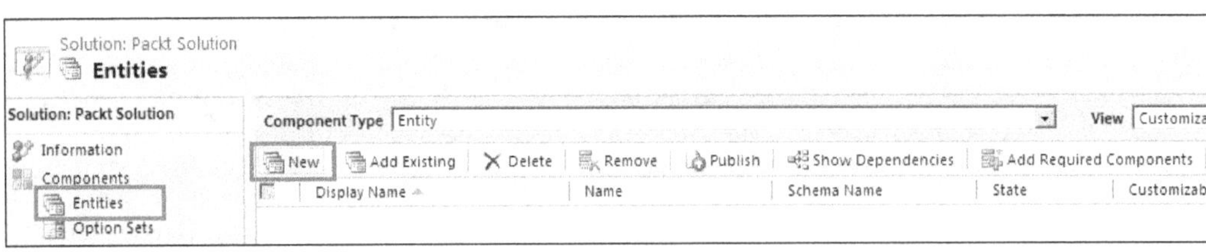

5. On the **New Information** page, under the **General** tab, provide the following information:

Property name	Description	Mandatory during entity creation	Cannot be modified after entity creation	Can be modified after entity creation	
				Only Once	Anytime
Display Name	This is the singular name for the entity.	√			√
Plural Name	The plural name of the entity. This name will appear in the Sitemap depending on the **Areas that display this entity** settings for the entity.	√			√
Name	This is the schema name for the entity. This name should be used when accessing this entity using the Dynamics CRM 2011 SDK. The name of a custom entity will be prefixed by the **Prefix** setting of the publisher of the unmanaged solution, which has created the custom entity.	√	√		
Description	We can provide the description and justification for this custom entity.				√
Ownership	This setting defines the ownership of the entity. Once the entity is saved the **Ownership** property cannot be changed.	√	√		
Define as an activity	Select this option if you want to create a custom activity type entity.	√	√		
Display in Activity Menus	If **Define as an activity** property is selected, a subsetting **Display in Activity Menus** will be enabled. Select this setting if you want this custom activity type to appear grouped with the existing activity types under the activity entity views.	√	√		
Areas that display the entity	This setting controls in which sections of the Sitemap the entity will be displayed. The standard areas are Workplace, Sales, Marketing, Service, Settings, and Resource Center. But if the Sitemap has been customized, the navigation group options may vary.				√

Property name	Description	Mandatory during entity creation	Cannot be modified after entity creation	Can be modified after entity creation	
				Only Once	Anytime
Communication and Collaboration					
Notes	Determines whether notes or attachments can be associated to a record of this entity.			√	
Activities	Determines whether activities (for example, Phone Call, Appointment, Task, Letter, and so on) associated can be linked to this entity record using the activities' **Regarding** field.	√	√		
Connections	Determines whether connections can be established with these entity records.			√	
Sending e-mail	Can be used for e-mailing. If selected, a **Single Line of Text** attribute with **Display Name** as `E-mail Address` will be added to the entity's attribute list.			√	
Mail Merge	Determines whether this entity will support the Mail Merge process and templates.				√
Document Management	Determines whether the entity supports SharePoint-based document management.				√
Queues	Determines whether a record of this entity can be sent to a queue. Once this setting is enabled, the **Automatically move records to the owner's default queue when a record is created or assigned** subsetting will be enabled. Select this subsetting only if you want to automatically send every record to the record owner's default queue, post the creation or assignment. This setting, however, can be modified anytime.			√	
Data Services					
Duplicate Detection	Determines whether duplicate detection rules can be created against this entity.				√
Auditing	Determines whether records of this entity will be audited.				√

Property name	Description	Mandatory during entity creation	Cannot be modified after entity creation	Can be modified after entity creation	
				Only Once	Anytime
Outlook & Mobile					
Mobile Express	Determines whether the entity supports the Mobile Express form. If users want to access the data of this entity in their mobile, enable this option.				√
Reading pane for CRM in Outlook	Determines whether a user is allowed to set up their Outlook to show a preview of the records of this entity in their Outlook reading pane.				√
Offline capability for CRM for Outlook	Determines whether this entity will support the offline capability for Outlook.				√

> The **Notes**, **Connections**, **Activities**, **Sending e-mail**, and **Queues** options cannot be disabled post entity creation. Hence, proper care should be taken during entity creation. Unless it is required, do not enable them during entity creation. We can enable them in the future as required.

6. In the **Primary Field** section, create the primary field of the entity providing all the required information.

> Every entity is required to have one primary field. This field will be used to name the records of this entity. A primary field can only be a `Single Line of Text` attribute with a maximum of 4000 number of characters, 100 being the default. Once the entity is created, the primary field's properties cannot be changed from the **Primary Field** tab. However, **Display Name**, **Length**, and **Requirement Level** of this field can be changed by navigating to the list of **Fields** of the entity.
>
> The lookup view of this entity will only contain the primary field as its first column. This field or its column order cannot be removed or altered from the lookup view.

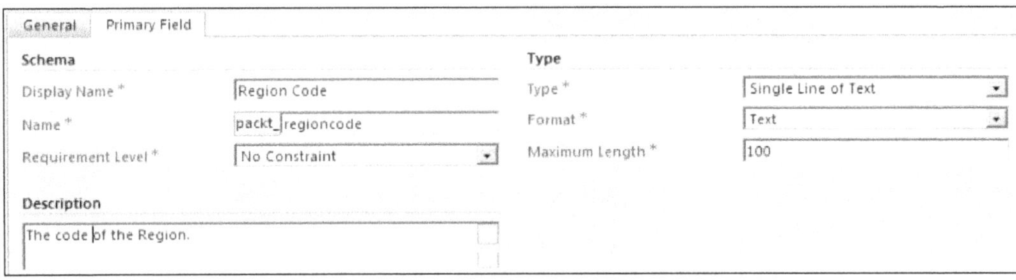

7. Thereafter, click on the **Save and Close** button in the top ribbon to create and save a new entity.
8. Then click on the **Publish** button in the newly created entity's ribbon menu.
9. In the **Primary Field** section, create the primary field of the entity providing all the required information as shown in the following screenshot:

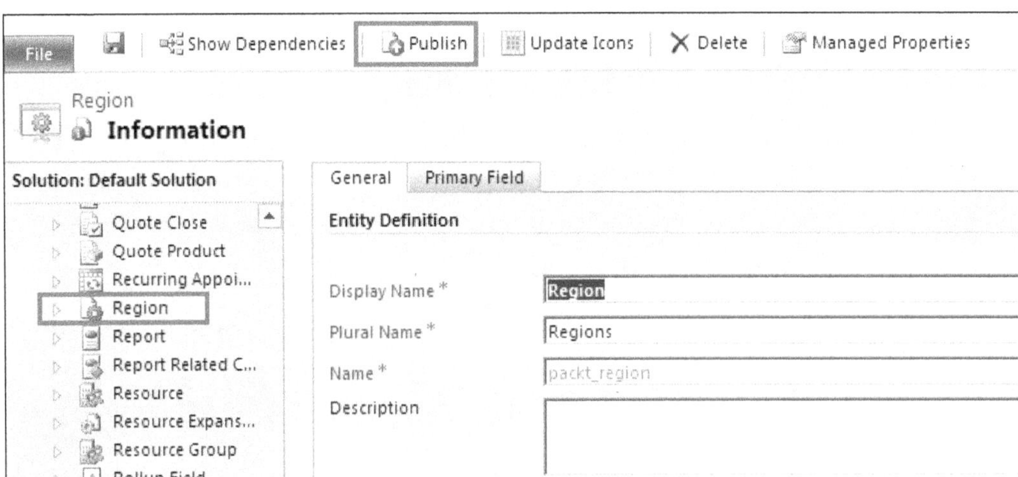

How it works...

A custom entity can be created in the default solution or in any unmanaged solution. In this recipe, we have discussed how to create a custom entity in an unmanaged solution, as this is recommended. To create a custom entity in a default solution, open the default solution by navigating to **Settings** | **Customization** | **Customizations** | **Customize the Entity**. Thereafter, the same recipe can be followed from step 4 onwards.

> In Dynamics CRM 2011 Online, only 200 custom entities can be created.

Custom entities support almost every feature of the business entities. Some of the main functionalities supported by a custom entity are as follows:

- Forms, views, and reports
- Relationships for custom entities can be defined
- Publish, export, and import the new entities and their associated forms and views
- Plugins, workflows, or dialogs can also be created against a custom entity
- Client-side events function in the same manner as those for system entities
- We can secure a custom entity in the same way as other Microsoft Dynamics CRM 2011 entities
- The security privileges available for organization-owned custom entities are as follows: create, read, write, delete, append, and append to
- The security privileges available for user-owned custom entities are as follows: create, read, write, delete, append, append to, assign, and share
- A custom entity can be extended using the `ISV.config` file in the same manner as system entities
- The filtered views for a custom entity are available to be used in the same manner as for system entities
- The entity can be included in the dataset that Microsoft Dynamics CRM 2011 for Microsoft Office Outlook users can take offline

Following the same recipe we can create custom activity type entities and privileges as well:

- **Custom activity entity**: To create a custom activity type entity, enable the **Define as an Activity Entity** property. If we wish this new entity to be grouped with the existing activities, we have to enable the **Display in Activity Menus** option as well.

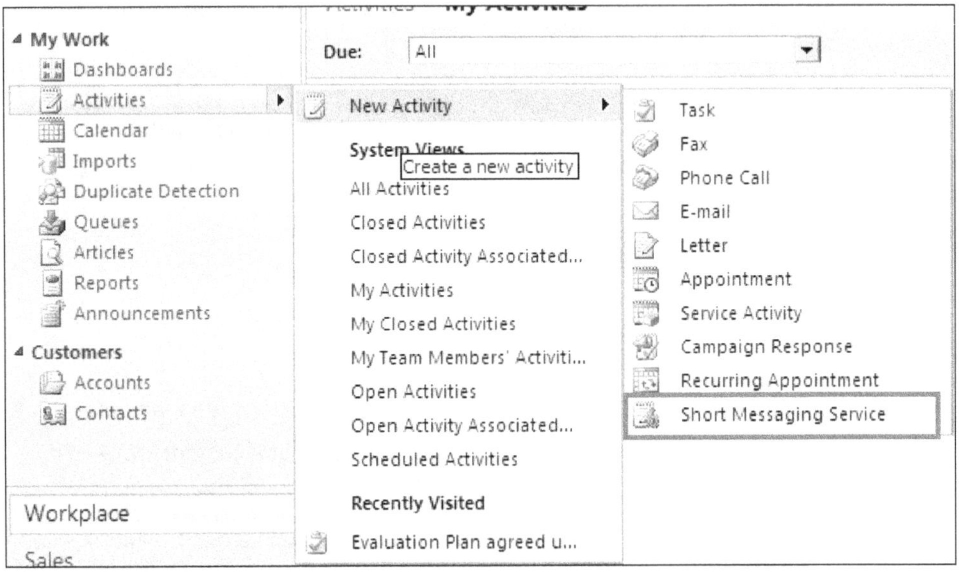

Custom activity entity records automatically qualify to be sent to a queue. However, we can determine whether we want the records to be sent to the record owner's default queue post record creation or assignment by choosing the **Automatically move records to the owner's default queue when a record is created or assigned** option.

The custom activity type entities are always user- or team-owned. Moreover, not all the entity settings are available for custom activity entities. Only the following settings are available for custom activities:

- **Display Name**
- **Plural Name**
- **Name**
- **Description**
- **Define as an activity**
- **Display in Activity Menus**
- **Document Management**
- **Duplicate Detection**

- **Auditing**
- **Mobile Express**
- **Reading pane for CRM in Outlook**

> Custom activities do not synchronize with Microsoft Outlook.

Customizable settings of a custom entity as well as a business entity can be modified by navigating to the entity section in the solution. A custom entity can also be deleted permanently from the Dynamics CRM 2011 system by using the **Delete** button.

- **Custom entity privileges**: After creation of a custom entity, the entity name will start appearing under the **Custom Entities** tab in any security role. However, except for the **System Administrator**, no other security role will have any access defined for the custom entity. Hence, post entity creation, security roles have to be updated to provide access to the custom entity:

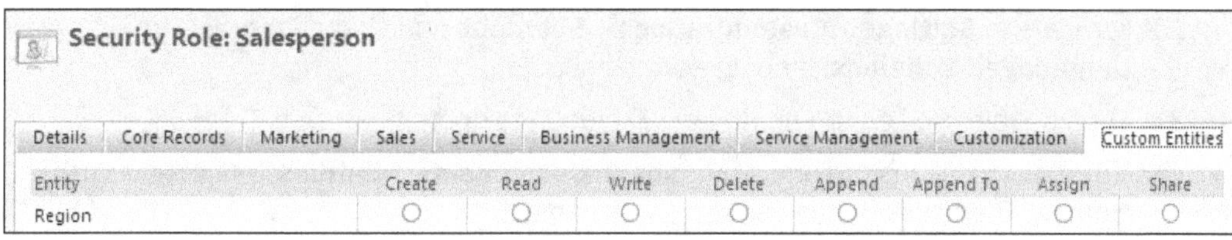

Like other system-defined activities, custom activity entities also share the same privileges as defined for the **Activity** entity under any security role. Hence, for custom activities there is no need to modify any security role.

With the custom entity creation, there will be a set of fields automatically created for it. If the entity is user- or team-owned, two fields, **Owner** and **Owning Team**, will be created automatically to store the user or the team owning the entity record respectively.

Every entity in Dynamics CRM 2011 will have the **Status** (**Activity Status** in case of an **Activity** entity) and **Status Reason** fields. Only the **Display Name** value of these fields can be edited. The **Status** field for a custom entity has only two values, **Active** and **Inactive**. By default, every record when created has **Status** as **Active**. When it is deactivated, the **Status** field changes to **Inactive**. Only active records of an entity can be searched using **Quick Find View**; however, **Advanced Find View** can list even inactive records. **Status Reason** is a dependent pick list and its values changes depending on the value of the **Status** field.

Finally, only custom entities can be deleted from the system. To delete a custom entity from the Dynamics CRM 2011 system, navigate to **Settings** | **Customization** | **Customizations** | **Customize the System** and then click on the **Entities** component and select the entity to be deleted. Click on **Delete** in the toolbar and then click on **OK** to confirm the deletion.

Updating the icon of an entity

After creating an entity in the Dynamics CRM 2011 system, the default icon is linked to any entity. This default icon can be modified to a more appropriate icon. In this recipe, we will discuss how to update the icon of a custom entity.

How to do it...

Please perform the following steps to update the icon of a custom entity:

1. Log in to the Dynamics CRM 2011 system as a system administrator or with a relevant security role.
2. Navigate to **Settings** | **Customizations** | **Solutions** and change the view to **Unmanaged Solutions**, if not already selected.
3. Then double-click on the unmanaged solution to open it.
4. Navigate to the custom entity by going to **Components** | **Entities** | **<Custom Entity Name>**. Then click on the custom entity name.
5. Then the top ribbon will refresh and the **Update Icons** button will be visible. Click on this button as shown in the following screenshot:

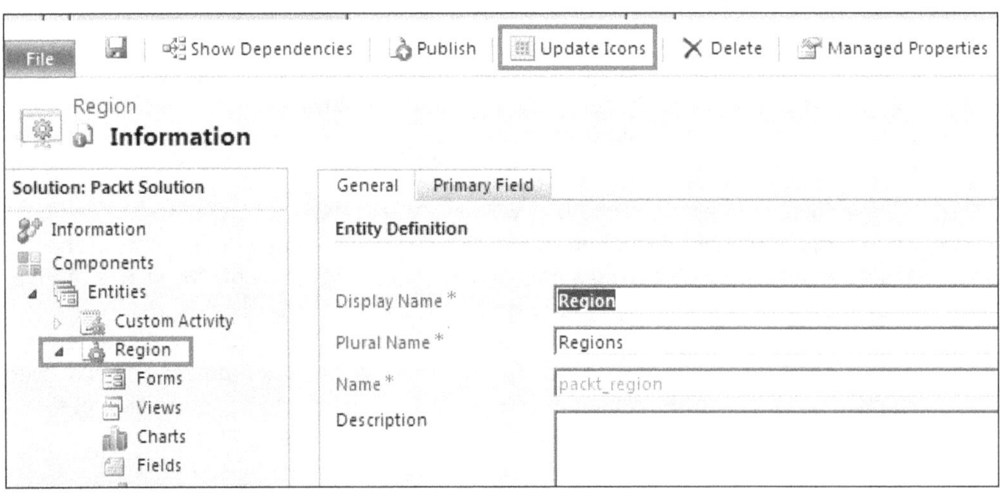

6. The **Select New Icons** page will appear. In this form, we can select two icons to be displayed in the following areas of Dynamics CRM 2011:

Icon	Description	Image resolution	Image size (maximum)	Property
Icon in a web application	This icon will appear for the custom entity in the Dynamics CRM Web User Interface	16 x 16 pixel	10 KB	`IconSmallName`
Icon for entity forms	This icon will appear for the custom entity in the custom entity's forms	32 x 32 pixel	10 KB	`IconMediumName`

> There exists an icon with an image resolution of 66 x 48 pixel and image size of 10 KB with the property name `IconLargeName`. But this icon is not used in Microsoft Dynamics CRM 2011.

7. To select a new icon for a web application, click on the **New Icon** lookup under the **Icon in Web Application** section. The **Lookup Record** web dialog will pop up. In this dialog, select the icon web resource (if it already exists) and then click on the **OK** button.

   If the icon has not already been added as a web resource, we have to first add it as a web resource and then we can select it here. To add the icon file as a new web resource, click on the **New** button as shown in the following screenshot:

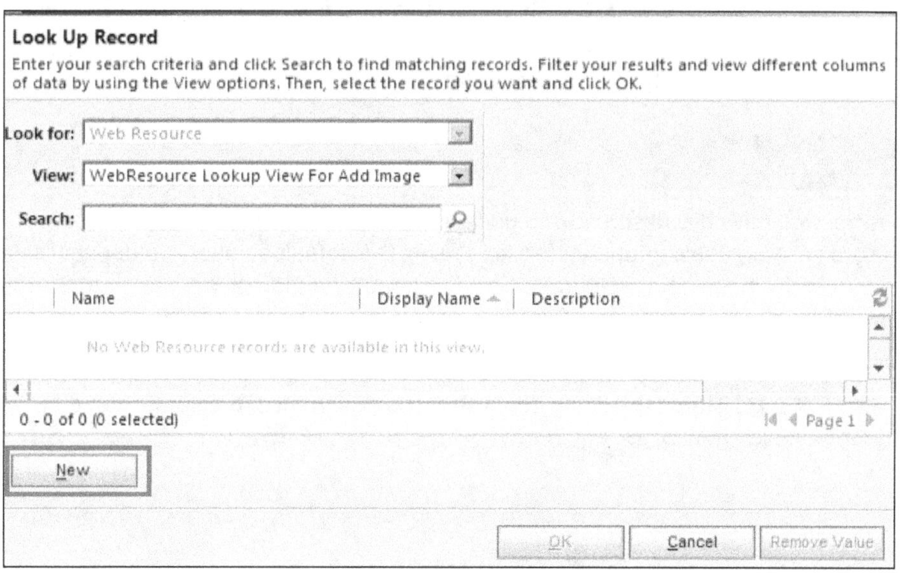

The **Web Resource: New** page will appear. On this page provide the **Name** and **Display Name** values, and the content type of the icon. Then click on the **Save and Close** button in the top ribbon as shown in the following screenshot:

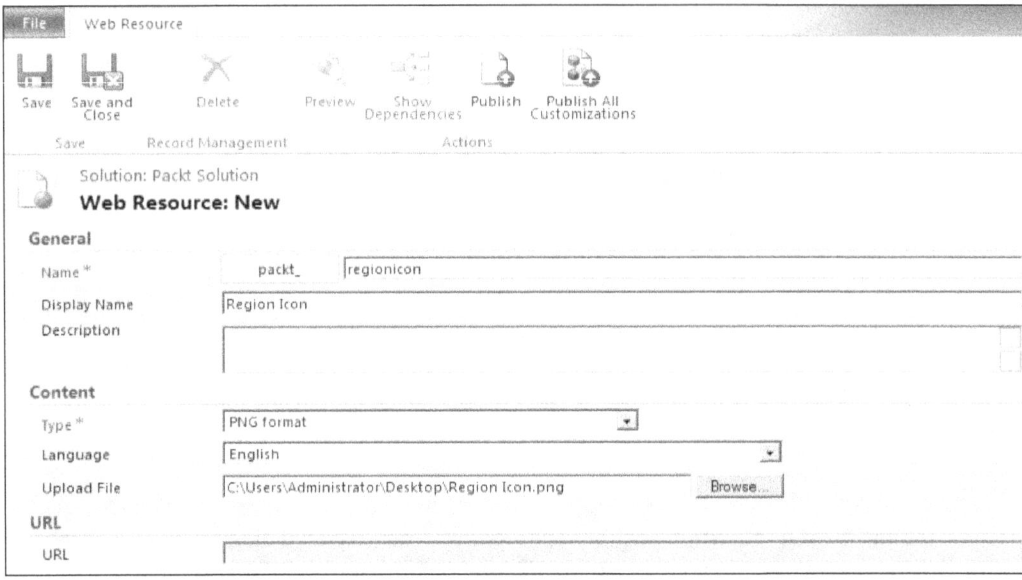

8. Now we can find the icon web resource in the **Look Up Record** web dialog. Select the icon web resource and click on **OK** to proceed.
9. Add the icon for **Icon in Entity Forms** by following steps 7 to 9.
10. Thereafter, click on the **OK** button on the **Select New Icons** page to save and close the selections.
11. The icon of the entity will now be updated.

How it works...

In this recipe, we have discussed how to update the icon of a custom entity using an unmanaged solution. We can update the icon using the default solution. To update the icon of a custom entity in a default solution, open the default solution by navigating to **Settings** | **Customization** | **Customizations** | **Customize the System**. Thereafter the same recipe can be followed from step 4 onwards.

Dynamics CRM 2011 stores the icons into web resources. Hence, the same icon can be re-used for multiple entities, as required.

> Icons of a system entity or business entity cannot be updated. Only icons of custom entities can be updated.

Creating a custom field for an entity

In Dynamics CRM 2011, we can create custom fields or attributes to satisfy the needs of the business processes. New fields or attributes can be added to a business entity as well as a custom entity. In this recipe, we will discuss how to add a custom field to an entity.

How to do it...

Perform the following steps to create a new attribute for an entity:

1. Log in to the Dynamics CRM 2011 system as a system administrator or with a relevant security role.
2. Navigate to **Settings** | **Customizations** | **Solutions** and change the view to **Unmanaged Solutions**, if not already selected.
3. Then double-click on the unmanaged solution to open it.
4. Navigate to the entity to which the custom field needs to be added by going to **Components** | **Entities** | **<Entity Name>**.
5. Then expand the **Entity** section and click on **Fields**. Then click on **New** in the **Fields** page's toolbar as shown in the following screenshot:

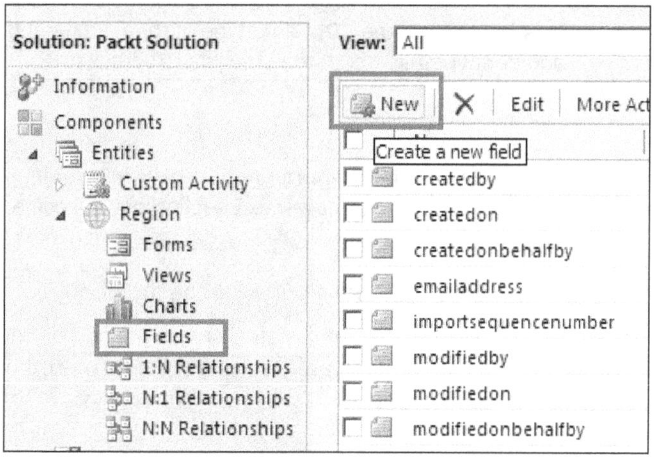

6. A **New for <Entity Name>** page will appear. Provide the following details about the attributes or fields to create the field:

Property name	Description
Display Name	This is the display name of the attribute. This name will appear in the CRM UI for this attribute when added to any form (form label can be modified), view, charts, or reports.
Name	This is the schema name of the attribute. This name should be used when accessing this attribute using the Dynamics CRM 2011 SDK.
Requirement Level*	This determines the requirement level of the attribute, when it is added to the entity forms. There are three possible values for this: ▸ **No Constraint** ▸ **Business Recommended** ▸ **Business Required**
Searchable*	This defines whether this attribute is searchable.
Field Security	This defines whether this field can be part of a field-level security profile. Read more about field-level security in the *Creating a field-level security profile* recipe of *Chapter 3, Administering Microsoft Dynamics CRM 2011*.
Auditing	This determines whether this field can be audited. Read more about field-level auditing in the *Enabling auditing in the Dynamics CRM 2011 system* recipe of *Chapter 4, Data Management*.
Description	This is the description for the field.
Type*	This will contain the CRM data type of the field. Post type selection, additional details about the type would be asked.

> Read more about the **Requirement Level**, **Searchable**, and **Type** settings in the *How it works...* section of this recipe.

7. Thereafter, click on the **Save and Close** button in the top ribbon.
8. To publish the change, click on the entity name and then click on the **Publish** button in the top ribbon. Unless the changes are published, the new attribute will not be visible in the entity forms or charts:

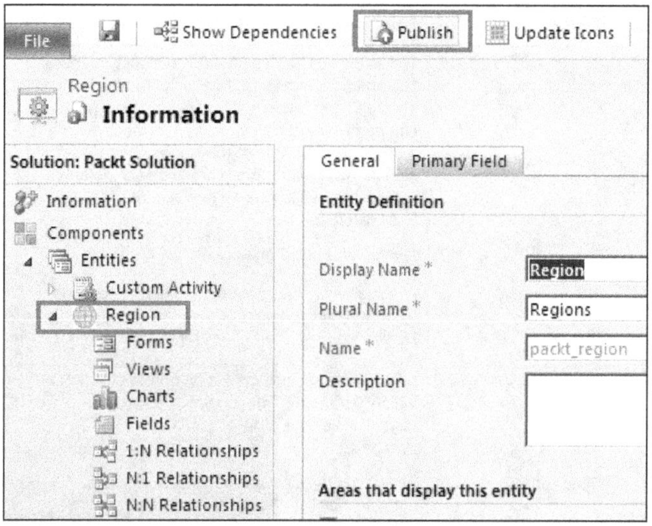

How it works...

New attributes can be added for business entities as well as custom entities. However, for system entities no new attribute can be added.

The new attribute can be of the following CRM data types:

Type	Format	Description	Constraints
Single Line of Text SQL data type: `nvarchar`	E-mail	Allows only properly formatted e-mail addresses. After population, if the user clicks on the field, it launches an e-mail to the specified address. This will display a hyperlink.	Maximum length: 4000.
	Text	Allows text in a single line.	
	Text Area	Allows text in multiple lines.	
	URL	Allows only formatted URL. After population, if the user clicks on the field it launches the website. This will display a hyperlink.	
	Ticker Symbol	Converts the entered text into a hyperlink. If the user clicks on the hyperlink, it launches Microsoft Value Central with details about the stock.	
Option Set SQL data type: `int`		Single select list of options. This is an HTML select control, often referred to as a combobox or drop-down list. We can define the integer value corresponding to a text value. The integer value is what is stored into the database.	

Type	Format	Description	Constraints
Two Options SQL data type: `bit`		This is the Yes/No type field. The display names **Yes** and **No** can be modified to some other pair such as True/False or Always/Never. This field can be displayed as a checkbox, combobox, or a drop-down list. One of the values must be set as a default value. Unless modified the default value will be used when a new record of the entity is created. A value of 0 and 1 is stored in the database.	
Whole Number SQL data type: `int`	None	Accepts any whole number (positive or negative without a decimal point) within the specified range.	The minimum value is -2,147,483,648 and the maximum value is 2,147,483,647.
	Duration	Allows you to select a duration from a pick list, which increments from one minute to three days. The value is stored in minutes in the database.	
	Time zone	Allows you to select a time zone from a pick list. The pick list displays time zones and time zone names. The value is stored as a time zone code in database. All the available time zone codes are stored in the `TimeZoneDefinitionBase` table of the `<OrganizationName>_MSCRM` database.	
	Language	Allows you to select a language from the installed languages from a pick list.	
Floating Point Number SQL data type: `float`		Allows a floating point number within the range and precision specified.	The minimum value is -1,000,000,000 and the maximum value is 1,000,000,000. Precision is up to 5 digits.
Decimal Number SQL data type: `decimal`		Allows a decimal number within the range and precision specified. Decimal types take more space in database, but provide more precision than **Floating Point Number**.	Precision up to 10 digits.
Currency SQL data type: `money`		Accepts a money value within the specified range. Adding a money field, automatically adds another extra field with same name but prefixed with `Base` to handle a multicurrency configuration. The base attribute stores the value of the money attribute in the base currency. Each entity that has a `money` attribute must also have the `Currency` and `Exchange Rate` attributes. If these attributes do not already exist, they will be created when a new `money` attribute is added to an entity.	The minimum value is -922,337,203,685,477 and the maximum value is 922,337,203,685,477. The `money` attribute supports up to four decimal places.
Multiple Lines of Text SQL data type: `Nvarchar(max)`		Allows multiline texts up to 100,000 characters.	

Type	Format	Description	Constraints
Date and Time SQL data type: `datetime`	Date Only	Accepts a date value. Provides a `Calendar` control to select a date.	
	Date and Time	Accepts a date and time value. Provides both a `Calendar` control to select a date and a `Time` control to select time.	
Lookup SQL data type: `Uniqueidentifier`		Allows you to select a record from another entity. Creating this field will create a N:1 or many-to-one relationship with another entity.	

The **Requirement Level** setting determines how important the field is in the business process. There are three possible settings:

- **Business Required**: This field should be mandatorily populated and there will be a red asterisk next to the field in the form. But if data is entered using **Import Data Wizard** or via the Dynamics CRM 2011 SDK, then such a field can be left blank.
- **Business Recommended**: Though this field need not be populated to save the form data, it is an important field in the business process and there will be a blue plus sign next to the field in the form.
- **No Constraint**: This is the default setting. It is a regular field with no constraints. Providing a value for such a field is optional.

> **System Required** is a system-defined requirement level. This is used for some system-defined fields and cannot be used for any custom fields. Unlike the **Business Required** fields, **System Required** fields restrict a user from creating a record from both UI and programmatic ways without providing the field's value.
>
> **Potential Customer** in an Opportunity entity is a **System Required** field as well as the **Owner** field in any entity.

Make a field searchable if you want the **Searchable** field to be available for querying Dynamics CRM to retrieve data. By default, most of the out-of-the box fields and all the custom fields are searchable. Nonsearchable fields will not be available when creating the **filter criteria** for system views, user views, advanced find views, or others.

The **input method editor mode** (**IME mode**) allows Dynamics CRM to work with Chinese, Korean, and Japanese characters. If we don't intend to use any of the languages, we can safely leave the default setting for this attribute. The listed languages have more characters than other keyboards and IME allows a sequence of characters to represent a single character in these languages. The options for IME mode setting are:

- **auto**: This specifies that the IME mode is not changed.

- **inactive**: This specifies all characters entered without IME mode, but the mode can be deactivated. For `Date and Time` type fields, the default is **inactive**.
- **active**: This specifies all characters entered in IME mode, but the mode can be deactivated. For name-related fields and addresses, the default is **active**.
- **disabled**: This specifies that the IME mode is disabled and cannot be activated. For number type fields such as `Currency`, `Whole Number`, and `Floating Point Number`, the default is **disabled**.

There's more...

After creating a custom field, a few properties can be modified. Even most of the system-defined existing fields can be modified. The following is a list of properties of any field that cannot be modified post creation:

- The **Name** value of a field. This is the schema name of the field and hence cannot be edited. However, **Display Name** of a field can be modified.
- The **Type** property of a field cannot be modified. If we want to change the data type of a field, the exiting field has to be deleted and recreated with the correct data type.

Creating a global option set

A global option set provides us with the mechanism to define an option set once and re-use it in various fields of different entities in the system. By using the global option set feature, there is no need to redefine the same option set separately each time it is used. The Dynamics CRM 2011 system provides us with a set of global option sets out of the box. We should explore these existing ones before creating a new one. The list of existing global option sets can be found at `http://msdn.microsoft.com/en-in/library/gg328546.aspx`.

In this recipe, we will discuss how to create a custom global option set.

How to do it...

Perform the following steps to create a global option set:

1. Log in to the Dynamics CRM 2011 system as a system administrator or with a relevant security role.
2. Navigate to **Settings** | **Customizations** | **Solutions** and change the view to **Unmanaged Solutions**, if not already selected.
3. Then double-click on the unmanaged solution to open it.
4. Navigate to the global option sets by going to **Components** | **Option Sets**. Then click on the **New** button in the actions toolbar.

5. The **Option Set New** page will appear. Please provide the following details about the global option set on this page:
   - **Display Name**: The Display name of the option set
   - **Name**: The unique schema name of the option set
   - **Description**: The description of the option set
6. Thereafter, click on the add button (a green plus sign) under the **Options** section to add option texts in the option set. Populate the following fields for each option:
   - **Label**: The display text for the option. This can be modified any time after creation.
   - **Description**: A description about the option. This is optional.
   - **Value**: This will be autopopulated with a predefined value. This value is based on the **Option Value Prefix** value of the publisher of this solution. Every time an option value is added to the global option set, a unique value is created by autoincrementing the number after **Option Value Prefix**.

   > In a default solution, the **Option Value Prefix** value will be 10,000.

   Although, this value can be edited, it is best practice to accept the autogenerated value.

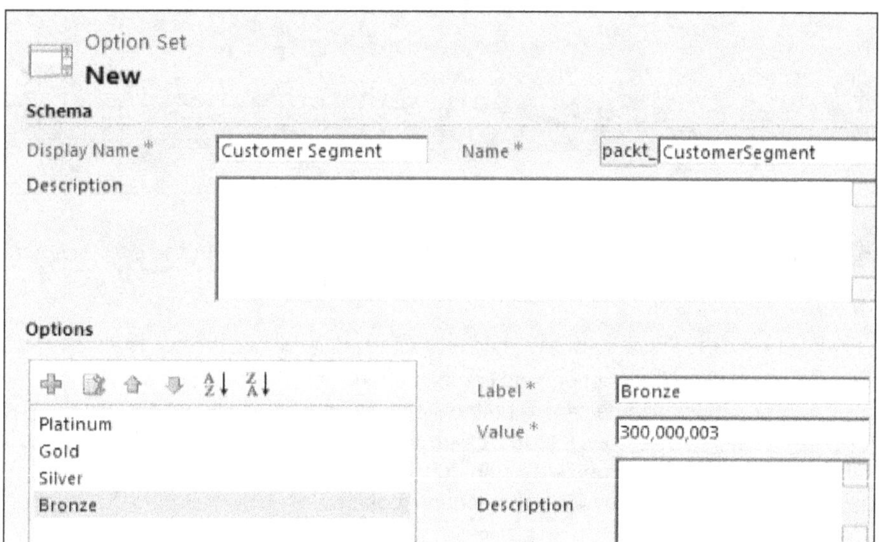

7. After adding all the option texts, click on the **Save and Close** button in the top ribbon.
8. Then, select the option set added in the list of options sets and click on the **Publish** button in the actions menu as shown in the following screenshot:

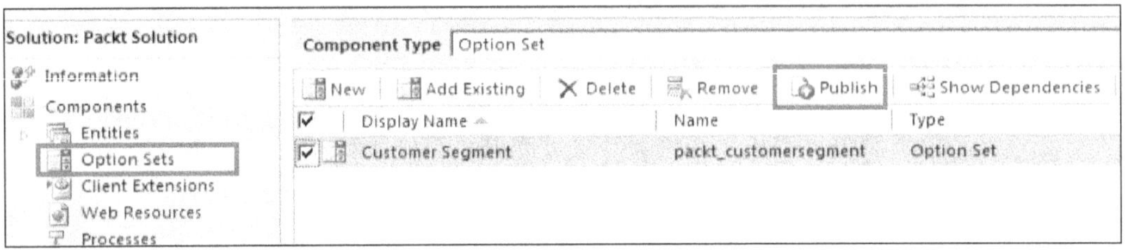

How it works...

Global option sets are available to be used in every entity form. The label of every option text is the display format for the option and the value part is a numerical value and is what gets stored in the database.

To use a global option set for an entity field, navigate to the entity **Fields** section of an unmanaged solution or default solution and click on **New**. In the new custom field form provide/specify the **Type** value as `Option Set` and set the **Use Existing Option Set** field to **Yes**. Finally, set the **Option Set** value to the global option set. Then save and close the form:

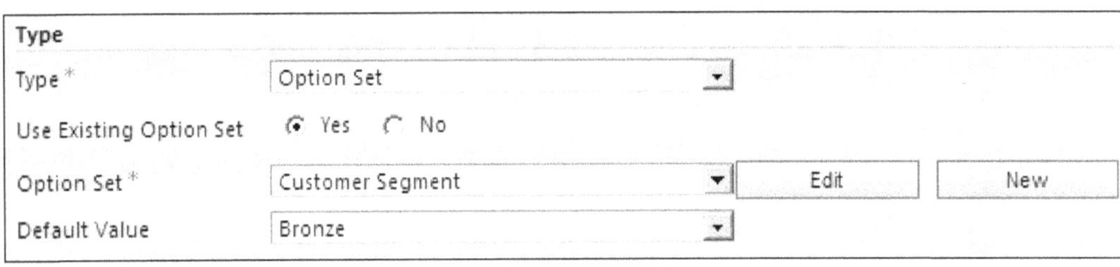

The global option set can be modified by clicking on the **Edit** button in the previous screenshot or a new one can be created by clicking on the **New** button.

> Not all existing option sets can be edited. Only those option sets that are customizable can be edited. To check whether a global option is customizable, navigate to **Components** | **Option Sets** of the solution and check the **Customizable** column value for the option set. Set the **View** drop-down box to **All** in the actions toolbar.

A global option set can be deleted permanently from the Dynamics CRM system using the **Delete** button in the toolbar menu of the global option set.

Creating a new one-to-many (1:N) or many-to-one (N:1) relationship

In this recipe, we will discuss the various entity types possible between two entities in Dynamics CRM 2011 and how to create a one-to-many or many-to-one relationship between two entities.

Getting ready

Dynamics CRM 2011 supports two types of relationships between two entities:

- **One-to-many (1:N) or many-to-one (N:1)**: An example of this relationship would be, an Account can have many Leads linked to it. If it is viewed from the other side, the relationship would be many Leads can be linked to one Account.
- **Many-to-many (N:N)**: An example of this relationship would be, an Account can be linked to many Marketing Lists and a Marketing List can have many Accounts.

These are illustrated in the following diagram:

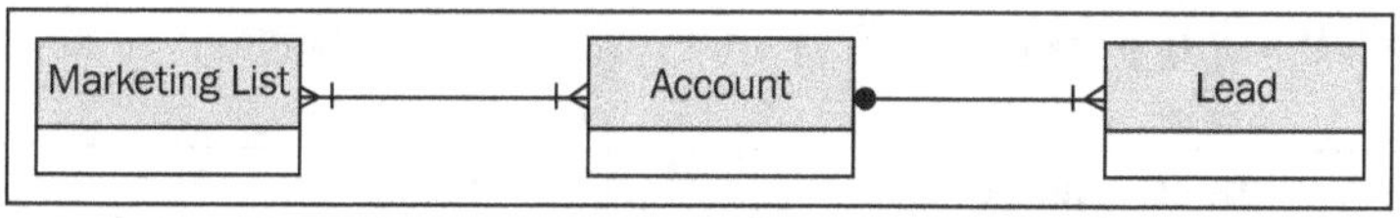

The **1:N self-referencing** relationship is also supported. An example would be an Account can be the parent of many other Accounts. The **Parent Account** field in the **Account** entity represents a 1:N self-referential relationship.

The **1:1** relationship type is not supported in Dynamics CRM 2011.

How to do it...

Let us consider a scenario where we will create a one-to-many (1:N) relationship between a custom entity **Region** and a business entity **Account**. This relationship can be viewed as many-to-one (N:1) between **Account** and **Region** as well. The same recipe can be followed to create a one-to-many (1:N) or many-to-one (N:1) relationship between any two entities.

Please follow the next steps to create a new one-to-many (1:N) relationship between **Region** and **Account**:

1. Log in to the Dynamics CRM 2011 system as a system administrator or with a relevant security role.
2. Navigate to **Settings** | **Customizations** | **Solutions** and change the view to **Unmanaged Solutions**, if not already selected.

3. Then double-click on the unmanaged solution to open it.
4. Navigate to the **Region** entity's **1:N Relationships** section by going to **Components** | **Entities** | **Region** | **1:N Relationships**.
5. Then click on the **New 1-to-Many Relationship** button in the actions toolbar as shown in the following screenshot:

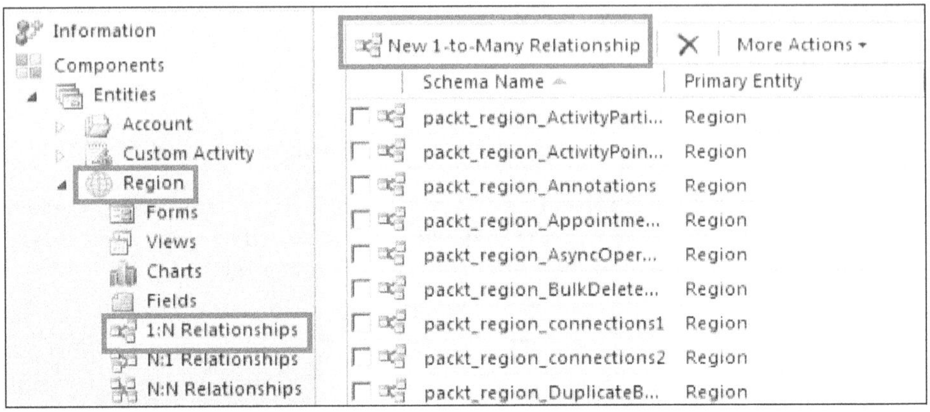

6. The **Relationship New** page will open. Provide the following details on this page:

Settings	Description
Relationship Definition	
Primary Entity	This is the primary or parent entity in the relationship. In a 1:N relationship creation, this would be the current entity and would not be modifiable. In an N:1 relationship creation, this field would be a drop-down list of all available entities.
Related Entity	This is the child entity in the relationship. In a 1:N relationship creation, this field would be a drop-down list of all the available entities. But in an N:1 relationship creation, this would be the current entity and would not be modifiable.
Name	This is the schema name for the relationship. Dynamics CRM autopopulates the name, which can be modified.
Lookup Field	
Display Name	This is the name of the lookup field that will appear on the related or child entity records.
Name	This is the schema name of the lookup field.
Requirement Level	This is the requirement level for the lookup field.
Description	This field will bear a description of the lookup field.

Settings	Description
Navigation Pane Item for Primary Entity	
Display Option	This determines whether a link for the list of child records will be visible in the parent entities record. We can select from the following options: ▸ **Do not Display**: This means the primary entity form will not display this relationship ▸ **Use Custom Label**: This means the primary entity form will display a custom label in the form ▸ **Use Plural Name**: This means the primary entity form will display the plural name of the child entity
Display Area	This is the display area in the parent entity's form where the link to child records list would appear. We can select from the following options: ▸ **Details**: The **Details** area of the navigation pane of the parent entity form will display the link for a list of associated child entity records ▸ **Marketing**: The **Marketing** area of the navigation pane of the parent entity form will display the link for a list of associated child entity records ▸ **Sales**: The **Sales** area of the navigation pane of the parent entity form will display the link for a list of associated child entity records ▸ **Services**: The **Services** area of the navigation pane of the parent entity form will display the link for a list of associated child entity records
Custom Label	If **Use Custom Label** is selected in **Display Option**, provide a label here.
Display Order	Within each of the navigation pane areas we can control the display order. The entity relationship with the lowest value will appear above the others.
Relationship Behavior	
Type of Behavior	This defines how changes made to the parent record will affect the child record.

These settings are illustrated in the following screenshot:

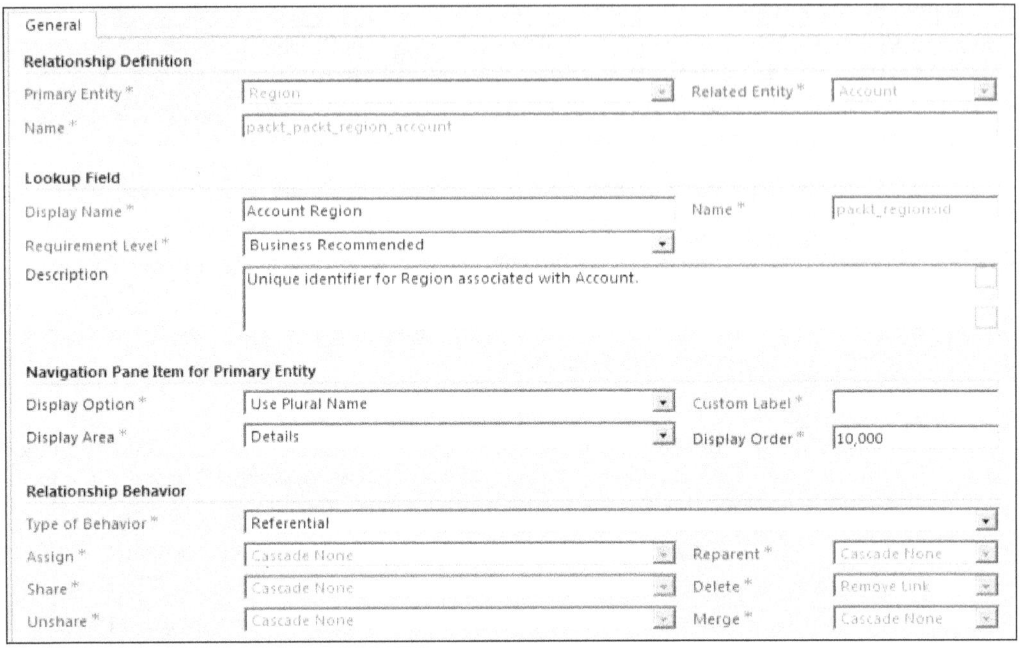

7. Then click on the **Save and Close** button in the top ribbon to create the new relationship and save it.

How it works...

One-to-many or many-to-one relationships are common in the Dynamics CRM system. If an entity "X" is linked to another entity "Y" via a one-to-many relationship, the entity "Y" is linked to the entity "X" via the many-to-one relationship. Despite the fact that there are two separate relationship options, that is, 1:N and N:1, it is not needed to create both for any two entities. Once we create one of these relationships, the other one automatically exists.

When we create lookup fields in an entity, a many-to-one relationship is automatically created between the current entity and the entity to be looked up.

The **type of behavior** is a very important feature of one-to-many or many-to-one relationship. This, however, does not exist for many-to-many relationships. The type of behavior decides how the change made to the parent entity will cascade down to the related child entity records for various actions. The possible types of behavior are as follows:

Type of behavior	Description
Parental	This cascades all changes from the parent record to child records.
Referential	This does not cascade any change from the parent record to the child records. This is the default behavior type.
Referential, Restrict Delete	This does not cascade any change from the parent record to the child record; however, it does prohibit parent records from being deleted if there are associated child records.
Configurable Cascading	This allows us to set the cascading behavior rules for six behavior actions.

Behavior actions are six different actions that are performed on the related or child entity records when the same action has been performed on a primary entity record. The six behavior actions are as follows:

- **Assign**
- **Share**
- **Unshare** (revoking **Share**)
- **Reparent** (associating with a new parent record)
- **Delete**
- **Merge**

Different **cascading behavior rules** can be applied to each of the six behavior actions:

- **Cascade All**: This cascades changes made to the parent record to all child records
- **Cascade Active**: This cascades changes made to the parent record to all active child records
- **Cascade User-owned**: This cascades changes made to the parent record to all child records having the same owner as of the parent record
- **Cascade None**: This does not cascade the change to the child record
- **Remove Link**: When the parent record is deleted, this rule removes the link of the parent record from the child record, instead of deleting the child records
- **Restrict**: This does not allow the parent record to be deleted if it contains any associated child records

The following table describes the applicable **Behavior Actions** options against **Behavior Rules**:

Behavior Actions	**Assign**	**Share**	**Unshare**	**Reparent**	**Delete**	**Merge**
Behavior Rules						
Cascade All	√	√	√	√	√	√
Cascade Active	√	√	√	√		
Cascade User-owned	√	√	√	√		
Cascade None	√	√	√	√	√	
Remove Link					√	
Restrict					√	

Creating a new many-to-many (N:N) relationship

In the previous recipe, we discussed how to create a one-to-many relationship between two entities and in this recipe, we will discuss how to create a many-to-many (N:N) relationship between two entities.

How to do it...

Let us consider a scenario where we will create a many-to-many relationship between a custom entity **Region** and a business entity **Account**. This means a Region can be linked to many Accounts and many Regions can be linked to one Account. The same recipe can be followed to create a many-to-many relationship between any two entities.

Perform the following steps to create a new many-to-many relationship between **Region** and **Account**:

1. Log in to the Dynamics CRM 2011 system as a system administrator or with a relevant security role.
2. Navigate to **Settings** | **Customizations** | **Solutions** and change the view to **Unmanaged Solutions**, if not already selected.
3. Then double-click on the unmanaged solution to open it.
4. Navigate to the **Region** entity's many-to-many relationships section by going to **Components** | **Entities** | **Region** | **N: N Relationships**.
5. Then click on the **New Many-to-Many-Relationship** button in the actions toolbar as shown in the following screenshot:

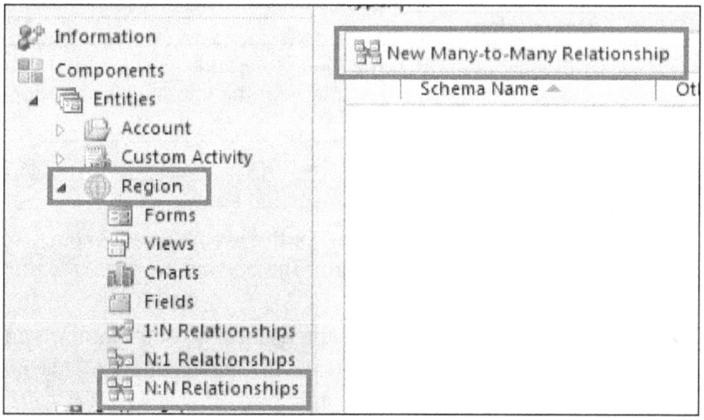

6. The **Relationship New** page will open. Provide the following details on this page:

Setting	Description
Current Entity	
Entity Name	This is the name of the current entity.
Display Option	This determines how a link for the list of associated entities would be visible in a current entity form. We can select from the following options: ▸ **Do not Display**: This means that the current entity form will not display this relationship ▸ **Use Custom Label**: This means that the current entity form will display a custom label in the form ▸ **Use Plural Name**: This means that the current entity form will display the plural name of the child entity
Display Area	This is the display area in the current entity's form where the link to associated records list would appear. We can select from the following options: ▸ **Details**: The **Details** area of the navigation pane of the current entity form will display the link for list of associated entity records ▸ **Marketing**: The **Marketing** area of the navigation pane of the current entity form will display the link for list of associated entity records ▸ **Sales**: The **Sales** area of the navigation pane of the current entity form will display the link for list of associated entity records ▸ **Services**: The **Services** area of the navigation pane of the current entity form will display the link for list of associated entity records
Custom Label	If **Use Custom Label** is selected in **Display Option**, provide a label here.

Setting	Description
Display Order	Within each of the navigation pane areas we can control the display order. The entity relationship with the lowest value will appear above the others.
Other Entity	
Entity Name	This is the name of the associated entity.
Display Option	This determines how a link for the list of current entities would be visible in an associated entity form. The options are similar to the current entity display options.
Display Area	This is the display area in the associated entity form where the link to current records list would appear. The options are similar to the current entity display area.
Custom Label	If **Use Custom Label** is selected in **Display Option**, provide a label here.
Display Order	Within each of the navigation pane areas we can control the display order. The entity relationship with the lowest value will appear above the others.
Relationship Definition	
Name	This is the schema name of the relationship.
Relationship Entity Name	This is the schema name of the relationship entity.

This is illustrated in the following screenshot:

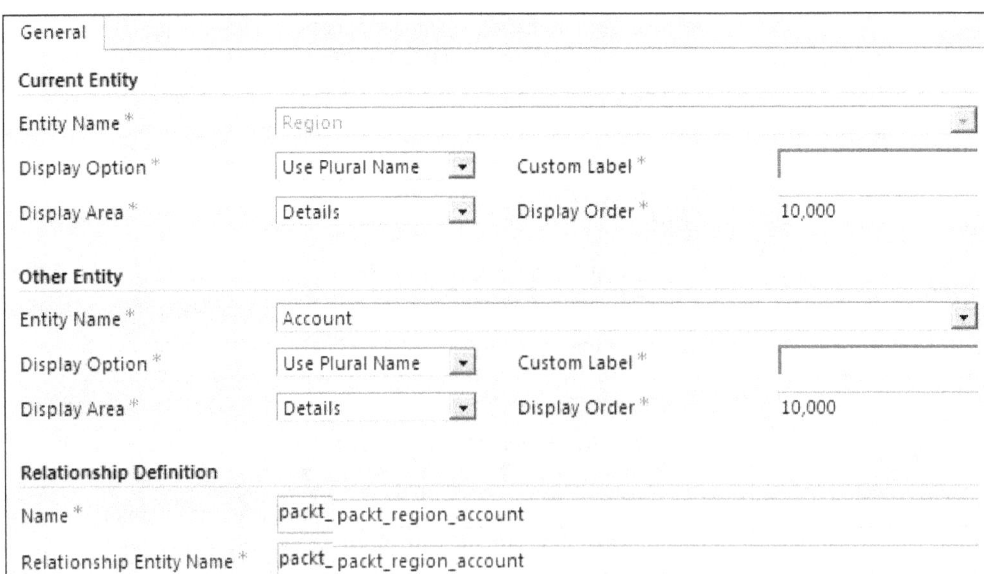

7. If **Display Option** for **Current Entity** or **Other Entity** is set as **Do not Display**, an advanced find query cannot be created from the related entity using the N:N relationship. The following table describes this behavior in detail:

Display Option for Current Entity (Region)	Display Option for Other Entity (Account)	Advanced find query can be created from the entity
Use Custom Label / Use Plural Name	**Use Custom Label / Use Plural Name**	Both **Region** and **Account**
Do not Display	**Use Custom Label / Use Plural Name**	**Region** alone
Use Custom Label / Use Plural Name	**Do not Display**	**Account** alone
Do not Display	**Do not Display**	None

8. Then click on the **Save and Close** button in the top ribbon to create the new relationship and save it.

How it works...

Many-to-many relationships enable you to establish a link between many records of one entity and many records of another entity. Unlike one-to-many relationships, there is no lookup field on either entity. Related records using a many-to-many relationship can be considered peers and the relationship its reciprocal. A many-to-many relationship may also be **self-referential**. As there is no cascading behavior involved in many-to-many relationships, we can allow an individual record to have a reference to itself.

With an N:N relationship, we cannot import data using **Import Data Wizard** and link them using the N:N relationship. For example, we cannot import a set of accounts and associate them with different **Region** records.

Moreover, we cannot execute any workflow against an N:N relationship. For example, we cannot execute a notification workflow when an Account is added to a Region.

Finally, in an advanced find query, the columns of only one entity from an N:N relationship alone can be added. For example, if we are creating an advance find query for the **Region** entity, only the **Region** entity columns can be added for a query defined using the native N:N relationship.

There's more...

The N:N relationship defined in this recipe, is usually known as the **native many-to-many relationship**. There is another way to create a many-to-many relationship between two entities in Dynamics CRM 2011 and it is known as a **manual many-to-many relationship**. Using a combination of two N:1 relationships, which shares a common **intersect entity**, a manual N:N relationship can be established between the two entities.

In this recipe our native N:N relationship is where one Region can be linked to many Accounts and many Regions can be linked to one Account. Now, instead of creating a direct N:N relationship, we can introduce an intersection entity called "Office" between the Region and Account entity. We can create an N:1 relationship between the intersect entity "Office" and Region as there can be many offices in one Region. Another N:1 relationship can be created between the intersect entity "Office" and the Account entity as many Offices can be linked to one Account or, in other words, an Account can have many Offices:

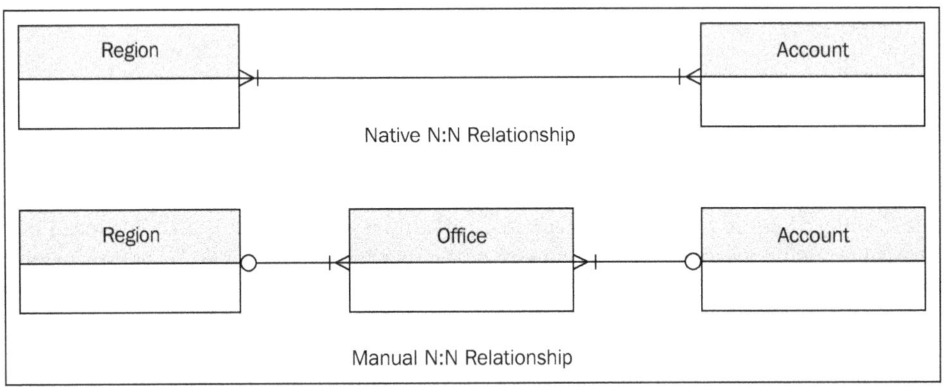

In one sense both these types of N:N relationships are the same. But in Dynamics CRM 2011, the manual N:N relationship provides some additional benefits and hence, it is worth considering. The benefits with manual N:N relationships are as follows:

- Data can be imported using **Import Data Wizard** and linked to each other. Manual N:N relationships are based on two lookup fields (N:1 relationships). Lookup fields are supported in data import using **Import Data Wizard**.
- Workflows can be executed on the intersect entity (Office). Hence, it is possible to find out when an Account's Office is added to a Region.
- An advanced find view on the intersect entity (Office) can include columns from both the Region and Account entities.

Creating a relationship field mapping

When we establish a one-to-many or many-to-one relationship between two entities, Dynamics CRM 2011 allows us to create field mappings to reduce the data entry required when a record is created within the context of a primary record. In this recipe, we will discuss how to create relationship field mapping in the Dynamics CRM 2011 system.

How to do it...

Let us consider that we have created a one-to-many relationship between two entities Account and Office, where one Account (primary entity) can have many Offices (related entity). Both of these entities have a **Website** field. Using relationship mapping we want to make sure that when an office record is created from the associated view on an Account form, the account record's website entry gets automatically populated to the office record.

Please perform the following steps to create a field mapping:

1. Log in to the Dynamics CRM 2011 system as a system administrator or with a relevant security role.
2. Navigate to **Settings** | **Customizations** | **Solutions** and change the view to **Unmanaged Solutions**, if not already selected.
3. Then double-click on the unmanaged solution to open it.
4. Navigate to the primary entity's (**Account**) one-to-many relationships section by going to **Components** | **Entities** | **Account** | **1:N Relationships**.
5. In the actions toolbar, select **Mappable** in the **Type** drop-down list.
6. The view will display a list of mappable relationships with this entity. Double-click on the relationship against which the field mapping is to be added.
7. On the **Relationship** form, click on **Mappings** under the **Common** section.
8. This will display a list of existing field mappings for this relationship.
9. To create a new field mapping, click on the **New** button in the actions toolbar.
10. With this the **Create Field Mapping From <Primary Entity> to <Related Entity>** page will appear.

11. Select the source field from **Source Entity Fields** and target field from **Target Entity Fields** as shown in the following screenshot:

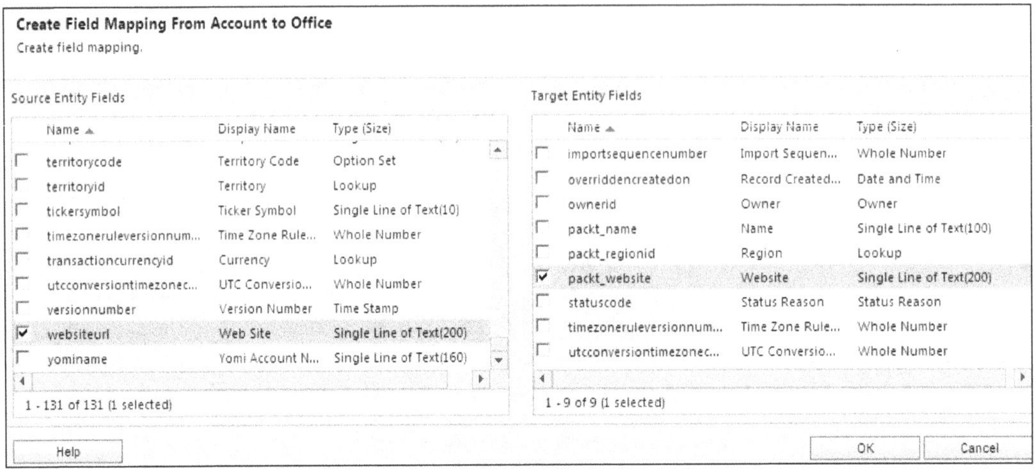

12. Click on **OK** to save the changes.
13. Click on **Save and Close** in the **Relationship** form.
14. Click on **Publish All Customizations** to publish the changes.

How it works...

As stated earlier, relationship field mappings reduce the data entry effort when a related entity record is created from a primary entity record form. In our example, if we open an account record having data for the **Website** field and then create an office record from this account form using associated view, we can see that the office record's **Website** field is automatically populated with the same URL copied from the account record. This is shown in the following screenshot:

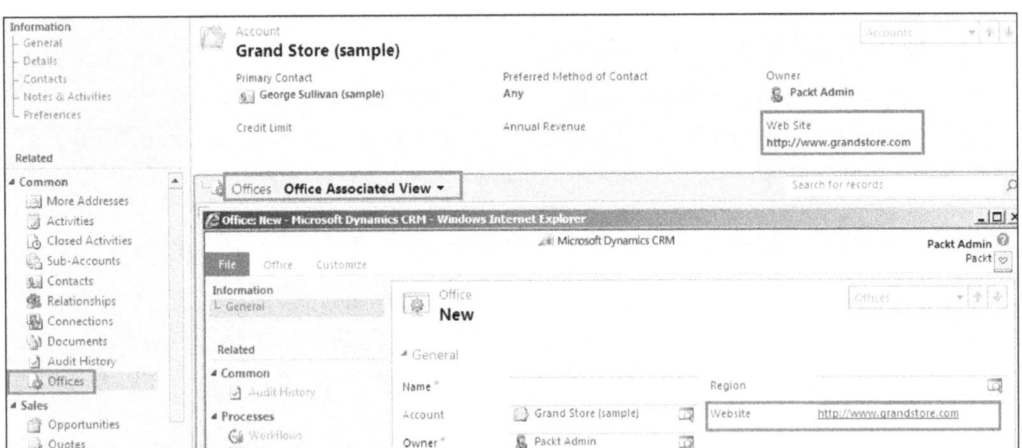

The requirements for entity field mapping are as follows:

- Both the source and target fields must have the same data type and format.
- One target field can only be mapped on one source field, but one source field can be mapped to multiple target fields.
- Only editable fields available on the source entity form are available for mapping.
- If both source and target fields are text fields, the target field length must be equal to or greater than source field length.
- If both source and target fields are option sets, each of the source option numeric value must match the target option numeric value.

See also

In this chapter, we have discussed in detail entity creation and their relationships. In the next chapter, we will delve into the entity forms and views. Some of the interesting recipes in the next chapter are as follows:

- Creating a role-based form
- Creating a new public view
- Creating a user's personal view

7

Form and View Customizations

Forms and views enable the display of the entity data to the users. In the previous chapter, we have discussed the recipes for creating and customizing an entity. Here we will delve into the recipes for creating and customizing entity forms and views. Forms are the most commonly used platform to display data inside the Dynamics CRM system. Hence, forms should be carefully designed and implemented.

In this chapter, we will discuss the following recipes:

- Creating and customizing an entity main form
- Controlling form behavior using JScript
- Customizing the process-driven form (Dynamics CRM 2011 Online only)
- Creating and customizing the mobile form
- Configuring a form to be role-based
- Creating and customizing a public view
- Customizing search criteria for a Quick Find view
- Creating a user's personal view
- Deactivating or deleting a user's personal view

Introduction

Forms are probably the most important visual element of the Dynamics CRM 2011 interface. To find the underlying data in every entity record, the user has to open the form. Dynamics CRM 2011 supports two types of forms:

- **The main form**: Dynamics CRM 2011 uses this form to allow the user to enter and view data within the Dynamics CRM 2011 web user interface as well as the Dynamics CRM 2011 within Microsoft Outlook interface.

> One main form per entity exists by default. However, multiple main forms can be created for an entity. Dynamics CRM 2011 supports role-based forms, which means separate forms can be visible depending on the security roles of the current user. Usually, multiple main forms are created when role-based forms have to be supported.

- **The mobile form**: Dynamics CRM 2011 uses this form when a user is accessing CRM from a mobile device that is compatible with HTML 4.0 using a URL such as <CRM_server> /m, where <CRM_server> is the path of Microsoft Dynamics CRM 2011 Server. A separate form for mobile devices is useful considering the limited space usually available on a mobile screen. A mobile form does not store data on a mobile device.

  If users try to access Dynamics CRM 2011 from an unsupported browser, they will be redirected to the mobile form.

  The following table outlines the browsers supported by Microsoft Dynamics CRM 2011:

Browser	Version / other requirements
Internet Explorer	IE7 (only for the on-premises version) IE 8, IE9 IE10 (desktop mode only)
Mozilla Firefox	Latest publicly released version running on Windows 8, Windows 7, Windows Vista, or Windows XP
Google Chrome	Latest publicly released version running on Windows 8, Windows 7, Windows Vista, or Windows XP
Apple Safari	Latest publicly released version running on Mac OS X 10.7 (Lion) or 10.8 (Mountain Lion)

Detailed information about supported browsers can be found at http://technet.microsoft.com/en-us/library/hh699710.aspx.

Dynamics CRM 2011 also supports special variants of the main form, as follows:

- **The read-optimized form**: Dynamics CRM 2011 has another type of form called the read-optimized form. Introduced in Update Rollup 7, this form is designed for the fast display of a record by disabling the ribbon and form scripts. This form displays the record in the read-only mode. Read-optimized forms are disabled by default and can be enabled by going to **System** | **Administration** | **System Settings** | **Customization** | **Form Mode**.

  Update Rollup 12 has introduced the following changes in read-optimized forms:

  - The navigation pane for read-optimized forms is now enabled and the navigation pane can be expanded or collapsed.
  - Support for web resources has been added. A new setting in the web resource properties, called **Show this Web Resources in Read Optimized form**, has been added. This setting must be enabled for the web resources to display in the read-optimized form. If the web resource depends on form resources, which are not available in a read-optimized form, we should not display it.

> Read-optimized forms honor all field-level security and role-based form definitions. If an entity has more than one form enabled, the read-optimized form uses the form that the user last used.

- **The process-driven form**: The December 2012 Service Update (Polaris update) of Dynamics CRM 2011 has introduced an enhanced read-optimized form, commonly known as the process-driven form for the Account, Contact, Lead, Opportunity, and Case entities. This new type of form is very useful, especially for touch devices, as the new form is designed to contain everything in one form; there is no need to open multiple pop ups. However, this new form type cannot be used for any entity other than the entities listed above.

  For the Account, Contact, Lead, Opportunity, and Case entities, in addition to the **Information** form, there will be a new form with the same name as that of the entity. The <entity name> form will always display using the updated presentation, regardless of the settings for read-optimized forms. However, if read-optimized forms are enabled for the organization, the information form will also display using the updated presentation.

  These new forms are not available in an on-premises deployment of Microsoft Dynamics CRM 2011.

Form editor

We need to use a form editor to customize a form within Dynamics CRM 2011. The form layout definition is actually stored as an XML file called `Form Xml` in the `SystemForm` entity. The `customization.xml` file exported with an unmanaged solution contains the definition of the entity forms.

Creating and customizing an entity main form

Almost all the business entities have a customizable main form. The Activity entity does not have any form and some entity forms such as the Case Resolution entity form are not customizable. When a custom entity is created, one main and one mobile form are added automatically. In this recipe, we will focus our discussion on how to customize a main form.

Getting ready

Dynamics CRM 2011 introduced a flexible layout for form design. The following diagram outlines the typical main form layout within the Dynamics CRM 2011 system:

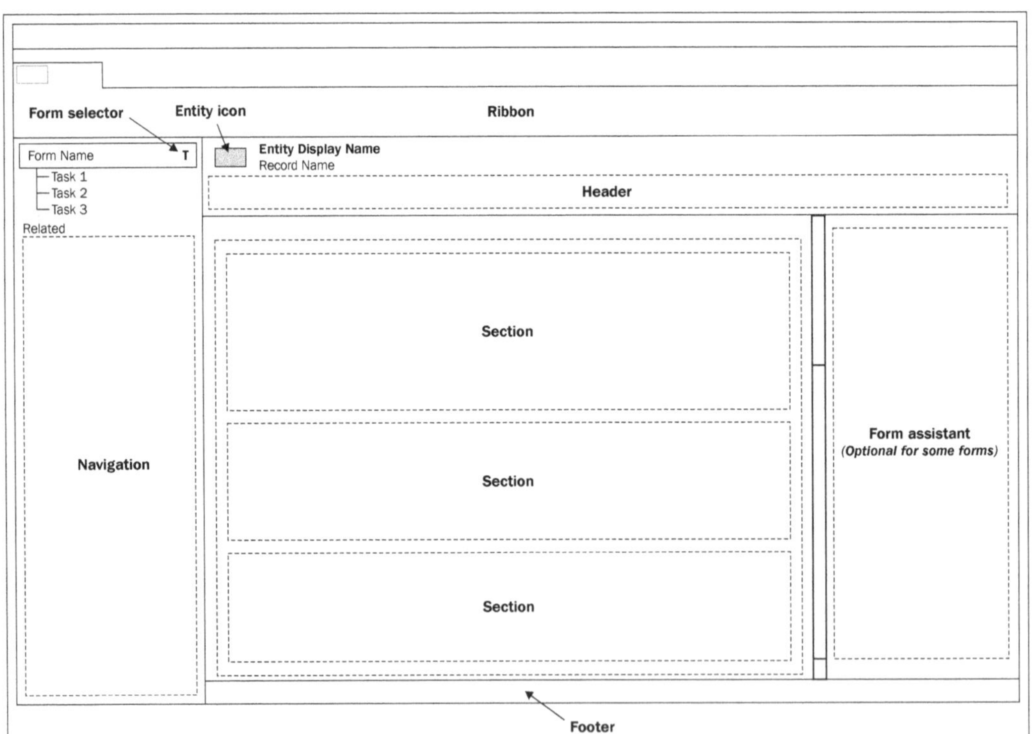

The major visible components of a standard main form are as follows:

- **Ribbon**: This is the top area of the form. We cannot customize this using the form editor. We can find more information on how to customize the form ribbon in the next chapter.
- **Entity icon**: This displays the **Icon for Entity Form** icon of the entity. It is a 32 x 32 pixel image and can be updated for an entity. Please refer to the *Updating the icon of an entity* recipe in *Chapter 6, Entity Customization*, to modify the entity icon displayed in entity forms.
- **Header and footer**: The header and footer are two read-only areas of the form layout. These two sections remain static when a user scrolls through the form data displayed by the various tabs and sections. So any data that is required to be available to the user irrespective of any scrolling, can be included in these sections.
- **Form selector**: When an entity has multiple forms and the current user's security role has access to more than one form, the form selector is displayed. The user can use the form selector to choose a form from multiple forms available to them.
- **Navigation**: This section allows users to navigate to related records of the current record. We can add, modify, delete, or reorganize the link to the related entity records using the form editor. We can also include links to URLs or web resources by adding navigation links using the form editor.
- **Form assistant**: It helps when we set values for lookup fields. Dynamics CRM 2011 has introduced improved capabilities to filter data returned in the lookup dialog. Hence, the form assistant is no longer useful; the form assistant has been turned off for all except the following three entity forms:
    - Case
    - Product
    - Service activity
- **Tabs and sections**: Tabs and sections allow grouping and laying out of controls in a form. A tab can contain multiple sections. Each form can have a maximum of 100 tabs. Tabs have a vertical collapse/expand feature.

We will now take a look at the various form-body elements that can be added or associated with an entity form:

- **Field**: Each field represents an attribute of the entity. A field can be added to a form using the form editor and the form editor allows us to add the same field multiple times in a form. Each instance of a field in a form is known as a **control**. The appearance and behavior of a control is driven by the type and formatting options of the attribute as well as display and formatting properties set on the control, using the form editor.

- **Tab and section**: As previously discussed, tabs and sections are used for grouping the controls in the form. A tab can contain multiple sections within it. Each tab or section can be assigned a name. We can choose to display the name of the tab or section on the form or include a separator line at the top of the tab or section, underneath the name.

  A tab can have one column or two columns; when two columns are specified, the width of each column is a percentage of the width of the tab. A section, on the other hand, may have up to four columns and we can control the width available for control labels to be displayed in the section as well as how labels for controls in the section should be aligned.

- **Spacer**: The **Spacer** element provides extra space between fields and controls in the form. This is used to improve the control layout in a section.
- **Sub-Grid**: **Sub-Grid** allows us to display a list of records, charts, or both.

> The first four subgrids can be populated with data in a form when it loads. If more than four subgrids exist on a form, the remaining subgrids require some user or form script action to retrieve data. This is for performance optimization.

- **IFRAME**: This control provides the HTML iFrame element in the form. Using the control, we can host another web page within the Dynamics CRM 2011 entity form. The form editor provides the ability to set regular iFrame properties along with properties specific to Dynamics CRM 2011.
- **Web Resource**: This control displays a form-enabled web resource to be displayed on the page. A form-enabled web resource includes a web page (HTML), image (JPG, PNG, GIF, ICO), or Silverlight (XAP) resource. The web resource contents are hosted within Dynamics CRM 2011.
- **Notes**: If the entity uses notes and attachments, we can add the **Notes** control into the form. This control can only be added if the entity has **Notes** enabled in the entity definition.
- **Navigation Link**: This control is available only within the **Navigation** section of the form. This control allows us to add a link to an external URL or web resource.

How to do it...

In this recipe, we will first discuss how to create a new main form and then discuss the form-customization options. The customization steps can be carried out on any main form.

The entity main form can be customized by carrying out the following tasks:

- Editing tabs
- Editing sections
- Editing fields
- Editing header and footer
- Adding subgrids
- Adding iFrames
- Adding web resources
- Editing the Navigation area
- Editing form properties
- Making the form non-customizable

In this recipe, we will discuss all the previously stated tasks one after the other. Please follow these steps to customize the main form for an entity:

1. Log in to the Dynamics CRM 2011 system as a system administrator or with a relevant security role.
2. Navigate to **Settings** | **Customizations** | **Solutions** and change the view to **Unmanaged Solutions**, if not already selected.
3. Then double-click on the unmanaged solution to open it.
4. On the expanded **Solution** page, navigate to **Components** | **Entities** | **<Entity>** | **Forms**.

The next step is to create a new main form; this can be done in two ways. We will discuss both of these here:

- **Creating an entirely new main form**: Go to **New** | **Main Form** in the actions toolbar. This will create a new form by copying the existing main form. When the new form pops up, click on the save button to save the form.

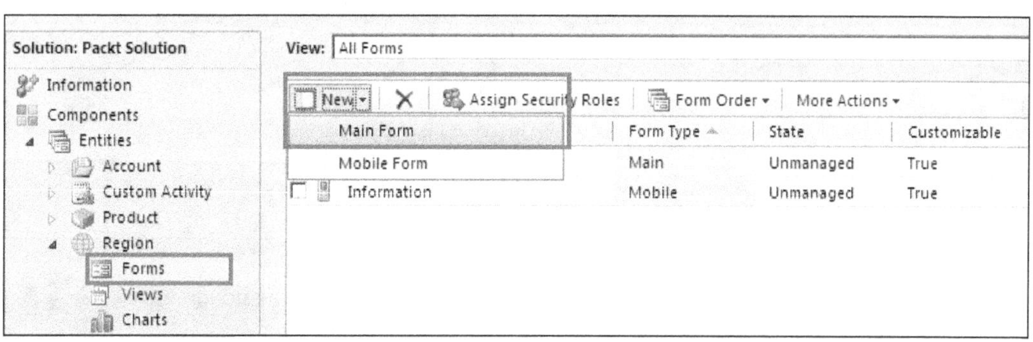

- **Creating a new form from an existing form**: Open the existing form by double-clicking on it. When the form launches, click on **Save As** in the top ribbon. When the **Save As -- Webpage Dialog** window pops up, provide data for the **Name** and **Description** fields of the new form. Finally, click on the **OK** button to save the new form as shown in the following screenshot:

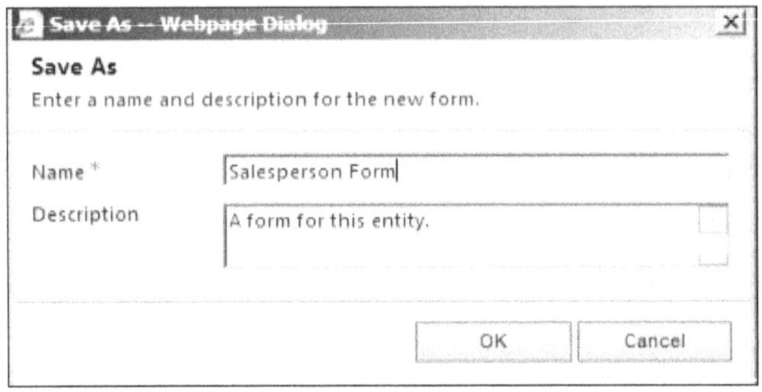

> Any newly created main form will be assigned only to the system administrator and system customizer security roles by default. If this form is to be used by users having other security roles, assign the form to additional security roles by following the *Configuring a form to be role-based* recipe in this chapter.

To customize a main form, open the form by double-clicking on it in the forms list.

The next step is to discuss the editing of tabs in the form. Tabs are collapsible controls that can contain section controls. The following two points will demonstrate adding a new tab and editing tab properties:

- **Adding a new tab in the form**: Click on **Body** in the form ribbon and then click on the **Insert** tab in the form. In the **Insert** tab, under the **Tab** group, select **One Column** to create a one-column tab, or **Two Columns** to create a two-column tab:

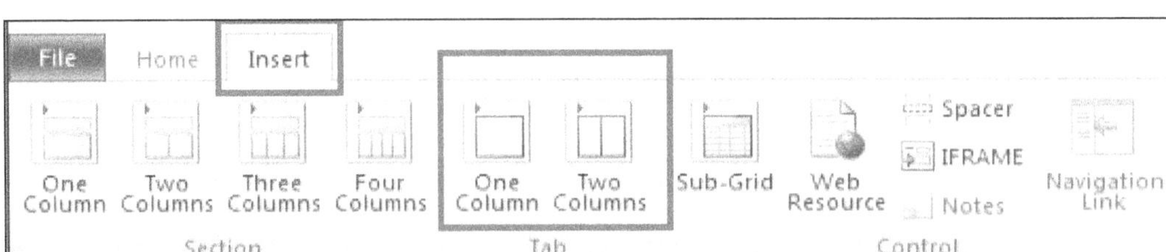

  If we add a tab, Dynamics CRM 2011 will automatically add a section for each column.

> To remove any control in an entity form, use the *Delete* key on the keyboard. Alternatively, the **Remove** button in the ribbon can also be used.

- **Editing tab properties**: Select the tab control and then click on the **Change Properties** button in the form ribbon. The **Tab Properties** page will open with the following properties being modifiable:

Tab property	Description
Under the **Display** tab	
Name	The unique name of the tab.
Label	The display label for this tab. This text will appear on the form.
Show the label of this tab on the Form	This determines whether the label defined for this tab will be displayed on the form. Select this option to enable the display of the tab's label on the form.
Expand this tab by default	If selected, the tab control will be displayed in expanded mode by default.
Visible by default	If selected, the tab control will be visible by default in the form.
Under the **Formatting** tab	
Select tab layout	Choose between **One Column** and **Two Columns** to define the layout of the tab.
Column 1 width	If the **Two Columns** option is selected in the tab layout, we can specify the width of column 1 as a percentage.
Column 2 width	If the **Two Columns** option is selected in the tab layout, we can specify the width of column 2 as a percentage.
The **Events** properties	
	Scripts libraries can be linked to the tab. The scripts functions will be called on the `TabStateChange` event.

Next we will see the editing of a section in a tab. A section contains fields in the form. The following two sections will demonstrate adding a section in a form and editing the section's properties:

- **Adding a section in the form**: Select the tab control where the new section is to be added and then click on the **Insert** tab in the form ribbon. Thereafter, click on **One Column**, **Two Columns**, **Three Columns**, or **Four Columns** under the **Section** group depending on whether a section with one, two, three, or four columns is to be added.

- **Editing section properties**: Select the section control and then click on the **Change Properties** button in the form ribbon. The **Section Properties** page will open and the following properties will be modifiable:

Section property	Description
Under the **Display** tab	
Name	The unique name of the tab.
Label	The display label for this tab. This text will appear on the form.
Show the label of this section on the Form	This determines whether the label defined for this section will be displayed on the form. Select this option to enable the display of the section's label on the form.
Show a line at top of the section	If selected, a divider line will be displayed underneath the name of the section.
Width	Specify the width of the label area of the fields in this field. The width must be set between 50 and 250 pixels.
Visible by default	If selected, the section control will be visible by default on the form.
Lock the section of the Form	If selected, the section would be locked in the form.
Under the **Formatting** tab	
Layout	Choose from among **One Column**, **Two Columns**, **Three Columns**, and **Four Columns** to define the layout of the section control.
Field label alignment	Select between the **Left** and **Right** alignments for the field labels in the section control.

Next we will take a look at editing a field in the section:

- **Adding a field in a section**: Select the section where the field has to be added. Thereafter, find the field in the right-hand side **Field Explorer** pane. By default, the **Field Explorer** pane displays all unused fields in the form. If we want to add a field that is already used in the form, uncheck the **Only show unused fields** checkbox as shown in the following screenshot:

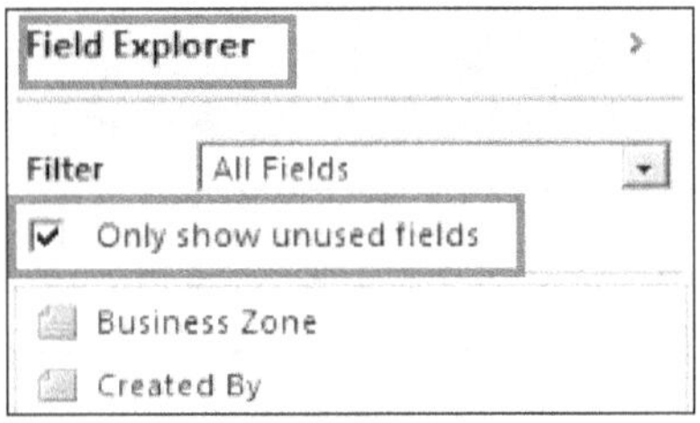

After selecting the field in **Field Explorer**, move the field by pressing the left mouse button and drop the field in the intended column of the section. The red line on top of the column indicates that the column has been selected. Now drop the field on the selected column.

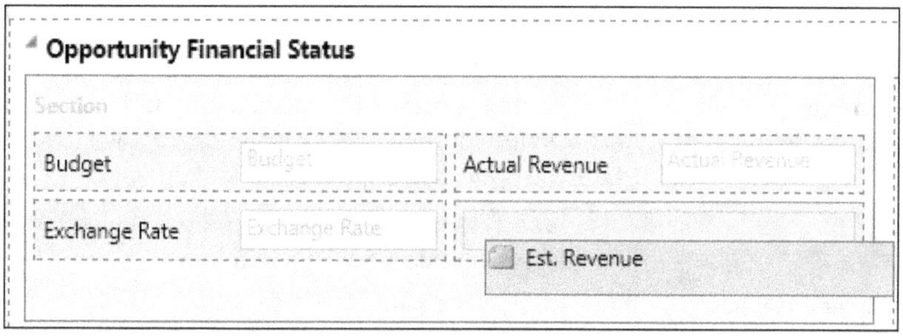

- **Editing field properties**: To edit the form-level properties of the field, select the field and then click on the **Change Properties** button in the form ribbon. Then the **Field Properties** pop up will open and the following properties can be modified:

Field property	Description
Under the **Display** tab	
Label	Here you can edit the display name of the field on the form. By default, the display name of the field will be displayed there, which can be edited to provide a new display name for the field on the form.
Display Label on the form	This determines whether the display name of the field is to be displayed in the form.
Field is read-only	This determines whether a field is to be read-only for the users in the form.
Lock the field on the form	This determines whether the field is to be locked on the form.
Visible by default	This determines the default visibility of the control in the form.
Under the **Formatting** tab	
Layout	This determines the width of this field on the form. The width of a field depends on the layout settings of the section it is in.
The **Details** properties	
	This tab displays the details of the field definition. Click on the **Edit** button to modify those properties of the field definition that can be modified.
The **Event** properties	
	Script libraries can be linked to the tab. The scripts' functions will be called on the `OnChange` event.

If the field is of type `Lookup` (N:1 relationship with another entity), then there exists an additional set of properties in the **Field Properties** list. These properties can be set to save the user's time, find the appropriate parent record, or to restrict the user to select among a subset of records in the parent entity. The following form-level properties of the lookup field can be edited:

Property name	Description
Turn off automatic resolutions in the field	If this setting is disabled (not selected) and if a user enters a partial value for the lookup field and tabs away, Dynamics CRM 2011 will try to autopopulate the lookup field. This property is not supported for process-driven forms of Microsoft Dynamics CRM 2011 Online.
Disable most recently used items for this field	If this setting is disabled (not selected), Dynamics CRM 2011 will automatically provide a list of recently selected values for the user to choose from. This property is not supported for process-driven forms of Microsoft Dynamics CRM 2011 Online.
Related Record Filtering	This setting provides a way to limit the list of records that the user can choose from. The list under the **Only show records where** heading displays all the potential relationships that can be used to filter this lookup. Once a record is selected, the list under the **Contains** heading will display all relationships that connect the related entity (selected in the first list) to the target entity. Select the **Allow users to turn off filter** checkbox to provide users with the option to turn off the filter defined here. This makes it possible for them to view a wider range of records.
Additional properties	This setting controls how much search flexibility the user will have in terms of changing among various views and searching the record with a search box. Select the **Display Search Box in lookup dialog** checkbox if you want a search box to be available in the lookup. In the **Default View** list, select the default view for which results will be displayed in the lookup. Finally, choose the views we want users to have access to in the lookup, using the **View Selector** list.

- **Adding a new entity field and then adding it to the form**: A new field can also be created and then added to the entity from the form. To create a new field, click on the **New Field** button at the bottom of the **Field Explorer** pane. This will launch the new field pop up. Thereafter, follow the *Creating a custom field for an entity* recipe in *Chapter 6, Entity Customization*, to add the new field in the entity.

Next we will delve into editing headers and footers.

To edit the header or footer of the form, click on the **Header** or **Footer** button in the form ribbon and the section will be focused automatically. Then click on **Change Properties** in the ribbon. The **Header Properties** or **Footer Properties** page will pop up and we can edit the following settings:

Header/footer property	Description
Under the **Display** tab	
Width	Specify the width field label area here. The width must be set between 50 and 250 pixels.
Lock the section of the Form	This setting is selected by default and cannot be modified. This setting determines whether the section would be locked in the form or not.
Under the **Formatting** tab	
Layout	Here you can choose from among **One Column**, **Two Columns**, **Three Columns**, and **Four Columns** to define the layout of the header/footer control.
Field Label Alignment	Select from the **Left** (default), **Right**, or **Center** alignment for the field labels in the header/footer control.
Field Label Position	Select between **Side** (default) and **Top** to specify whether the field label in this section will be on the left-hand side or above the field.

Fields can be added to the header or footer controls in the same way they are added in any section control in the form.

Next we will look at how to add subgrids. The **Sub-Grid** control displays related entity records in the form body, using the following steps:

1. Select the section control where the subgrid is to be added in the form.
2. Then click on the **Sub-Grid** button under the **Insert** tab in the form ribbon. This will bring up the **List or Chart Properties** page, where we can specify the following properties of a subgrid:

Subgrid property	Description
Under the **Display** tab	
Name	The unique name of the subgrid control.
Label	The display text of the subgrid. This text will be displayed on the form.
Display label on the Form	Select to confirm that the **Label** text will be displayed on the form.

Subgrid property	Description
Data Source	This specifies the primary data source of the subgrid. The **Records** list allows us to select between **Only Related Records** (to set only entities having a relationship to the current entity) and **All Record Types** (to set all available entities). We can choose the related entity from the **Entity** list. This list content will vary based on the earlier list's selection. The **Default View** list allows us to choose which view is to be displayed in the subgrid.
Display Search Box	Select this setting to display the search box in the subgrid.
Display Index	Select this setting to display the alphabetic index record selector in the subgrid. This property is not supported for process-driven forms of Microsoft Dynamics CRM 2011 Online.
View Selector	Select this setting to display the view selector in the subgrid. This property is not supported for process-driven forms of Microsoft Dynamics CRM 2011 Online.
Chart Options	Select whether to display a chart selector along with a default chart or show only a specified chart in place of the subgrid. This property is not supported for process-driven forms of Microsoft Dynamics CRM 2011 Online.
Under the **Formatting** tab	
Layout	Choose from among **One Column**, **Two Columns**, **Three Columns**, and **Four Columns** to define the layout of the subgrid control.
Number of Rows	Select the maximum number of rows to be displayed in the subgrid control. The number of rows has to be between 2 and 250.
Automatically expand to use available space	Select this setting to enable automatic expansion of the subgrid to use available space in the form.

iFrames or Inline Frames are HTML documents embedded inside the Dynamics CRM entity form. The following steps will guide you through adding an iFrame in the form:

1. Select the section control where the iFrame is to be added in the form.
2. Then click on the **IFRAME** button under the **Insert** tab in the form ribbon. This will bring up the **Add an IFRAME** page, where we can specify the following properties of an iFrame:

iFrame property	Description
Under the **General** tab	
Name	The unique name of the iFrame control.
URL	The URL of the HTML document to be displayed in the iFrame control.
Pass record object-type code and unique identifier as parameters	Select this option to pass contextual information entity object-type code and the record's unique identifier to the iFrame. Read more about this in the *How it works...* section of this recipe.
Label	Here, specify the display text for the iFrame.
Display label on the Form	Select this setting to display the label on the form.
Restrict cross-frame scripting, where supported	This checkbox is selected by default. We can remove this restriction only if we are certain that the HTML document/site we are using as the target of the iFrame can be trusted.
Visible by default	Select this setting to make the iFrame visible by default on the form.
Under the **Formatting** tab	
Layout	Choose from among **One Column**, **Two Columns**, **Three Columns**, and **Four Columns** to define the layout of the iFrame control.
Number of Rows	Select the maximum number of rows the iFrame control occupies on the form. The number of rows has to be between 1 and 40.
Automatically expand to use available space	Select this setting to enable automatic expansion of the iFrame control to use the available space in the form.
Scrolling	Select the scrolling option for the iFrame content display.
Display Border	Specify whether a border for the iFrame control is to be displayed.

Web resources represent files that can be used to extend the Microsoft Dynamics CRM 2011 web application, such as HTML files, Image files, JScript library, and Silverlight applications. The following steps can be used to add a web resource in the form:

1. Select the section control where the web resource is to be added in the form.
2. Then click on the **Web Resource** button under the **Insert** tab in the form ribbon. This will bring up the **Add Web Resource** page, where we can specify the following properties of a web resource:

Web resource property	Description
Under the **General** tab	
Web Resource	Lookup to find a form-enabled web resource.
Name	The unique name for the web resource.
Label	Specify the display text for the web resource here.
Display label on the Form	Select this setting to display the label on the form.
Visibility by default	Select this setting to make the web resource visible by default on the form.
Show this web resource in Read-Optimized Form	Select this setting if the web resource is to be displayed in the read-optimized form.
Under the **Formatting** tab	
Layout	Choose from among **One Column**, **Two Columns**, **Three Columns**, and **Four Columns** to define the layout of the web resource control.
Number of Rows	Select the maximum number of rows the web resource control occupies on the form. The number of rows has to be between 1 and 40.
Automatically expand to use available space	Select this setting to enable automatic expansion of the web resource control to use the available space in the form.
Scrolling	Select the scrolling option for the web resource content display.
Display Border	Specify here whether a border for the web resource control is to be displayed.
The **Dependencies** properties	
	Select the fields from the **Available fields** list that are required by the web resource, and then click on the (add selected records) button to move the selected fields to the **Dependent fields** list.

The navigation area displays entities that are related to the current entity. Each relationship has a **Label** property and in this navigation section this **Label** property is displayed by default. However, the display name for the related entity can be changed. This display name does not update the **Label** property of the relationship. In order to edit the navigation area, perform the following steps:

1. Select the **Navigation** button in the form ribbon.
2. The navigation section will be enabled. Then click on any relationship label and select **Change Properties** to edit the display text. This will bring up the **Relationship Properties** page.
3. Modify the **Label** field here.

Next we will edit the form properties; in order to do this, click on the **Form Properties** button in the form ribbon and the **Form Properties** page will pop up. The following properties can be edited there:

Form property	Description
The **Event** properties	
	Add or remove the JScript libraries that will be available for the form or field events.
Under the **Display** tab	
Form Name	The display name for the form. Modify this to rename the form.
Description	Specify a description for this form here.
Show navigation items	Select this setting to display the page navigation in the form.
The **Parameters** properties	
	Add query string parameters to be passed to the form. Click on the green plus sign to add a query string. We have to provide a **Name** value and select a **Type** value of the query string parameter.
The **Non- Event Dependencies** properties	
	Select the fields from the **Available fields** list that are required by any external, non-event scripts, and then click on the (add selected records) button to move the selected fields to the **Dependent fields** list. These fields will not be removable from the form.

Lastly, making a form non-customizable restricts any future customization of the form. Therefore, to make a form non-customizable, perform the following steps:

1. Select the **Managed Properties** button in the form ribbon.
2. The **Managed Properties of System Form: Form** web page dialog will pop up. In this page, mark **Customizable** as **False**.

> After making any changes to an entity form, the form has to be saved and published. Use the **Publish** button in the form ribbon to publish the changes.

How it works...

Web resources and iFrames are not displayed using the Microsoft Dynamics CRM 2011 for Outlook reading pane, but iFrames are displayed in read-optimized forms. When the **Pass record object-type code and unique identifier as parameters** setting is enabled, iFrames allow the form to pass the following contextual parameters to itself:

Parameter name	Description
`typename`	The name of the entity.
`type`	This takes in the entity type code, which is an integer value to uniquely identify an entity in a specific organization.
`Id`	A GUID that represents a record.
`orgname`	The organization's name.
`userlcid`	The user's language code.
`orglcid`	The organization's language code.

The list of **entity type codes** can be found at `http://msdn.microsoft.com/en-us/library/gg328086.aspx`. The key points about entity type codes are as follows:

- Type codes below 10,000 are reserved for out-of-the-box entities.
- Custom entities will have a type code greater than or equal to 10,000.
- Custom entities' type codes might change during solution import. Hence the type codes of a custom entity might be different in the development and test environments.
- The entity codes are stored in the Dynamics CRM database and can be retrieved from the `EntityView` table of the `<OrganizationName>_MSCRM` database.

Controlling form behavior using JScript

Form scripting allows us to perform a variety of actions such as enforcing custom field validation and automation and displaying values for calculated fields within a form in the Microsoft Dynamics CRM 2011 system. Most of the time, performing actions on data that is available on the client side offers better performance than using methods, which require data to be saved by the user, and then performing actions on the web server.

Dynamics CRM 2011 forms support scripts written using JScript and can be associated with the following two form events:

- `OnLoad`: This event is triggered when the form is loaded. This event is usually used to initialize the form for use.
- `OnSave`: This event is triggered when a user tries to save the form data. This event is usually used for data validation. Scripts associated with this event can cancel the save before it is sent back to the server.

Additionally, each field in a Dynamics CRM 2011 form provides access to the `OnChange` event. This event is triggered whenever a user changes data in the field or clicks a different form element (meaning, the field loses focus). This event can be used to validate the field data, perform calculations to change other fields, or implement dynamic pick lists (drop-down lists).

Update Rollup 12 and December 2012 Service Update (Polaris update) have introduced the following exceptions to the behavior of triggering the `OnChange` event for the **Two-Option** fields that are formatted to use radio buttons or checkboxes:

- If a Two-Option field is formatted to use radio buttons, the `OnChange` event occurs immediately without requiring that field to lose focus.
- If a Two-Option field is formatted to use checkboxes, the `OnChange` event occurs immediately without requiring that field to lose focus, except when the browser is Internet Explorer 7 or 8.

The `OnChange` event does not fire if the field value is modified programmatically using the `setValue` method. To handle this scenario, we can use the `fireOnChange` method in the code.

How to do it...

Please perform the following steps to add scripts in a Dynamics CRM form:

1. Log in to the Dynamics CRM 2011 system as a system administrator or with a relevant security role.
2. Navigate to **Settings** | **Customizations** | **Solutions** and change the view to **Unmanaged Solutions**, if not already selected.

3. Then double-click on the unmanaged solution to open it.
4. In the expanded solution page, navigate to **Components** | **Entities** | **<Entity>** | **Forms**. Double-click on the form where the script is to be used.
5. When the form designer opens up, click on **Form Properties** in the form ribbon.
6. In the **Form Properties** dialog, click on the **Add** button in the actions toolbar of the **Form Libraries** section.
7. The **Look Up Record** view will open up, and from this view the web resources can be added to the form library. Select a JScript web resource from the grid, if the JScript web resource is already added.

   Otherwise, click on the **New** button present at the bottom-left side of the view to add a new web resource. The **Web Resource: New** page will appear. In this page, provide the following information:

Web resource property	Value to be provided
Under the **General** tab	
Name	The schema name of the script-type web resource
Display Name	The display name of the web resource. Optional but recommended
Description	Optionally enter some descriptive text about the web resource
Under the **Content** tab	
Type	Select **Script (JScript)** from the drop-down list
Language	Select the language of the web resource from the drop-down list
Uploaded File	Click on the **Browse** button if you wish to upload the already saved JScript file

   Then click on the **Text Editor** button associated with **Type**. This will bring up the **Edit Content** dialog. Add the JScript methods in the **Source** section.

8. After adding the JScript to the web resource, click on the **Save** button in the **Web Resource: New** form ribbon. Thereafter, publish this web resource by clicking the **Publish** button in the ribbon. Finally, close the form.
9. Click on **OK** in the **Look Up Record** dialog. Now we can find the web resource added to the form libraries.
10. Below **Form Libraries**, in the **Event Handlers** section, choose the following options:
    - **Control**: Select **Form** to add a script to form events. Select any form fields to add a script to the field event.
    - **Event**: If the **Form** control was selected, then we have to select between the `OnLoad` and `OnSave` events depending on which event we want to add our script to.

11. Thereafter, click on the **Add** button in the **Event Handlers** section. The **Handler Properties** window will pop up. In the **Details** tab, provide the following inputs:
    - **Library**: Select an item from the form library
    - **Function**: Select the JScript method to be called from the selected library
    - **Enabled**: Select the **Enabled** checkbox to make the JScript method available to be called by a field event
    - **Pass execution context as first parameter**: Select this option if the execution context is to be passed as the first parameter
    - **Comma separated list of parameters that will be passed to the function**: A comma separated list of parameters to be passed to the JScript method
12. Then, in the **Dependencies** tab, add the fields using the (add selected records) button, which is used by the current script, from the **Available fields** list to **Dependent fields**.

> Up to 50 event handlers per event can be defined. Each handler is executed in the order that it is displayed on the **Events** tab of the form element's properties dialog box.

13. Finally, save and publish the form.
14. The script can be tested in three modes of a form: create, update, and read-only. In the form designer ribbon, click on **Preview** and then select **Create Form**, **Update Form**, or **Read-Only Form**.

How it works...

Scripts are added to a form or form fields to implement behaviors that are not available out of the box with Dynamics CRM 2011. Microsoft Dynamics CRM 2011 recommends the use of the `Xrm.Page` object model methods to access the form elements. Though for backward compatibility Dynamics CRM 2011 still supports `crmForm`, this support is expected to be withdrawn in the next major release of Microsoft Dynamics CRM.

Update Rollup 12 and December 2012 Service Update (Polaris update) support browsers other than Internet Explorer. Hence it is required that form scripts should also support W3C standards so that the script can also work in other browsers. This requires removal of dependencies on **HTML components** (**HTC**) that are specific to Internet Explorer. To identify potential issues with custom JScript libraries, Microsoft has released a tool known as **Microsoft Dynamics CRM 2011 Custom Code Validation Tool**. It is highly recommended to validate any custom JScript using this tool before applying them. The tool can be downloaded from the following URL:

`http://www.microsoft.com/en-us/download/details.aspx?id=30151`

However, to continue support for HTC, Update Rollup 12 and December 2012 Service Update (Polaris update) have both introduced an organization-level setting called **Include HTC support in Microsoft Dynamics CRM Forms**. For Microsoft Dynamics CRM 2011 Online organizations, the setting is turned "off" by default. But for on-premises organizations, the setting is turned "on" by default.

To modify the value of this setting, navigate to **Settings** | **System** | **System Settings** | **Customization** and then select or unselect the **Include HTC support in Microsoft Dynamics CRM Forms** setting.

> Enabling HTC support will not allow the newer versions of Internet Explorer to provide the best possible performance. Internet Explorer 10 does not support HTC components. Support for HTC will be removed in the next major release of Microsoft Dynamics CRM.

Modifying Microsoft Dynamics CRM 2011 application pages or forms using jQuery is not supported. The only supported use of jQuery in the Microsoft Dynamics CRM 2011 is the use of the `jQuery.ajax` method to retrieve data from the REST endpoint.

There's more...

In addition to the events discussed in this recipe, Microsoft Dynamics CRM 2011 supports two more events:

- `TabStateChange`: This event is triggered when a tab is expanded or collapsed
- `OnReadyStateComplete`: This event is triggered when the contents of any iFrame have completed loading

Customizing the process-driven form (Dynamics CRM 2011 Online only)

In this recipe, we will discuss how to customize the process-driven forms available in Microsoft Dynamics CRM 2011 Online.

Getting ready

The process-driven forms introduced in the Polaris update of Microsoft Dynamics CRM 2011 uses most of the elements described in the standard form. However, there are a few changes as shown in the following diagram:

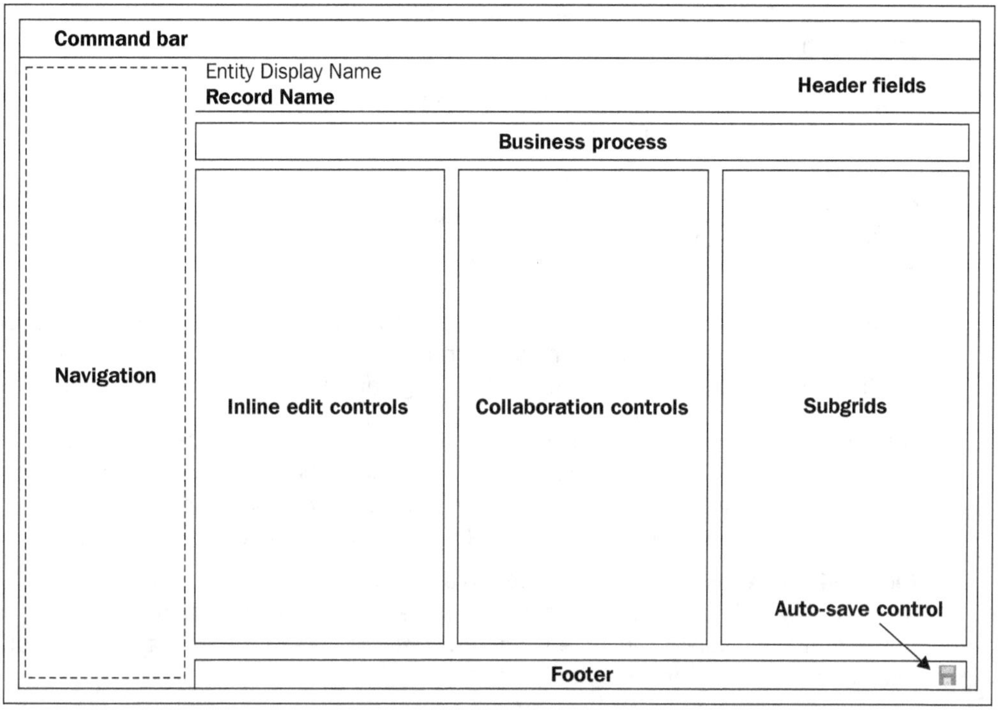

The following are the changes introduced in this new type of form:

- **Command bar**: A process-driven form does not have any ribbon; instead, it has a fixed set of commands for each entity and these are known as **command bar controls**. Some important features of command-bar controls are as follows:
    - These controls are record states (**Active/Inactive**) and are permission-aware (security-role access). These commands do not render if the user does not have proper permissions and they also display a different set of commands in different states.
    - Command controls cannot be extended. Any ribbon customization done will not be applied in these process-driven forms.

> Read more about ribbon customization in *Chapter 8, Site Map and Ribbon Customization*.

    - Command bar controls are not solution-aware.

The command bar provides a **Switch to Classic** option that displays the record in the edit-form mode.

- **Header fields**: The header fields in this process-driven form are displayed differently, but defined in the form in the same way as that of the standard main form.

> Unlike a standard form, a process-driven form's header fields allow editing.

However, a process-driven form can only display a maximum of 4 fields in the header area. Hence, if the header contains more than one row, additional header fields will not be visible in this mode. Header fields, being part of the form, are solution-aware.

- **Business processes**: This is a newly introduced feature in Lead, Opportunity, and Case entity forms. These controls cannot be viewed in the form editor. The existing business processes can be edited from the process-driven form itself; however, new business processes cannot be created. These controls are not solution-aware.
- **Inline edit controls**: Entity fields added to a process-driven form will be displayed in a new way. A field has to be selected to make it active for edit and thus prevents accidental modifications. Inline edit controls are solution-aware. A Bing Map control is also added as part of inline edit controls.
- **Collaboration controls**: Collaboration controls rendered in a process-driven form display the following tabs:
    - **Posts (Activity Feed/Yammer)**
    - **Activities**
    - **Notes**

  These controls are user-permission-aware and display based on the security role of the user.

  The form editor will only display the **Notes** control, which can be removed or added to the form. The other two controls are only viewed in the process-driven form and cannot be customized.

- **Subgrids**: The process-driven form displays subgrids with a new lighter look and feel and provides some inline editing capabilities. The records in a subgrid can be deleted inline. Subgrids are part of the form and hence are solution-aware.
- **The auto-save control**: The auto-save control appears on the bottom-right corner of the form and it automatically saves the record after record creation. Some important properties of this control are as follows:
    - After the first edit, the auto-save fires every 30 seconds
    - Auto-save retrieves any changes and displays them in the form without reloading it

- Only data that has been changed since the last save is saved
- The field currently being edited is not saved
- Closing the form automatically saves the record
- Command bar actions such as **New**, **Create**, or **Qualify** also save the record

> Each time an auto-save fires, it is actually an update to the record. Hence, any workflow or plugin registered against the `Update` event will trigger. Therefore, the workflow or plugin should be developed and registered in a way that it is triggered on the changing of some specific field values and not just on any field update.

How to do it...

The following controls can be modified using the same steps as those used during the creation of the main form:

- Tabs and sections
- Fields
- Header and footer
- Subgrids
- iFrames
- Web resources
- The navigation area
- Form properties

The **SOCIAL PANE** control, which displays **Posts**, **Activities**, and **Notes**, is locked in the form and cannot be customized or removed.

However, process-driven forms have a few additional controls that can be customized:

- Bing Map
- Lync or Skype
- Yammer

In this recipe, we will discuss all the stated tasks one after the other. For process-driven form customization, the **Form Editor** application can also be invoked from the command bar of any entity record with the new form.

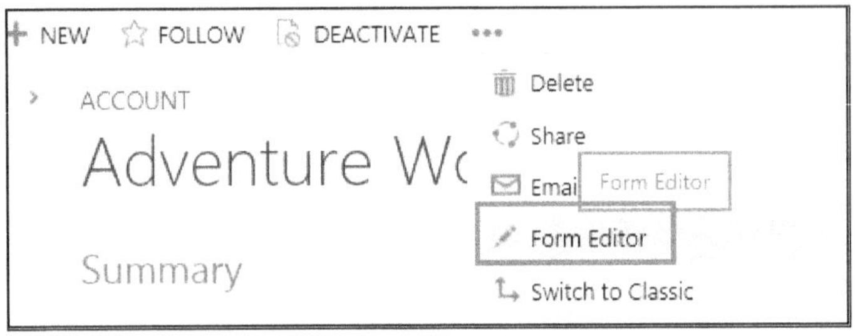

Please perform the following steps to customize the process-driven form for an entity. Firstly, you need to log in to the Dynamics CRM 2011 system as a system administrator or with a relevant security role.

We will now take a look at configuring the Bing Map display. The Bing Map control displayed in the process-driven form is locked in the form and cannot be modified or removed. The map is linked to display `Address1` and this setting too cannot be altered.

- We can disable or enable Bing Maps by navigating to **Settings** | **System** | **Administration** | **System Settings** | **General** and configuring the **Show Bing Maps on forms** setting.

Process-driven forms support Skype and Lync calls from the Dynamics CRM 2011 form itself, using the **Click to Call** feature:

- **To enable the Lync call feature**:
    1. We have to ensure that the Lync client is installed on the local machine and the Lync add-on is enabled in the Internet Explorer. Go to **Tools** | **Manage add-ons** in Internet Explorer. The following screenshot is what you will see:

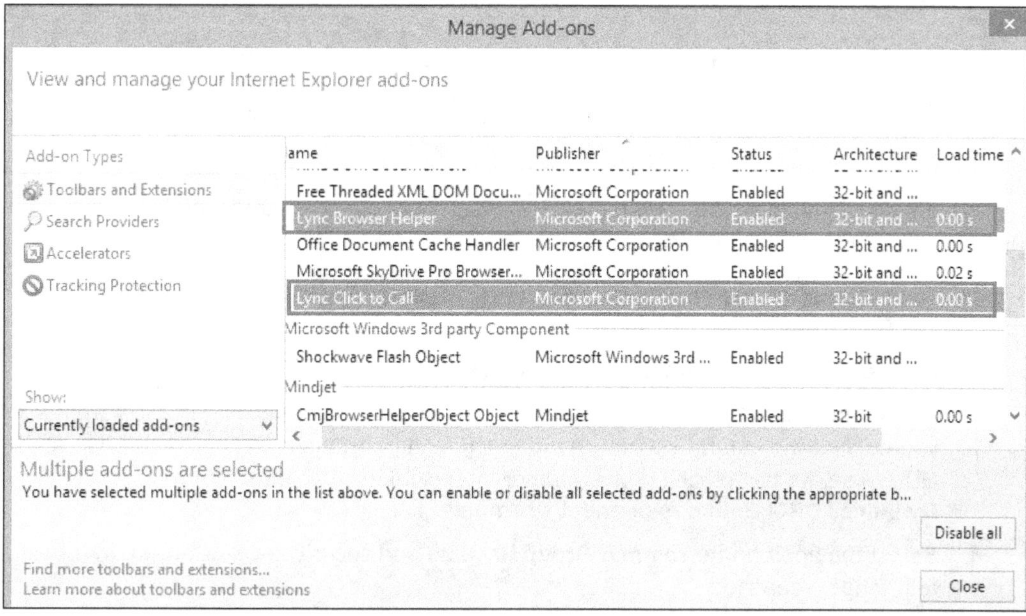

2. Then navigate to **Settings** | **System** | **Administration** | **System Settings** | **General** and set the **Select provider for Click to** call setting to **Lync**.

- **To enable the Skype call feature**:

  1. We have to ensure that the Skype client is installed on the local machine. Then navigate to **Settings** | **System** | **Administration** | **System Settings** | **General**.

  2. Set the **Select provider for Click to call** setting to **Skype**.

> If the Lync/Skype add-on recognizes the number format, it inserts a telephone icon (for Lync) / Skype icon (for Skype) before the phone number. When the add-on is disabled or not installed, a hyperlink on the phone number will be visible.

To make calls from Microsoft Dynamics CRM 2011 Online, any phone number must be of the <country/region code><area code><number> format. However, during data entry, a user may not enter the phone number in the stated format. Hence, Dynamics CRM 2011 Online provides a system-wide setting to enable country/region code prefixing.

This setting can be enabled by navigating to **Settings** | **System** | **Administration** | **System Settings** | **General** and selecting the **Enable country/region code prefixing** checkbox, and then specifying the country/region code, such as +91, in **Country/Region Code Prefix**.

> This organization-wide setting can be overridden by the user's preferred setting. But if a user specifies a different country/region prefix in the record, it will override the user-level and organization-level prefixes.

Lastly, we will look into configuring Yammer. The Polaris update has introduced Yammer integration with Dynamics CRM 2011 Online.

1. To configure Yammer, navigate to **Settings** | **System** | **Administration** | **Yammer Configuration**.
2. On the **Yammer Disclaimer** page, click on **Continue**.
3. The **Yammer configuration** page will appear. If you are already logged into Yammer, you will find the enterprise Yammer network along with the groups already populated. Otherwise, we have to log on to Yammer by clicking on the **Authorize Microsoft Dynamics CRM Online to connect to Yammer** link.
4. Select the appropriate **Yammer Group ID** value and security level as shown in the following screenshot:

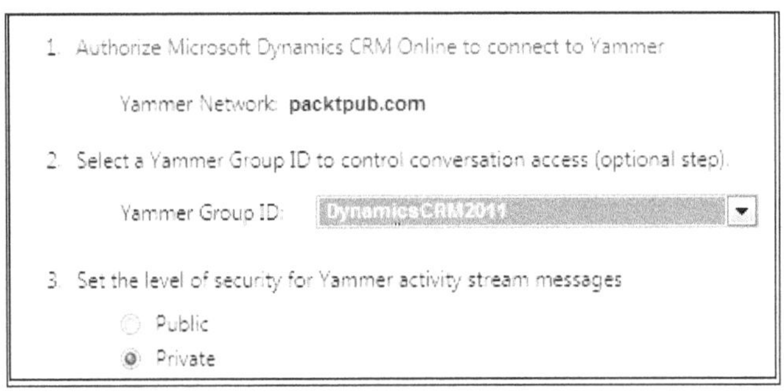

5. The next screen will display a confirmation message (**Congratulations, your system is configured for Yammer!**) about the Yammer integration with Dynamics CRM 2011.
6. Thereafter, we have to enable the rule configurations for Yammer. Navigate to **Settings** | **System** | **Administration** | **Post Rule Configurations**. Select the rule we want to enable and then click on the **Enable for Yammer** button in the ribbon.

> Connecting to Yammer is a one-way process. After the connection is established, it cannot be undone.

How it works...

In Microsoft Dynamics CRM 2011 Online, the new process-driven forms will be displayed for Account, Contact, Lead, Opportunity, and Case entities irrespective of the read-optimized mode setting.

Some of the important features of a process-driven form are as follows:

- Process-driven forms support web resources having the **Show this Web Resources In Read Optimized form** setting enabled.

> Except for the `Xrm.Page.ui.getFormType` method, the `Xrm.Page.ui` object is not available in process-driven forms. As a performance enhancement, web resources and parts of the `Xrm.Page` object model are loaded asynchronously for process-driven forms. As a result, if any script in the web resource depends on some `Xrm.Page` objects, such an object may not be available when a script runs. In addition, there is no public event to indicate that the parts of the `Xrm.Page` object are available. To counter this, scripts in the web resource should implement a strategy to query the `Xrm.Page` object to determine whether the objects to be used are available before using them.

- Process-driven forms do not support any type of event handler to be configured in the form definition. If an event handler is applied to these forms, they will appear as edit forms.
- The changes made to a record are saved automatically in process-driven forms. This auto-save behavior is not configurable.

The **Click to Call** functionality uses the `skype:` (for a Skype call) and `tel:` (for a Lync call) protocols that enable the direct call functionality for the numbers entered in the out-of-box phone number fields in Microsoft Dynamics CRM Online. When a phone number in a record is clicked, Microsoft Dynamics CRM 2011 opens Skype or Lync and dials the phone number automatically.

Skype and Lync clients and applications are not supported on iPad and other mobile devices. For the Click to Call feature, the supported Lync version is Lync 2013/2010 and the Skype version is Skype 6.0 or later.

The Yammer integration with Dynamics CRM 2011 is not available with on-premises Microsoft Dynamics CRM 2011 installations. Moreover, Yammer and activity feeds cannot be used simultaneously.

The following are a few important features of the Yammer integration:

- User posts created via the Dynamics CRM 2011 Online user interface are stored in Yammer, not in the Dynamics CRM system.
- Auto posts are created and stored in the Dynamics CRM system. Some auto posts are also stored in Yammer in addition to Dynamics CRM.
- Users are followed in Yammer only, not within Dynamics CRM.
- Objects other than the user are followed in both Dynamics CRM and Yammer. Yammer connection must be enabled before we can follow objects in Yammer.
- If the default Yammer group for users to post from the Dynamics CRM organization is deleted in Yammer, the Yammer group association with the Dynamics CRM organization has to be changed.
- If the **Post to Yammer Activity Stream** rule is set to **True** in Post Rules Configuration, that activity will post to Yammer.

Creating and customizing the mobile form

In this recipe, we will discuss how to create and customize the Mobile Express form. Dynamics CRM 2011 allows us to create multiple mobile forms.

How to do it...

In this recipe, we will first discuss the steps to create a new Mobile Express form and then we will discuss the customization options of a Mobile Express form.

1. Log in to the Dynamics CRM 2011 system as a system administrator or with a relevant security role.
2. Navigate to **Settings** | **Customizations** | **Solutions** and change the view to **Unmanaged Solutions**, if not already selected.
3. Then double-click on the unmanaged solution to open it.
4. In the expanded solution page, navigate to **Components** | **Entities** | **<Entity>** | **Forms**.
5. To create a new Mobile Express form, go to **New** | **Mobile Form** in the actions toolbar.
6. To customize a mobile form, double-click on the mobile form to be customized. Then follow the next steps in either of the previous scenarios.

7. The **Mobile Entity: <Entity Plural Name>** form will appear. Add here the fields that should be present in the Mobile form, from the **Available Attributes** list to the **Selected Attributes** list using the **Add** and **Add All** buttons.

   The **Remove** and **Remove All** buttons can be used to remove a field from the **Selected Attributes** list to the **Available Attributes** list. That means we are removing the field from the mobile form.

   We can move a field up or down in the mobile form UI by selecting a field in the **Selected Attributes** list and then using the **Move Up** or **Move Down** button.

   Finally, a field can be marked as read-only in the edit mode of the mobile form by selecting the field in the **Selected Attributes** list and then clicking on the **Read Only** button.

8. To rename the form, click on the **Form Properties** button in the actions toolbar of the **Mobile Entity: <Entity Plural Name>** form. This will bring up the **Form Properties** page. Edit the **Form Name** and **Description** properties. Click on **OK** to save the changes.
9. Click on **Save and Close** in the **Mobile Entity: <Entity Plural Name>** form.
10. Finally, publish the entity.

How it works...

Newly created mobile forms will only be assigned to the system administrator and system customizer security role. If this new form has to be used by users having another security role, the new mobile form has to be assigned to the relevant security roles by following the *Configuring a form to be role based* recipe of this chapter.

The **Go Mobile** privilege under the **Business Management** tab of a security role defines whether the security role has access to mobile forms.

Finally, for any entity to be available in Mobile Express, the **Mobile Express** setting should be in the enabled state for the entity.

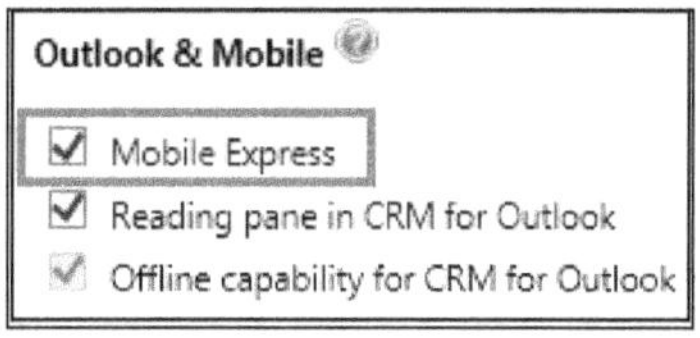

Configuring a form to be role-based

Dynamics CRM 2011 supports security-role-based forms. A form can be linked to a single or a set of security roles. This recipe will help us understand how to achieve this.

How to do it...

Please perform the following steps to configure a form to be role-based:

1. Open the unmanaged solution from the solution section.
2. In the expanded solution page, navigate to **Components** | **Entities** | **<Entity>** | **Forms**.
3. Select the form and then click on the **Assign Security Roles** button for main forms and the **Assign Role** button for mobile forms, from the actions menu:

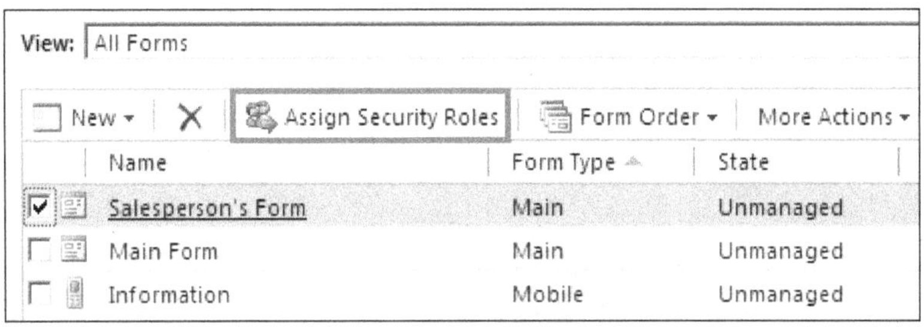

4. Then a web pop up, **Assign Security Roles: <Form Name>**, will launch. In this pop up, first select the **Display only to these selected security roles** option. Thereafter, select the security roles this form is to be associated with.
5. Then click on the **Enable for fallback** option if you want this form to be a fallback form for those security roles that do not have any form configured.

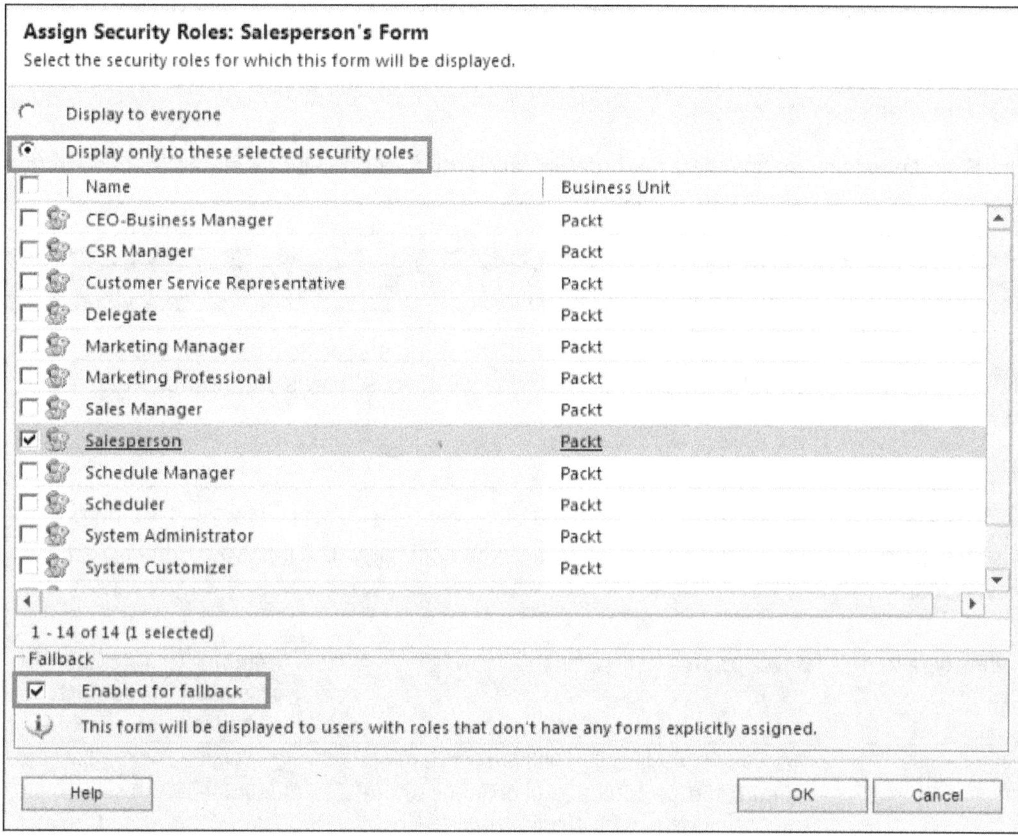

6. Finally, click on the **OK** button to save the settings.
7. To set the **Form Order** for the available forms, click on the **Form Order** pop up in the actions toolbar and then select **Main Form Set**.
8. The **Form Order** pop up will appear. Use the up and down arrows to set the order of the forms. Finally, click on the **OK** button to save the changes.

How it works...

When we have more than one main form defined for an entity, we can select which forms the users will be able to see based on their security roles.

Because each entity must be able to display a form for any user, at least one form must be designated as a fallback form—a form visible to users whose security roles do not have any forms explicitly assigned to them.

If an entity has only one main form, the **Enable for fallback** option cannot be deselected from the form. After we create a second main form for the entity, we will be able to clear the **Enabled for fallback** option for one of them. The system will always make sure that at least one form is enabled for fallback.

The **Form Order** pop up specifies the order in which the forms will be displayed to a user if the user's security role has access to multiple forms.

Creating and customizing a public view

Entity views are presaved queries to retrieve data by using a specific filter and displaying those using predefined columns. In this recipe, we will discuss views and how to create a new public view.

Getting ready

Every entity in Dynamics CRM can have only six types of views. The following table lists these view types:

View type	Description	Number of views permitted	Action permitted
Public view	This view is available to all users. The filter criteria, sorting criteria, and columns of the existing views can be customized; new public views can be created as well.	Zero to unlimited	Create, Update, and Delete
Default public view	The default public view is the default view for all users when they initially navigate to the entity. Any public view can be made as the default public view. There has to be one default public view.	One	Update only
Quick Find view	This view type controls the Quick Find settings for the entity. When a user conducts a search using the search box in any view, the result view will contain the columns of Quick Find view only.	One	Update only
Advanced Find view	This view is displayed when the user initiates a new Advanced Find view for the entity. No filter cannot be created for this view. However, sorting criteria and columns can be defined for this view.	One	Update only

View type	Description	Number of views permitted	Action permitted
Associated view	This is the view used on related lists when a subgrid of items from this entity is visible on a parent entity (or on the navigation pane). Because the parent entity automatically sets the filtering, this view does not allow customization of the filter. However, sorting criteria and columns can be defined for this view.	One	Update only
Lookup view	This is the view used on lookup fields on child entities of the current entity. The filter for this entity cannot be edited, but the columns and sorting can be edited. The filter can be edited from the form of the child entity.	One	Update only

Only public views for an entity can be created and the other view types can only be customized. In this recipe, we will figure out how to create a public view for an entity.

How to do it...

There can be multiple public views created for any entity. Dynamics CRM 2011 automatically creates a few public views and other types of views for an entity. In this recipe, we will discuss how to create and/or customize any public view. The following customization activities will be discussed here:

- Editing the filter criteria
- Modifying the columns of the view
- Rearranging the column order
- Renaming the view
- Making the view the default public view of the entity

Please perform the following steps to create and/or customize any public view:

1. Log in to the Dynamics CRM 2011 system as a system administrator or with a relevant security role.
2. Navigate to **Settings | Customization | Solutions** and double-click on the unmanaged solution to open it.
3. In the expanded solution page, navigate to **Components** | **Entities** | **<Entity>** | **Views**.

4. To create a new public view, click on **New** in the actions toolbar as shown in the following screenshot:

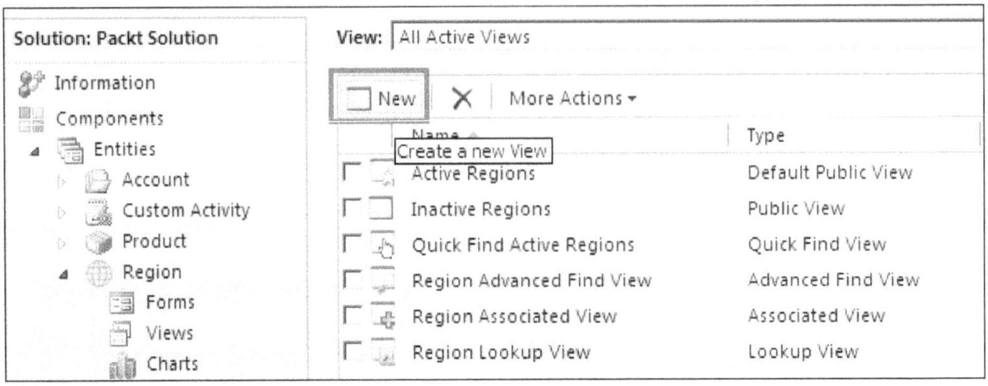

5. The **Provide Information for this view** pop up will now appear. Provide the following details in this page and then click on **OK** to save the settings:
   - **Name**: Name of the new view
   - **Description**: Description of the view

6. To edit the filter criteria for the view, click on the **Edit Filter Criteria** button in the **Common Tasks** toolbar as shown in the following screenshot:

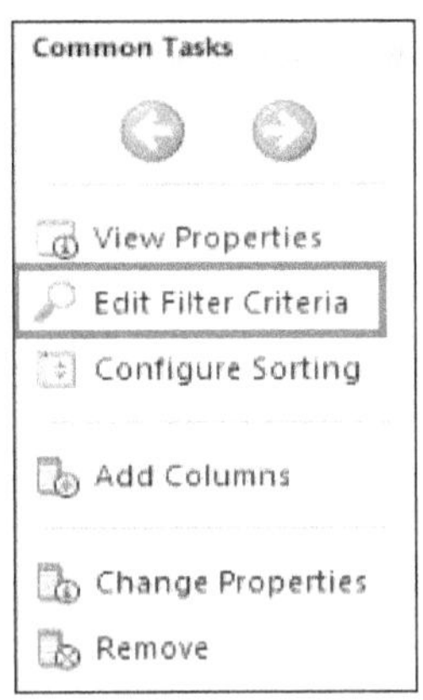

7. The **Edit Filter Criteria** pop up will now appear. Create a new filter criteria here and then click on the **OK** button to save the changes:

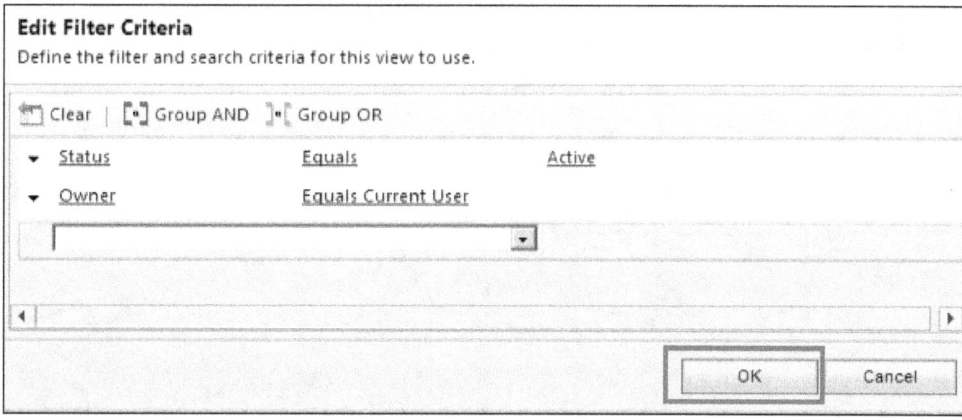

8. To modify the columns of the view, click on the **Add Columns** button in the **Common Tasks** toolbar. The **Add Columns** page will now appear.
9. Select the required columns and then click on the **OK** button to save the changes.

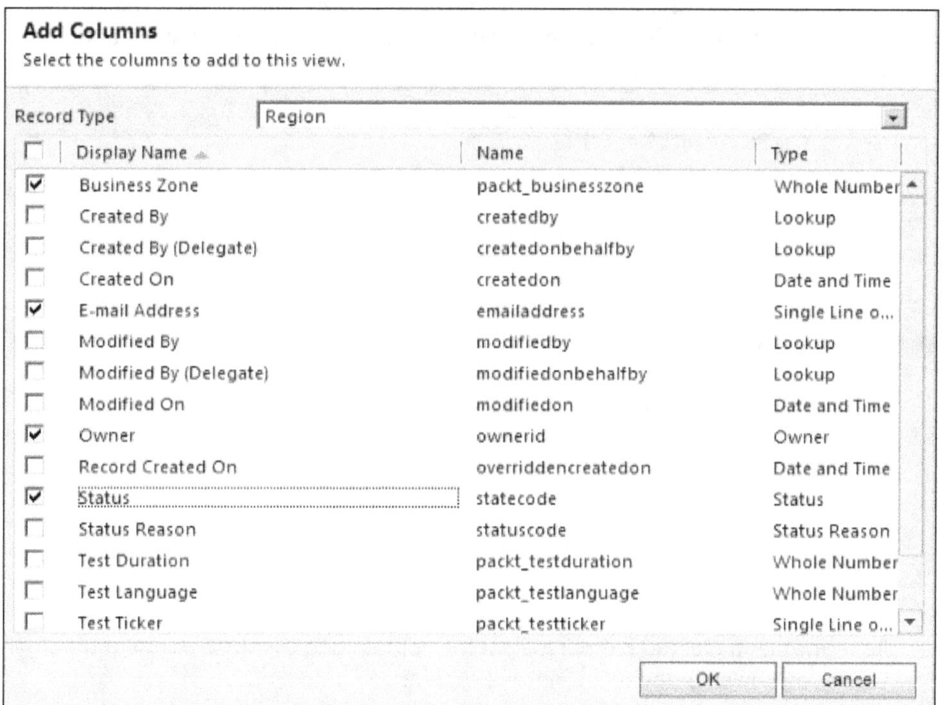

10. To resize any column, select the column in the view and then click on the **Change Properties** button in the **Common Tasks** toolbar.

11. The **Change Column Properties** web dialog will now appear. Modify the column width and then click on the **OK** button to save the changes. Follow this steps to modify the width of the other columns if required.

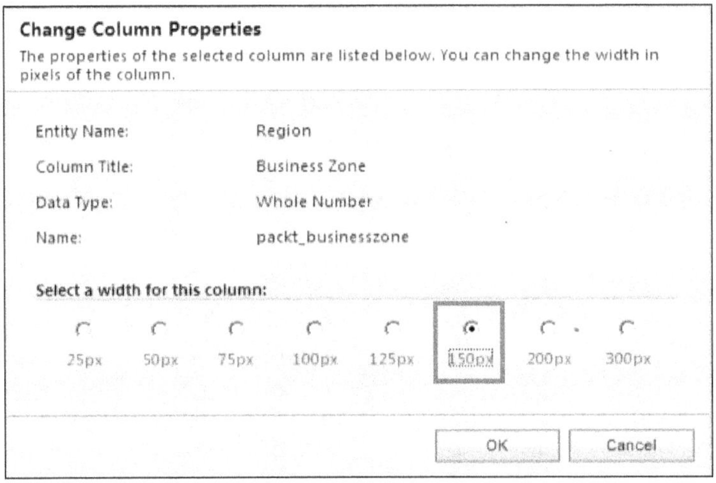

12. To rearrange the column order, select the column and then use the right or left green arrows as shown in the following screenshot:

13. To configure the sorting order for the view, click on the **Configure Sorting** button in the **Common Tasks** toolbar. The **Configure Sort Order** web page will appear. On this page, set the sort order for the view and then click on the **OK** button to save the changes.

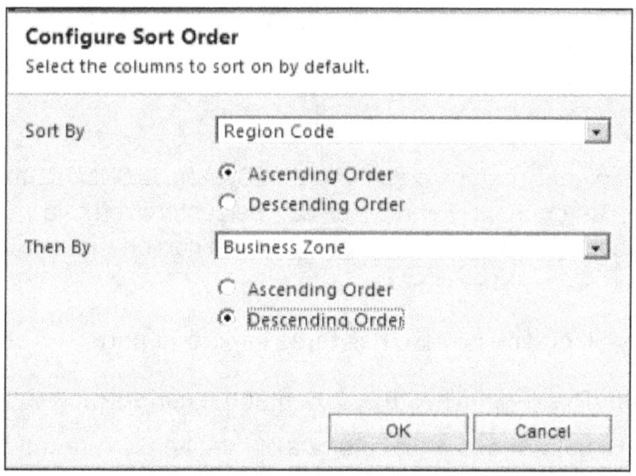

14. To rename a public view, click on the **View Properties** button in the **Common Tasks** toolbar. The **Provide Information for this view** page will appear; modify the **Name** and/or **Description** fields of the current view and then click on the **OK** button to save the changes.

> After performing any of the previous customization steps, save the view using the **Save and Close** button.

15. To make a public view the default public view for an entity, in the entity views select the public view to be set as the default public view and then go to **More Actions** | **Set Default** in the actions toolbar.

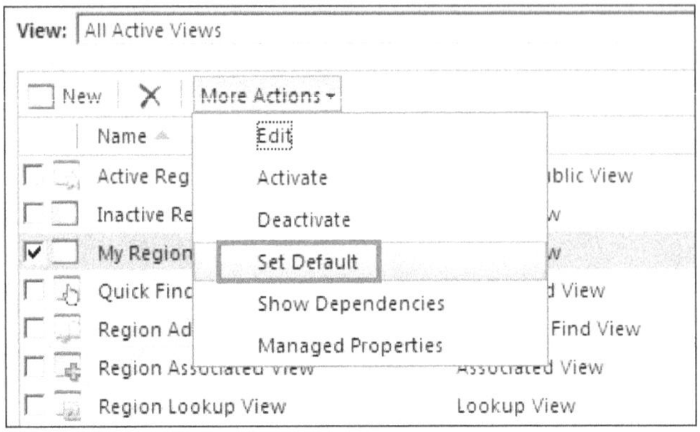

16. Finally, we have to publish the entity.

How it works...

Only public views for an entity can be created within Dynamics CRM. Other types of views are created by the system automatically and these can be customized to a certain extent. There can exist multiple public views for an entity, but only one can be the default public view at any point in time.

A public view, like any other type of view, has three important parts:

- **Filter criteria**: This determines the data that the current view will display
- **Columns**: This determines what columns of the filtered data will be displayed
- **Sorting criteria**: This determines the sorting algorithm of the data to be displayed

These three parts define the data that is displayed by any public view.

Customizing search criteria for the Quick Find view

In the Dynamics CRM 2011 system, Quick Find view is used as the search basis for all grid-view quick searches, as well as lookup searches within lookups to an entity in other forms. In this recipe, we will discuss how to customize the Quick Find view search criteria.

How to do it...

Perform the following steps to add or remove fields according to the search criteria for an entity:

1. Log in to the Dynamics CRM 2011 system as a system administrator or with a relevant security role.
2. Navigate to **Settings** | **Customization** | **Solutions** and change the view to **Unmanaged Solutions**, if not already selected. Then double-click on the unmanaged solution to open it.
3. In the expanded solution page, navigate to **Components** | **Entities** | **<Entity>** | **Views**.
4. Double-click on **Quick Find View**.
5. When the Quick Find view page opens up, click on the **Add Find Columns** button in the **Common Tasks** toolbar:

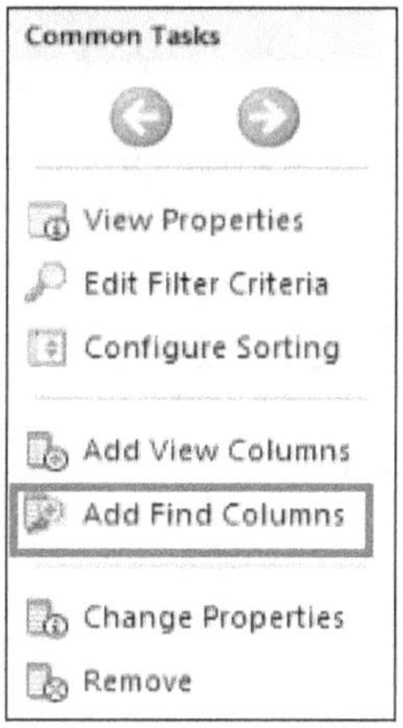

6. The **Add Find Columns** web pop up will appear. On this page, add or remove the fields and then click on the **OK** button to save the changes.

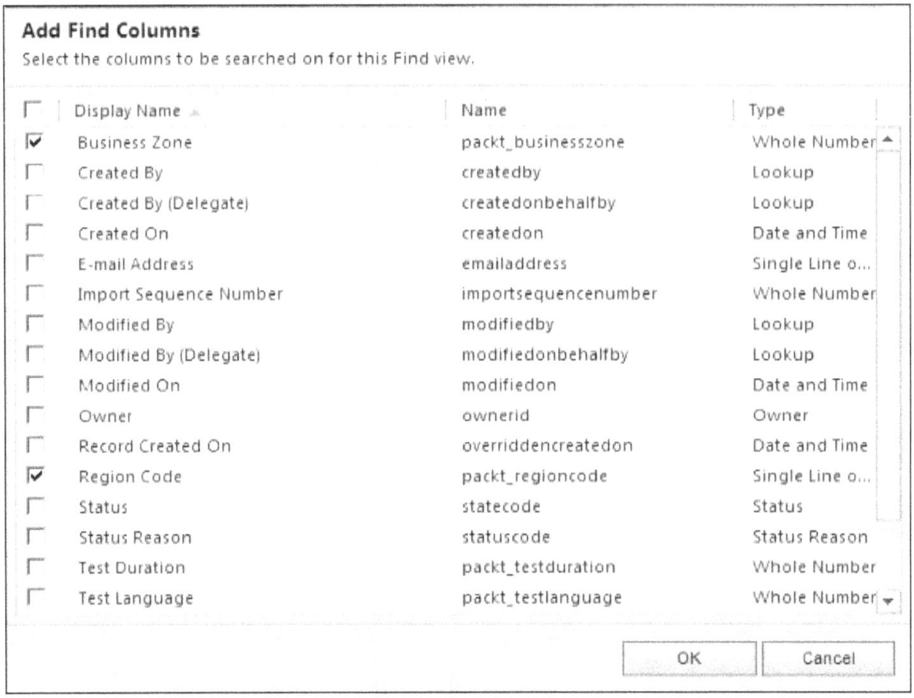

7. Then click on the **Save and Close** button in the view ribbon.
8. Finally, publish the entity.

How it works...

The Quick Find view is used for searching records in an entity grid. By default, the Account entity records can be searched using the **Account Name** and **Account Number** fields in the entity grid. If we try to search account records by **City**, no records will be displayed in the **Search Results** grid. Now if we add the **Address1: City** field in the Quick Find view, we will be able to search account records using the **City** field in the CRM grid.

Creating a user's personal view

The Dynamics CRM 2011 system allows users to create their personal views in the system. In this recipe, we will discuss how to create a personal view.

How to do it...

Perform the following steps to create an Advanced Find view:

1. Log in to the Dynamics CRM 2011 system with the credentials of the user who wishes to create the personal view.
2. Then click on the **Advanced Find** button in the top ribbon of the Dynamics CRM 2011 as shown in the following screenshot:

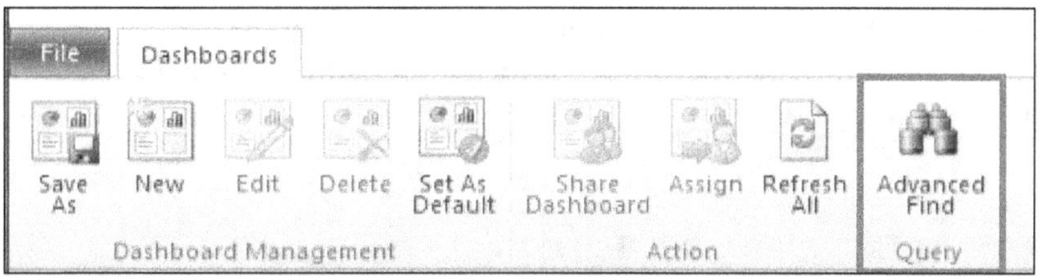

3. When the **Advanced Find** view web page appears, select the entity from the **Look For** drop-down list.
4. Then click on the **Query** button in the ribbon and create the new filter criteria for the Advanced Find view:

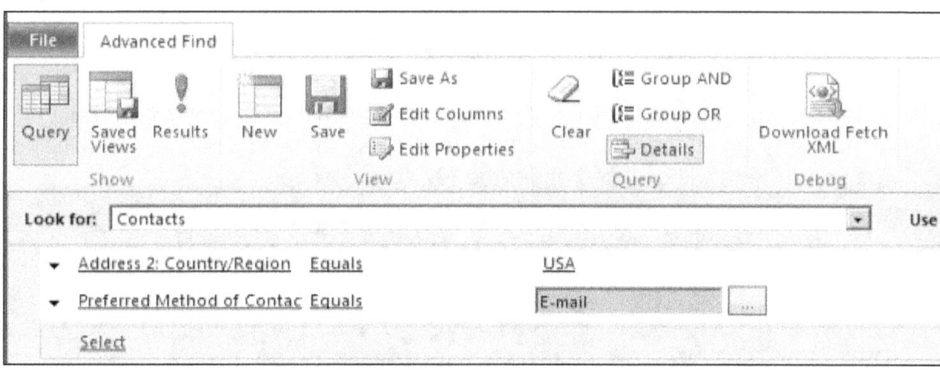

5. Optionally, you can click on the **Results** button to check the result of the view definition and can correct the filter criteria if required:

6. Click on the **Advanced Find** tab and then click on the **Save** button in the top ribbon.

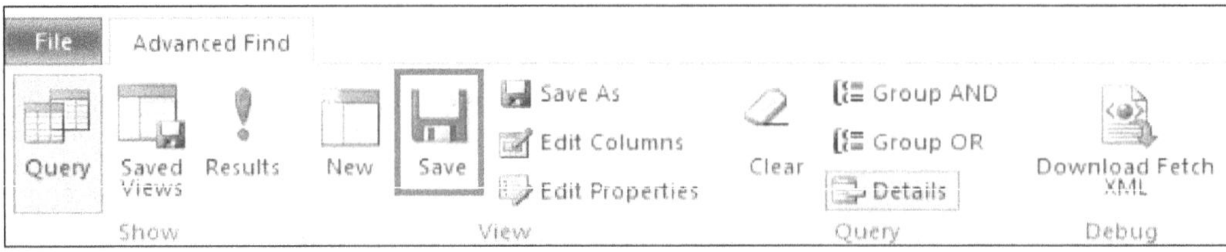

7. The **Provide Information for This View** page will appear; provide the name and the description of the view and then click on the **OK** button to save the changes as shown in the following screenshot:

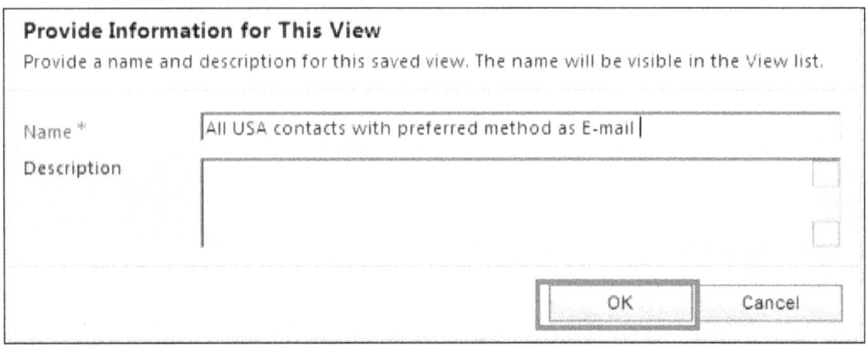

8. This view is saved as a personal view now. We can access this view by navigating to the **Entity** link in the Site Map and then clicking on the view's drop-down list. The saved views will be listed under the **My Views** section.

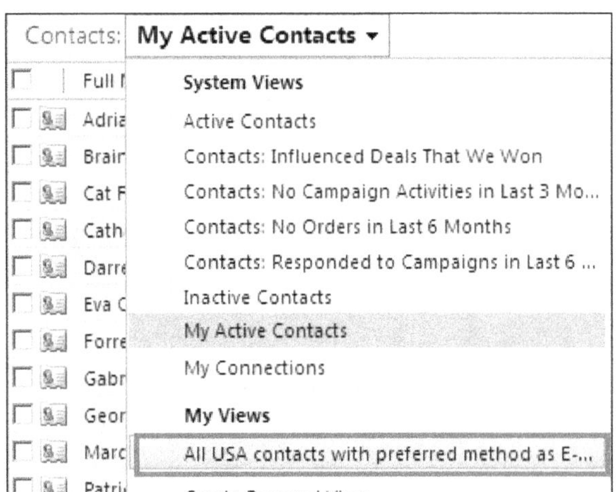

How it works...

Personal views are views accessible only to the user who has created it and users with whom this view has been shared by the creator. In Dynamics CRM 2011, views are not security-role-based. Hence, personal views are useful as these views can be shared with a specific set of users and other users cannot access this view in the system.

Personal views cannot be included in any unmanaged or managed solution. Hence personal views cannot be exported from any organization and imported to another organization as part of the solution export/import process.

Deactivating or deleting a user's personal view

In this recipe, we will discuss how to deactivate or delete a personal view created by a user.

How to do it...

Perform the following steps to delete a user's personal view:

1. Log in to the Dynamics CRM 2011 system with the credentials of the user who is the owner (creator) of the personal view to be deactivated or deleted.
2. Then click on the **Advanced Find** button in the top ribbon of the main Dynamics CRM page.

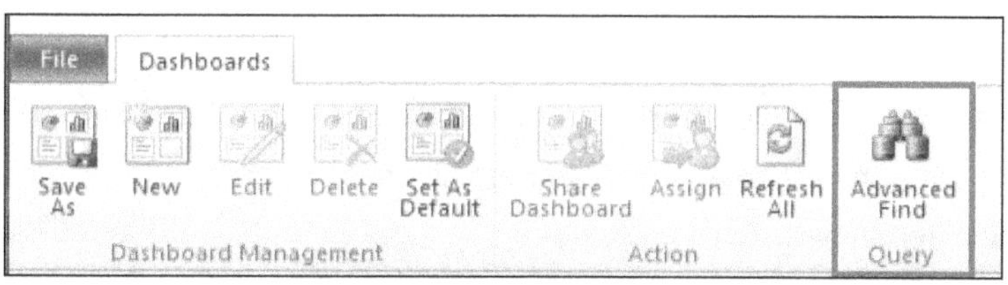

3. Click on the **Saved Views** button in the top ribbon.

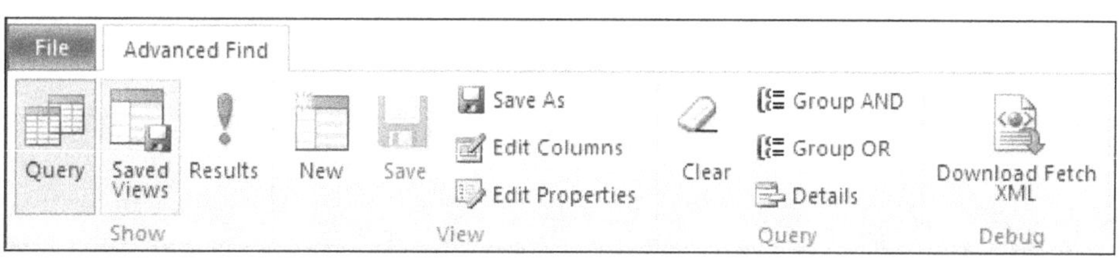

4. In the **Saved Views** grid, select the saved view to be deactivated or deleted. Then click on the **Deactivate** or **Delete Saved View** button:

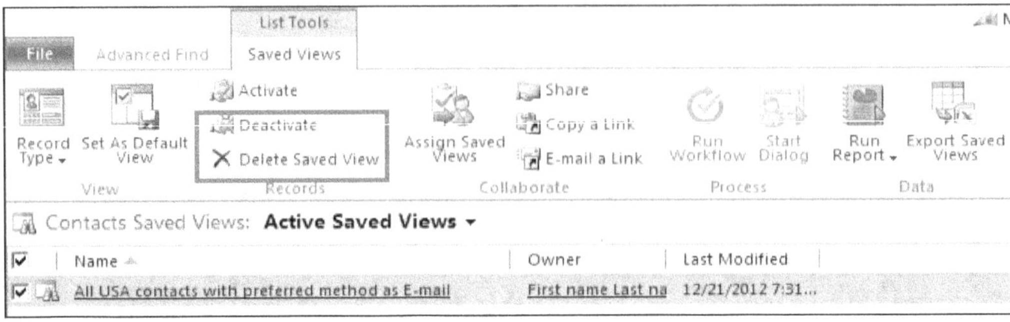

How it works...

Personal views can either be deactivated or deleted if they are not useful anymore. Only the owner of the personal view record or the user who has created the personal view can deactivate or delete any personal view. Once a personal view is deactivated or deleted, the view will be unavailable to all those users to whom the view have been shared.

See also

In this chapter, we have discussed various recipes of the entity form and view customization. In the next chapter, we will discuss the recipes for Site Map and ribbon customization. Some of the interesting recipes in the next chapter are:

- Editing the Site Map
- Adding a new button to an existing group for all entities
- Adding a new button to an existing group of a specific entity
- Hiding a ribbon button

8

Site Map and Ribbon Customizations

The **Site Map** and the **Ribbon** constitute the visual components of the Dynamics CRM 2011 system and control the navigation. After customizing entity forms and views, we will now discuss how to customize the Site Map and the ribbon.

In this chapter, we will discuss the following recipes:

- Editing the Site Map
- Preparing for editing the ribbon
- Adding a new button to an existing ribbon group for all entities
- Adding a new button to an existing ribbon group of a specific entity
- Hiding a ribbon button
- Importing the modified ribbon's definition

Introduction to Site Map and Ribbon

Dynamics CRM 2011 includes an application navigation control system called Site Map, which allows us to control the application navigation structure. The application navigation is created as an in-memory representation of the Site Map. Site Map evaluated together with security privileges control the display navigation options in the application. If the security privileges do not provide read access to an entity specified in the Site Map, that navigation option will not be displayed.

The Site Map is a node in the `customizations.xml` file of an exported unmanaged solution. We can edit the navigation options by editing the Site Map XML in the `customization.xml` file. The following customization options are available with Site Map:

- **Edit Labels**: Editing the title or label displayed in the navigation structure
- **Add or Change Icon**: Adding a new icon or editing an existing icon displayed on the Site Map
- **Add or Remove Elements**: Adding a new element in the navigation structure or removing an existing element from it
- **Add new pages to an Area**: Adding an external page to an area of the application

The following diagram displays the application navigation structure of Dynamics CRM 2011 Web UI:

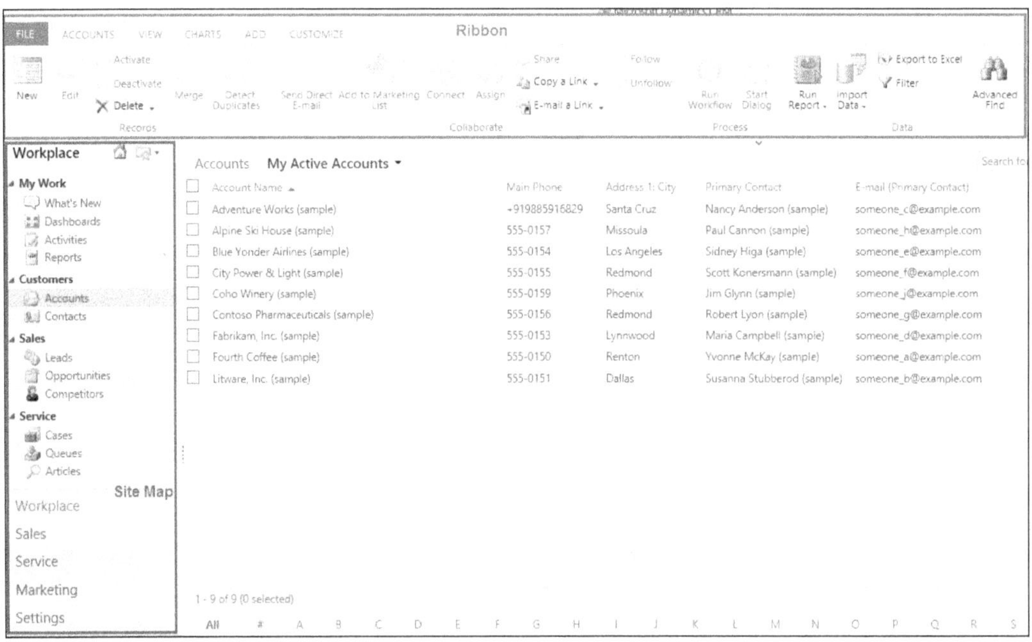

Microsoft Dynamics CRM 2011 contains ribbons for the master page as well as for all other entity views. The ribbons of the Dynamics CRM 2011 system can be classified as the following:

- **Entity ribbon**: Dynamics CRM 2011 uses an entity ribbon template for all entities. Each system entity has a separate `<RibbonDiffXml>` definition that builds upon the entity ribbon template definition.

- **Grid ribbon**: The grid ribbon is displayed for the entity homepage where a grid is displayed with a list of entity records corresponding to the entity view selected.
- **Sub-grid ribbon**: When a list of records for a different entity is displayed within a sub-grid on the form of another entity or in a chart, the ribbon will change when the user places the cursor on the grid. This ribbon is known as the sub-grid ribbon.
- **Form ribbon**: Each entity can have multiple forms. But each of the forms will display the form ribbon of the entity.
- **Jewel**: The jewel is the blue tab with the label **File** that appears on the far-left side of the ribbon. The jewel is also displayed on the entity form.
- **Basic home tab**: This tab is displayed on the main application ribbon whenever an alternative tab is not defined because of entity context or a display rule that suppresses it for specific pages. For example, this tab is displayed when we view the **Microsoft Dynamics CRM 2011 Resource Center**.
- Other ribbons: There are several other special-purpose ribbon tabs and a contextual group that are defined by Microsoft Dynamics CRM 2011. For example, the Advanced Find tab, Dashboard Editor tab, Form Editor tab, and Dashboard Homepage tab.

When Microsoft Dynamics CRM 2011 is accessed within the Microsoft Outlook 2003 or 2007 versions, the Outlook application does not display any ribbon for Dynamics CRM 2011 pages. However, when accessed via the Microsoft Outlook 2010 or 2013 version, Outlook supports the Dynamics CRM 2011 ribbon.

The definition of the ribbon is contained within an XML file named `applicationribbon.xml`. This file can be exported and viewed but cannot be modified directly. We can only modify the ribbon by defining how we want it to be changed. The changed definitions can be authored as part of the ribbon XML and these changes are applied on the default definition during runtime.

Editing the Site Map

In this recipe, we will discuss how to edit the Site Map to customize the navigation within the Dynamics CRM 2011 system.

Getting ready

Site Map has a complex XML structure and to edit it we need to export the XML from the Dynamics CRM 2011 system. After editing, we need to import the XML back for the changes to take effect. This task requires much care, otherwise the XML structure may get corrupted and make the edited Site Map unusable. The XML Schema of the Site Map can be found at `http://msdn.microsoft.com/en-in/library/gg334271.aspx`.

To help us in customizing the Site Map, **Microsoft Dynamics CRM Lab** has released a Site Map editor that can be downloaded and used for free. Here we will discuss both the alternatives of editing the Site Map. However, the preferred approach would be to edit the Site Map using the Site Map editor to minimize the risk of editing the Site Map incorrectly.

Another important thing to remember is to export and save the default Site Map before making any changes to it. This is recommended because if the Site Map creates serious issues after editing, it can be reverted to the default state.

How to do it...

As part of our Site Map customization, the first step would be to save the default Site Map. Follow these steps to export and save the default Site Map:

1. Log in to the Dynamics CRM 2011 system as a system administrator or with any other relevant security role.
2. Navigate to **Settings** | **Customizations** | **Solutions**. Create a new unmanaged solution and open the solution form.
3. Then include the Site Map component by clicking on **Add Existing** in the **Actions** toolbar.

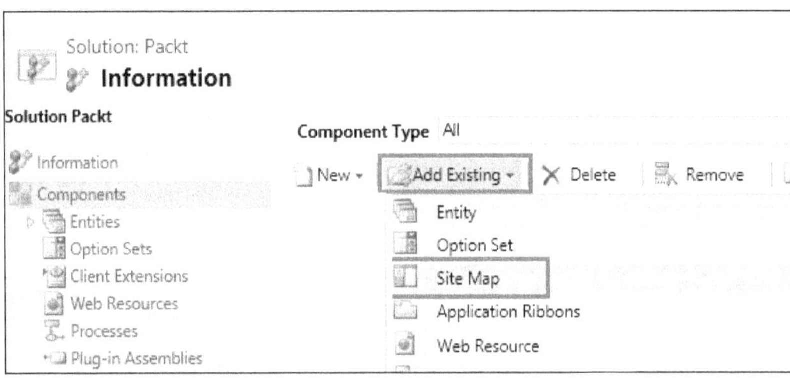

4. Then click on **Save and Close** to close the solution.
5. Thereafter, export this solution and save the solution's ZIP file in a safe location for future use.

The next step is to edit the Site Map. As discussed earlier, Site Map can be edited in two ways:

- It can be edited manually
- It can be edited using the SiteMap Editor released by Microsoft Dynamics CRM Lab

Follow these steps to edit the Site Map manually:

1. Navigate to **Settings** | **Customizations** | **Solutions**. Export the Site Map solution created earlier in this recipe as part of saving the default Site Map before editing it as an unmanaged solution.
2. Now extract the files from the compressed solution file. Then open the `customizations.xml` file from the extracted location using any XML editor such as Microsoft Visual Studio 2012.

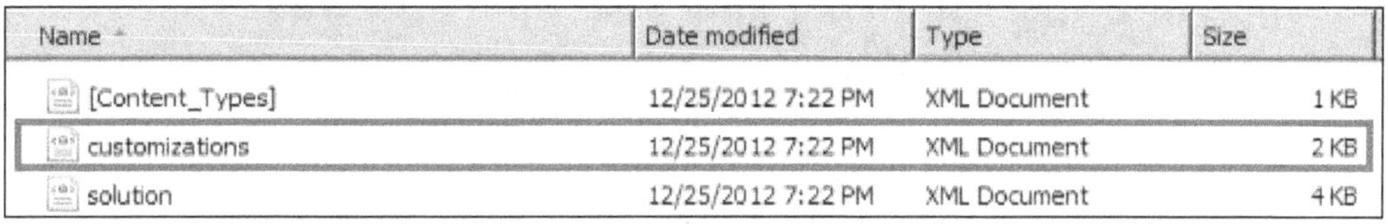

3. Locate the `SiteMap` node by going to `ImportExportXml/SiteMap/SiteMap`. The following image displays the SiteMap XML in an exported `customizations.xml` file:

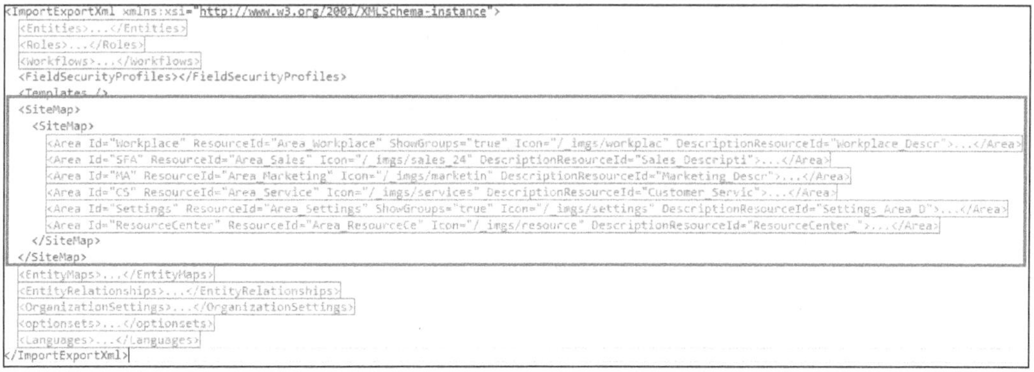

The Site Map XML structure is as follows:

```
<Area URL="string" Id="string" ShowGroups="true|false">
  <Titles>
    <Title LCID="string" Title="string"/>
  </Titles>
  <Descriptions>
      <Description LCID="string" Description="string"/>
  </Descriptions>
```

```
<Group Description="string"
        DescriptionResourceId="string"
        Icon="string"
        Id="string"
        IsProfile="" ["0" | "1" | "true" | "false"]
        License="string="
        ResourceId="string="
        Title="string="
        Url="string=">
    <Titles />
    <Descriptions />
    <SubArea AvailableOffline=""
            CheckExtensionProperty="string"
            Client="" Description="string"
            DescriptionResourceId="string"
            Entity="string"
            GetStartedPanePath="string"
            GetStartedPanePathAdmin="string"
            GetStartedPanePathAdminOutlook="string"
            GetStartedPanePathOutlook="string"
            Icon="string"
            Id="string"
            License="string"
            OutlookShortcutIcon="string"
            PassParams=""
            ResourceId="string"
            Sku=""
            Title="string"
            Url="string">
      <Titles />
      <Descriptions />
      <Privilege/>
    </SubArea>
  </Group>
</Area>
```

Downloading the example code

You can download the example code files for all Packt books you have purchased from your account at `http://www.packtpub.com`. If you purchased this book elsewhere, you can visit `http://www.packtpub.com/support` and register to have the files e-mailed directly to you.

The following table describes some of the important nodes and attributes of the SiteMap XML:

Site Map node	Node attributes	Description
`Area`		This specifies an area that will appear in the Dynamics CRM 2011 navigation pane. The default areas are `Workplace`, `SFA` (Sales), `MA` (Marketing), `CS` (Service), `Settings`, and `ResourceCenter`.
	`ResourceId`	This is internally used by Dynamics CRM 2011.
	`ShowGroups`	Determines whether the groups of subareas are displayed in the navigation pane.
	`Icon`	A 16 x 16 pixel icon that will be displayed in the Navigation pane for this area.
	`DescriptionResourceID`	This is internally used by Dynamics CRM 2011.
`Group`		This specifies a group of subareas.
	`Id`	A unique identifier for the `Group` element.
	`ResourceId`	This is internally used by Dynamics CRM 2011. We need to use the `Group/Titles/Title` element to set the text to display for this group.
	`DescriptionResourceId`	This is internally used by Dynamics CRM 2011. We need to use the `Group/Descriptions/Description` element for adding any description for this group.
	`IsProfile`	Determines whether this `Group` element represents a user-selectable profile for the workplace. This only applies to groups within the `Workplace` area.
`SubArea`		This specifies a navigation option within an area.
	`Id`	A unique identifier for this `SubArea` element. The valid values are `a-z`, `A-Z`, `0-9`, and underscore (_)
	`Icon`	This specifies a URL for a 16 x 16 pixel image to be displayed for the `SubArea` element.
	`ResourceId`	This is internally used by Dynamics CRM 2011. We need to use the `SubArea/Titles/Title` element to set the text to be displayed for this `SubArea` element.
	`Url`	This specifies a URL or HTML web resource for a page to be displayed in the main frame of the application when this subarea is selected.
	`DescriptionResourceId`	This is internally used by Dynamics CRM 2011. We need to use the `SubArea/Descriptions/Description` element for any description.
	`AvailableOffline`	This controls whether `SubArea` is available offline.
	`GetStartedPanePath`	This specifies the path to the **Get Started** page for this subarea.
	`GetStartedPanePathOutlook`	This specifies the path to the **Get Started** page for this subarea when Microsoft Dynamics CRM 2011 for Outlook is in use.
	`GetStartedPanePathAdminOutlook`	This specifies the path to the **Get Started** page for this subarea if the user is logged in as an administrator and Microsoft Dynamics CRM 2011 for Outlook is in use.

Site Map node	Node attributes	Description
Privilege		This determines whether a subarea will be displayed based on the privileges defined in any security role assigned to the user.
	Entity	This specifies the name of the entity to check privileges for. A valid value has a length greater than 1.
	Privilege	The privilege to check. Valid values include `Read`, `Write`, `Append`, `AppendTo`, `Create`, `Delete`, `Share`, `Assign`, `All`, `AllowQuickCampaign`, and `UseInternetMarketing`. Multiple values can be used separated by a comma and not containing spaces.

Edit the Site Map XML file as per requirements. After editing, create a new compressed ZIP file, including the extracted solution files and the edited `customizations.xml` file.

1. Then navigate to **Settings** | **Customizations** | **Solutions**. Click on **Import** and import the created ZIP file.
2. When importing finishes, click on **Close**.
3. Then publish the solution by clicking on the **Publish** button.

Microsoft Dynamics CRM Lab has released a Site Map editor that can be downloaded and used for free. The SiteMap Editor can be downloaded from the following location: `http://pinpoint.microsoft.com/en-us/applications/microsoft-dynamics-crm-sitemap-editor-12884928049`

After downloading the package, follow these steps to edit the Site Map using the SiteMap Editor:

1. Navigate to **Settings** | **Customization** | **Solutions**. Click on **Import** and import the downloaded file (`SiteMapEditormanaged.zip.cab`).
2. The preceding step will install the SiteMap Editor in the current Dynamics CRM 2011 system. To verify the installation, open the solution form by double-clicking on the Microsoft Dynamics CRM SiteMap Editor solution by going to **Settings** | **Customization** | **Solutions**; then click on **Configuration** to load the editor.

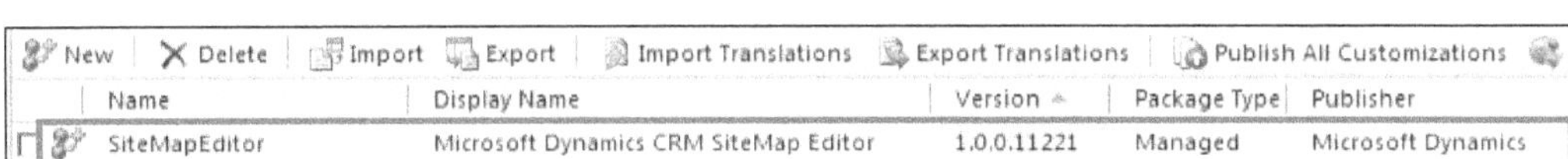

We can see that the areas, subareas, and groups are loaded on the navigation pane, and the editing pane is on the right-hand side:

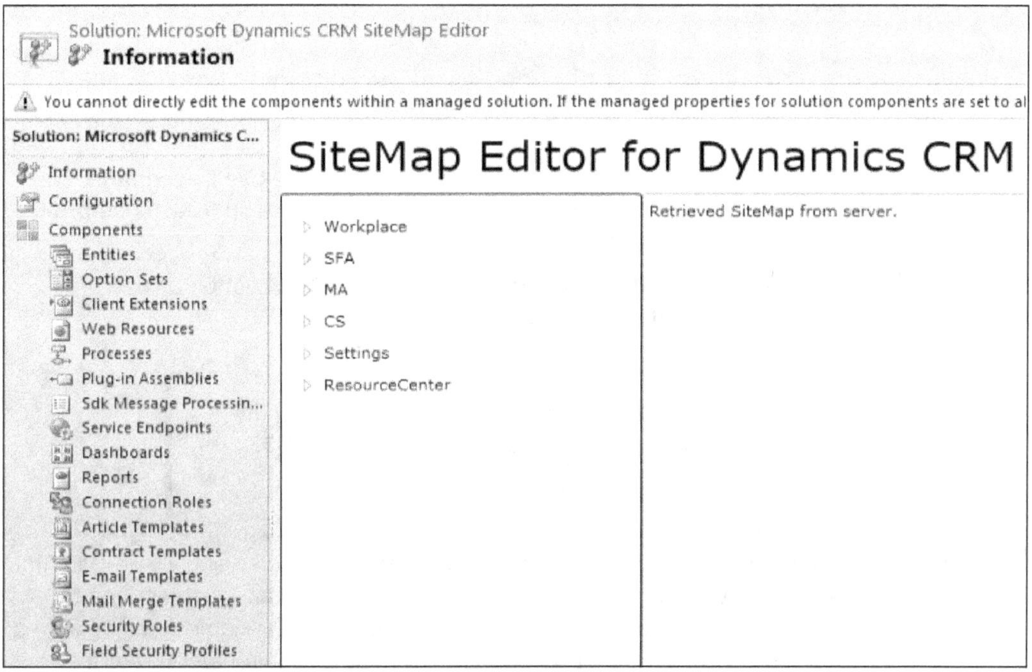

3. Using this editor, we can now edit the Site Map of the current CRM organization. We will discuss the following three editing options with the SiteMap Editor:
    - **Editing Labels** (**titles and descriptions**): To edit the title, uncheck the **Use Resource ID for Title** checkbox.

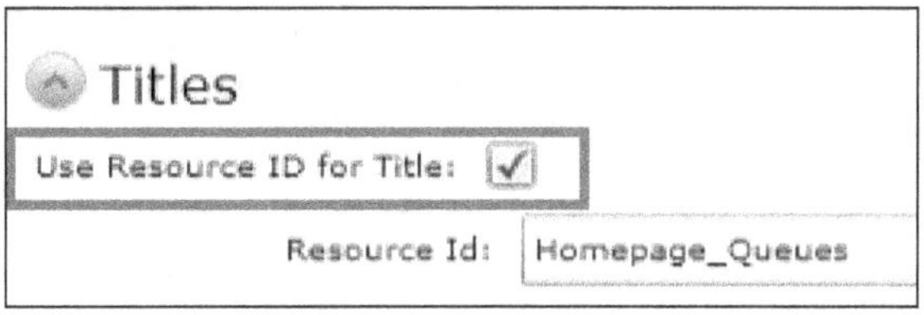

Then click on the **New Title** button and enter the new title.

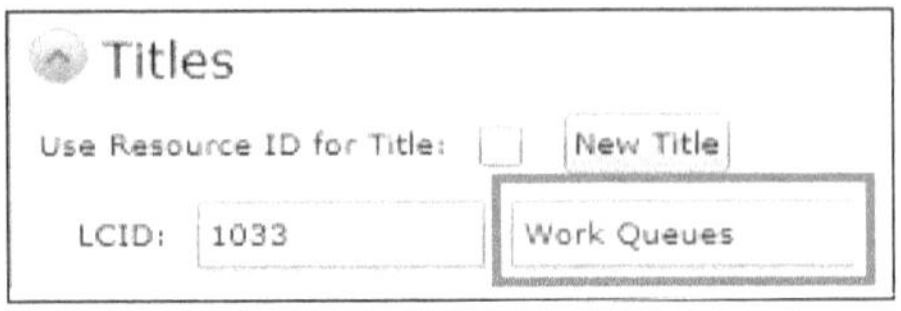

In a similar way, to edit the description, uncheck the **Use Description Resource ID for Description** checkbox and then click on **New Description** and enter the descriptive text.

To delete an added title or description, click on the **X** button on the right-hand side of the title/description string.

> The **LCID** or **Locale ID** is the language ID of the Dynamics CRM 2011 system. The value 1033 refers to English—United States (en-US).

- **Adding an element to the Site Map**: To add a new element, we have to first select another element at the same level (a sibling) and then click on the **+** button at the bottom of the navigation pane. The new element will be added next to the selected sibling. Then provide all the required details for the new element.

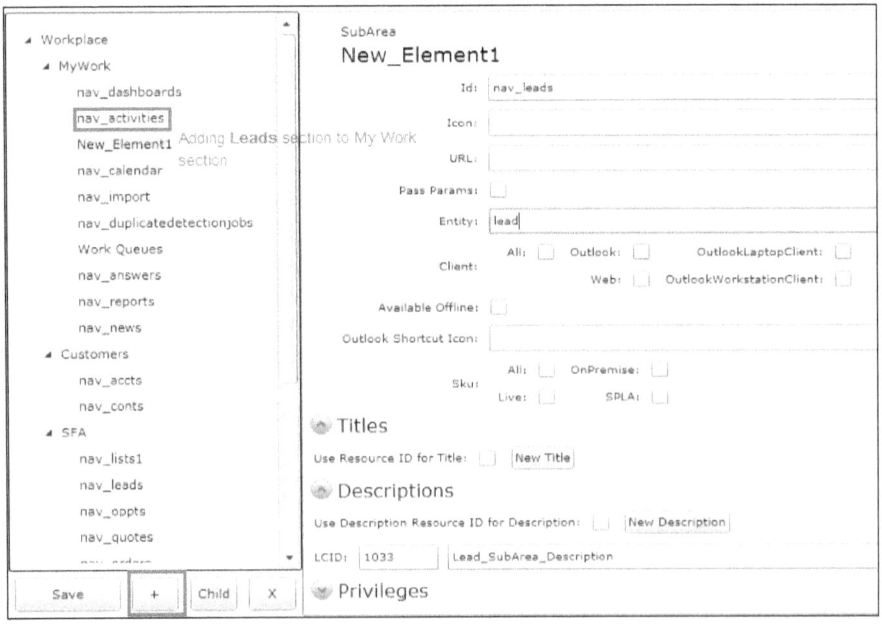

- **Removing an element from the Site Map**: To remove an element, select the element and click on the **X** button on the left-hand side navigation pane. If the element is a parent element, this action will also remove all subelements under it.

4. After editing the Site Map using the editor, click on the **Save** button in the left-hand side navigation pane. Once the changes are saved, we have to click on the **Publish All Customizations** button of the Microsoft Dynamics CRM SiteMap Editor solution.

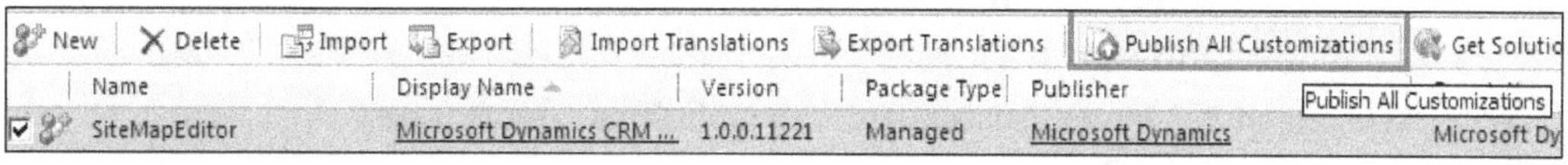

How it works...

Site Map is the navigation framework of the Dynamics CRM 2011 system. In this recipe, we have discussed how to edit the Site Map. The Site Map is saved as an XML in the Dynamics CRM 2011 system and manipulating it manually will be error-prone. Hence utmost care is required when manually manipulating it.

When adding an element to the Site Map, we have to ensure that every element has a unique ID attribute value; otherwise, the solution import will fail. Before removing an element from the Site Map, the best practice is to consider editing the security roles for users to control the Site Map.

Preparing for editing the ribbon

In this recipe, we will discuss how to customize the ribbon within the Dynamics CRM 2011 system.

Getting ready

To add any changes to the definition of the ribbon, the first step is to export the current definition of the ribbon; as a best practice, it is always advised to save the existing ribbon definition before making any changes. The saved ribbon definition can be helpful for reverting to the previous definition if any modification is causing serious issues to the system. After editing the ribbon definition, the solution has to be imported back for the changes to be applied. Hence, ribbon customization actually has three steps, as follows:

1. Exporting the ribbon definition as a Solution (this step will be covered in this recipe).
2. Editing the ribbon definition (this step will be covered in the next recipe, *Adding a new button to an existing ribbon group for all entities*).

3. Importing back the modified ribbon definition and applying the changes (this step will be covered in the recipe after the next one, *Importing the modified ribbon definition*).

How to do it...

Follow these steps to export the current ribbon definition from the Dynamics CRM 2011 system:

1. Log in to the Dynamics CRM 2011 system as a system administrator or with any other relevant security role.
2. Navigate to **Settings** | **Customization** | **Solutions**. Create a new unmanaged solution.

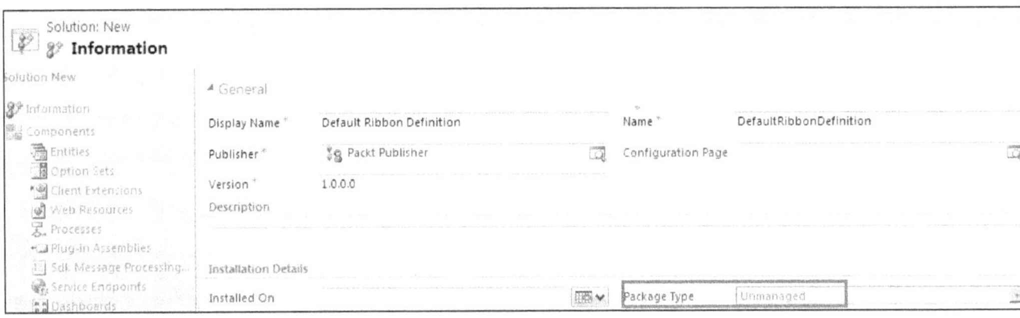

3. After creating the unmanaged solution, if we want to edit the ribbon for the specific entity or entities then click on **Add Existing** and add the required entity or entities.

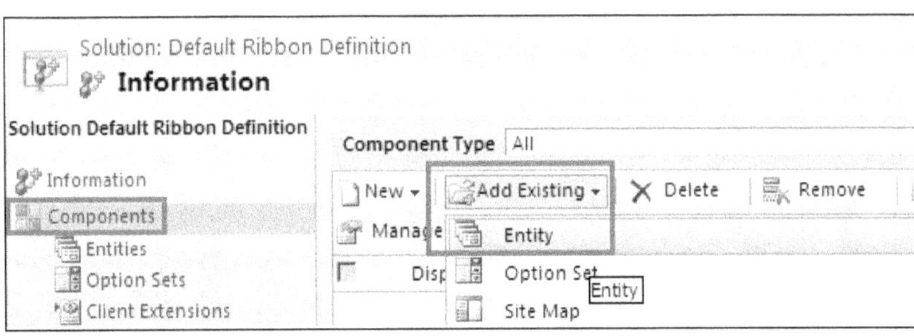

For the purpose of editing the entity ribbons, there is no need to include the required components; but if we intend to export this solution and apply it to another system, we should include the required components.

4. If we intend to edit the global ribbon or add a custom group to all entities, we have to include the **Application Ribbons** component to the solution by clicking on **Add Existing** in the **Actions** menu.

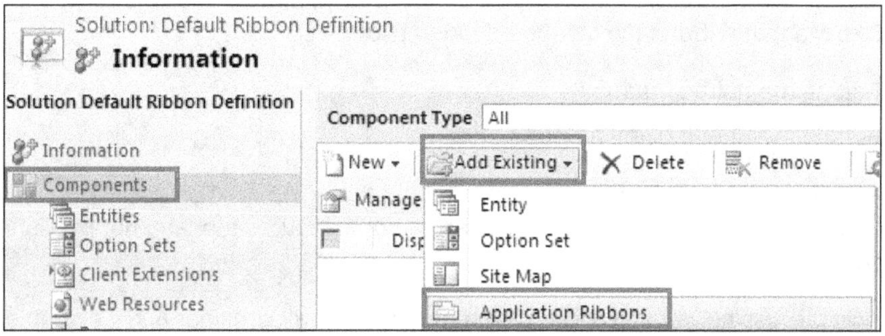

5. Finally, click on **Save and Close**.
6. Thereafter, export the solution as an unmanaged solution by clicking on the **Export** button in the **Solutions** actions menu:

7. Save the compressed Solution file.

How it works...

The ribbon definition has to be exported to edit it. For this purpose, an unmanaged solution is created with the existing ribbon definitions and a copy of this solution has to be preserved for any future rollback operation. To prepare the ribbon for editing, we need to extract a copy of the exported compressed unmanaged solution file. The extracted folder will have a file with the name `customizations.xml`. This file contains the ribbon definitions and will be edited to include the modified ribbon definitions. Post this editing, the solution folder will be compressed again and imported back into the Dynamics CRM 2011 system.

Adding a new button to an existing ribbon group for all entities

Like the Site Map, the ribbon too can be edited in two ways:

- Editing the ribbon manually
- Editing the ribbon using a ribbon editor.

There are multiple ribbon editor solutions available at `www.codeplex.com`. But unlike the SiteMap Editor, these ribbon editor tools are an open source tool and not published by Microsoft.

Here, we will discuss how to edit the ribbon manually. We will consider a few examples to illustrate how to edit the ribbon. Editing a ribbon can be done manually by modifying the `customization.xml` file of the exported solution.

Getting ready

The following is what we wish to achieve in this recipe:

- Add a button with the title `Bing` in the form of every entity
- The button should appear in the **Process** group of the main tab
- When the user clicks on this button, it should launch `www.bing.com`

The following screenshot shows how the final output will look:

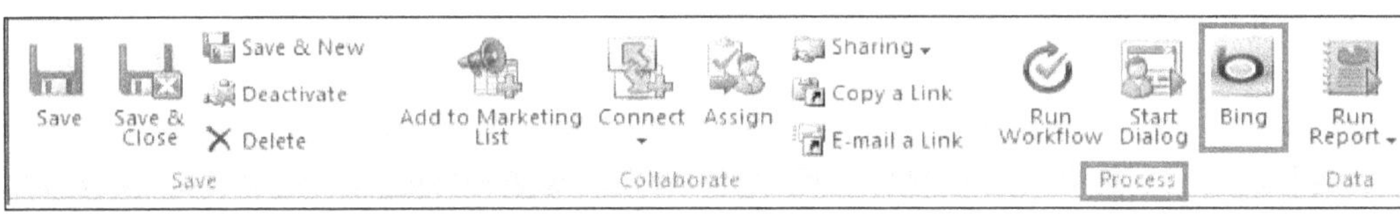

How to do it...

Follow these steps to add a new button (`Bing`) to an existing group (**Process**) for all entities:

1. Log in to the Dynamics CRM 2011 system as a system administrator or with any other relevant security role.
2. Export the ribbon Solution as described in the *Preparing for editing the ribbon* recipe.

3. The image file for the `Bing` button has to be added to the default solution before adding the ribbon. We will add two PNG images for the new `Bing` button in the web resources of the default solution. Let us name the images as follows:
    - A 16 x 16 pixel PNG file with the web resource name `packt_icons/Bing16.png`
    - A 32 x 32 pixel PNG file with the web resource name `packt_icons/Bing32.png`

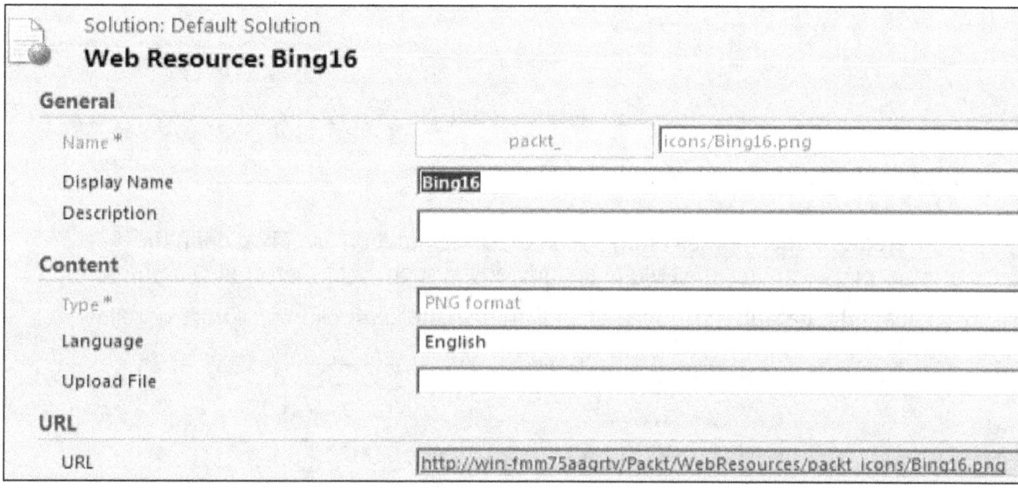

4. The next step is to identify the ID of the existing ribbon group with display name **Process** in all entity forms. We can refer to the Dynamics CRM 2011 SDK for identifying the ID of the group. The ribbon definitions are available under the `SDK\Resources\ExportedRibbonXml` location.

   The ID value of the **Process** group controls in the entity forms' main tab is `Mscrm.Form.{!EntityLogicalName}.MainTab.Workflow`

The following image shows the **Process** group ID in the ribbon from the `SDK\Resources\ExportedRibbonXML` file:

```
      <Button Id="Mscrm.Form.{!EntityLogicalName}.CopySelected" ToolTipTitle="$Resources:Ribbon.HomepageGrid.Record.Shortcut.Copy
      <Button Id="Mscrm.Form.{!EntityLogicalName}.SendSelected" ToolTipTitle="$Resources:Ribbon.HomepageGrid.Record.Shortcut.Send"
    </Controls>
  </Group>
  <Group Id="Mscrm.Form.{!EntityLogicalName}.MainTab.Workflow" Command="Mscrm.Enabled" Sequence="45" Title="$Resources:Ribbon.Homepa
    <Controls Id="Mscrm.Form.{!EntityLogicalName}.MainTab.Workflow.Controls">
      <Button Id="Mscrm.Form.{!EntityLogicalName}.RunWorkflow" ToolTipTitle="$Resources:Ribbon.HomepageGrid.Data.Workflow.RunWorkfl
      <Button Id="Mscrm.Form.{!EntityLogicalName}.RunScript" ToolTipTitle="$Resources:Ribbon.HomepageGrid.Data.InteractiveWorkflow.R
    </Controls>
  </Group>
  <Group Id="Mscrm.Form.{!EntityLogicalName}.MainTab.ExportData" Command="Mscrm.Enabled" Sequence="50" Title="$Resources:Ribbon.Home
    <Controls Id="Mscrm.Form.{!EntityLogicalName}.MainTab.ExportData.Controls">
      <FlyoutAnchor Id="Mscrm.Form.{!EntityLogicalName}.Reports" ToolTipTitle="$Resources:Ribbon.HomepageGrid.Data.Report.RunReport"
    </Controls>
  </Group>
 </Groups>
</Tab>
<Tab Id="Mscrm.Form.{!En" Command="Mscrm.Form.{!En" Title="$Resources:Ribb" Description="$Resources:Ribb" Sequence="20">...</Tab>
<Tab Id="Mscrm.Form.{!En" Command="Mscrm.Form.{!En" Title="$Resources:Ribb" Description="$Resources:Ribb" Sequence="30">...</Tab>
<Tab Id="Mscrm.HomepageG" Command="Mscrm.HomepageG" Title="{!EntityPluralD" Description="{!EntityPluralD" Sequence="100">...</Tab>
```

5. Thereafter, decompress or unzip the exported solution file. Then open the `customizations.xml` file in an XML editor such as Microsoft Visual Studio.
6. Locate the default `RibbonDiffXml` node in the `customizations.xml` file:

```
<RibbonDiffXml>
  <CustomActions />
  <Templates>
    <RibbonTemplates Id="Mscrm.Templates">
    </RibbonTemplates>
  </Templates>
  <CommandDefinitions />
  <RuleDefinitions>
    <TabDisplayRules />
    <DisplayRules />
    <EnableRules />
  </RuleDefinitions>
  <LocLabels />
</RibbonDiffXml>
```

7. Edit the `<LocLabels>` node in the `RibbonDiffXml` section to define the button name and tool tip.

```
<LocLabels>
  <LocLabel Id="Packt.all.Bing.LabelText">
    <Titles>
      <Title languagecode="1033" description="Bing" />
    </Titles>
  </LocLabel>
  <LocLabel Id="Packt.all.Bing.ToolTip">
    <Titles>
      <Title languagecode="1033" description="Launch Bing Application." />
    </Titles>
  </LocLabel>
</LocLabels>
```

8. Now we will define a `CommandDefinition` element for the new button.

```
<CommandDefinitions>
  <CommandDefinition Id="Packt.form.Bing">
    <EnableRules />
    <DisplayRules />
    <Actions>
      <Url Address="http://www.bing.com" />
    </Actions>
  </CommandDefinition>
</CommandDefinitions>
```

The `<Actions>` tab defines the action that will happen when the user clicks on the button. As we intend to launch a URL, we have defined a URL within the `<Actions>` node. We can use the `<Url>` node for any kind of URL navigation. We can use a relative URL if we want to launch a Dynamics CRM 2011 page URL or an HTML page added as a web resource.

> We can also execute a JavaScript function when the button is clicked. Add the JavaScript as a web resource and then refer to the web resource in the `Actions` node as shown in the following screenshot:

```
<Actions>
  <JavaScriptFunction FunctionName="launchBing" Library="$webresource:packt_scripts/formActions.js" />
</Actions>
```

9. Now we will define the `<CustomActions>` element for the button. Here, we will associate the `Labels`, `Actions`, and `Icons` defined before with the new button. With this step, we have completed the new button definition.

```
<CustomActions>
  <CustomAction Id="Packt.all.form.Bing.CustomAction"
                Location="Mscrm.Form.{!EntityLogicalName}.MainTab.Workflow.Controls._children"
                Sequence="30">
    <CommandUIDefinition>
      <Button Id="Packt.{!EntityLogicalName}.form.Bing.Button"
              Command="Packt.form.Bing"
              LabelText="$LocLabels:Packt.all.Bing.LabelText"
              ToolTipTitle="$LocLabels:Packt.all.Bing.LabelText"
              ToolTipDescription="$LocLabels:Packt.all.Bing.ToolTip"
              TemplateAlias="o1"
              Image16by16="$webresource:packt_icons/Bing16.png"
              Image32by32="$webresource:packt_icons/Bing32.png" />
    </CommandUIDefinition>
  </CustomAction>
</CustomActions>
```

10. The final, modified `RibbonDiffXml` node should look like the following code:

```
<RibbonDiffXml>
  <CustomActions>
    <CustomAction
Id="Packt.all.form.Bing.CustomAction"
Location="Mscrm.Form.{!EntityLogicalName}.MainTab.
Workflow.Controls._children"
           Sequence="30">
      <CommandUIDefinition>
        <Button Id="Packt.{!EntityLogicalName}.form.Bing.Button"
                Command="Packt.form.Bing"
                LabelText="$LocLabels:Packt.all.Bing.LabelText"
                ToolTipTitle="$LocLabels:Packt.all.Bing.LabelText"
          ToolTipDescription="$LocLabels:Packt.all.Bing.Tool Tip"
                TemplateAlias="o1"
                Image16by16="$webresource:packt_icons/Bing16.png"
               Image32by32="$webresource:packt_icons/Bing32.png"/>
      </CommandUIDefinition>
    </CustomAction>
  </CustomActions>
  <Templates>
    <RibbonTemplates Id="Mscrm.Templates"/>
  </Templates>
  <CommandDefinitions>
    <CommandDefinition Id="Packt.form.Bing">
      <EnableRules />
      <DisplayRules />
      <Actions>
        <Url Address= "http://www.bing.com" />
      </Actions>
    </CommandDefinition>
  </CommandDefinitions>
  <RuleDefinitions>
    <TabDisplayRules />
    <DisplayRules />
    <EnableRules />
  </RuleDefinitions>
  <LocLabels>
    <LocLabel Id="Packt.all.Bing.LabelText">
      <Titles>
        <Title languagecode="1033" description="Bing" />
      </Titles>
    </LocLabel>
```

```
        <LocLabel Id="Packt.all.Bing.ToolTip">
          <Titles>
            <Title languagecode="1033" description="Launch Bing
                                  Application." />
          </Titles>
        </LocLabel>
      </LocLabels>
    </RibbonDiffXml>
```

11. Then import the modified solution by following the *Importing the modified ribbon definition* recipe of this chapter.

The final outcome of this recipe will be a new **Bing** button added to the **Process** group of all entity forms, as shown in the following screenshot:

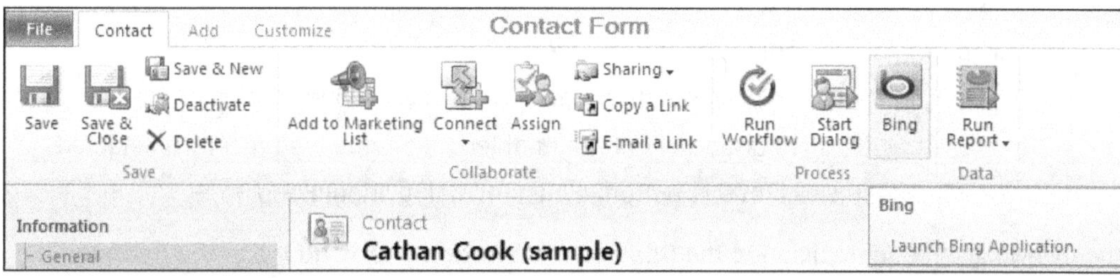

How it works...

The new ribbon button is added to all entity forms' ribbons. If we intend to add this same button to a specific entity ribbon form (for example, the Account entity form), the ID of the ribbon section is required to be used in the `Mscrm.Form.account.MainTab.Workflow` format. It is clear that we have to replace the `{!EntityLogicalName}` part with the specific entity name. Ribbon changes will fail if an incorrect ID is used during the new button definition.

In addition, the web resources referred to in the button definition (PNG images and JScripts) have to be present before importing the solution having the new button definition. Otherwise, the solution import will fail.

Adding a new button to an existing ribbon group of a specific entity

In this recipe, we will add a new button to an existing ribbon group for a specific entity.

Getting ready

The following is what we wish to achieve in this recipe:

- Add a new button (**Change Lead Rating**) in both the Lead form ribbon as well as the Lead grid ribbon
- This button should appear in the **Actions** group on the right-hand side of the **Qualify** button
- This button should only appear in the web client
- This button should only appear if the record has already been saved
- In the lead grid, this button will only be enabled if just one lead record is selected
- When the user clicks on this button, a custom dialog should pop up

The following screenshot displays the **Change Lead Rating** button added to the **Actions** ribbon group of the Lead record:

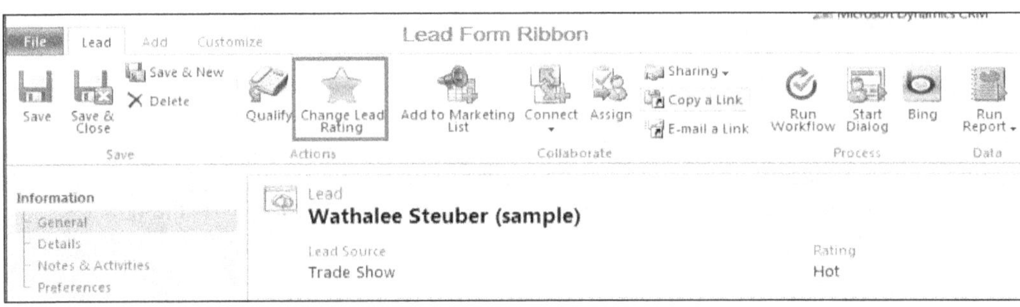

The following screenshot displays the **Change Lead Rating** button added to the **Actions** ribbon group of the Lead grid ribbon and is enabled when only one record is selected:

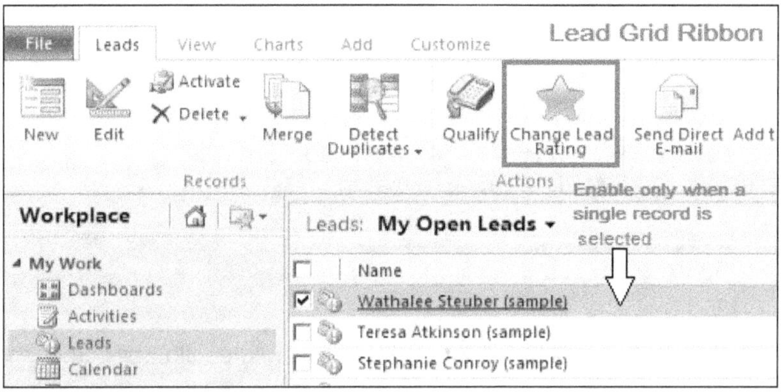

How to do it...

Follow these steps to add a new button (**Change Lead Rating**) as defined in the preceding scenario:

1. Log in to the Dynamics CRM 2011 system as a system administrator or with any other relevant security role.
2. Create the new custom dialog (**Change Lead Rating**) that will be launched via the custom button.

   The *Creating a dialog using the Dynamics CRM 2011 web interface* recipe can be found in *Chapter 10, Processes*, of this book.

3. Export the ribbon solution as described in the *Preparing for editing the ribbon* recipe. Include the custom dialog and the concerned entity (Lead, in this case) into this solution before exporting.
4. Then create the following JScript file and add it as a web resource to the default solution. Name the web resource as `packt_scripts/ChangeLeadRating.js`.

```
function LaunchModalDialog(dialogId, typeName, recordId) {
    var serverUrl = Xrm.Page.context.getServerUrl();
    recordId = recordId.replace("{", "");
    recordId = recordId.replace("}", "");
    dialogId = dialogId.replace("{", "");
    dialogId = dialogId.replace("}", "");

    // Load modal dialog
    var serverUri = serverUrl + '/cs/dialog/rundialog.aspx';
    var mypath =   serverUri +
```

```
        '?DialogId=%7b' +
                dialogId.toUpperCase() +
        '%7d&EntityName=' +
    typeName +
    '&ObjectId=%7b' +
    recordId +
    '%7d';

        // First item from selected leads only
        window.showModalDialog(mypath);

        // Reload form.
        window.location.reload(true);
    }
```

The window for creating the JScript file is shown in the following screenshot:

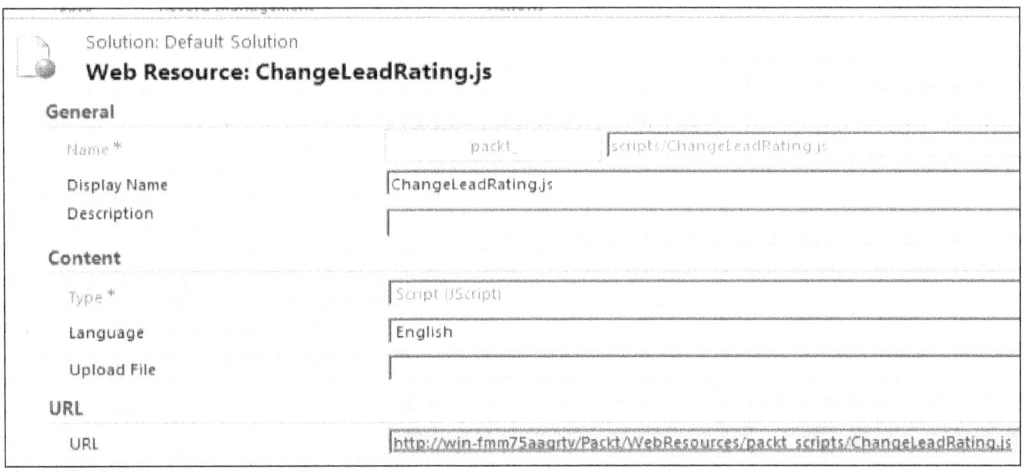

5. Thereafter, we will add two PNG images for the new **Change Lead Rating** button in the web resources of the default solution. Let us name the images as follows:
   - A 16 x 16 pixel PNG file with the web resource name `packt_icons/LeadRating16.png`
   - A 32 x 32 pixel PNG file with the web resource name `packt_icons/LeadRating32.png`

The window for adding the PNG files is shown in the following screenshot:

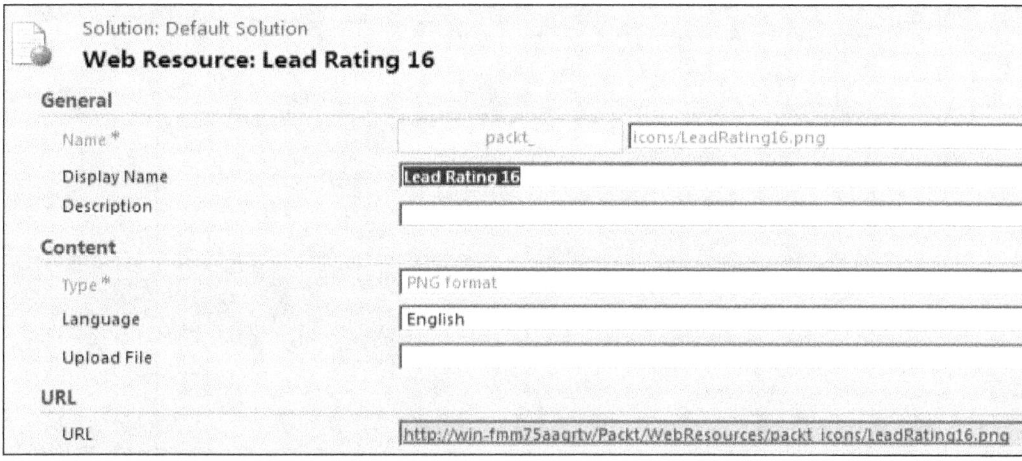

6. The next step is to identify the ID of the existing ribbon group with display name **Actions** for the Lead form ribbon and the Lead grid ribbon.
   - We can refer to the Dynamics CRM 2011 SDK for identifying the ID of the group. The ribbon definitions are available under the `SDK\Resources\ExportedRibbonXml` location.
   - The ID of the **Actions** group for the Lead form ribbon is as follows:

```
<Group Id="Mscrm.Form.lead.MainTab.Actions"
       Command="Mscrm.Enabled"
       Sequence="30"
       Title="$Resources:Ribbon.HomepageGrid.MainTab.Actions"
       Image32by32Popup="/_imgs/ribbon/Actions_32.png"
       Template="Mscrm.Templates.Flexible3">
```

   - The ID of the **Actions** group for the Lead grid ribbon is as follows:

```
<Group Id="Mscrm.HomepageGrid.lead.MainTab.Actions"
       Command="Mscrm.Enabled"
       Sequence="20"
       Title="$Resources:Ribbon.HomepageGrid.MainTab.Actions"
       Template="Mscrm.Templates.Flexible4"
       Image32by32Popup="/_imgs/ribbon/Actions_32.png">
```

7. Thereafter, decompress the exported solution file. Then open `customizations.xml` in an XML editor such as Microsoft Visual Studio.

8. Locate the default `RibbonDiffXml` node in `customizations.xml` under the Lead entity section as shown in the following screenshot:

```
<Entities>
  <Entity>...</Entity>
  <Entity>
    <Name LocalizedName="Lead" OriginalName="Lead">Lead</Name>
    <ObjectTypeCode>4</ObjectTypeCode>
    <FormXml>...</FormXml>
    <RibbonDiffXml>
      <CustomActions />
      <Templates>
        <RibbonTemplates Id="Mscrm.Templates">
        </RibbonTemplates>
      </Templates>
      <CommandDefinitions />
      <RuleDefinitions>
        <TabDisplayRules />
        <DisplayRules />
        <EnableRules />
      </RuleDefinitions>
      <LocLabels />
    </RibbonDiffXml>
```

9. Edit the `<LocLabels>` node in the `RibbonDiffXml` section to define the button name and tool tip.

```
<LocLabels>
  <LocLabel Id="Packt.lead.ChangeLeadRating.LabelText">
    <Titles>
      <Title languagecode="1033"
             description="Change Lead Rating" />
    </Titles>
  </LocLabel>
  <LocLabel Id="Packt.lead.ChangeLeadRating.ToolTip">
    <Titles>
      <Title languagecode="1033"
             description="Launches Change Lead Rating dialog." />
    </Titles>
  </LocLabel>
</LocLabels>
```

10. Now we will edit the `RuleDefinitions` node to define the display and enable rules to support the following requirements, as described in the *Getting ready* section of this recipe:
    - This button should only appear in the web client
    - This button should only appear if the record has already been saved
    - In the Lead grid ribbon, this button will only be enabled if only one Lead record is selected

The `RuleDefinitions` node is shown in the following screenshot:

```
<RuleDefinitions>
  <TabDisplayRules />
  <DisplayRules>
    <DisplayRule Id="Packt.lead.form.FormStateNotNew.DisplayRule">
      <FormStateRule State="Create" InvertResult="true" />
    </DisplayRule>
    <DisplayRule Id="Packt.lead.WebClient.DisplayRule">
      <CrmClientTypeRule Type="Web" />
    </DisplayRule>
  </DisplayRules>
  <EnableRules>
    <EnableRule Id="Packt.lead.WebClient.EnableRule">
      <CrmClientTypeRule Type="Web" />
    </EnableRule>
    <EnableRule Id="Packt.lead.form.NotNew.EnableRule">
      <FormStateRule State="Create" InvertResult="true" />
    </EnableRule>
    <EnableRule Id="Packt.lead.grid.OneSelected.EnableRule">
      <SelectionCountRule AppliesTo="SelectedEntity" Maximum="1" Minimum="1" />
    </EnableRule>
  </EnableRules>
</RuleDefinitions>
```

11. Now we will define `CommandDefinition` for the new button. The `CommandDefinition` element for the button in the Lead form ribbon will be as follows:

```
<CommandDefinition Id="Packt.lead.form.ChangeLeadRating.Command">
  <EnableRules>
    <EnableRule Id="Packt.lead.WebClient.EnableRule" />
    <EnableRule Id="Packt.lead.form.NotNew.EnableRule" />
  </EnableRules>
  <DisplayRules>
    <DisplayRule Id="Packt.lead.form.FormStateNotNew.DisplayRule" />
    <DisplayRule Id="Packt.lead.WebClient.DisplayRule" />
  </DisplayRules>
  <Actions>
    <JavaScriptFunction FunctionName="LaunchModalDialog" Library="$webresource:packt_scripts/ChangeLeadRating.js" >
      <StringParameter Value="fa252917-737e-4e5d-8d1c-c143c29f34e7" />
      <StringParameter Value="lead" />
      <CrmParameter Value="FirstPrimaryItemId" />
    </JavaScriptFunction>
  </Actions>
</CommandDefinition>
```

The `CommandDefinition` element for the new button in the Lead grid ribbon will be as follows:

```
<CommandDefinitions>
  <CommandDefinition Id="Packt.lead.grid.ChangeLeadRating.Command">
    <EnableRules>
      <EnableRule Id="Packt.lead.WebClient.EnableRule" />
      <EnableRule Id="Packt.lead.grid.OneSelected.EnableRule" />
    </EnableRules>
    <DisplayRules>
      <DisplayRule Id="Packt.lead.WebClient.DisplayRule" />
    </DisplayRules>
    <Actions>
      <JavaScriptFunction FunctionName="LaunchModalDialog" Library="$webresource:packt_scripts/ChangeLeadRating.js" >
        <StringParameter Value="fa252917-737e-4e5d-8d1c-c143c29f34e7" />
        <StringParameter Value="lead" />
        <CrmParameter Value="FirstSelectedItemId" />
      </JavaScriptFunction>
    </Actions>
  </CommandDefinition>
```

The `<Actions>` tab defines the action that will happen when the user clicks on the button. In this example, a JavaScript function with the name `LaunchModalDialog` will be called when the user clicks on the button. We have already defined and added this JScript to the web resources. The JavaScript method expects three parameters, which are passed to the method using the `StringParameter` and `CrmParamater` nodes.

12. Finally, we have to define the `CustomActions` element for the new button. The `CustomAction` element for the button in the Lead form will be as shown in the following screenshot:

```
<CustomAction Id="Packt.lead.form.ChangeLeadRating.CustomAction"
              Location="Mscrm.Form.lead.MainTab.Actions.Controls._children"
              Sequence="10">
  <CommandUIDefinition>
    <Button Id="Packt.lead.form.ChangeLeadRating.Button"
            Command="Packt.lead.form.ChangeLeadRating.Command"
            LabelText="$LocLabels:Packt.lead.ChangeLeadRating.LabelText"
            ToolTipTitle="$LocLabels:Packt.lead.ChangeLeadRating.LabelText"
            ToolTipDescription="$LocLabels:Packt.lead.ChangeLeadRating.ToolTip"
            TemplateAlias="o1"
            Image16by16="$webresource:packt_icons/LeadRating16.png"
            Image32by32="$webresource:packt_icons/LeadRating32.png" />
  </CommandUIDefinition>
</CustomAction>
```

The `CustomAction` element for the button in the Lead grid will be as follows:

```
<CustomAction Id="Packt.lead.grid.ChangeLeadRating.CustomAction"
              Location="Mscrm.HomepageGrid.lead.MainTab.Actions.Controls._children"
              Sequence="10">
  <CommandUIDefinition>
    <Button Id="Packt.lead.grid.ChangeLeadRating.Button"
            Command="Packt.lead.grid.ChangeLeadRating.Command"
            LabelText="$LocLabels:Packt.lead.ChangeLeadRating.LabelText"
            ToolTipTitle="$LocLabels:Packt.lead.ChangeLeadRating.LabelText"
            ToolTipDescription="$LocLabels:Packt.lead.ChangeLeadRating.ToolTip"
            TemplateAlias="o1"
            Image16by16="$webresource:packt_icons/LeadRating16.png"
            Image32by32="$webresource:packt_icons/LeadRating32.png" />
  </CommandUIDefinition>
</CustomAction>
```

13. The final, modified `RibbonDiffXml` node should look as follows:

```
<RibbonDiffXml>
  <CustomActions>
    <CustomAction
Id="Packt.lead.grid.ChangeLeadRating.CustomAction"
Location="Mscrm.HomepageGrid.lead.MainTab.Actions.
Controls._children"
Sequence="10">
      <CommandUIDefinition>
        <Button Id="Packt.lead.grid.ChangeLeadRating.Button"
                Command="Packt.lead.grid.ChangeLeadRating.Command"
LabelText="$LocLabels:Packt.lead.ChangeLeadRating.
LabelText"
ToolTipTitle="$LocLabels:Packt.lead.
ChangeLeadRating.LabelText"
ToolTipDescription="$LocLabels:Packt.lead.
ChangeLeadRating.ToolTip"
                TemplateAlias="o1"
                Image16by16="$webresource:packt_icons/
LeadRating16.png"
                Image32by32="$webresource:packt_icons/
LeadRating32.png" />
      </CommandUIDefinition>
    </CustomAction>
    <CustomAction
Id="Packt.lead.form.ChangeLeadRating.CustomAction"
Location="Mscrm.Form.lead.MainTab.Actions.Controls.
```

```
_children"
Sequence="10">
      <CommandUIDefinition>
        <Button Id="Packt.lead.form.ChangeLeadRating.Button"
                Command="Packt.lead.form.ChangeLeadRating.Command"
LabelText="$LocLabels:Packt.lead.ChangeLeadRating.
LabelText"
ToolTipTitle="$LocLabels:Packt.lead.
ChangeLeadRating.LabelText"
ToolTipDescription="$LocLabels:Packt.lead.
ChangeLeadRating.ToolTip"
                TemplateAlias="o1"
Image16by16="$webresource:packt_icons/LeadRating16.png"
Image32by32="$webresource:packt_icons/LeadRating32.png" />
      </CommandUIDefinition>
    </CustomAction>
  </CustomActions>
  <Templates>
    <RibbonTemplates Id="Mscrm.Templates"/>
  </Templates>
  <CommandDefinitions>
    <CommandDefinition
Id="Packt.lead.grid.ChangeLeadRating.Command">
      <EnableRules>
        <EnableRule Id="Packt.lead.WebClient.EnableRule" />
        <EnableRule Id="Packt.lead.grid.OneSelected.EnableRule" />
      </EnableRules>
      <DisplayRules>
        <DisplayRule Id="Packt.lead.WebClient.DisplayRule" />
      </DisplayRules>
      <Actions>
        <JavaScriptFunction FunctionName="LaunchModalDialog"
Library="$webresource:packt_scripts/ChangeLeadRating.js" >
          <StringParameter Value="fa252917-737e-4e5d-8d1c-
c143c29f34e7" />
          <StringParameter Value="lead" />
          <CrmParameter Value="FirstSelectedItemId" />
        </JavaScriptFunction>
      </Actions>
    </CommandDefinition>
    <CommandDefinition
Id="Packt.lead.form.ChangeLeadRating.Command">
      <EnableRules>
        <EnableRule Id="Packt.lead.WebClient.EnableRule" />
```

```
        <EnableRule Id="Packt.lead.form.NotNew.EnableRule" />
      </EnableRules>
      <DisplayRules>
        <DisplayRule
Id="Packt.lead.form.FormStateNotNew.DisplayRule" />
        <DisplayRule Id="Packt.lead.WebClient.DisplayRule" />
      </DisplayRules>
      <Actions>
        <JavaScriptFunction FunctionName="LaunchModalDialog"
Library="$webresource:packt_scripts/ChangeLeadRating.js" >
          <StringParameter Value="fa252917-737e-4e5d-8d1c-
c143c29f34e7" />
          <StringParameter Value="lead" />
          <CrmParameter Value="FirstPrimaryItemId" />
        </JavaScriptFunction>
      </Actions>
    </CommandDefinition>
  </CommandDefinitions>
  <RuleDefinitions>
    <TabDisplayRules />
    <DisplayRules>
      <DisplayRule
Id="Packt.lead.form.FormStateNotNew.DisplayRule">
        <FormStateRule State="Create"
                       InvertResult="true" />
      </DisplayRule>
      <DisplayRule Id="Packt.lead.WebClient.DisplayRule">
        <CrmClientTypeRule Type="Web" />
      </DisplayRule>
    </DisplayRules>
    <EnableRules>
      <EnableRule Id="Packt.lead.WebClient.EnableRule">
        <CrmClientTypeRule Type="Web" />
      </EnableRule>
      <EnableRule Id="Packt.lead.form.NotNew.EnableRule">
        <FormStateRule State="Create" InvertResult="true" />
      </EnableRule>
      <EnableRule Id="Packt.lead.grid.OneSelected.EnableRule">
        <SelectionCountRule AppliesTo="SelectedEntity"
                            Maximum="1"
                            Minimum="1" />
      </EnableRule>
    </EnableRules>
  </RuleDefinitions>
```

```
    <LocLabels>
      <LocLabel Id="Packt.lead.ChangeLeadRating.LabelText">
        <Titles>
          <Title languagecode="1033"
                 description="Change Lead Rating" />
        </Titles>
      </LocLabel>
      <LocLabel Id="Packt.lead.ChangeLeadRating.ToolTip">
        <Titles>
          <Title languagecode="1033"
                 description="Launches Change Lead Rating dialog" />
        </Titles>
      </LocLabel>
    </LocLabels>
  </RibbonDiffXml>
```

14. Then import the modified solution by following the *Importing the modified ribbon definition* recipe of this chapter.

The final outcome of this recipe will be a new **Change Lead Rating** button added to the **Actions** group of the Lead form and the Lead grid ribbons.

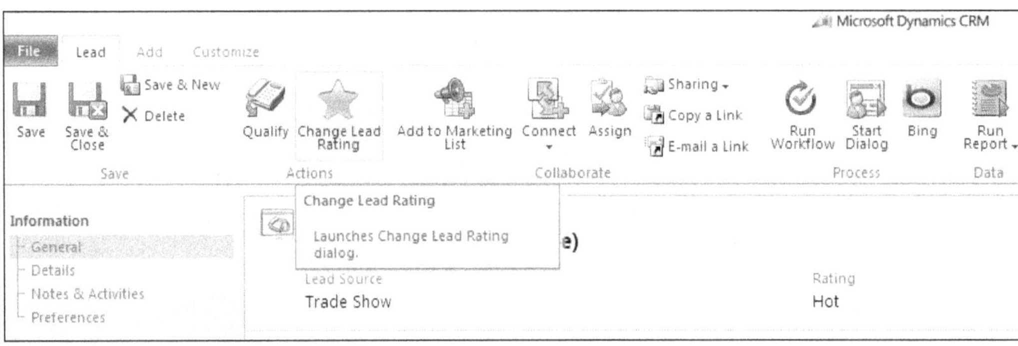

Lead form ribbon

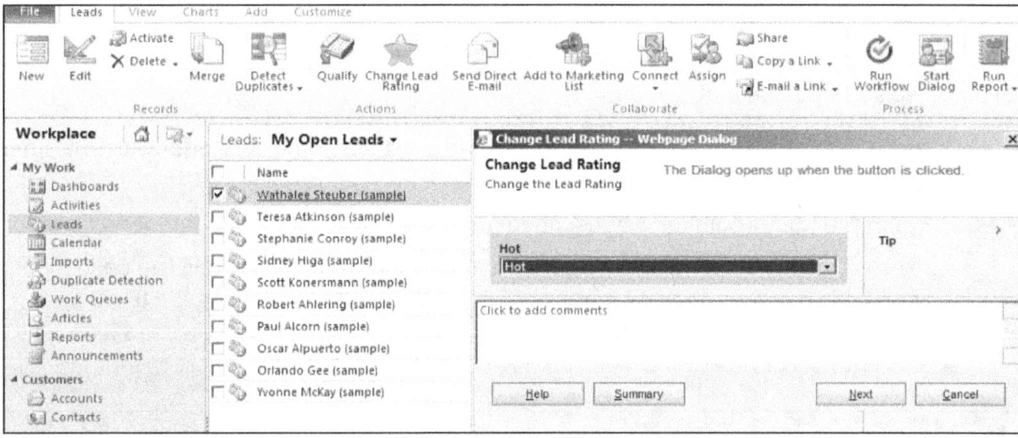

Lead grid ribbon

How it works...

In this recipe, we have discussed how to open a dialog from a custom ribbon button as well as how to add this new button in an entity's form ribbon as well as grid ribbon, along with certain other conditions. This recipe can be used to add new buttons in different groups of the ribbon. The ID of the group will vary along with the ribbon group.

Hiding a ribbon button

In this recipe, we will discuss how to hide a ribbon button.

Getting ready

The following is what we wish to achieve in this recipe:

- Remove the **Queue Item Details** button from the form ribbon of **Case**.

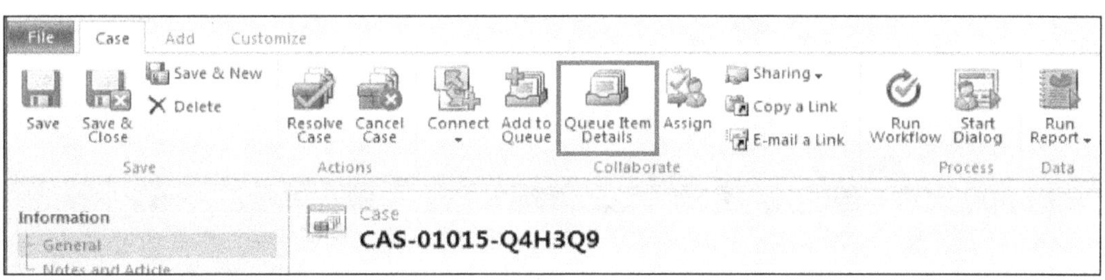

How to do it...

Follow these steps to hide a ribbon button:

1. Log in to the Dynamics CRM 2011 system as a system administrator or with any other relevant security role.
2. Export the ribbon solution as described in the *Preparing for editing the ribbon* recipe.
3. The next step is to identify the ID of the **Queue Item Details** button in the Case ribbon. We can refer to the Dynamics CRM 2011 SDK for identifying the ID of the group. The ribbon definitions are available under the `SDK\Resources\ExportedRibbonXml` location. The file is shown in the following screenshot:

```
<Button Id="Mscrm.Form.incident.QueueItemDetail"
        ToolTipTitle="$Resources:Ribbon.HomepageGrid.queueitem.MainTab.Actions.QueueItemDetail"
        ToolTipDescription="$Resources:Mscrm_SubGrid_queueitem_MainTab_Actions_QueueItemDetail_ToolTipDescription"
        Command="Mscrm.QueueItemDetail"
        Sequence="32"
        Alt="$Resources:Ribbon.HomepageGrid.queueitem.MainTab.Actions.QueueItemDetail"
        LabelText="$Resources:Ribbon.HomepageGrid.queueitem.MainTab.Actions.QueueItemDetail"
        Image16by16="/_imgs/Workplace/QueueItemDetails_16.png"
        Image32by32="/_imgs/Workplace/QueueItemDetails_32.png"
        TemplateAlias="o1" />
```

4. Thereafter, decompress the exported solution file. Then open the `customizations.xml` file in an XML editor such as Microsoft Visual Studio.
5. Locate the default `RibbonDiffXml` node in `customizations.xml` under the Case entity, as shown in the following screenshot:

```
<Entity>
  <Name LocalizedName="Case" OriginalName="Case">Incident</Name>
  <ObjectTypeCode>112</ObjectTypeCode>
  <FormXml>...</FormXml>
  <RibbonDiffXml>
    <CustomActions/>
    <Templates>
      <RibbonTemplates Id="Mscrm.Templates"></RibbonTemplates>
    </Templates>
    <CommandDefinitions />
    <RuleDefinitions>
      <TabDisplayRules />
      <DisplayRules />
      <EnableRules />
    </RuleDefinitions>
    <LocLabels />
  </RibbonDiffXml>
```

6. Define `HideCustomAction` with the `Location` attribute as the **Queue Item Details** button ID. The final `RibbonDiffXml` element will look as follows:

```
<RibbonDiffXml>
  <CustomActions>
    <HideCustomAction
Location="Mscrm.Form.incident.QueueItemDetail"
HideActionId="Packt.Form.incident.QueueItemDetail.
HideAction" />
  </CustomActions>
  <Templates>
    <RibbonTemplates Id="Mscrm.Templates"/>
  </Templates>
  <CommandDefinitions />
  <RuleDefinitions>
    <TabDisplayRules />
    <DisplayRules />
    <EnableRules />
  </RuleDefinitions>
  <LocLabels />
</RibbonDiffXml>
```

7. Then import the modified solution by following the *Importing the modified ribbon definition* recipe of this chapter.
8. The final outcome of this recipe will be a hidden **Queue Item Details** button in the Case form as shown in the following screenshot:

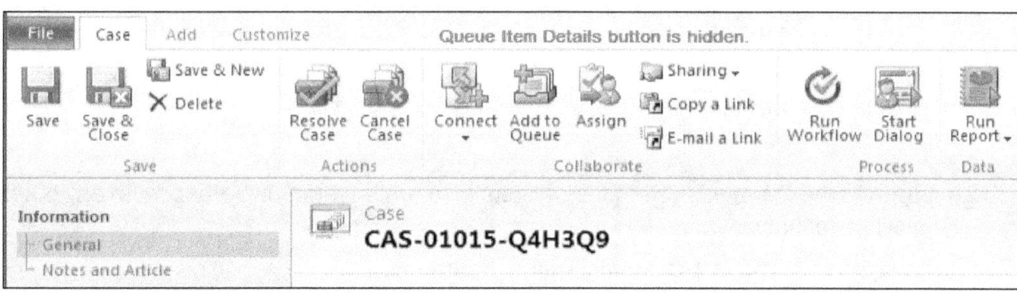

How it works...

In this recipe, we have discussed how to hide an existing ribbon button. The `HideCustomAction` element only removes a specified node from the ribbon; using this approach may not be advisable for every situation.

> If we intend to hide a button that is associated with a security role, we must try to adjust the entity security role to hide the button. If we intend to replace an existing ribbon element with a custom one, we can overwrite the element by using `CustomAction` with a `Location` attribute value identical to the existing element.

Importing the modified ribbon definition

In the previous recipes, we have learned how to edit the ribbon definition for various scenarios. After editing the ribbon definition, the modified ribbon definition has to be imported back to the Dynamics CRM 2011 system. This recipe will describe how to achieve this.

How to do it...

Follow these steps to import the modified ribbon definition from the Dynamics CRM 2011 system:

1. Compress the `Solution` folder, which contains the files shown in the following screenshot, to a ZIP file. The `customizations.xml` file should contain the modified ribbon definitions.

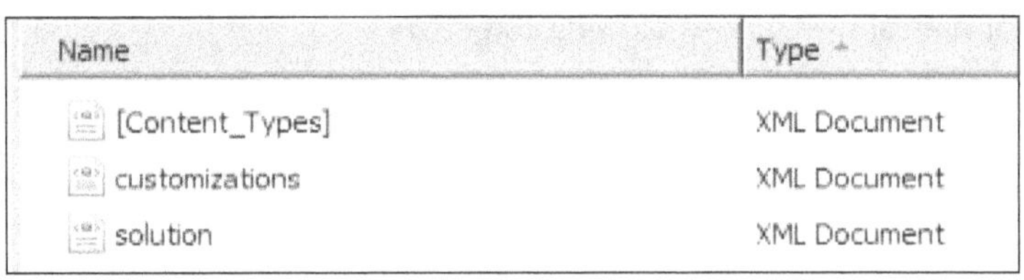

2. Log in to the Dynamics CRM 2011 system as a system administrator or with any other relevant security role.
3. Navigate to **Settings** | **Customization** | **Solutions**.
4. Click on the **Import** button in the **Actions** menu to import the modified solution.

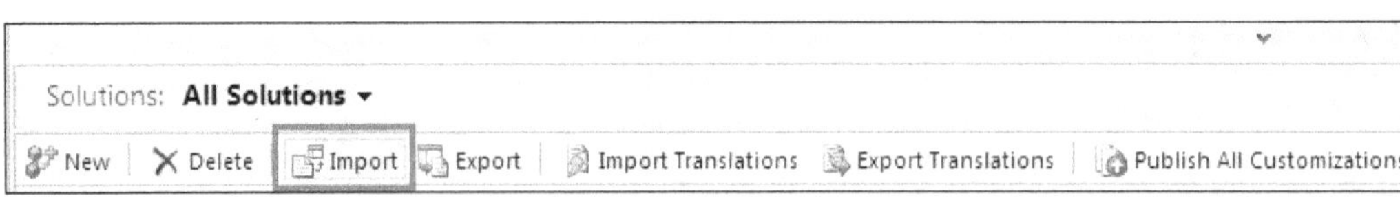

5. After importing, we have to publish the changes by selecting the imported solution and clicking on the **Publish All Customizations** button in the **Actions** menu.

How it works...

After modifying the ribbon definition, it has to be reimported so that the changes can take effect. If the ribbon definition's modification is not done with care, then during import the modified ribbon definition may throw errors or may cause serious issues after solution import. In such a case, the exported default ribbon definition solution can be imported to go back to the default state of the ribbon.

See also

In this chapter, we have discussed various recipes regarding Site Map and ribbon customization. In the next chapter, we will discuss the integration of SharePoint and Microsoft Word with the Dynamics CRM 2011 system. The interesting recipes in the next chapter will be:

- *Creating Mail Merge templates using Microsoft Word*
- *Integrating Microsoft SharePoint with Dynamics CRM 2011*

9
Office and SharePoint Integration

Microsoft Dynamics CRM 2011 allows a very strong integration with Microsoft Office and Microsoft SharePoint. In *Chapter 4, Data Management* we discussed how data can be exported from Dynamics CRM 2011 to Microsoft Excel. Microsoft Dynamics CRM 2011 can be accessed when integrated with Microsoft Outlook. In this chapter, we will discuss how Microsoft Dynamics CRM 2011 provides a strong integration with Microsoft Word via Mail Merge templates. Microsoft Dynamics CRM 2011 also supports integration with Microsoft SharePoint for better collaboration and document management.

In this chapter, we will delve into the following recipes:

- Creating Mail Merge templates using Microsoft Word
- Integrating Microsoft SharePoint with Dynamics CRM 2011

Introduction

There is a usual requirement to quickly create documents populated with data from Dynamics CRM 2011. Dynamics CRM 2011 supports the creation of predefined templates that can then be published to users. Such templates are known as **Mail Merge** templates and can be used to quickly create documents that include information from records in the Dynamics CRM 2011 system. Using the Mail Merge functionality of Dynamics CRM 2011, we can create Microsoft Office Word templates for sending letters, faxes, envelopes, and e-mail messages.

Although Dynamics CRM 2011 has the ability to attach a document with records, it does not provide a good document management solution. The document versions cannot be maintained, documents cannot be searched, and it also takes a lot of manual effort to find the exact document that we were looking for. Integrating Dynamics CRM 2011 with SharePoint allows us to use SharePoint as a document management solution.

Creating Mail Merge templates using Microsoft Word

In this recipe, we will discuss how to create a Mail Merge template based on Microsoft Word that can extract data from a Dynamics CRM 2011 system and create a letter, form, e-mail, fax, and so on.

How to do it...

The steps to create a Mail Merge template using Microsoft Word within a Dynamics CRM 2011 system are as follows:

1. Log in to the Dynamics CRM 2011 system as a system administrator or as a relevant security role.
2. Navigate to **Settings** | **Business** | **Templates** | **Mail Merge Templates**.
3. Click on the **New** button in the **Actions** menu.

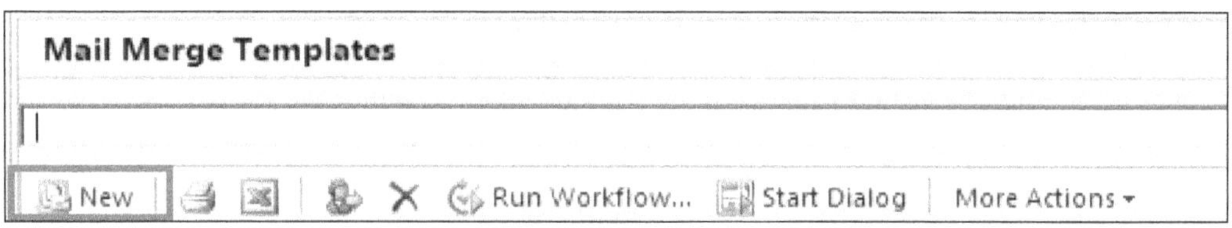

4. On the **New** page of **Mail Merge Templates**, provide the following information:
    - **Name**: This is the name of the Mail Merge template. Use a descriptive name that will be easy to understand.
    - **Description**: This is the description of the Mail Merge template.
    - **Associated Entity**: This is the entity against which the Mail Merge template will be linked.

> The creation of a Mail Merge template is enabled only for the following business entities: Account, Case, Contact, Lead, Opportunity, and Quote. For custom entities, the Mail Merge setting can be enabled from navigating to **General** | **Communication & Collaboration** from the entity.
>
> Mail Merge can be used to list the members in a marketing list. On opening a marketing list and navigating to the **Add** tab in the ribbon, we will find the **Mail Merge on List Members** option that can be used by Mail Merge to list members.

- **Language**: This is the language of the Mail Merge template. The drop-down box will only display the languages installed in the Dynamics CRM 2011 system.
- **Ownership**: The ownership of the Mail Merge template record can also be selected. By default, the logged-in user will be selected as the template owner, which can be changed.

5. Then, click on the **Save** button in the top ribbon to save the settings.
6. After saving the template, click on the **Data Fields** button under the **Select data fields** section on the page.

7. This will bring up the **Add Columns** web dialog with the default fields selected. We have to choose the fields/columns we intend to use in the Mail Merge template. We can even choose fields from the **Related** entities. Only the fields included here will be available for the Mail Merge template.

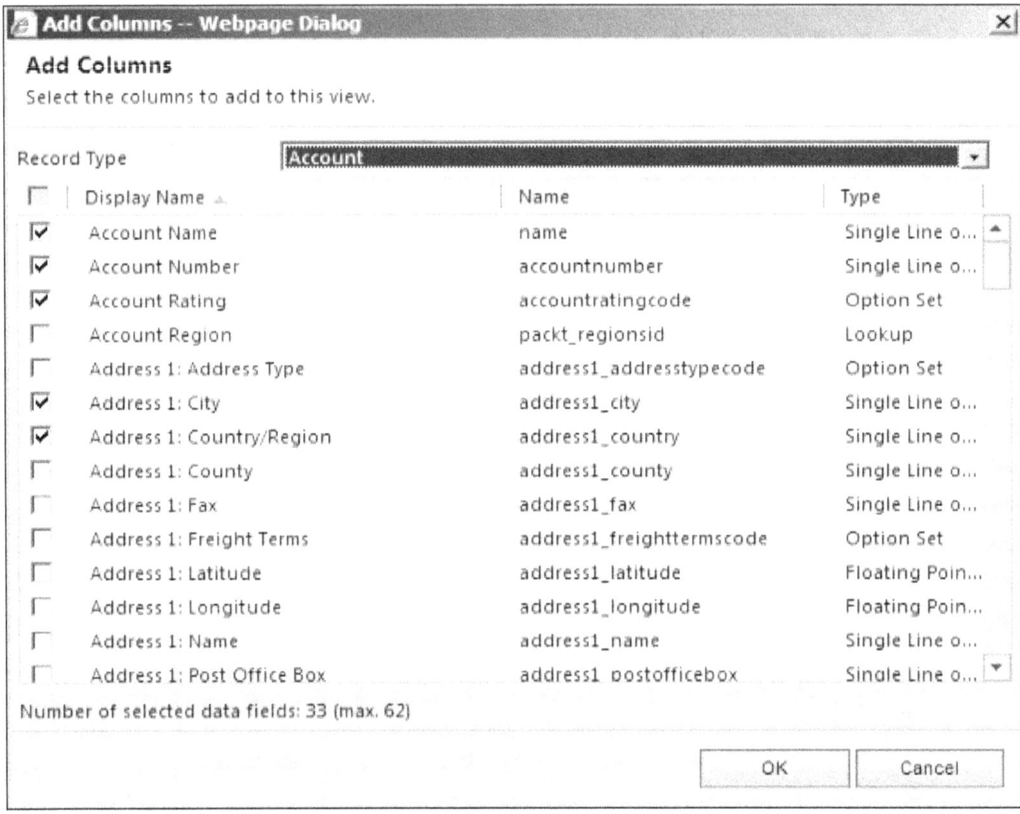

8. Then click on the **OK** button to close the screen. Thereafter, click on the **Save** button in the top ribbon to save the changes.
9. Then click on the **Create Template in Word** button in the top ribbon.

10. This will prompt us to **Open** or **Save** a Microsoft Word document. Click on the **Open** button to open the document. If prompted by Microsoft Word, accept any security questions to allow macros and document editing in Word.

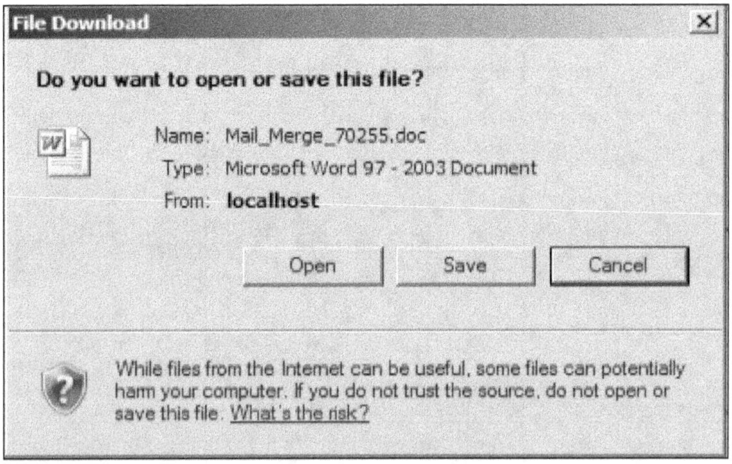

11. When the Microsoft Word document opens up, click on the **Add-Ins** tab and then click on the **CRM** button.

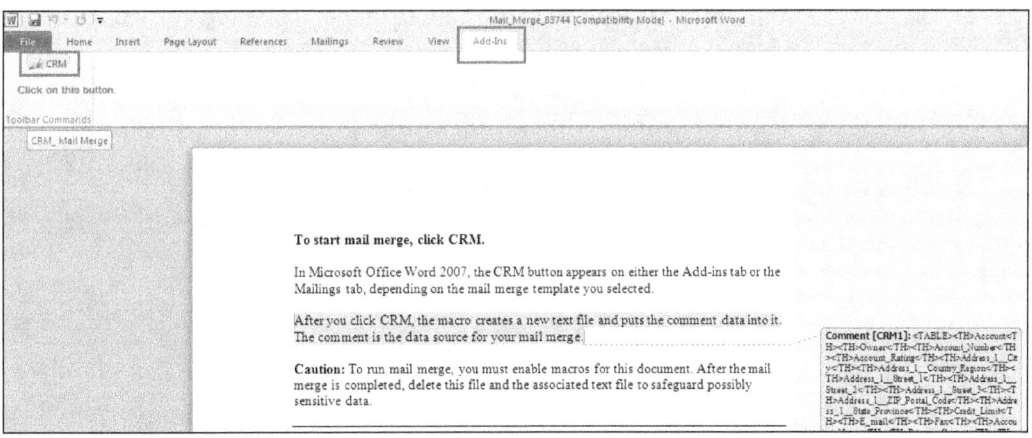

12. Click on the **OK** button if prompted to confirm the list of recipients.

13. Now we will be left with a blank document. On the right-hand side of the document, there will be a **Mail Merge** task pane. Click on the **Next: Starting document** link at the bottom of that pane.

14. Click on the **Step x of 6** link located at the bottom of the **Mail Merge** task pane until it reaches the **Step 4 of 6** stage as follows:

15. Now we can create our Mail Merge template from the blank document. Some pointers to develop the Mail Merge template are as follows:
    - We can use **Insert Merge Field** under the **Mailings** tab to insert fields from Dynamics CRM 2011 into the document.

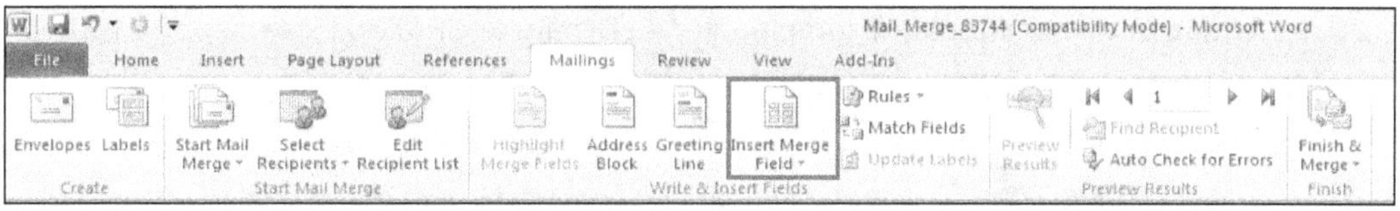

    - We can use the **Address Block** and **Greeting Line** buttons under the **Mailings** tab as well. If we do this, we need to be sure to click on the **Match Fields** button (also in the **Mailings** tab) first in order to choose the correct fields from Dynamics CRM 2011.

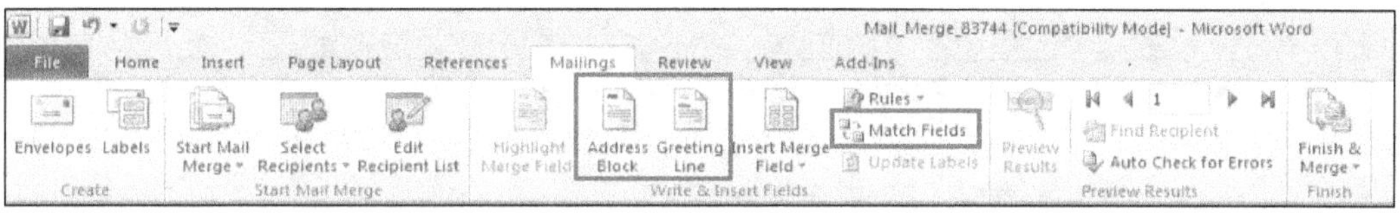

> Although fields may appear as text based on field names, some field names actually contain a unique ID number. Hence, extra care needs to be taken when selecting fields.

16. A sample Mail Merge document may look like the following screenshot:

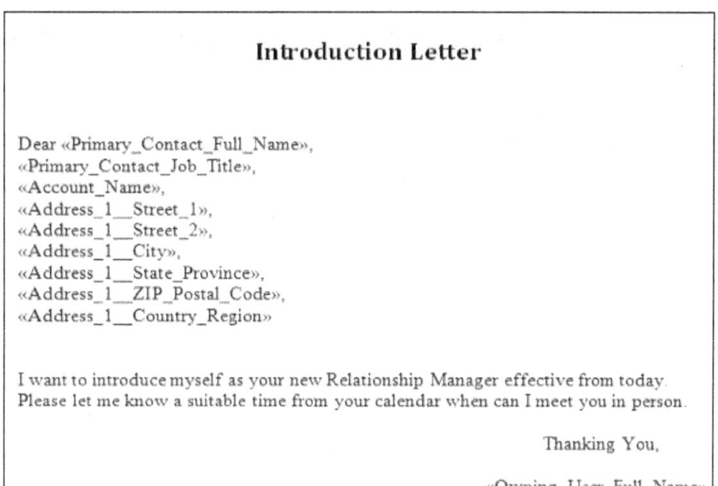

Introduction Letter

Dear «Primary_Contact_Full_Name»,
«Primary_Contact_Job_Title»,
«Account_Name»,
«Address_1__Street_1»,
«Address_1__Street_2»,
«Address_1__City»,
«Address_1__State_Province»,
«Address_1__ZIP_Postal_Code»,
«Address_1__Country_Region»

I want to introduce myself as your new Relationship Manager effective from today. Please let me know a suitable time from your calendar when can I meet you in person.

Thanking You,

«Owning_User_Full_Name»

17. After authoring the template, click on the remaining step links at the bottom of the **Mail Merge** task menu to complete the merge activity. Thereafter, save the Microsoft Word document to the local drive and exit from Microsoft Word.
18. Now click on the **Browse** button under the **File Attachment** section on the Dynamics CRM 2011 page. Then browse the created Mail Merge template and click on the **Attach** button to attach the template to the Dynamics CRM 2011 system.

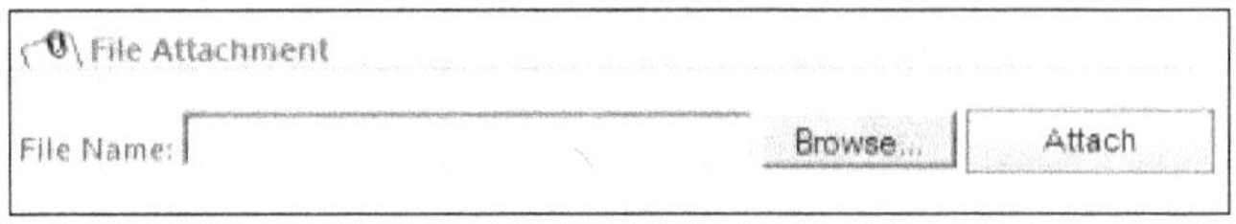

19. Thereafter, click on the **Save** button in the top ribbon again to save the changes.
20. Now if we intend to make this Mail Merge template available to the whole organization, we need to navigate to **Actions** | **Make Available to Organization** in the top ribbon.

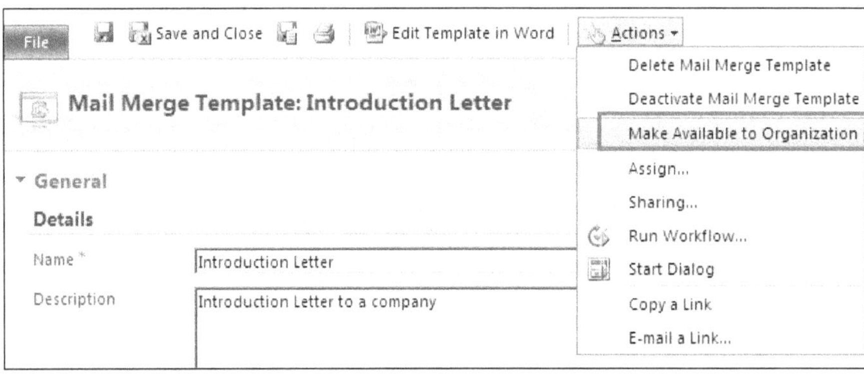

This will bring up the **Make Available to the Organization** page. Click on **OK** to make this template available to the organization.

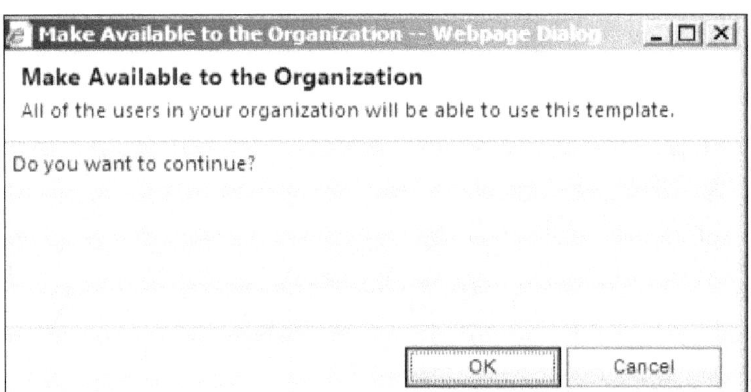

21. Then, click on the **Save** and **Close** buttons in the top ribbon to close the Mail Merge template page.
22. Now we have to activate the Mail Merge template. We can do this by selecting the template and then navigating to **More Actions** | **Activate** in the **More Actions** menu.

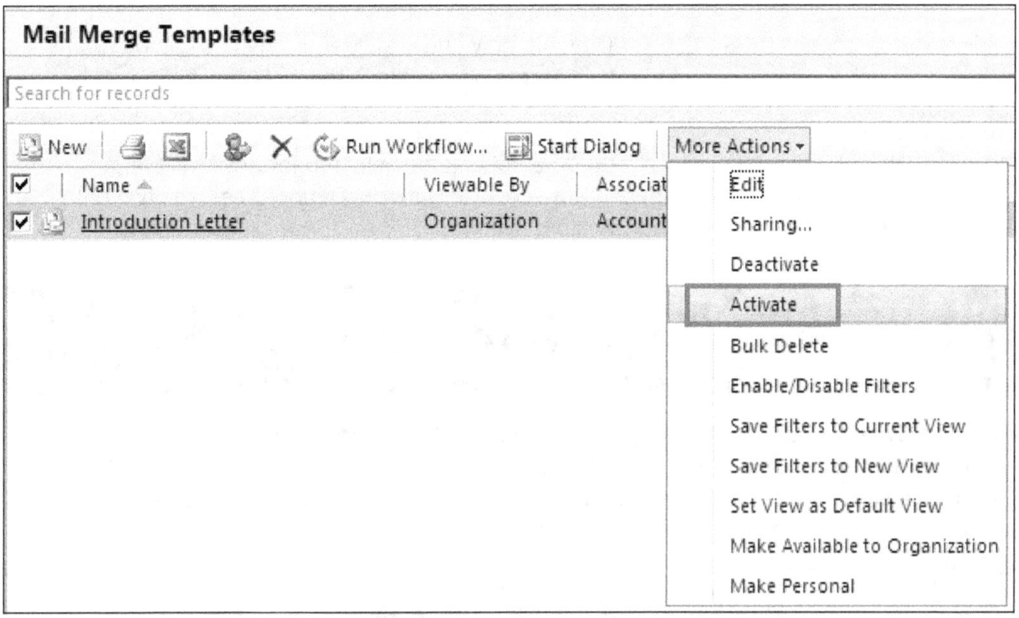

23. This will bring up the **Confirm Mail Merge Template Activation** page. Click on the **OK** button to activate the Mail Merge template.

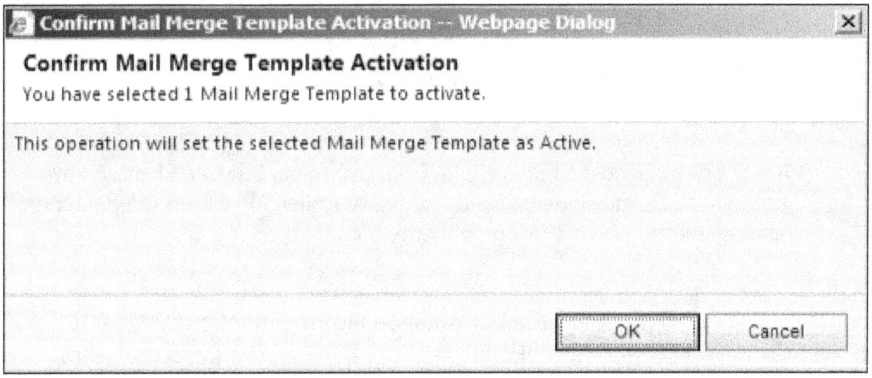

How it works...

Mail Merge templates are very useful when a letter or form has to be sent to the customer. Mail Merge helps to pull data from the Dynamics CRM 2011 system and populate it into the letter automatically. This letter in turn can be sent via e-mail or can be printed as well.

In Microsoft Dynamics CRM 2011 for Outlook, only one Mail Merge process can be run at a time; however, we can run multiple Mail Merge processes in the web application at the same time.

Microsoft Office Word supports up to 64 data fields to be selected for any Mail Merge template. If using Microsoft Dynamics CRM 2011 for Outlook, Outlook reserves two data fields to store the primary key and the record owner.

Integrating Microsoft SharePoint Server (2010/2013) with Dynamics CRM 2011

Microsoft Dynamics CRM 2011 along with Microsoft SharePoint server provides a very strong contextual document management functionality to Dynamics CRM 2011 users. This provides enhanced productivity to the Dynamics CRM users. Dynamics CRM 2011 allows attaching documents to virtually any records and viewing them in the context of a Dynamics CRM record.

To use the Document Management functionality with SharePoint, one of the following SharePoint editions is required, and must be installed, running, and at least one SharePoint site collection configured and available for Microsoft Dynamics CRM 2011:

- Microsoft SharePoint 2013
- Microsoft SharePoint 2010
- Microsoft Office SharePoint Server (MOSS) 2007

> The user who accesses SharePoint from Dynamics CRM 2011 must have appropriate permissions on SharePoint Site Collection where the document management functionality components are installed.

Document Management is an out-of-the-box functionality in Dynamics CRM 2011, and so once the integration with SharePoint is set up, Dynamics CRM 2011 users can easily create, modify, download, and delete documents of SharePoint from the Dynamics CRM 2011 interface.

How to do it...

When we install Microsoft Dynamics CRM 2011, SharePoint Server integration is enabled by default. However, the Dynamics CRM 2011 administrator has to configure the integration between Dynamics CRM 2011 and SharePoint. In this recipe, we will discuss SharePoint Server 2010 or 2013 integration with Dynamics CRM 2011.

The following tasks have to be carried out by the Dynamics CRM administrator:

- Install Microsoft Dynamics CRM 2011 List Component for Microsoft SharePoint Server.
- Select the entities in Microsoft Dynamics CRM 2011 for which we want to create and manage documents on SharePoint Server.
- Specify the URL of a site or site collection on SharePoint Server 2010. This URL is used to automatically create folders and document libraries on SharePoint.

The previously mentioned activities have to be done by a user having the System Administrator security role in the Dynamics CRM 2011 system. The Dynamics CRM 2011 administrator user setting up Document Management settings in Dynamics CRM 2011 requires that the administrator has a minimum of the **Read**, **Design**, and **Contribute** permissions to create document libraries in SharePoint.

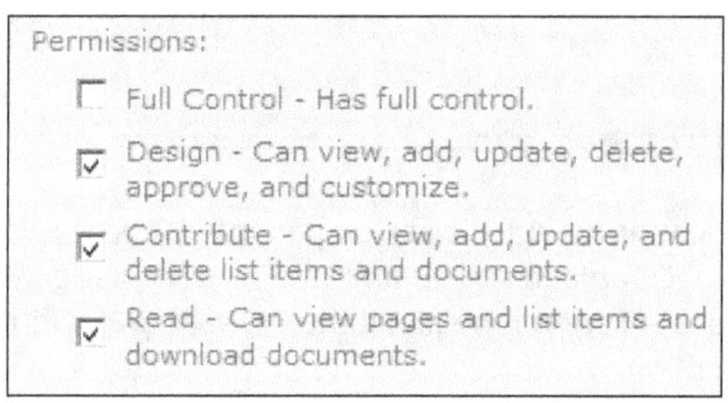

We will install Microsoft Dynamics CRM 2011 List Component for Microsoft SharePoint Server by performing the following steps:

1. Navigate to **Settings** | **System** | **Document Management** and click on the **Install List Component** option. This will take us to the Microsoft Download Centre.

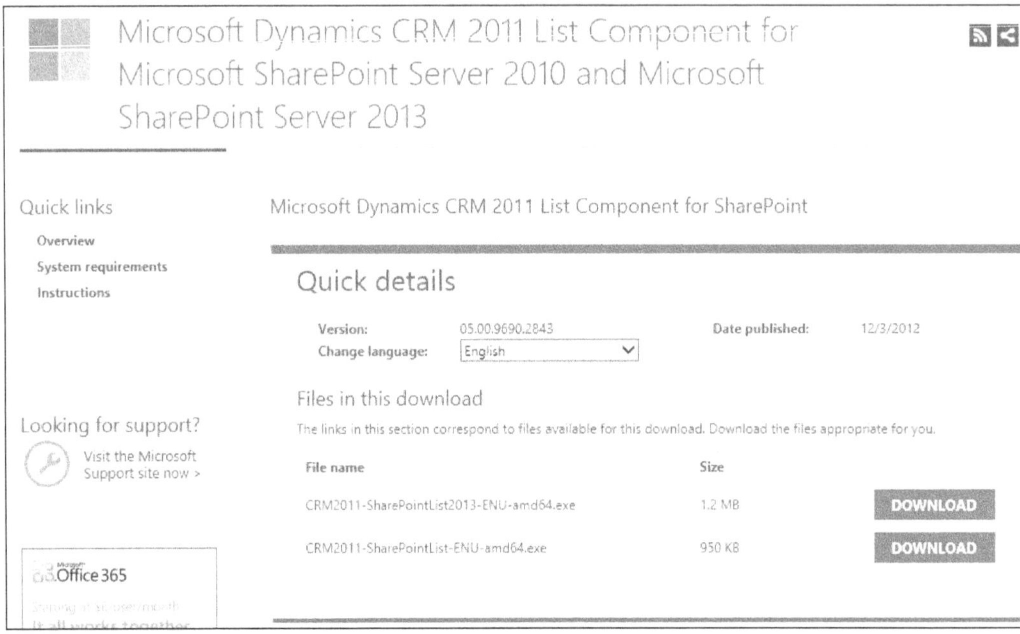

2. The download location includes List Components for both SharePoint 2010 and SharePoint 2013. Download the appropriate version, navigate to the downloaded file, and then double-click on the file. If the browser offers to **run** the downloaded file, select the **Run** option.
3. In the **Setup for Microsoft Dynamics CRM 2011 SharePointList** page, accept the Microsoft Software License Terms and then click on **Continue**.
4. Now we will be prompted to select a folder to store the extracted files. Select a folder and then click on the **OK** button.
5. Finally, **The extraction is complete** message will appear. Click on the **OK** button.
6. The extraction location will contain the following three files:
   - `AllowHtcExtn.ps1`
   - `crmlistcomponent.wsp`
   - `mscrmsharepointeula.txt`

Now copy these extracted files to SharePoint Server. To install Microsoft Dynamics CRM 2011 List Component on Microsoft SharePoint Server, the user must be a SharePoint Site Collection administrator.

Please perform the following steps in SharePoint Server:

1. Start **Windows PowerShell** from the **Start** menu in SharePoint Server:

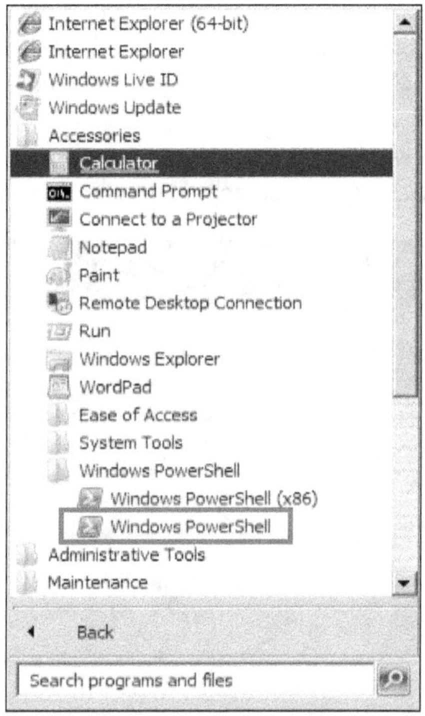

[The next two steps (steps 2 and 3) are not required for SharePoint Online.]

2. In the PowerShell window, change the directory location to the SharePoint List Component (the extracted files folder) folder. Thereafter, type the following command and press the *Enter* key:

```
AllowHtcExtn.ps1 http://<server_name>:<port_number>
```

   Replace <server_name> with the SharePoint server name and <port_number> with the SharePoint port number.

The Microsoft Dynamics CRM 2011 List Component on Microsoft SharePoint Server uses the legacy `.htc` files that are not supported by default in SharePoint. So to enable the use of `.htc` extensions in SharePoint, the `AllowHtcExtn.ps1` command is executed using PowerShell.

1. After this command is executed, we need to reset IIS using the `iisreset` command.
2. Thereafter, browse the SharePoint website. If we are using SharePoint 2010, we'll navigate to **Site Actions** | **Site Settings**, and if we are using SharePoint 2013, we'll navigate to the **Settings** icon in the top-right corner and then click on **Site Settings**.
3. Then for SharePoint 2012, navigate to **Galleries** | **Solutions** or for SharePoint 2013, navigate to **Web Designer Galleries** | **Solutions**.

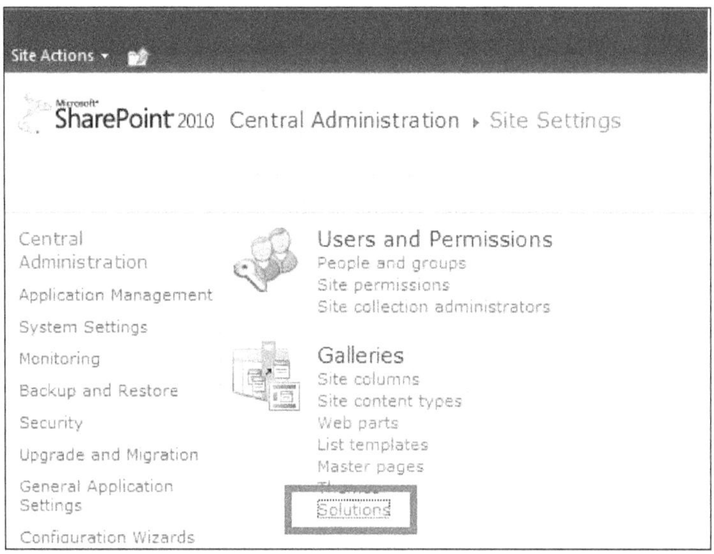

4. Click on **Upload Solution**. Then click on **Browse** and navigate to the **SharePoint List Component** folder we created earlier.
5. Select the `crmlistcomponent.wsp` file (extracted file folder), and click on **Open** and then on **OK**.
6. Thereafter, click on **Activate**. We can see the List Components in the list of activated solutions.

The next step would be to enable Document Management for the required entities for which Document Management has to be configured. Document Management can be enabled for those entities in Microsoft Dynamics CRM 2011 that can be customized.

> By default, Document Management is enabled only for the following entities in a new installation of Microsoft Dynamics CRM: Account, KbArticle, Lead, Opportunity, Product, and Quote.

Perform the following steps to enable Document Management for entities:

1. Log in to the Dynamics CRM 2011 system with the System Administrator security role.
2. Navigate to **Settings** | **System** | **Document Management** and click on **Document Management Settings**.

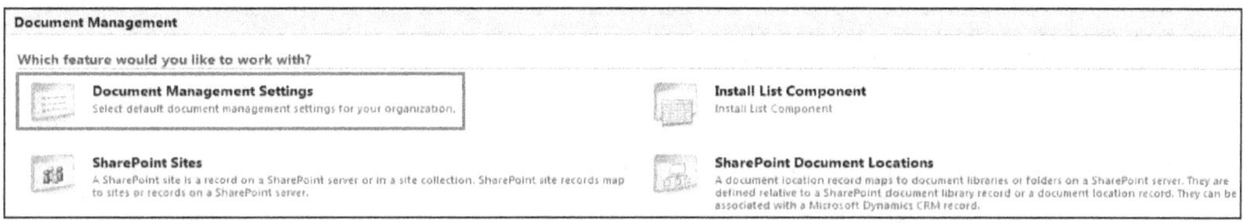

3. This will bring up the **Document Management Settings** window. Select the entities for which Document Management has to be enabled and provide the URL of the SharePoint site. Then click on the **Next** button to proceed.

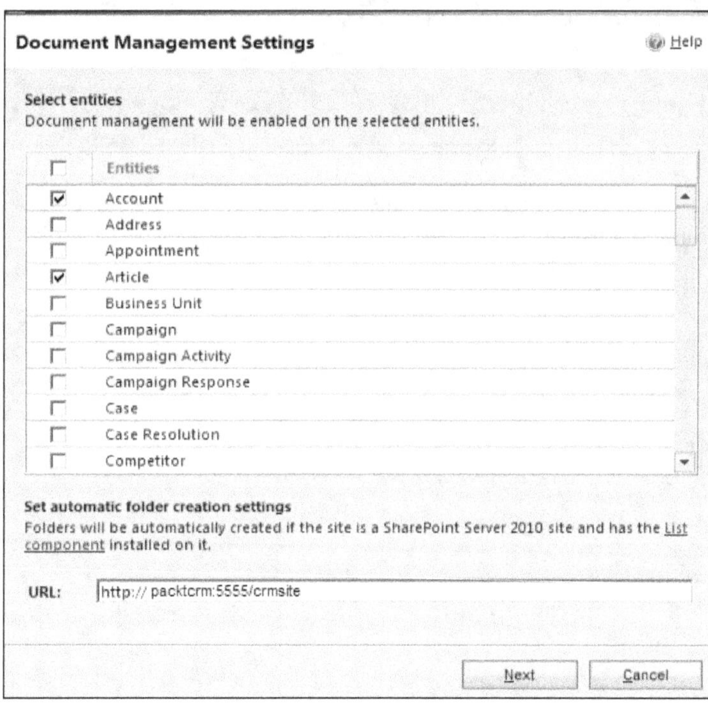

> Document Management settings for an entity have to be enabled to make the entity available to the previous **Document Management Settings** window. To enable Document Management for an entity, open the **Solutions** page and navigate to **Components** | **Entities** | **[Entity]**. The **Document Management Settings** wndow can be found under the **Communication & Collaboration** section in the **General** tab.

4. In the next window, we can define the folder structure. We have to select an entity name from the **Based on entity** drop-down box as the parent folder.

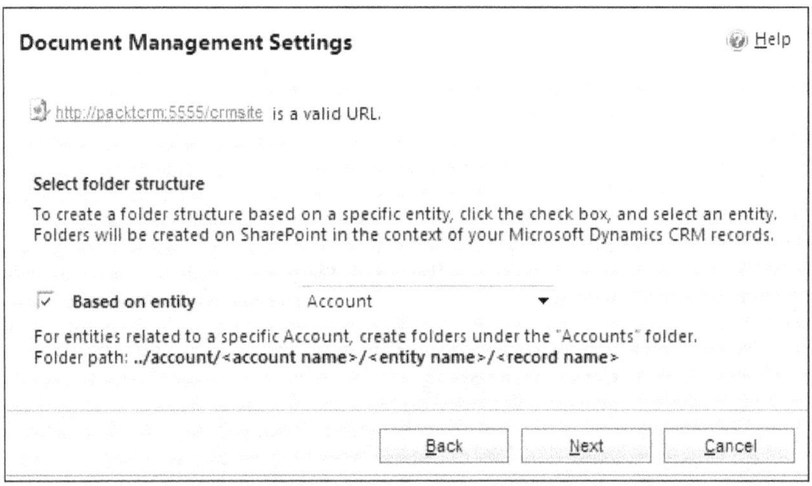

5. Finally click on the **Finish** button. This will automatically create folders inside SharePoint as follows:

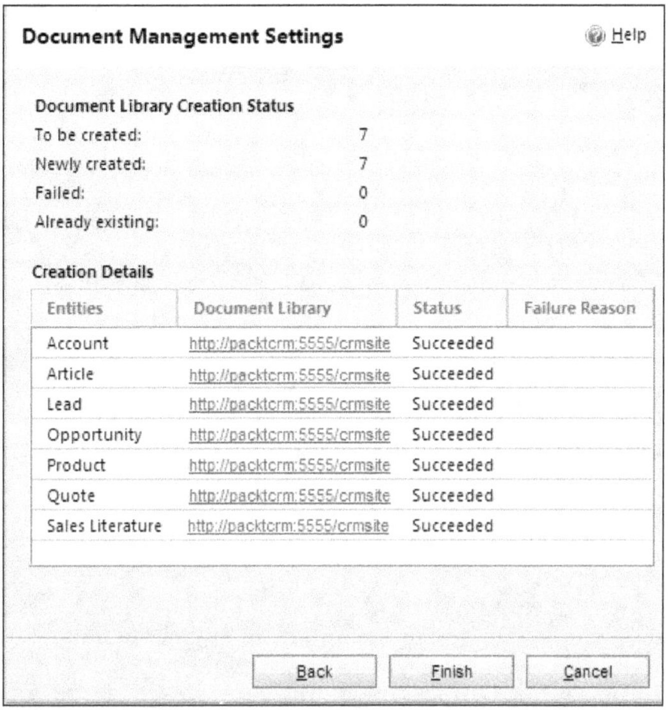

How it works...

This recipe will enable SharePoint-based Document Management with Dynamics CRM 2011. For the automatic creation of location records on SharePoint Server, we must use SharePoint Server 2010 or 2013, and Microsoft Dynamics CRM 2011 List Component for Microsoft SharePoint Server 2010/2013 must be installed on the target server that is running SharePoint Server.

10 Processes

Business processes are a vital part of any CRM software application. Dynamics CRM also provides means to create business processes within itself. In addition to this, Dynamics CRM 2011 provides a useful **software development kit** (**SDK**) for developing extensions and custom components to achieve the functionality that the standard behavior of the application does not provide. In this chapter, we will delve into some of the recipes that deal with automated processes and extensions.

The following recipes will be discussed in this chapter:

- Creating a workflow using the Dynamics CRM 2011 web interface
- Creating a dialog using the Dynamics CRM 2011 web interface
- Querying Dynamics CRM data in a dialog
- Monitoring the workflow execution status

Introduction to processes

Dynamics CRM 2011 supports two types of business processes: **automated** processes, which rely on communication among system components; and **interactive** processes, which rely on users to start and run the processes and allow them to make appropriate decisions during the execution of the processes.

Processes in Dynamics CRM 2011 are built using **Windows Workflow Foundation**. Dynamics CRM 2011 allows us to create such business processes using the following two components:

- **Workflows**: These are the automated asynchronous business processes that can be initiated either automatically or by a user. Workflows can be created either using the Dynamics CRM 2011 Web application or using Microsoft Visual Studio with Windows Workflow Foundation and Dynamics CRM 2011 SDK. The second type is usually known as **custom workflows**.

- **Dialogs**: These are the interactive synchronous business processes that can only be initiated by a user. Dialogs are built using a dialog wizard.

Though both workflows and dialogs help us to build business processes within the Dynamics CRM 2011 system, there exist some significant differences between them. Let us have a look at some of these differences:

Workflows	**Dialogs**
Workflows are asynchronous.	Dialogs are synchronous.
They are either initiated by events or run on demand.	They always run on demand.
They are background processes.	They are wizard-like processes that run in the foreground and allows users to make appropriate selections during the execution.
They do not require user interaction to finish.	They always require user interaction to finish.
Triggers are supported.	Triggers are not supported.
They can run on multiple records at a time.	They can run on only a single record at a time.
They cannot build interactive queries on CRM data.	They can build interactive queries on CRM data.

> Dynamics CRM 2011 Online did not support custom workflows until the release of the Microsoft Dynamics CRM December 2012 service update (Polaris update). The Polaris release has introduced add-ons to create custom workflows for Dynamics CRM 2011 Online organizations.
>
> Moreover, up to 200 workflows can be created in a Microsoft Dynamics CRM 2011 Online service.

Creating a workflow using the Dynamics CRM 2011 web interface

In this recipe, we will discuss how to create a workflow using the Dynamics CRM 2011 web interface.

Getting ready

Before we start creating the workflow, we need to understand a few basic concepts about workflows.

Workflow availability – There are three types of workflows that can be made available:

- **Automated workflows**: Such a workflow is executed as soon as the trigger conditions specified in the workflow logic are met
- **On-demand workflows**: Such a workflow is available to the user, and the user has to apply it to records from a toolbar or menu
- **Child workflows**: Such a workflow is contained within and executed by another workflow, known as the **parent workflow**

> A single workflow can be made available in any combination of these three types.

Workflow scope – A workflow can have any of the following scopes:

- **User**: The workflow will only execute on the records owned by the workflow owner
- **Business unit**: The workflow will only execute on the records owned by a user within the same business unit of the workflow owner
- **Parent-child business unit**: The workflow will only execute on the records owned by a user within the same business unit or in the child business units of the workflow owner
- **Organization**: The workflow will execute on any records.

Workflow logic – Every workflow will have some logic that will determine what kind of action a workflow will take on the records. Workflow logic includes the following elements:

- **Stage**: A workflow stage groups workflow steps. This makes the logic clear and readable. However, stages do not affect workflow logic. Workflow stage descriptions appear as headings in system job forms, which display the progress of a workflow job. Stage descriptions can also appear in reports.
- **Step**: Workflow steps define a unit of business logic within a workflow. These steps can be conditions, actions, other steps, or a combination of these elements.

  The following types of steps can be added to a workflow logic:

  - **Check condition**: This is a logical if-then statement in a workflow logic.
  - **Conditional branch**: This is a logical else-if-then statement in a workflow logic.
  - **Default action**: This is a logical else statement in a workflow logic.
  - **Wait condition**: This enables a workflow to pause itself until the criteria defined in the wait condition have been met. The workflow will start again automatically.

- **Parallel wait branch**: This defines an alternative wait condition with a set of additional steps to be executed when the initial criterion is met. This prevents workflows from waiting indefinitely until the wait criteria are met. It is very useful to create timeout logics in the workflow.
- **Custom step**: Such a step has to be created using Dynamics CRM 2011 SDK and then can be used in a workflow logic.

- **Action** - This defines the actions to be performed when a condition is met in a workflow logic. The following actions can be included in a workflow logic:
    - Creating a record
    - Updating a record
    - Assigning a record
    - Sending an e-mail notification
    - Starting a child workflow
    - Changing the status of a record
    - Stopping the current workflow
    - Performing a custom workflow action

How to do it...

Please perform the following steps to create a workflow using the Dynamics CRM 2011 web interface.

First we will have a look at how to create a new process in the web interface:

1. Log in to the Dynamics CRM 2011 organization as a system administrator or a user with rights to create workflows.
2. Navigate to **Settings** | **Customization** | **Solutions** and change the view to **Unmanaged Solutions** if not already selected.
3. Then double-click on the unmanaged solution to open it.
4. On the expanded solution page, navigate to **Components** | **Processes**.
5. Click on the **New** button in the actions toolbar.
6. The **Create Process** web page dialog will open. Fill in the required details in this dialog.
    - Provide a relevant process name in the **Process name** textbox
    - Select the primary entity that we want to use in this workflow from the **Entity** drop-down list

- From the **Category** list, select **Workflow**
- In the **Type** section, select whether we want to create a completely new process or want to re-use an existing template

> If we want to view details about the process template, select the process template and then click on **Properties**.

Finally, click on **OK** to close the web page dialog.

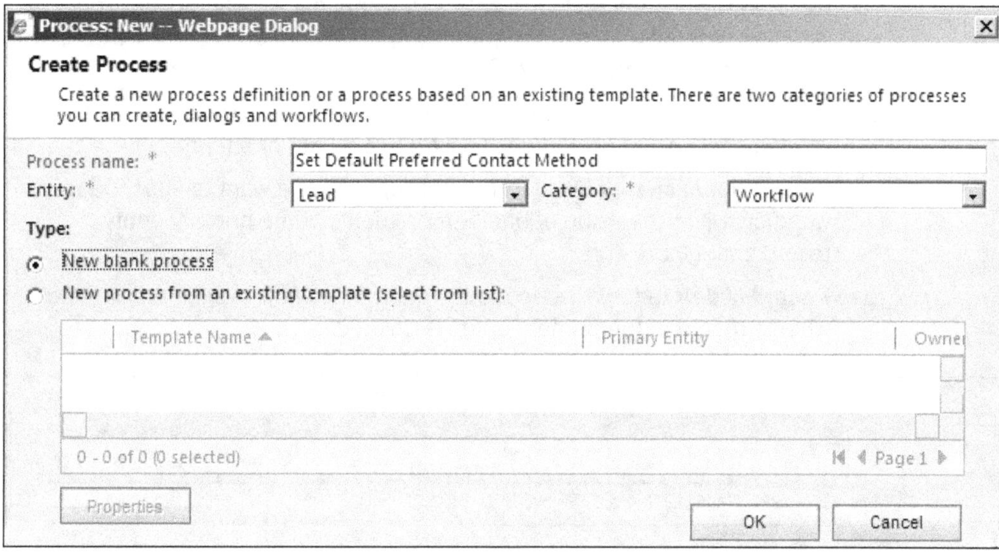

7. Thereafter, a web page with **Process:< Workflow Name>** will appear. In this page, we have to set the following workflow properties:
    - If the workflow has to be renamed, provide the new name in the **Process Name** textbox.
    - From the **Activate As** list, select **Process** if the workflow is to be activated to automate a business process or **Process Template** if the workflow is to be activated as a template.
    - In the **Available to Run** section, select the workflow availability criteria. We can select more than one criterion here from the following:
    - **As an on-demand process**: Select this if the workflow has to be executed on an on-demand basis by a user.
    - **As a child process**: Select this if the workflow is to be available as a child workflow.

- In the **Scope** drop-down list, select the access level that matches the workflow scope to be set.

  The items available in the list depend on the privileges that have been assigned to the user's security role for the workflow's primary entity.

- In the **Start when** section, select the events that will trigger the workflow execution. The following events are available:
- **Record is created**: We'll select this option if we want to start the workflow when a record of the workflow's primary entity is created.
- **Record status changes**: We'll select this option if we want to start the workflow when the status of a primary entity record changes, for example from Active to Inactive.
- **Record is assigned**: We'll select this option if we want to start the workflow when a primary entity record is assigned to a user or a team.
- **Record fields change**: We'll select this option if we want to start the workflow when the value of one or more fields of the primary entity record changes.
- **Record is deleted**: We'll select this option if we want to start the workflow when a record of the primary entity is deleted.

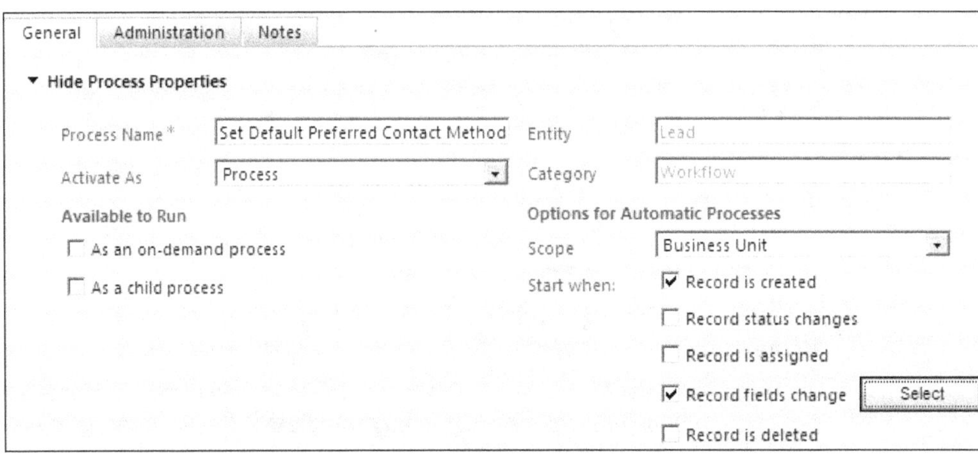

8. If **Record fields change** is selected, specific fields of the primary entity are required to be set by clicking on the **Select** button associated beside this option. After making the selection, click on the **OK** button to close the web page:

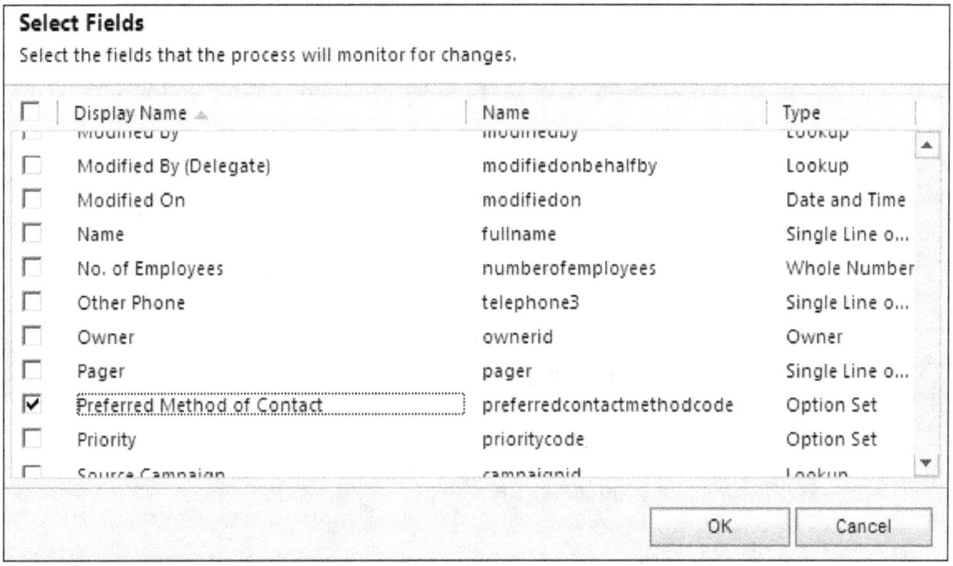

Next we will add the workflow logic. We can add the workflow **stages**, **steps**, and **actions** in any order, but they have to be combined sequentially depending on the workflow logic intended to be built.

- **Workflow stage**:
    1. Click on the **Add Step** tab and then select the **Stage** option in the workflow logic toolbar as shown in the following screenshot:

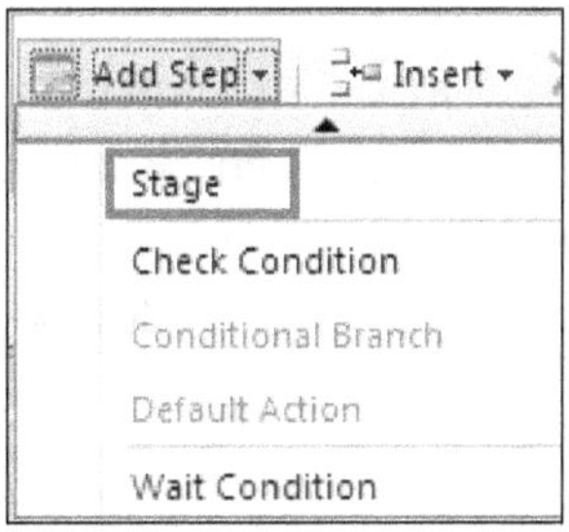

    2. Click on **OK** in the message box that pops up.
    3. Then enter a stage description.
    4. If a stage is added to a workflow, all the steps must be contained within a stage.

- **Workflow step**:

  1. Click on the **Add Step** option in the workflow logic toolbar and then select one of the following options: **Check Condition** or **Wait Condition**.

     > These options can be added at any level of the workflow logic.

  2. If the check condition is added to a workflow logic, either **Conditional Branch** or **Default Action** can be added to the parent step. To add either of these options to the workflow logic, we must select the **If** line in a check condition or the **Otherwise, if** line in a conditional branch.

     > It is not possible to create more than six levels of conditional branching.

  3. In case a wait condition is added to a workflow logic, the **Parallel Wait Branch** step can be added to the parent step.
  4. Once the workflow steps are added, click on **<condition> (click to configure)**. The **Specify Condition** web dialog will pop up. In this page, specify the conditions for the step. Repeat the following steps to add multiple conditions.
  5. In the first column, select either the primary entity or the related entity.
  6. In the second column, select a field from the entity selected in the previous step.
  7. In the third column, select a logical operator.
  8. In the last column, enter the values that we want to use as the criteria for the condition.
  9. Once all the conditions are added, click on **Save and Close**.

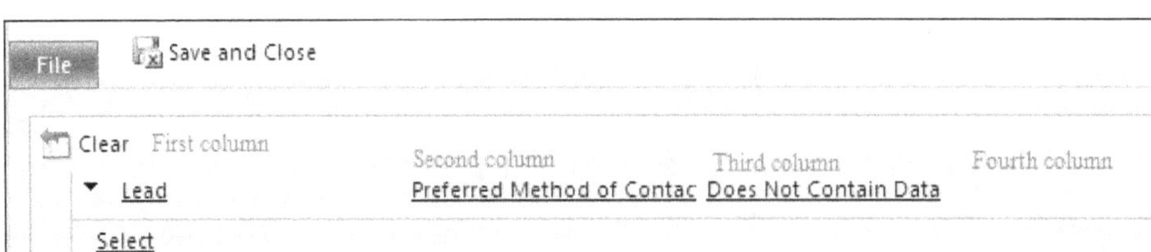

- **Workflow action**:
    1. Click on the **Add Step** option in the workflow logic toolbar and then select one of the following options:
        - **Create a record**
        - **Update a record**
        - **Assign a record**
        - **Send an e-mail notification**
        - **Start a child workflow**
        - **Change the status of a record**
        - **Stop the current workflow**
    2. Then enter the description for the step.
    3. If a **Set Properties** button appears next to the newly added action, click on **Set Properties** and specify details about the entity that this step in the workflow is taking action on.

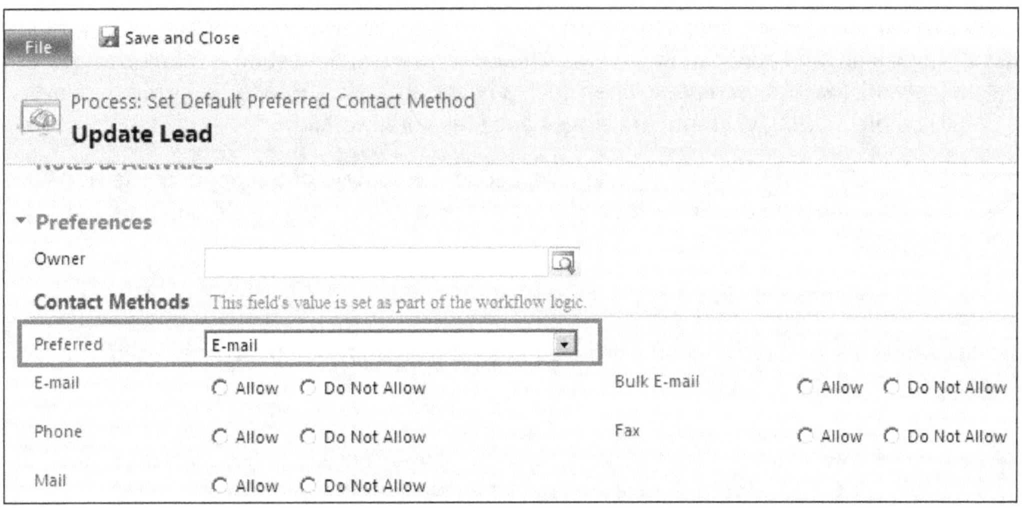

4. After creating a workflow, we have to activate it. If activated workflows are not available for use, click on the **Save** button in the top toolbar to save the workflow first and then click on the **Activate** button to activate it. Click on **OK** when the confirmation dialog pops up.

   Once activated, the workflow properties and logic are read-only. To edit these, we have to deactivate the workflow using the **Deactivate** button in the top toolbar.

A workflow having stage, step, and action would look like this:

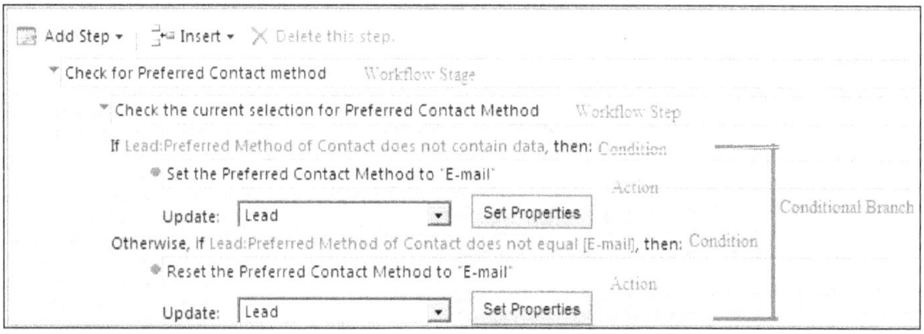

How it works...

Workflows are very useful tools for building business process within the Dynamics CRM 2011 system. In this recipe, we have discussed the building blocks of a workflow. Using these elements of a workflow, complex workflows can be built.

There are a few important things to remember when building a workflow. Workflow logic built using stage, step, and action cannot be easily restructured, and most of the time we have to delete the workflow and recreate it when such a necessity arises. Hence, you have to think carefully before starting to create the stages and steps of a workflow.

Another important thing is that if we use a wait condition to wait for a timeout in the workflow logic, we cannot change the timeout condition. We have to delete the condition and then add a new condition.

If workflows are not activated, they are unavailable for use.

Workflows can be backed up and transferred from one organization to another using Dynamics CRM 2011 Solution.

> If we want to remove the completed workflows from system jobs, we can make use of the **Automatically delete completed workflow jobs (to save disk space)** feature of Dynamics CRM 2011. This feature can be selected from the **Administration** tab in the workflow. By selecting this option, we can save some disk space.

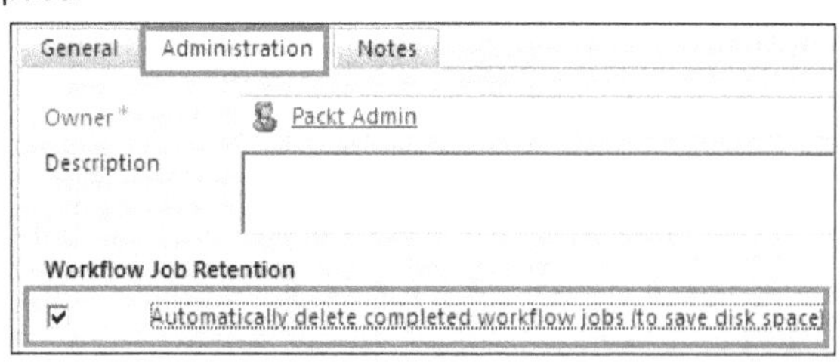

Creating a dialog using the Dynamics CRM 2011 web interface

In this recipe, we will delve into how to create a dialog using the Dynamics CRM 2011 web interface.

Getting ready

Before we start the dialog creation recipe, let us first discuss some basic concepts around a dialog.

Dialog availability - There are two types of dialog that can be made available:

- **On-demand dialog**: Such a dialog is initiated by a user on a CRM record
- **Child dialog**: Such a dialog only starts from within another dialog

> A single dialog can be made available in any combination of these two types.

Input arguments and variables - A dialog uses input arguments and variables to store and pass on data to another dialog.

- **Input arguments**: Input arguments are used only in child dialogs to pass on data to the parent dialog. Input arguments can be of the following types:
    - Text
    - Integer
    - Float
    - Date and Time
    - Date only
    - Lookup

- **Variables**: A variable stores data that can be accessed later on from the steps in the dialog. Variables are also of the same data types as those of input arguments.

> - Variables in dialogs have a global scope and can be accessed for any step in the dialog
> - Variables can be used as data slugs in the workflow logic for different action steps in the dialog
> - Variables can be used to maintain a running counter for determining a score based on responses in prompt and response steps
> - Variables can also be used for computational values that can be used in a dialog by using the assign value step

Dialog logic – Dialog logic can be built using the following elements:

- **Stages**: Like workflow stages, dialog stages also group the dialog pages and steps. This makes the logic clear and readable. However, stages do not affect the dialog logic.
- **Pages**: A page offers a visual interface to the dialog and is the basic unit of a dialog. A dialog can have more than one page, and every page can have multiple prompts and responses. When a dialog is run, the pages appear in the same sequence in which they are defined in a dialog.

> We *must* add at least one page in a dialog.

- **Prompt and response steps**: They allow for the user to be questioned and gather responses. For any prompt, the following types of responses can be defined in a dialog:
  - **None**: No response is required for this prompt
  - **Single Line**: This provides the user with a textbox with a length of 255 characters
  - **Multiple Line of Text (Text Only)**: This provides the user with a textbox to enter multiple lines of text
  - **Option Set (radio buttons)**: This provides the user with a set of radio-button-based options with a predefined set of choices or from data returned by a CRM Query Data step
  - **Option Set (picklist)**: This provides the user with drop-down list based options with a predefined set of choices or from data returned by a CRM Query Data step

- **Date and Time**: This provides the user with a calendar and a drop-down list to select a date and time from
- **Date Only**: This provides the user with a calendar to select a date from
- **Lookup**: This provides the user with an option to select a related record using the lookup field

We can also insert hyperlinks in the prompt or tip text or in an e-mail created using the **Send E-mail** action to provide the dialog users with a link to external content, any existing CRM records, or any CRM records that are created during the current dialog session.

> We must add at least one prompt and response in a dialog.

- **Workflow logic**: A dialog can also use workflow logic elements. The following workflow logic elements can be used in a dialog:
  - The check condition step
  - Actions that include the following:
    - **Query CRM Data**
    - **Assign Value**
    - **Create Record**
    - **Update Record**
    - **Assign Record**
    - **Send E-mail**
    - **Link Child Dialog**
    - **Start Child workflow**
    - **Change Status**
    - **Stop Dialog**
  - Custom workflow actions

How to do it...

Perform the following steps to create a dialog using the Dynamics CRM 2011 web interface:

1. Log in to the Dynamics CRM 2011 organization as a system administrator or a user with rights to create dialogs.
2. Navigate to **Settings** | **Customization** | **Solutions** and change the view to **Unmanaged Solutions**, if not already selected.

3. Then, double-click on the unmanaged solution to open it.
4. On the expanded solution page, navigate to **Components** | **Processes**.
5. Click on the **New** button in the actions toolbar.
6. The **Create Process** web page dialog will open. Fill in the required details in this dialog:
    - Provide a relevant process name in the **Process name** textbox
    - Select the primary entity that we want to use in this dialog from the **Entity** drop-down list
    - In the **Category** list, select **Dialog**
    - In the **Type** section, select whether we want to create a completely new process or re-use an existing template

      If we want to view details about the process template, select the process template and then click on **Properties**.

   Finally, click on **OK** to close the web page dialog.

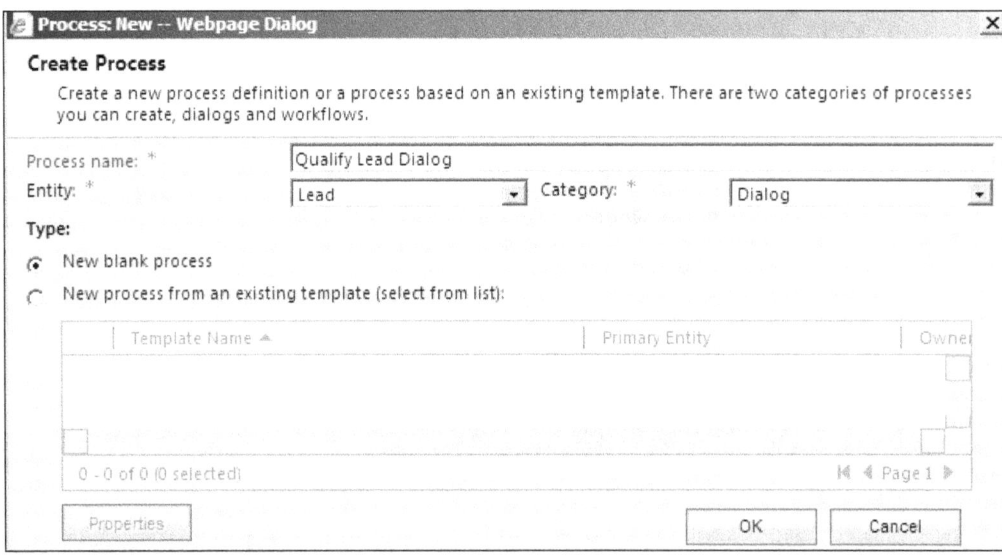

7. Thereafter, a **Process:< Dialog Name>** web page will appear. In this page, we have to set the **dialog properties**.
    - If the dialog has to be renamed, provide the new name in the **Process Name** textbox.

- From the **Activate As** list, select **Process** (if the dialog is to be activated to automate a business process) or **Process Template** (if the dialog is to be activated as a template).
- In the **Available to Run** section, select the dialog availability criteria. We can select more than one criterion here from the following:
- **As an on-demand process**: If the dialog has to be executed on an on-demand basis by a user
- **As a child process**: If the dialog is to be available as a child dialog

  By default the **As an on-demand process** option is already selected.

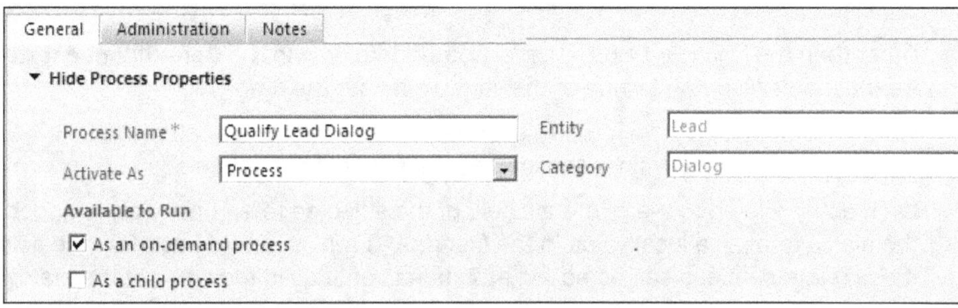

8. Let us now find out how to add variables in a dialog. Variables are added to store data within a dialog, to be used later. To do so, click on the **Add** button in the **Variables** section. This will launch the **Add or Modify Properties** page:

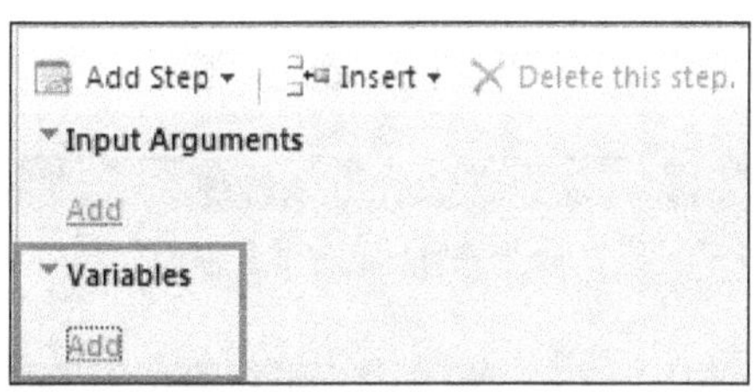

9. Furnish the following details in this page:
   - **Name**: Insert a unique name for the variable. The name should be clear enough so that the variable can be easily identifiable later when we want to use it in the dialog.

- **Data Type**: Select the data type of the variable from the following available data types:

Data type	Description
`Text`	Stores alphanumeric values
`Integer`	Stores numeric values
`Float`	Stores floating numeric values
`Date and Time`	A calendar and option set control used for storing date and time values
`Date Only`	A calendar and option set control used for storing date values
`Lookup`	A relationship field used for selecting a related record

Other than the `Lookup` fields, for every other data type in the **Default Value** textbox, we must enter a default value of the variable as per the data type.

For the `Lookup` fields, we must select a reference entity and a reference field. This combination determines the entities the variable can refer to.

Each entity related to the reference field of the selected reference entity is added in the dialog form as a local value in the first drop-down list under **Look for**. The fields of these related entities can be added as dynamic entities in the steps of the dialog.

For example, if we select the **Lead** entity and **Customer** as **Reference Entity** and **Reference Field** respectively, the entity drop-down list under **Look for** will include Account and Contact. This is because the **Customer** field of the **Lead** entity is related to both the Account and the Contact records. The fields for the local values of Account and Contact can be used as dynamic values in the next steps.

10. Finally, to save the changes click on the **OK** button.

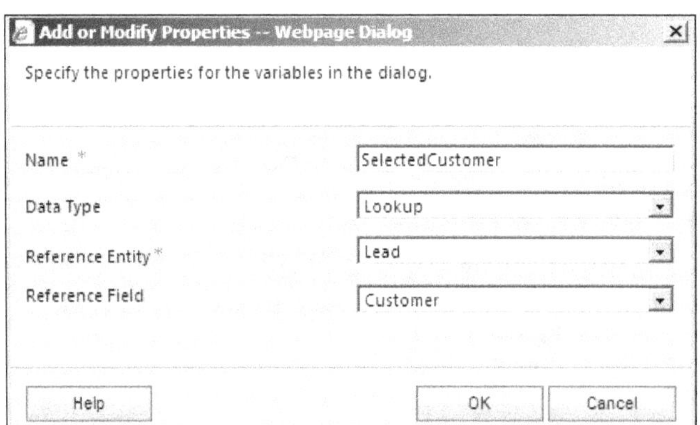

11. If we are designing a child dialog, we can add an input argument in the dialog. Input arguments can only be added to a child dialog.

An input argument is added in the same way that a variable was added in the last step of this recipe. The only difference is that to add an input argument, we have to click on the **Add** button of the **Input Arguments** area and not of the **Variables** area as shown in the following screenshot:

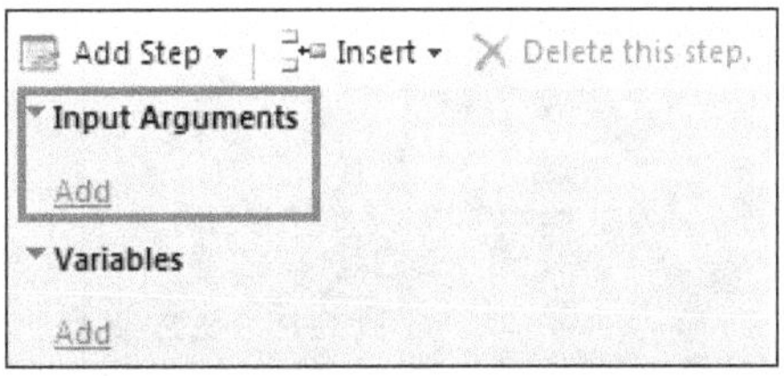

12. After learning how to add variables / input arguments, now it is time to check how to add stages in a dialog. A stage in a dialog is added in the same way as it is added to a workflow. First we need to click on the **Add Step** tab and then select the **Stage** option in the process toolbar as shown in the following screenshot:

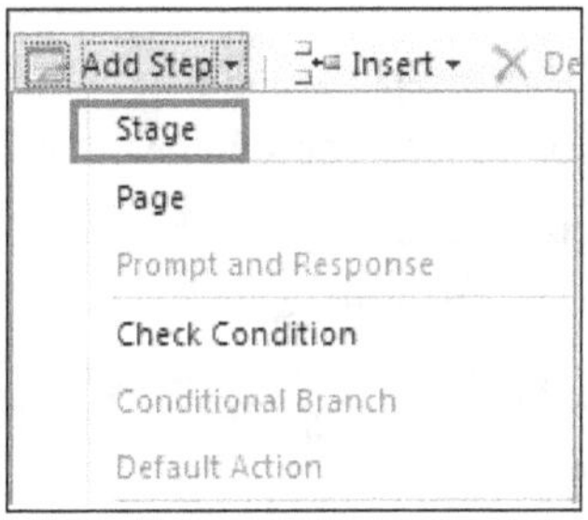

13. Click on **OK** in the message box that pops up.
14. Then enter a stage description.
15. The next element of a dialog is a page. To add a page in the dialog, under the steps click on the section where we want to add the page.
16. Then click on **Add Step** in the process logic toolbar and select **Page**.
17. Finally, we have to enter a page description.

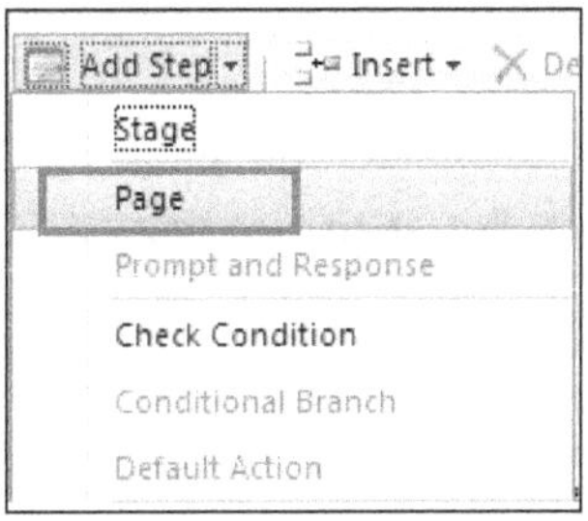

18. Once a page is added, a Prompt and Response element can be added to it. To add a prompt and response step in a dialog, we need to select the line where we want to add a prompt and response, then click on **Add Step** in the process logic toolbar, and select **Prompt and Response** as shown in the following screenshot:

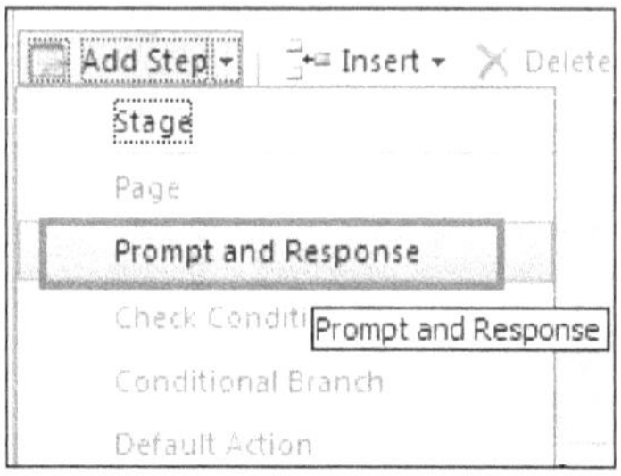

19. Under the steps, click on **Set Properties**.
20. The **Define Prompt and Response** page will appear. Provide the following details on this page:
    - Under the **Prompt Details** section:

      Provide a question or instructions for the prompt in the **Prompt Text** area.

      Provide an optional tip to help clarify the prompt in the **Tip Text** area.
    - Under the **Response Details** section:

      For the Response Type setting, select a response type from the available types listed here:
        - **None**
        - **Single Line**
        - **Option Set (radio buttons)**
        - **Option Set (picklist)**
        - **Multiple Lines of Text (Text Only)**
        - **Date and Time**
        - **Date Only**
        - **Lookup**

      For the **Data Type** setting for the **Single Line**, **Option Set (radio buttons)**, or **Option Set (picklist)** response type, we can select any of the following data types:
        - **Text**
        - **Integer**
        - **Float**

For the **Default Value** setting, an optional default value can be provided for the **Single Line**, **Multiple Lines (Text Only)**, **Date and Time**, or **Date Only** response type.

For the **Lookup** response type, we need to select a reference entity and a reference field.

Finally, for option set response types select any of the following for **Provide Values**:

- **Define Values**: This enables us to define our own values to the response
- **Query CRM Data**: This enables us to provide values from a record in Dynamics CRM

Select **Log Response** if you want to log the response so that it can be used in another place in the dialog

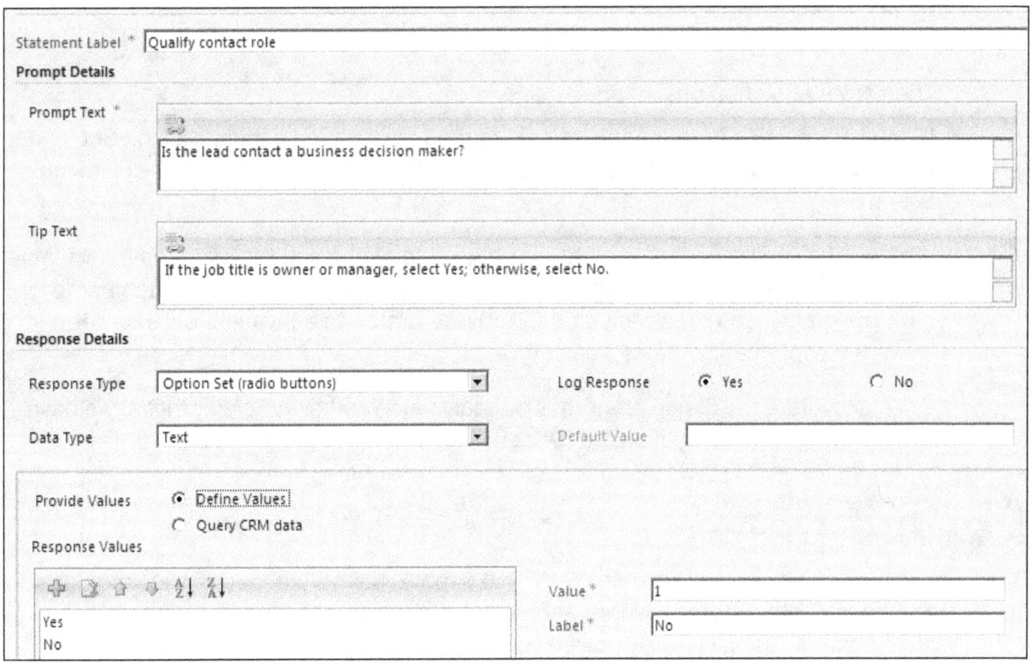

21. Then click on **Save and Close**.
22. The next element that can be included in a dialog logic is a conditional step. A conditional step can be added to the dialog in the same way it is done for workflows. Please refer to step 10 of the *Creating a workflow using the Dynamics CRM 2011 web interface* recipe.

23. The final element that can be added to a dialog is an action. To add an action to a dialog, under **Steps** click where we want to add the action.

    Then click on **Add Step** and select any of the following actions from the process logic toolbar:

    - **Query CRM Data**
    - **Assign Value**
    - **Create Record**
    - **Update Record**
    - **Assign Record**
    - **Send E-mail**
    - **Start Child Workflow**
    - **Link Child Dialog**
    - **Change Status**
    - **Stop Dialog**

    Then enter an action description.

    If a **Set Properties** button appears next to the newly added action, click on **Set Properties** and specify details about the entity that this step in the dialog is taking action on.

24. Like workflows, after a dialog creation we have to activate it. Dialogs are not available for use unless activated. Please click on the **Save** button first in the top toolbar to save the dialog, and then click on the **Activate** button to activate it. Click on **OK** when the confirmation dialog pops up.

    Once activated, the dialog properties and logic are read-only. To edit these, we have to deactivate the dialog using the **Deactivate** button in the top toolbar.

How it works...

A dialog is a type of process in Dynamics CRM 2011 that displays the input forms and data that a user needs at each step while interacting with a customer or following a process that requires user input. A dialog is a very powerful tool to have branching logic that is based on input from the person stepping through a case, phone call, or any other customer interaction.

A dialog can only be run through the Microsoft Dynamics CRM 2011 web application and is not supported in Microsoft Dynamics CRM 2011 for Microsoft Office Outlook with offline access.

After developing a dialog, the dialog can be accessed via the following URL:

```
http://CRMServer_Name/Org_Name/cs/dialog/rundialog.aspx?DialogId=Dial
ogID&EntityName=EntityLogicalName&ObjectId=EntityObjectId
```

Here we will see the following:

- `CRMServer_Name` is the name of the Microsoft Dynamics CRM server
- `Org_Name` is the organization name
- `DialogID` is GUID of the dialog that we want to run
- `EntityLogicalName` is the entity logical name of the primary entity of the dialog that we want to run
- `EntityObjectId` is the GUID of the primary entity record

> We might try to split a complex dialog into child dialogs and invoke all of those child dialogs from a parent dialog. However, that is not supported.

Querying Dynamics CRM data in a dialog

In this recipe, we will find out how to retrieve Dynamics CRM data and use them in a dialog.

Getting ready

Sometimes, in the **Prompt and Response** section we would like the user to select a response from existing CRM data. Here we will discuss how we can retrieve CRM data and display them in a dialog.

There are two basic ways to achieve this: one using the `Lookup` variables in a dialog and the other using the **Query CRM Data** action. Let us have a look at both the approaches here.

How to do it...

Perform the following steps to query CRM data and display the data in a dialog:

1. Open the dialog designer page where CRM data has to be queried.

   Now, we will delve into both the approaches of retrieving CRM data one by one. First, we will find out how to query CRM data using a `lookup` field.

2. To configure a `Lookup` response type in the **Prompt and Response** page, we have to provide a reference entity and the reference field.

Let us take an example here. Assume that we want to provide a lookup to a user to select from existing accounts to associate it with a lead record in a dialog. The following screenshot displays the **Prompt and Response** page configuration for this example:

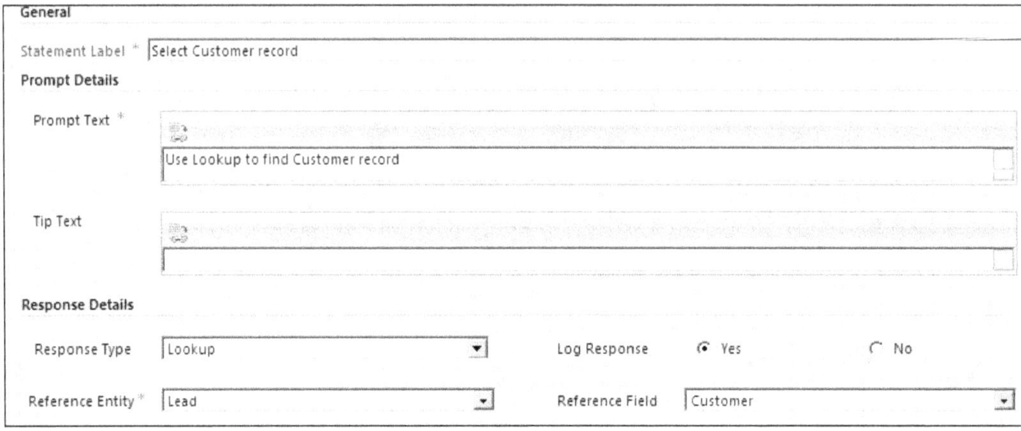

> We can observe that the **Reference Field** drop-down box shows only those fields that are a parent of the **Lead** entity type. Hence, using this method we can query only the parent entity records in a dialog.

3. The following screenshot illustrates the user experience when the dialog runs:

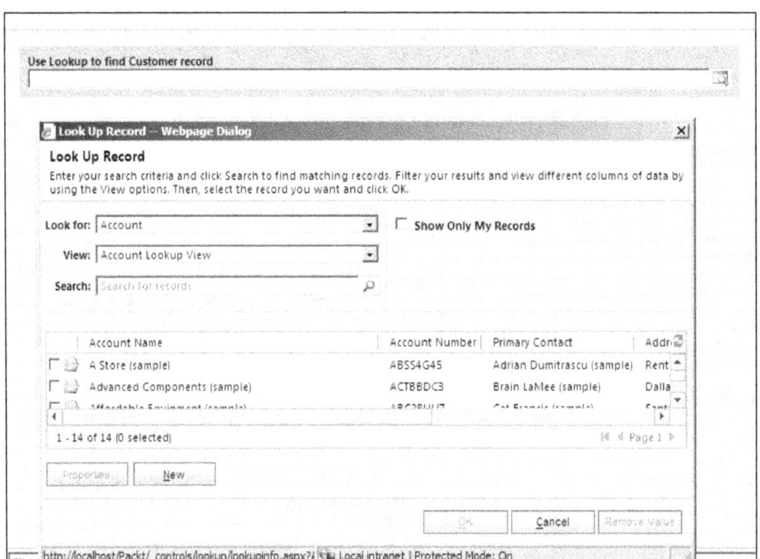

4. Let us now discuss how to query CRM data using the Query CRM Data action. To use this action, let us take an example of allowing a dialog user to select a Contact whose City is already selected by the user in a previous step in the dialog.
5. The next step is to add a variable (**City**) to store the user-provided city. The following screenshot displays how that can be done:

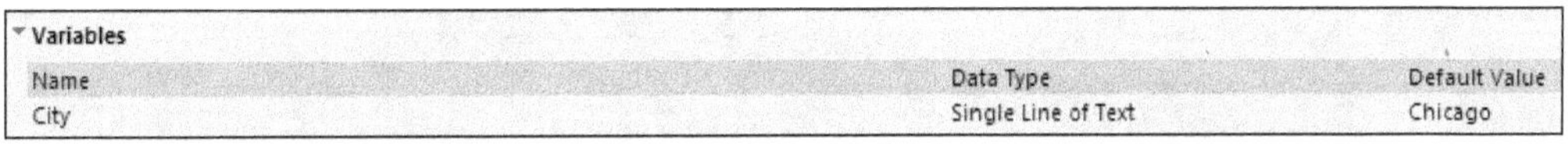

6. Then, add a prompt and response for requesting the user to enter the city information. A default value is selected as the default value of the added **City** variable.

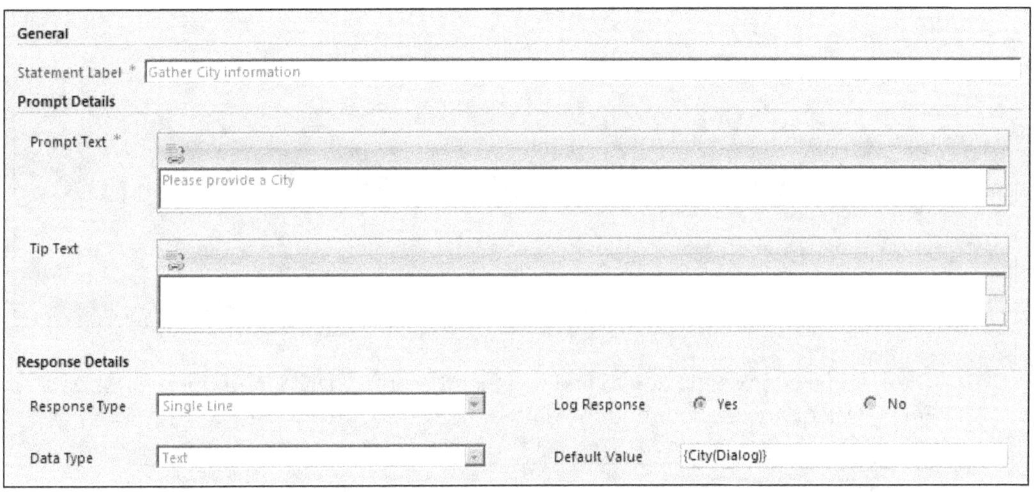

7. Then, we have to assign the user-provided city to the **City** variable, after which we have to add an assign value action to the dialog:

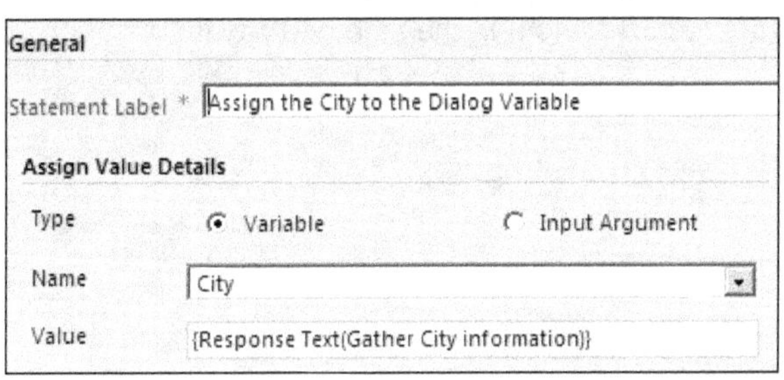

8. Thereafter, we have to add and define the Query CRM Data action. In the dialog, we would use the user-provided city information as shown in the following screenshot:

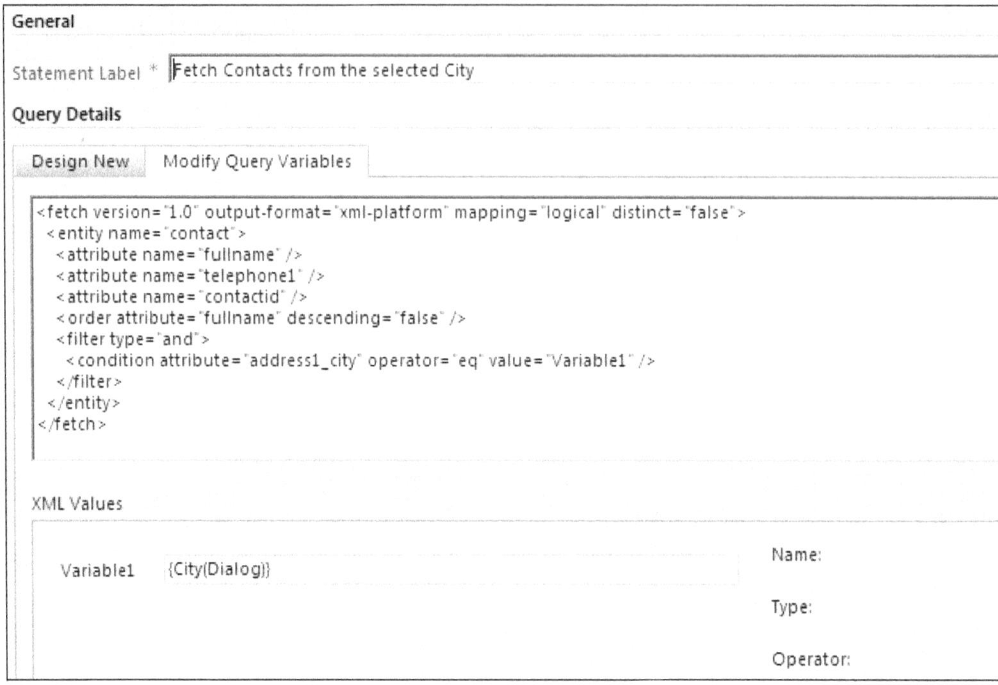

9. Then, add a check condition to find whether the previously added Query CRM Data Fetch XML query has returned the data or not:

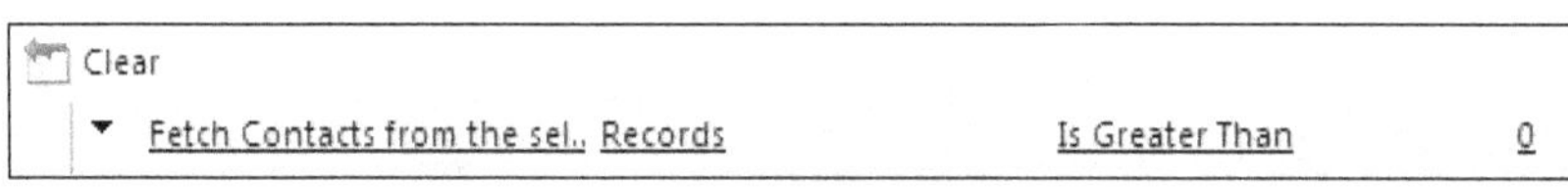

10. If the data has been returned, we will add a prompt and response to allow the user to select a Contact record matching the selected city information:

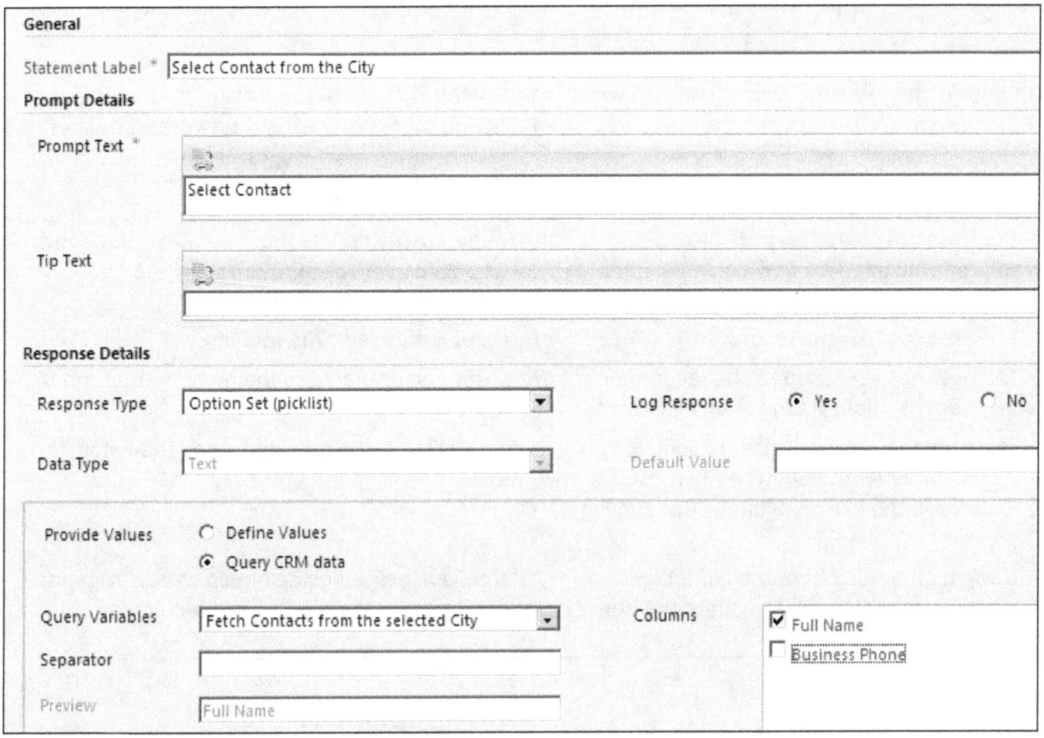

11. The final dialog steps look like the following screenshot:

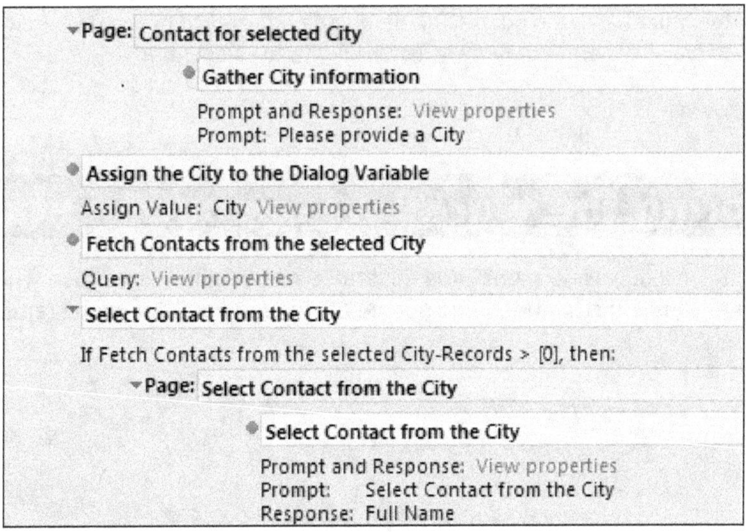

How it works...

In this recipe, we have discussed two ways to query the CRM data to be used in a dialog. Both ways have their own pros and cons. The following table compares the two approaches:

The Lookup field	The Query CRM data action
The user can search records on any columns included as view columns in the quick find view.	This approach presents the user with an option set populated with data returned by the query. The user cannot search records.
The user can sort the records.	The user cannot sort the records.
The user has access to all the records of the response field via the available views.	The user can only access the records returned by the query.
This approach can only use the lookup view defined for the entity; a filtered list to perform the lookup against cannot be provided.	A filtered list can be provided using the Fetch XML query.
Navigation around hundreds of records is relatively easy using the out-of-the-box entity view grid.	As data is displayed using option sets, navigation around hundreds of records is difficult.

With these comparative differences, the lookup field approach should be used when we want users to be able to search and select a record interactively. On the other hand, the query CRM data approach should be used when we want to provide users with more structured data to select from.

Monitoring the workflow execution status

In this recipe, we will delve into monitoring the status of a workflow execution. The following section will brief you on the the need and source of the workflow execution status.

Getting ready

The need to know the execution status of a workflow is very important. As workflows are asynchronous in nature, they do not execute when they are run; rather, workflows are queued up and run in an asynchronous nature. The status of workflow execution can be determined from system jobs.

How to do it...

Perform the following steps to determine the status of a workflow execution:

1. Log in to the Dynamics CRM 2011 organization as a system administrator or a user with appropriate rights on the **System Jobs** entity.
2. Navigate to **Settings** | **System** | **System Jobs**.
3. The **System Job** views will list every record of the type **System Job**, including workflows.
4. To filter the workflow records, click on the **More Actions** tab in the actions toolbar as shown in the following screenshot:

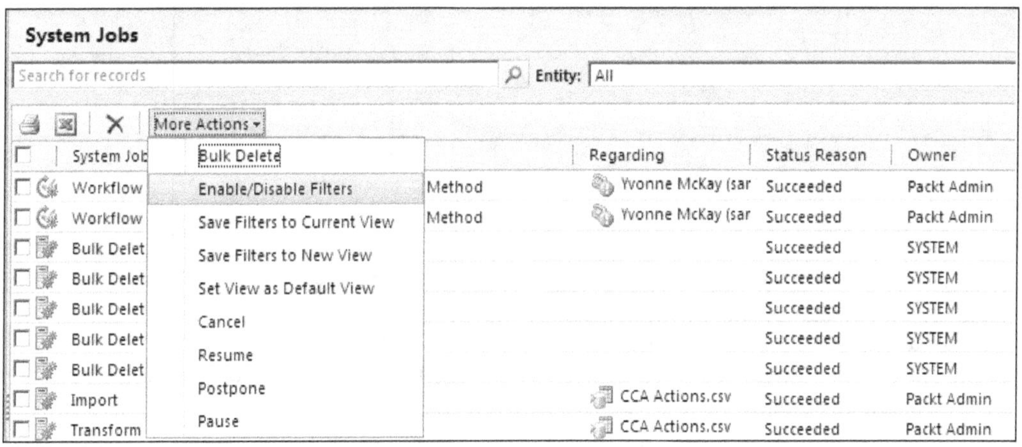

5. Then, a drop-down icon will appear against all the columns in the current view. Click on the icon next to **System Jobs Type**, and then select only **Workflow** and click on **OK** to apply the filter as shown in the following screenshot:

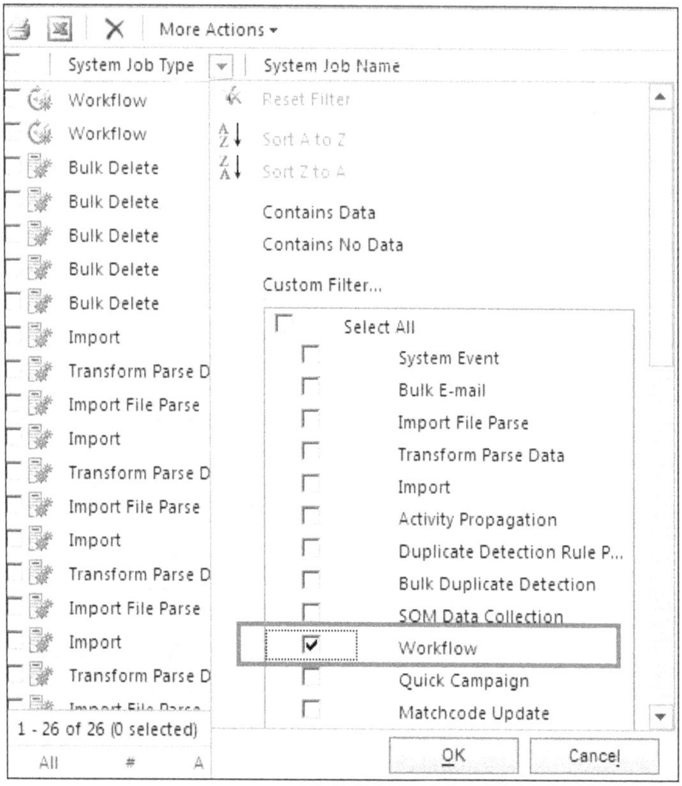

6. Once the workflows are filtered, check the **Status Reason** column. This column will tell us the status of the workflows. We can apply a filter to this column using the previous step.
7. The following actions can be performed on a **Workflow** system job:
   - **Cancel**
   - **Resume**
   - **Postpone**
   - **Pause**

To perform any of these actions on a workflow, select the workflow from the list and then click on **More Actions** in the actions toolbar. Then select any one of the actions as shown in the following screenshot:

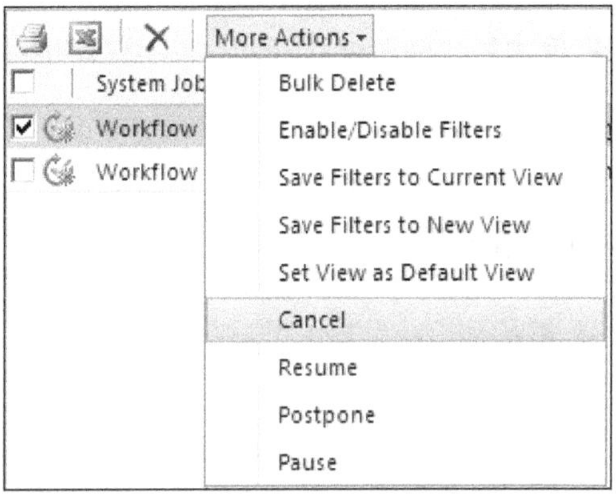

How it works...

If there is a problem with a workflow, it can be canceled, postponed, paused, or resumed. However, there are a few restrictions around this.

A canceled workflow cannot be resumed.

No action can be applied on a workflow that has been successfully completed.

Each time a workflow rule is triggered, a system job is created. These jobs carry a status, and when a failure is experienced, they are stamped with an error code and an error message and are set to a **Waiting** status.

A workflow with a wait condition can also be displaying the status **Waiting**. But unless the system job is stamped with an error message, all waiting workflows *may not* have an error.

> If a system job fails, the details about which steps failed and what the problems may have been can be viewed as well. To do so, at first the system job record has to be opened. To display details about system job failures, the cursor has to be moved over the warning symbols.
>
> To view system job failures in a format that can be printed or copied and pasted, click on the **Print** button.

There could be a number of reasons why Dynamics CRM workflow instances fail to complete. It is important to regularly check for failed workflows to ensure the integrity of the system.

A failed workflow instance can indicate:

- A workflow rule operating under a user context that has insufficient permissions assigned
- A badly written workflow logic
- Environmental issues / timeouts / system errors
- Asynchronous service-related issues

Index

Symbols

1:1 relationship type 237
1:N self-referencing relationship 237
<httpRuntime> element 198

A

access levels 135
Active/Active SQL Server clustering 10
Active Directory Federation Services (AD FS)
  about 111
  URL 122
activity 216
Activity Monitor 88
activity parties 216
Administrative access mode 144
Advanced Find view 284
AND operation 177
Append access rights 138
Append To access rights 138
application navigation control system 297
application pool 22
applicationribbon.xml file 299
Application Service 10
Application service account
  about 20-22
  permissions 11
Associated view 285
Asynchronous Processing Service 10
Asynchronous Processing service account 20
auditing
  about 183
  enabling, in Dynamics CRM 2011 183-187
audit management 159
audit records
  cleaning 188
  viewing 188
automated processes 351
automated workflows 353
autonumbering formats
  configuring 150, 151
auto-save control
  about 274
  properties 274

B

base currency 23
behavior actions 241
Bing Map control 274
browser support, Microsoft Dynamics CRM 2011
  Apple Safari 252
  Google Chrome 252
  Internet Explorer 252
  Mozilla Firefox 252
Bulk Deletion Wizard
  about 159
  used, for cleaning data 172-175
bulk record deletion 172
business entities
  about 216
  types 216
business processes
  about 274, 351
  automated processes 351
  interactive processes 351
business units
  about 132
  considerations, for deleting 134
  considerations, for disabling 134
  creating 133

button
adding, to ribbon group for entites 310-315
adding, to ribbon group of specific entity 316-327

C

cascading behavior rules 241
Case Resolution entity form 254
certificate 108, 109
certification authorities (CAs) 109
child business unit
about 133
creating 133
child dialog 361
child workflows 353
Claims-based authentication (AD FS)
configuring, for Microsoft Dynamics CRM 2011 111-121
Click to Call feature 276, 279
client access information 144
Client Access License (CAL) 144
collaboration controls 274
command bar controls
about 273
features 273
components
deleting, from managed solution 208, 209
components, standard main form
entity icon 255
footer 255
form assitant 255
form selector 255
header 255
navigation 255
ribbon 255
sections 255
tabs 255
composite entity 216
configuration, autonumbering formats 150, 151
configuration, Claims-based authentication (AD FS)
for Microsoft Dynamics CRM 2011 111-121
configuration database 66
configuration, error notification preferences 157, 158
configuration, fiscal year settings 156
configuration, Internet-facing Deployment (IFD) 122-126
configuration, Microsoft Dynamics E-mail Router 44-52
configuration, role-based forms 282, 283
configuration, security roles 135-138
configuration, system-wide settings 152-156
control 255
CREATE DATABASE permissions 76
CRM 2011 Maintenance Job Editor 96
CRM Application Pool Account
SPN, configuring for 57
CRM data types
Currency 232
Date and Time 233
Decimal Number 232
Floating Point Number 232
Lookup 233
Multiple Lines of Text 232
Option Set 231
Single Line of Text 231
Two Options 232
Whole Number 232
CRM (frontend roles) and AD FS
installing, on same server 111
installing, on separate servers 111
CRM Online 8
cross entity duplicate detection rule 177
custom activities
settings 224
custom activity type entities
creating 224
custom administrator security role
creating 139-141
Custom Code Validation Tool 271
custom entities
about 216, 218
creating 218-223
functionalities 223
custom entity privileges
creating 225
Customer Experience Improvement Program 158
customer relationship management (CRM) 7
custom field
creating, for entity 229-234

customization options, Site Map 298
customizations.xml file 298
customization.xml file 254
custom workflows 351

D

data
cleaning, Bulk Deletion Wizard used 172-175
importing, into Dynamics CRM 2011 160-169
database server backup plan 67
Database Server backup strategy
types 67
data import 159, 160
data integrity 134
data management 159
Default public view 284
Default Publisher for <OrganizationUniqueName> 194
default solution 193
delta release
about 207
creating 207
deployment administrator
about 127
creating 127-131
deployment-level tracing
about 79
enabling 82, 83
Deployment Service 10
Deployment Web service account
about 20, 22
permissions 11
dialog
about 352
creating, Dynamics CRM 2011 web interface used 361-371
Dynamics CRM data, querying 371-376
input arguments 361
variables 362
versus workflows 352
dialog availability
about 361
child dialog 361
on-demand dialog 361
dialog logic
about 362
pages 362
prompt and response steps 362
steps 362
disabled business unit 134
domain controller 66
duplicate detection
about 159
settings 178, 179
duplicate detection jobs
scheduling 180-183
duplicate detection rules
creating 175-179
cross entity duplicate detection rule 177
single entity duplicate detection rule 177
Dynamics CRM 2011
about 7, 191
auditing, enabling 183-187
data, importing into 160-169
Microsoft SharePoint Server (2010/2013), integrating with 342-349
modified ribbon definition, importing from 330, 331
multiple users, adding in 146-148
ribbon, customizing 307
ribbon definition, exporting from 308, 309
team, creating 148-150
user, adding 142-145
Dynamics CRM 2011 data
exporting, to Microsoft Excel 170-172
Dynamics CRM 2011 Database Server
backing up 67-74
performance optimizing 87-97
recovering from failure 75-78
Dynamics CRM 2011 deployment
securing, SSL/HTTPS used 108-110
Dynamics CRM 2011 E-mail Router machine
tracing, enabling on 84
Dynamics CRM 2011 Installation User account
permissions 12
Dynamics CRM 2011 organization
system administrator, creating 132
Dynamics CRM 2011 performance counters
adding 85-87
Dynamics CRM 2011 Server
about 66
backing up 74, 75

Dynamics CRM 2011 Server failure
recovering from 78
Dynamics CRM 2011 Server infrastructure
components, for backup 66
Dynamics CRM 2011 Server performance
monitoring 85-87
optimizing 98-104
Dynamics CRM 2011 web interface
application navigation structure 298
used, for creating dialog 361-371
used, for creating workflows 352-360
Dynamics CRM administrator
tasks 343
Dynamics CRM data
querying, in dialog 371-376
Dynamics CRM form
scripts, adding 269-271
Dynamics CRM for Outlook
installing 28-35
Dynamics CRM language pack
installing 35-39
Dynamics CRM Server
installing 10-23

E

elements, entity forms
field 255
IFRAME 256
navigation link 256
notes 256
section 256
Spacer element 256
Sub-Grid 256
tab 256
web resources 256
EnableRetrieveMultipleOptimization (ERMO) 103
entities
about 137, 215
custom field, creating for 229-234
icon, updating of 226-228
types 215
entity field mapping
requisites 249
entity icon 255
entity-level access rights
customizing 135
entity main form
creating 254-258
customizing 254-268
entity ownership 217
entity ownership type
about 217
business unit 217
none 217
organization 217
user 217
entity ribbon 298
entity type codes 268
error notification preferences
configuring, in CRM system 157, 158
Exchange Server 66
execution status
monitoring, for workflows 376-380
executionTimeout attribute 198

F

failed workflow instance 380
fetch data processing extension 24
Fiber Channel 52
field
adding, in section 260
field-level security 135
field-level security profile
creating 141, 142
FileGrowth property 91
filter criteria 233
fiscal year settings
about 156
configuring, in CRM system 156
footer 255
form assistant 255
form behavior
controlling, JScript used 269-272
form editor 254
form ribbon 299
forms
about 252
creating, from existing form 258
main form 252

mobile form 252
section, adding 259
form selector 255
forms, modifications
auto-save control 274
business processes 274
collaboration controls 274
command bar controls 273
header fields 274
inline edit controls 274
subgrids 274
forward mailbox
about 44
setting up 48, 49
FQDN 57
full release 206
Fully Qualified Domain Name. *See* **FQDN**

G

global option set
about 234
creating 234-236
grid ribbon 299

H

hardware specifications, Microsoft Dynamics CRM 2011 Server 9
header 255
header fields 274
Help Text 36
HideCustomAction element 329
HTML components (HTC) 271

I

icon
updating, of entity 226-228
identity providers 121
IFRAME control 256
iFrames 265
iisreset command 346
Import Data Wizard
about 159
used, for importing data into Dynamics CRM 2011 160-169
information form 253
inline edit controls 274
input arguments, dialog 361
input method editor mode (IME mode) 233
installation, Dynamics CRM for Outlook 28-35
installation, Dynamics CRM language pack 35-39
installation, Dynamics CRM Server 10-23
installation, Microsoft Dynamics CRM E-mail Router
about 40-43
on multiple computers 52-54
installation, Microsoft Dynamics CRM Reporting Extensions 24-26
instant messaging (IM) 217
interactive processes 351
Internet-facing Deployment (IFD)
about 8, 111
configuring 122-126
Internet Information Services (IIS) 10
Internet Information Services (IIS) Manager console 109
intersect entity 246
item
adding, in unmanaged solution 196-198
deleting, from unmanaged solution 198, 199

J

jewel 299
JScript
used, for controlling form behavior 269-272

L

LCID 306
lookup field
versus Query CRM data action 376
Lookup view 285
Lync call feature
enabling 276

M

Mail Merge templates
about 333
creating, Microsoft Word used 334-342

main form
about 252
components 255
process-driven form 253
read-optimized form 253
managed service accounts 11
managed solution
about 192
components, deleting from 208, 209
updating 206, 207
manual many-to-many relationship 246
many-to-many (N:N) relationship
about 237
creating 242-246
many-to-one (N:1) relationship
about 237
creating 237-242
matchcode 177
maxRequestLength attribute 198
merge 205
Microsoft ASP.NET 4 10
Microsoft Dynamics CRM
deploying, on multiple servers 54-59
Microsoft Dynamics CRM 2011
administering 107
Claims-based authentication (AD FS), configuring for 111-121
Microsoft Dynamics CRM 2011 Deployment Manager 60, 108
Microsoft Dynamics CRM 2011 Online
process-driven form, customizing 272-279
Microsoft Dynamics CRM 2011 Resource Center 299
Microsoft Dynamics CRM 2011 Server
about 8
hardware specifications 9, 10
software specifications 9, 10
Microsoft Dynamics CRM 2011 Web Client 8
Microsoft Dynamics CRM Asynchronous Processing Service 96
Microsoft Dynamics CRM Asynchronous Processing service account
about 22
permissions 12
Microsoft Dynamics CRM Async Service counters 87
Microsoft Dynamics CRM Authentication counters 87
Microsoft Dynamics CRM Client counters 87
Microsoft Dynamics CRM Discovery counters 87
Microsoft Dynamics CRM E-mail Router
installing 40-43
installing, on multiple computers 52-54
Microsoft Dynamics CRM E-mail Router counters 87
Microsoft Dynamics CRM for Microsoft Office Outlook 8
Microsoft Dynamics CRM for Microsoft Office Outlook with Offline Access 8
Microsoft Dynamics CRM for Outlook
operating environments 29
software prerequisites 29
Microsoft Dynamics CRM Lab 300
Microsoft Dynamics CRM LocatorService counters 87
Microsoft Dynamics CRM Outlook Sync counters 87
Microsoft Dynamics CRM Platform counters 87
Microsoft Dynamics CRM Reporting Extensions
installing 24-28
Microsoft Dynamics CRM Sandbox Client counters 87
Microsoft Dynamics CRM Sandbox Host counters 87
Microsoft Dynamics CRM Sandbox Processing service account
about 22
permissions 12
Microsoft Dynamics CRM Server counters 87
Microsoft Dynamics CRM Service counters 87
Microsoft Dynamics E-mail Router
configuring 44-52
Microsoft Excel
Dynamics CRM 2011 data, exporting to 170-172
Microsoft SharePoint Server (2010/2013)
integrating, with Dynamics CRM 2011 342-349

Microsoft Word
used, for creating Mail Merge templates 334-342
miscellaneous privileges
customizing 136
Mobile Express for Microsoft Dynamics CRM 8
mobile form
about 252
creating 280, 281
customizing 280, 281
modified ribbon definition
importing, from Dynamics CRM 2011 330, 331
multiple servers
Microsoft Dynamics CRM, deploying on 54-59
multiple users
adding, in Dynamics CRM 2011 system 146-148
multiserver
versus single server 8

N

native many-to-many relationship 246
navigation 255
Navigation Link 256
Network Load Balancing (NLB) 55
Non-interactive access mode 144
Notes control 256

O

OnChange event 269
on-demand dialog 361
on-demand workflows 353
one-to-many (1:N) relationship
about 237
creating 237-242
OnLoad event 269
on-premises deployment 8
OnReadyStateComplete event 272
OnSave event 269
organization
creating, steps 60-62
details, editing 62, 63
organization units (OUs) 13

P

Parallel SCSI 52
parent business unit 133
parent workflow 353
performance counters 85
Microsoft Dynamics CRM Async Service counters 87
Microsoft Dynamics CRM Authentication counters 87
Microsoft Dynamics CRM Client counters 87
Microsoft Dynamics CRM Discovery counters 87
Microsoft Dynamics CRM E-mail Router counters 87
Microsoft Dynamics CRM LocatorService counters 87
Microsoft Dynamics CRM Outlook Sync counters 87
Microsoft Dynamics CRM Platform counters 87
Microsoft Dynamics CRM Sandbox Client counters 87
Microsoft Dynamics CRM Sandbox Host counters 87
Microsoft Dynamics CRM Server counters 87
Microsoft Dynamics CRM Service counters 87
Performance Monitor 85
performance objects 85
Performance Toolkit 9
personal view
creating, for user 292-295
deactivating, for user 295, 296
Plug-in Assembly 137
PrincipleObjectAccess (POA) 95
privacy 134
privileges 135, 137
PrivReportingGroup 20
PrivUserGroup 20
process-driven form
about 253
customizing, in Microsoft Dynamics CRM 2011 Online 272-279
profiles
setting up 45-47
public view
about 284

columns 290
creating 284-290
customizing 284-290
filter criteria 290
sorting criteria 290

Q

Query CRM data action
about 371
versus lookup field 376
Quick Find view 284
about 290
search criteria, customizing for 291, 292

R

Read access mode 144
read-optimized form 253
Read-Write access mode 144
relationship field mapping
creating 247-249
relying party 121
ReportingGroup 20
ribbon button
hiding 328, 329
ribbon component 255
ribbon definition
exporting, from Dynamics CRM 2011 308, 309
ribbon group, for entities
button, adding to 310-315
ribbon group, of specific entity
button, adding to 316-327
ribbons
about 297
customizing, within Dynamics CRM 2011 307
entity ribbon 298
form ribbon 299
grid ribbon 299
jewel 299
sub-grid ribbon 299
role-based forms
configuring 282, 283
role-based security 134
root business unit 133
RuleDefinitions node 321
Rule Deployment Wizard
running 50, 51
used, for configuring rules 50
rules
configuring, Rule Deployment Wizard used 50

S

Sandbox Processing Service 10
Sandbox Processing service account 20
scripts
adding, in Dynamics CRM form 269-271
SDK Message 137
SDK Message Processing Step 137
SDK Message Processing Step Image 137
search criteria
customizing, for Quick Find view 291, 292
SeAuditPrivilege 114
section
adding, in form 259
field, adding in 260
Secure Socket Layer (SSL) 110
Secure Token Service (STS) 111
security role name
modifying 135
security roles
about 135, 139
configuring 135-138
self-referential 245
Send E-mail action 363
server-level tracing
enabling 79-81
service accounts 10
service principal number (SPN) 11
SeServiceLogonRight 114
SetupClient.exe file 31
Short Message Service (SMS) 217
single entity duplicate detection rule 177
single server
versus multiserver 8
sink mailbox. *See* **forward mailbox**
Site Map
about 298, 299
customization options 298
editing 300-307
working 307

Site Map XML
attributes 303, 304
nodes 303, 304
structure 301
Skype call feature
enabling 277
SOCIAL PANE control 275
software development kit (SDK) 351
software specifications, Microsoft Dynamics CRM 2011 Server 9
Solution Framework 191
solution management 192
solution publisher
about 193
creating 193, 194
solutions
about 192
deleting 209, 210
exporting 200-203
importing 203, 204
types 192
Spacer element 256
SPN
configuring, for CRM Application Pool Account 57
SQLAccessGroup 20
SQL data processing extension 24
SQL Server Collation 18
SQL Server Reporting Services (SSRS) 10, 25
SQL Server service account 20
SSL/HTTPS
used, for securing Dynamics CRM 2011 deployment 108-110
SSRS service account 20
Sub-Grid 256
sub-grid ribbon 299
subgrids 274
Support User access mode 144
system administrator
about 131
creating, in Dynamics CRM 2011 organization 132
system administrators 127
system entities 215
system-wide settings
Audit 154
Auditing 152
Calendar 152, 153
configuring 152-156
Customization 152
E-mail 152, 154
Formats 152, 153
General 152, 153
Goals 152, 156
Marketing 152-154
Outlook 152, 155
Reporting 152, 156

T

tabs 255
TabStateChange event 272
team
about 148
creating, in Dynamics CRM 2011 148-150
top wins 205, 206
tracing
enabling, on Dynamics CRM 2011 E-mail Router machine 84
tracing methods
deployment-level tracing 79
server-level tracing 79
transaction currency 23
translations
about 210
exporting, from unmanaged solution 210, 211
importing, to unmanaged solution 212, 213
Two-Option fields 269

U

unmanaged solution
about 192
creating 195, 196
item, adding in 196-198
item, deleting from 198, 199
translations, exporting from 210, 211
translations, importing to 212, 213
Update rollup 10 141, 153
Update rollup 12 253
user
adding, in Dynamics CRM 2011 142-145
personal view, creating for 292-295

personal view, deactivating for 295, 296
user e-mail settings
configuring 49
User Principle Name (UPN) 119

V

variables, dialog 362
versioning 205
views
about 251
Advanced Find view 284
Associated view 285
Default public view 284
Lookup view 285
Public view 284
Quick Find view 284
virtual LAN (VLAN) 23
virtual private network (VPN) 122

W

web.config file 66, 198
web resource 256
Windows Communication Foundation (WCF) 8
Windows Identity Foundation (WIF) 121
Windows on Windows (WOW) 40
Windows Small Business Server 8
Windows Workflow Foundation 351
workflow action 354, 359, 360
workflow availability
about 353
automated workflows 353
child workflow 353
on-demand workflows 353
workflow logic
about 353
actions 354
check condition 353
conditional branch 353
custom step 354
default action 353
parallel wait branch 354
stage 353
steps 353
wait condition 353
workflows
about 351
creating, Dynamics CRM 2011 web interface used 352-360
execution status, monitoring 376-380
versus dialog 352
workflow scope
about 353
business unit 353
organization 353
parent-child business unit 353
user 353
workflow stage 353, 357
workflow steps 353, 358
World Wide Web Publishing Service (W3SVC) 10

Y

Yammer
configuring 278

[PACKT] enterprise
professional expertise distilled
PUBLISHING

Thank you for buying
Microsoft Dynamics CRM 2011 Cookbook

About Packt Publishing

Packt, pronounced 'packed', published its first book "*Mastering phpMyAdmin for Effective MySQL Management*" in April 2004 and subsequently continued to specialize in publishing highly focused books on specific technologies and solutions.

Our books and publications share the experiences of your fellow IT professionals in adapting and customizing today's systems, applications, and frameworks. Our solution-based books give you the knowledge and power to customize the software and technologies you're using to get the job done. Packt books are more specific and less general than the IT books you have seen in the past. Our unique business model allows us to bring you more focused information, giving you more of what you need to know, and less of what you don't.

Packt is a modern, yet unique publishing company, which focuses on producing quality, cutting-edge books for communities of developers, administrators, and newbies alike. For more information, please visit our website: `www.PacktPub.com`.

About Packt Enterprise

In 2010, Packt launched two new brands, Packt Enterprise and Packt Open Source, in order to continue its focus on specialization. This book is part of the Packt Enterprise brand, home to books published on enterprise software - software created by major vendors, including (but not limited to) IBM, Microsoft and Oracle, often for use in other corporations. Its titles will offer information relevant to a range of users of this software, including administrators, developers, architects, and end users.

Writing for Packt

We welcome all inquiries from people who are interested in authoring. Book proposals should be sent to `author@packtpub.com`. If your book idea is still at an early stage and you would like to discuss it first before writing a formal book proposal, contact us; one of our commissioning editors will get in touch with you.

We're not just looking for published authors; if you have strong technical skills but no writing experience, our experienced editors can help you develop a writing career, or simply get some additional reward for your expertise.

[PACKT] enterprise
professional expertise distilled
PUBLISHING

Microsoft Dynamics CRM 2011 New Features

ISBN: 978-1-84968-206-0   Paperback: 288 pages

Get up to speed with the new features of Microsoft Dynamics CRM 2011

1. Master the new features of Microsoft Dynamics 2011
2. Use client-side programming to perform data validation, automation, and process enhancement
3. Learn powerful event driven server-side programming methods: Plug-Ins and Processes (Formerly Workflows)

Microsoft Dynamics CRM 2011: Dashboards Cookbook

ISBN: 978-1-84968-440-8   Paperback: 266 pages

Over 50 simple but incredibly effective recipes for creating, customizing, and interacting with rich dashboards and charts

1. Take advantage of all of the latest Dynamics CRM dashboard features for visualizing your most important data at a glance
2. Understand how iFrames, chart customizations, advanced WebResources and more can improve your dashboards in Dynamics CRM
3. A highly practical cookbook bursting with a range of exciting task-based recipes for mastering Microsoft Dynamics CRM 2011 Dashboards

Please check **www.PacktPub.com** for information on our titles

www.ingramcontent.com/pod-product-compliance
Lightning Source LLC
LaVergne TN
LVHW080013210926
848481LV00011B/3007

9781849684521